Linking Artificial Intelligence With Corporate Social Responsibility and Ethical Leadership

Caglar Dogru
https://orcid.org/0000-0002-4215-8979
Ufuk University, Turkey

IGI Global
Scientific Publishing
Publishing Tomorrow's Research Today

Vice President of Editorial Melissa Wagner
Director of Acquisitions Mikaela Felty
Director of Book Development Jocelynn Hessler
Production Manager Mike Brehm
Cover Design Jose Rosado

Published in the United States of America by
IGI Global Scientific Publishing
701 East Chocolate Avenue
Hershey, PA, 17033, USA
Tel: 717-533-8845 | Fax: 717-533-7115
Website: https://www.igi-global.com E-mail: cust@igi-global.com

Library of Congress Cataloging-in-Publication Data

Names: Dogru, Caglar, 1983- editor.
Title: Linking artificial intelligence with corporate social responsibility and ethical leadership / [edited by] Caglar Dogru.
Description: Hershey, PA : IGI Global Scientific Publishing, [2027] | Includes bibliographical references and index. | Summary: "This book explores how AI can be aligned with CSR initiatives, helping organizations to not only drive profitability but also promote transparency, equity, and sustainability in their operations. By focusing on the integration of AI with CSR, this volume highlights how businesses can foster trust and accountability in a rapidly evolving digital landscape"-- Provided by publisher.
Identifiers: LCCN 2024061719 (print) | LCCN 2024061720 (ebook) | ISBN 9798369340998 (hardcover) | ISBN 9798369351789 (paperback) | ISBN 9798369341001 (ebook)
Subjects: LCSH: Social responsibility of business. | Leadership--Moral and ethical aspects. | Artificial intelligence.
Classification: LCC HD60 .L564 2025 (print) | LCC HD60 (ebook) | DDC 658.4/08--dc23/eng/20250228
LC record available at https://lccn.loc.gov/2024061719
LC ebook record available at https://lccn.loc.gov/2024061720

British Cataloguing in Publication Data
A Cataloguing in Publication record for this book is available from the British Library.

Editorial Advisory Board

Table of Contents

Detailed Table of Contents

In today's world, digitization, global competition, and evolving employee expectations have continuously heightened the demand for more strategic, rapid, and analytical approaches in the field of Human Resources Management (HRM) (Dulebohn & Johnson, 2021). At this juncture, artificial intelligence (AI) technologies, with their data processing, machine learning, and predictive analytics capabilities, play a pivotal role in shaping the future of HRM. In conclusion, the application of AI-driven solutions in HRM goes beyond merely expediting routine tasks. By fostering a data-oriented decision-making culture, AI contributes to a more strategic and agile HRM framework. Moreover, one must remember that the human element remains central to all HRM functions. AI outputs achieve their greatest impact when they are integrated with managerial expertise and the organization's core values (Eren, 2022). Consequently, the implementation of planned, ethical, and sustainable digital transformation strategies stands out as a comprehensive approach illuminating the future of HRM.

This chapter explores the strategic integration of Artificial Intelligence (AI) and Emotional Intelligence (EI) within Corporate Social Responsibility (CSR) practices. While AI enhances efficiency through data-driven insights, it lacks emotional depth and ethical awareness. EI complements this gap by fostering empathy, ethical reflection, and stakeholder sensitivity. Grounded in stakeholder theory, institutional theory, and organizational learning, the chapter presents a framework where AI and EI operate in synergy to strengthen CSR's ethical foundation and relational impact. By illustrating how emotionally intelligent leadership and responsible innovation can align with technological advancement, this chapter contributes to both theoretical development and practical application in responsible business transformation.

In a global environment where stakeholders believe ethical company practices, CSR reporting is vital for transparency. Traditional reporting methods often fail due to human data management, inaccuracies, and lack of real-time insights. AI has given businesses novel opportunities to rethink CSR strategy and reporting. This chapter examines how AI-driven systems might improve transparency and accountability through automated data gathering, better analytics, and insights that encourage corporate responsibility. It addresses the ethical implications, opportunities, and problems of AI-driven reporting systems and recommends best practices. The chapter discusses case studies of businesses using AI for CSR reporting to boost stakeholder confidence and uphold ethical leadership.

This section studies the strategic dimensions that Culture of Organizational plays for sustainable business practices through in the Horn of Africa which faces rapid economic development alongside special difficulties. The study analyzes data from 385 participants using KMO to check sample adequacy as well as CFA for measurement model validation as well as SEM based on AMOS software for variable relationship analysis. The study demonstrates that organizations through strong cultures lead the adoption of sustainable practices since they benefit from common values as well as shared organizational norms that drive environmental responsibility together through social equity standards. Organizations practicing adaptive cultures demonstrate better success rates in sustainability initiative implementation which strengthens their market position as well as organizational stability when encountering regional challenges. The study explores how these outcomes affect decision-making authorities as well as business executives who should establish sustainability as their fundamental strategy.

This study examines how financial markets react to CSR announcements by listed firms. Using event study methodology, we analyze abnormal returns and trading volumes around 237 CSR announcements by French companies between 2022 and 2024. Announcements fall into four categories: environmental, social, governance, and hybrid initiatives. Results show heterogeneous responses. Governance and hybrid announcements generate the strongest and most persistent abnormal returns and volumes, reflecting investor confidence. Environmental initiatives elicit moderate, delayed effects, while social ones trigger the weakest and most transient reactions. Findings highlight the market's differentiated valuation of CSR, favoring initiatives seen as strategically relevant or tied to governance. Evidence supports signaling and information asymmetry theories, indicating that transparent CSR communication enhances firm value by reducing investor uncertainty. The study also stresses the importance of aligning CSR with governance reforms and improving visibility of environmental and social efforts.

The rapid integration of Artificial Intelligence (AI) into digital learning platforms has revolutionized educational approach through personalized learning paths and predictive analytics. However, this technological leap brings significant ethical challenges, particularly regarding data privacy, algorithmic bias, and user transparency. This chapter explores the intersection of AI, data ethics, and Corporate Social Responsibility (CSR) within the context of digital education. It argues that for platform providers, data ethics is no longer merely a legal compliance issue but a core element of Digital CSR. The chapter examines the risks of data exploitation in educational environments and proposes a Responsible AI framework that aligns corporate profit with social educational goals. By analyzing current industry standards

Preface

INTRODUCTION

The accelerating integration of Artificial Intelligence into the fabric of modern enterprise has ushered in a transformative era—one defined not only by technological advancement, but also by profound ethical responsibility. As Editor of this volume, I am pleased to present a collection of scholarly and practical contributions that examine the vital intersection of Artificial Intelligence, Corporate Social Responsibility (CSR), and Ethical Leadership. This work emerges from a growing recognition that innovation, while powerful, must be guided by principles that safeguard societal well-being, human dignity, and environmental sustainability.

Artificial Intelligence is no longer confined to theoretical exploration or experimental application; it is embedded in the operational core of organizations across industries. From decision-making systems to customer engagement and predictive analytics, AI is reshaping how businesses function and compete. However, with this unprecedented capability comes an equally significant obligation: to ensure that these systems are designed, deployed, and governed in ways that are ethical, transparent, and socially responsible.

Corporate Social Responsibility has long served as a framework through which organizations evaluate their broader impact. In the context of AI, CSR must evolve to address new challenges—algorithmic bias, data privacy, accountability, and the societal consequences of automation, among others. This volume seeks to explore how organizations can extend their CSR commitments into the digital domain, ensuring that AI-driven innovation aligns with enduring ethical values rather than undermining them.

Central to this discussion is the role of Ethical Leadership. Leaders today are not only tasked with driving performance and innovation but also with navigating complex moral landscapes shaped by emerging technologies. They must ask difficult questions: How can AI be leveraged to advance fairness and inclusion? What governance structures are necessary to ensure accountability? How can organizations balance competitive advantage with ethical integrity? The chapters in this book engage directly with these questions, offering both conceptual frameworks and real-world insights.

The primary objective of this volume is to bridge the gap between technical progress and ethical responsibility. By bringing together interdisciplinary perspectives—from technology, business, ethics, and leadership—it provides a comprehensive examination of how AI can be responsibly integrated into organizational strategy. Contributors present case studies, models, and best practices that illuminate pathways toward responsible AI governance, emphasizing transparency, equity, and sustainability.

This book is intended as a resource for a diverse audience. Academics and researchers will find theoretical depth and emerging research directions. Business leaders and managers will gain practical guidance for implementing AI in ways that uphold organizational values. Policymakers and regulators will encounter perspectives that inform balanced and effective governance. Students and educators will discover a foundation for understanding one of the most critical challenges of our time: aligning technological innovation with ethical responsibility.

As Editor, I hope this volume not only contributes to academic and professional discourse but also inspires meaningful action. The future of AI is not predetermined; it will be shaped by the choices organizations and leaders make today. By fostering a collaborative and ethically grounded approach, we can ensure that AI serves as a force for good—advancing both business objectives and the broader interests of society.

It is with this vision that I present this work to you.

ORGANIZATION OF THE BOOK

As Editor of this volume, I am pleased to present the following chapter overview, which reflects the interdisciplinary depth and thematic coherence of the work. Each contribution examines Artificial Intelligence through the critical lenses of Corporate Social Responsibility and Ethical Leadership, while also extending into organizational, cultural, financial, and strategic dimensions of responsible innovation.

Chapter 1 examines the foundational role of ethical leadership in guiding the responsible adoption of Artificial Intelligence within organizations. It highlights how values-based leadership practices enable sustainable digital transformation by fostering accountability, transparency, and trust. Through a synthesis of literature and empirical findings drawn from leadership perspectives, the chapter demonstrates that ethical leadership is not only a governance necessity but also a critical enabler of data-driven organizational cultures. In addressing challenges such as algorithmic bias and transparency in decision-making, it establishes ethical leadership as central to ensuring responsible and sustainable AI integration.

Chapter 2 extends this discussion by positioning Corporate Social Responsibility as a key structural mechanism through which ethical AI practices are embedded within organizations. It explores how leadership influences the operationalization of ethical principles in AI systems, emphasizing transparency, fairness, and accountability. The chapter underscores the shifting reality in which ethical AI is no longer theoretical but increasingly institutionalized within corporate policies and practices, with leadership serving as the primary catalyst for this transformation.

Chapter 3 further develops the discourse on leadership by focusing on ethical decision-making frameworks in the age of Artificial Intelligence. It critically examines the governance challenges associated with AI adoption, including bias, privacy concerns, transparency, and the reduction of human agency. The chapter articulates core principles—fairness, inclusivity, accountability, and stakeholder engagement—as essential pillars for responsible AI leadership and emphasizes the need for robust ethical governance structures within organizations.

Chapter 4 expands the ethical discourse into a global context by exploring cross-cultural dimensions of AI ethics and leadership. It argues that ethical frameworks cannot be universally applied without considering cultural diversity and contextual moral interpretations. Drawing on international case examples, the chapter illustrates how concepts such as fairness, privacy, and dignity are understood differently across regions, thereby reinforcing the need for culturally intelligent leadership capable of navigating ethical complexity in a globalized AI landscape.

Chapter 5 turns attention to Human Resource Management, examining how Artificial Intelligence is reshaping workforce practices and organizational decision-making. It highlights the increasing reliance on AI-driven analytics for strategic HR functions while emphasizing the continued importance of human judgment and organizational values. The chapter concludes that sustainable HR transformation depends on integrating technological advancement with ethical awareness and human-centered leadership.

Chapter 6 introduces a synergistic framework that integrates Artificial Intelligence with Emotional Intelligence to enhance Corporate Social Responsibility initiatives. It argues that while AI provides analytical precision, Emotional Intelligence contributes empathy, ethical sensitivity, and relational awareness. By combining both dimensions, organizations can strengthen the ethical and human-centered foundations of CSR, ensuring that technological advancement remains aligned with stakeholder well-being and responsible innovation.

Chapter 7 explores the growing role of Artificial Intelligence in transforming Corporate Social Responsibility reporting systems. It demonstrates how AI-enabled tools enhance transparency, accuracy, and accountability through real-time data processing and advanced analytics. At the same time, it critically examines the ethical implications and governance challenges associated with automated reporting systems, while offering practical insights into how organizations can responsibly deploy AI to strengthen stakeholder trust.

Chapter 8 shifts the focus to organizational culture and its strategic influence on sustainable business practices within the Horn of Africa. It highlights how strong and adaptive organizational cultures facilitate the adoption of sustainability initiatives by embedding shared values and norms that promote environmental and social responsibility. The chapter further emphasizes that cultural adaptability enhances organizational resilience and strategic positioning in regions facing complex economic and developmental challenges.

Chapter 9 concludes the volume by examining financial market responses to Corporate Social Responsibility announcements. Through an empirical event study approach, it reveals that investor reactions vary significantly depending on the nature of CSR initiatives, with governance and hybrid strategies generating the strongest market confidence. The chapter demonstrates that CSR communication plays a critical signaling role in reducing information asymmetry and shaping investor perceptions of firm value, thereby reinforcing the strategic importance of transparent and well-aligned CSR practices.

Chapter 10 explores the ethical governance of data within AI-driven learning environments by examining the intersection of data ethics, digital Corporate Social Responsibility, and educational governance. It highlights the growing responsibility of institutions to ensure transparency, privacy protection, fairness, and accountability in the collection, analysis, and use of learner data. The chapter argues that effective AI-driven learning governance requires not only robust technological infrastructures but also ethically grounded policies that safeguard stakeholder rights while fostering trust, inclusivity, and responsible digital innovation in education.

Collectively, these chapters offer a comprehensive exploration of how Artificial Intelligence intersects with ethics, leadership, and corporate responsibility across multiple domains. As Editor, I trust that this volume will serve as both an academic resource and a practical guide for advancing responsible, inclusive, and ethically grounded innovation in the age of Artificial Intelligence.

CONCLUSION

In concluding this edited volume, I am reminded that the conversation surrounding Artificial Intelligence is no longer one of technological possibility alone, but of ethical necessity and organizational responsibility. Across the chapters in this book, a consistent and compelling narrative emerges: Artificial Intelligence, while transformative in its capabilities, derives its true legitimacy from the values that guide its design, deployment, and governance.

The contributions within this work collectively demonstrate that Corporate Social Responsibility and Ethical Leadership are not peripheral considerations in the age of AI—they are foundational pillars. Whether examined through organizational leadership, cultural contexts, human resource practices, financial markets, or CSR reporting systems, the central message remains clear: innovation must be anchored in accountability, transparency, and a deep commitment to societal well-being.

What this volume also makes evident is that there is no singular pathway to responsible AI. Instead, there exists a dynamic interplay between technology and human judgment, between data-driven systems and emotional intelligence, and between global frameworks and local cultural values. Ethical leadership, therefore, is not static; it is adaptive, reflective, and continuously responsive to the evolving complexities introduced by AI-driven transformation.

As Editor, I view this collection not as a definitive endpoint, but as a contribution to an ongoing and urgent dialogue. The ideas presented here are intended to provoke reflection, inform practice, and inspire further inquiry among scholars, practitioners, and policymakers alike. The responsibility of shaping ethical AI ecosystems does not rest with any single discipline or sector, but requires sustained collaboration across academia, industry, and governance structures.

Ultimately, the future of Artificial Intelligence will be defined not only by the sophistication of its algorithms, but by the integrity of the systems within which it operates. It is my hope that this volume encourages its readers to engage critically and constructively with that responsibility, and to advance a vision of innovation that is both technologically progressive and ethically grounded.

In bringing this work to completion, I extend my sincere appreciation to the contributors whose insights have shaped this discourse, and to the readers who will carry it forward into practice, research, and leadership.

Chapter 1
Ethical Leadership:
The Role of Leadership in Balancing Innovation and Responsibility

Giulia Pascuzzi
http://orcid.org/0009-0001-0058-120X
IULM University, Italy

Grazia Murtarelli
http://orcid.org/0000-0002-6602-8503
IULM University, Italy

Stefania Romenti
IULM University, Italy

ABSTRACT

This chapter examines the role of ethical leadership in the adoption of artificial intelligence (AI) within organizations, highlighting how a values-based approach supports responsible and sustainable integration. It begins with a literature review on the intersection of AI development and ethical leadership, followed by a multilevel case study. The study explores how ethical leaders can guide digital transformation while ensuring accountability and transparency. Empirical data is collected through surveys and interviews with leaders. The results show that one of the crucial elements for innovation is data culture, which implies the use of data at every decision-making level of the organization. In this context, ethical leadership emerges as an enabler to foster trust and acceptance of AI among employees. By addressing challenges such as algorithmic bias, governance, and decision-making transparency, the chapter demonstrates that ethical leadership is essential for sustainable AI use.

DOI: 10.4018/979-8-3693-4099-8.ch001

1. INTRODUCTION

This era is characterized by a profound technological and cultural transformation in which artificial intelligence (AI) together with robotics, predictive and generative models is redefining markets and business models. AI is now an integral part of people's daily lives: from healthcare and education to business management and communication. This transversal development in society brings with it a growing ethical, organizational and political complexity. This means a change in social relationships and the way people and organizations make decisions.

AI systems do indeed have a major influence on the decisions made by companies For example, artificial intelligence systems are used to decide who should be hired, which users can receive a credit line, and which content should be shown to which users. However, these decisions are often made in a kind of closed box, without people being aware of it. In other words, the decision-makers are not clear why the algorithm leads to one path being favored over others. In parallel with technological development, there is a growing awareness of the risks associated with algorithmic discrimination, the opacity of decision-making processes and the concentration of power in the hands of a few global players. There is also a growing awareness that artificial intelligence is not neutral but reflects values, interests and prejudices that are anchored in the data, models and contexts in which it is developed.

In this scenario, it is crucial to understand how to ensure that artificial intelligence is used in a deliberate and careful way. On the one hand, it requires leadership that is able to support and promote technological change; on the other hand, it requires a leadership that is not willing to abandon fundamental values such as equality, justice, inclusion, transparency and sustainability, and that is able to act on these premises. In this sense, ethical leadership proves to be a positive catalyst for these needs.

This chapter looks at the role of ethical leadership in promoting innovative, sustainable and ethical development. The first part examines the main ethical and organizational challenges arising from the adoption of AI, such as algorithmic discrimination (e.g. Jobin et al. 2019; Al-kfairy et al. 2024) and transparency in decision-making (Muneeza and Kunhibava 2024). This last point is particularly critical because it makes it difficult to understand, challenge or correct an automated decision, while also making it difficult to assign responsibility (Saxena, 2024). Finally, the increasing dependence on algorithms could impair humans' critical faculties and their ability to deal with certain situations, leading to human dependence on the machine or a lack of human autonomy (Jobin et al. 2019). Among all the technological challenges associated with the use of AI, this chapter focuses specifically on the development of a data-driven organizational culture. This decision is dictated by two fundamental factors: on the one hand, the awareness that data is the basis for the construction of artificial intelligence models and, on the other hand, the management need that emerged during the empirical assessment, which sees the implementation of a data-driven culture as a strategic advantage that can ensure the survival and development of the organization. The chapter then examines the evolution of the concept of leadership, which has undergone a profound development in recent decades: from the theories of the Great Man (Sacavém et al. 2019) to behavioral theories (Squires, 2018; Northouse, 2025) to transformational models (Bass, 1995) and servant leadership. In this process, the model of ethical leadership is evolving into a paradigm that meets the growing needs for legitimacy, consistency and trust. In this sense, the ethical leader becomes the guarantor of the organization's values, able to pursue a corporate vision and support technological change in an ethical and sustainable way. An ethical leader is characterized by the fact that their communication is consistent with their behavior, making them a role model for all.

The aim of the second part is to empirically understand whether ethical leaders can effectively support sustainable technological progress and, in particular, how the data is collected and used. To this end, 113 leaders, mainly based on the European continent, were asked to complete a questionnaire to understand the main challenges faced by the organizations they work for. In order to obtain a relational and contextualized picture of the phenomena studied, some participants were then invited to take part in focus groups. This created a space for authentic reflection on these issues.

Finally, the third part discusses the implications for management that emerge from the analysis of the reference literature and the qualitative and quantitative data. The first challenge for managers concerns the ability to disseminate ethical leadership within the organization. fact, this leadership style has proven to be a driving force to build trust, maintain the coherence of values and guide change, even in contexts characterized by strong tensions. It is therefore necessary to ensure that ethical leaders can grow and develop in an organization that rewards this type of behavior. The second challenge relates to fostering a mature and cross-functional data culture. Today, while managers recognize the potential of using data in decision-making processes, they face cultural and organizational barriers that value data as a control mechanism rather than a method for making more informed, less emotional decisions, for example. Against this backdrop, ethical leadership emerges as a means of integrating ethics and data. fact, leaders must be able to use numbers to construct credible narratives, promote collective deliberation, and legitimize the use of data as a lever for equity and broad accountability.

2. FRAMING AI & LEADERSHIP: CHALLENGES AND NEW PERSPECTIVES

The aim of this part of the chapter is first to provide an overview of the main challenges that the Academy has identified in the use of AI. In particular, the chapter focuses on the use of data and the importance of fostering a data-driven culture. Secondly, this section presents a development of the concept of leadership and the characteristics a leader should have to support innovation.

2.1 AI Challenges and Opportunities

This era is characterized by a rapid digital transformation, with the advent of artificial intelligence representing the greatest opportunity and challenge. Artificial intelligence is embedded in social, economic and environmental dynamics, contributing to the transformation of numerous sectors and representing a key vector for innovation. Artificial intelligence is seen as a possible solution to the problems of our time, such as social inequalities (Latonero, 2018) or better access to services. While science recognizes the positive aspects of this tool, it also questions its limitations and contradictions.

One of the first aspects studied to assess the risks of artificial intelligence is algorithmic discrimination. Indeed, systems learn on the basis of historical data and often make decisions based on prejudices and stereotypes found in the data itself. This is the case, for example, with personnel selection systems that can discriminate against applicants on the basis of their gender, ethnicity, age, etc. Another example is predictive algorithms in justice systems, which assign different risk values depending on the personal characteristics of the person under investigation. Essentially, algorithms that have been trained based on biased data can exacerbate this aspect and lead to decisions that are not inclusive. Another important point in this context is the fact that the development of this technology is tied to a few global players, which risks excluding other countries by further widening the technological gap and the possibility of non-inclusive responses (Saxena, 2024). Another challenge concerns the transparency of the decision. This is because when deep learning mechanisms are used, the why of the decision remains in the dark, a kind of black box. This is a major limitation in areas such as justice, credit and healthcare, where understanding the reasons behind the decision is essential. This dilemma also prompts reflection on the question of liability. Who is legally responsible in the event of damage caused by a decision made by an artificial intelligence algorithm? Without an appropriate legal and ethical framework, there is a risk that no one will take responsibility or blame a machine. This is part of the public responsibility that AI governance has for the appropriate norms, practices and tools to regulate its introduction and impact on society. However, several authors (e.g. Shoker, 2022; Mathur, 2024) point out the differences in regulation in different regions of the world. For example, Europe has proposed an AI law based on a risk-based approach, while other regions have opted not to impose strict regulations in order to encourage technological development. Countries have also taken different positions on data management (Wu, 2014). This point is key as AI feeds on vast amounts of data, which in some cases can be collected without explicit consent. Governance should therefore ensure digital sovereignty, i.e. the right of individuals and communities to control their own data. This requires clear accountability mechanisms, algorithmic checks and systems for redress and rectification when harm is done. This is one of the biggest contradictions in this area (Jobin et al., 2019): On the one hand, algorithms require large amounts of heterogeneous data to improve performance and model fairness; on the other hand, citizens and data owners more generally have a right to privacy and sovereignty over their data. Resolving this contradiction is essential for promoting ethical and sustainable solutions (Saxena, 2024). Another important point is the autonomy of people. Indeed, artificial intelligence is credited with the ability to be efficient and support decision-making; on the other hand, it can reduce the critical capacity of individuals and replace human judgment. These are issues of particular interest in areas such as education, health or public resource management (Jeeva et al., 2024).

It is also recognized that companies have a responsibility for data governance (Al-Ruithe et al., 2019). To best manage this responsibility, Janssen and colleagues (2020) suggest that organizations develop agile structures and widespread leadership that is able to communicate their decisions transparently. Finally, it is important to develop internal processes that can adapt to constant change (Otto, 2011). In this sense, the challenge is cultural: it requires a corporate culture based on trust, continuous learning and employee empowerment.

In essence, the introduction and development of artificial intelligence presents a series of complex and interconnected ethical challenges that touch on fundamental principles such as human dignity, justice, autonomy, transparency and accountability. These challenges are not abstract, but manifest themselves daily in real-world applications that affect the lives of millions of people.

Data Culture

Today, one of the biggest challenges for companies is to remain competitive in a constantly evolving market. In this sense, a data-driven approach, i.e. making decisions based on data, has proven to be one of the most important necessities in the organizational context. In fact, in a constantly evolving world, data culture is establishing itself as one of the most important strategic assets for innovation-oriented organizations. In this sense, tools based on artificial intelligence represent a fundamental catalyst, as they allow the management, analysis and enrichment of enormous amounts of heterogeneous and unstructured data, enabling a profound change in decision-making processes. In contrast to traditional approaches, artificial intelligence allows us to gain predictive insights from a large number of inputs, which can then be adapted to different scenarios. Data thus becomes an important support for entrepreneurial action and contributes to a data-driven revision of corporate strategy. In this sense, the ability to analyze large amounts of data in a complex and predictive way represents a real competitive advantage and strengthens the ability of companies to act in a proactive and personalized way towards their stakeholders (Davenport & Harris, 2017).

When an organization uses data in a mature way, it is able to integrate data into every business process, from the operational level to the decision-making and strategy level. This implies a change in the management approach, which also affects the corporate culture. In this sense, it is advisable to promote the conscious use of data in every business function (Wamba et al. 2017) and in every process and to develop transversal analytical capabilities. Karatzoglou et al. (2010) and others (e.g. Donkers et al., 2017; Ahani, et al. 2019) emphasize that the development of e.g. predictive performance models, intelligent recommendation systems and customer segmentation enables organizations to reduce costs and increase business responsiveness. In addition, the customer experience can be further personalized thanks to the data, which increases conversion and loyalty rates.

A particular element in a data-driven company is data governance, i.e. the set of policies, procedures and tools designed to ensure not only the quality of the data but also the security and integrity of the company's information. In this context, management plays a key role in defining a strategic vision that integrates data into every process and in ensuring regulatory compliance, transparency and respect for privacy (Kitchin, 2014). Furthermore, data can be used not only to improve business performance in terms of profit and competitiveness, but also for aspects of corporate social responsibility (CSR). Namely, data can be used to monitor ESG (environmental, social and governance) performance, e.g. to assess product life cycle and reparability, optimize energy consumption and reduce waste. When data is linked to the ethical aspects of business operations, it becomes a tool for social and environmental responsibility (Vaswani, 2024).

To summarize, in an ever-evolving world, data is a treasure trove of information which, if used intelligently, can transform the entire business process and give the company a real competitive advantage. In this sense, organizations that build an integrated view of data, promoting innovation, transparency and accountability, will be able to overcome complex challenges and seize new opportunities.

2.2 Framing Leadership

The concept of leadership is a much-discussed topic in academic and organizational circles, as it is considered one of the success factors for organizations (Sacavém et al. 2019). Furthermore, several authors have shown that different leadership styles can lead to better performance and innovation (Mohav, 2023).

However, the concept of leadership remains difficult to define (Silvia, 2016) and much depends on the angle from which we view this phenomenon.

To better understand this concept, in this part of the chapter we will look at the main developments of the concept of leadership in order to understand which aspects of it contribute to innovation and the responsible use of new technologies.

Evolution and Rise of Ethical Leadership

The earliest studies of leadership qualities viewed them as a natural gift (Stogdill, 1948), a set of personal and physical characteristics that can predict a person's effectiveness as a leader. Later studies investigated what qualities characterize an outstanding leader. The trait that has emerged most strongly from these studies is "trustworthiness", which is associated with four characteristic traits: Honesty, vision, the ability to inspire and competence (Posner & Kouzes, 1988). Other research sees charisma as a trait that not only predicts a good leader, but is also able to influence and motivate his or her followers (Deluga, 2001). Charismatic leaders are indeed carriers of enthusiasm and convey confidence (House, 1977). However, charismatic leadership has also encountered criticism, such as that of Deluga (2001), who distinguishes between socialized charismatic leaders - who align their vision with the inspirations of their group - and personalized leaders who manipulate people to achieve personal goals.

Another line of research focuses on the behavior of the leader. This line of research, called behavioral theory, extends the research from the individual unit of the leader to the people who must follow him, thus relating the behavior and attitudes of leaders to the reactions of their followers. This research identifies two types of behavior associated with leaders: task-oriented behavior, i.e. oriented towards tasks, results and the organization of work, as opposed to behavior that is more focused on people and their well-being (Den Hartog, 2015). Other research expands on this view by giving the phenomenon of leadership a broader perspective. Contingency theories take the whole context as a starting point and assume that leaders display different attitudes and behaviors depending on the context, the team they are working with and the external environment (Winston, 2001). Another interesting idea about leader behavior comes from Robinson et al. (2019), who coined the term "servant leadership" to describe a leader who thinks of others before themselves. The servant leader is someone who is able to help people grow, in turn transforming them into leaders. He is a generous person because he focuses on others and not on himself.

Another area of research is the relationship that develops between leader and follower. A seminal study in this area was transactional theory, which views the relationship between a leader and their team as a series of exchanges, rewards and punishments based on performance (Judge & Piccolo, 2004). A different perspective on the relationship is offered by transformational theory, which views followership as leading to higher levels of motivation, morale and performance. In other words, Bass's (1995) theory defines transformational leadership as the leader's ability to inspire, motivate and transform their employees and get them to transcend their individual interests for the good of the group or organization. This approach has a positive impact on employees, who report greater job satisfaction and an overall increase in the organization's performance. In this sense, transformational leadership is the process that facilitates the connection between leader and followers and increases the level of motivation and morale in both (Northouse, 2025). This leadership style is able to inspire and motivate, and is characterized by being high value, visionary and charismatic. Thanks to its ability to improve collaboration between groups and generate greater organizational commitment, several studies (Wiston 2001, Williams & Seaman, 2016) consider this leadership style particularly suitable for highly innovative contexts.

Finally, in recent years, the concept of ethical leadership has come strongly to the forefront of academic and management debate, presenting itself on the one hand as a possible promoter of organizational values towards internal stakeholders and at the same time as a guarantor towards external stakeholders (Hoogh & Harog, 2009). An ethical leader would counteract organizational opportunism and be able to guide change through shared moral values.

The most widely accepted definition of ethical leadership is that of Brown and Treviño (2006), according to which ethical leadership is the demonstration of normatively appropriate behavior through personal actions and interpersonal relationships and the promotion of such behavior among followers through two-way communication, reinforcement, and decision making. This definition has the advantage of combining different aspects of ethical leadership. On the one hand, it focuses on the behavior of the leader who builds an ethical organizational culture by translating values into coherent actions. It also highlights how an ethical leader develops a relationship with their followers that is able to inspire them to behave similarly in line with organizational values on the one hand, and to promote transparent communication that fosters the creation of virtuous circles of information on the other. However, this definition does not usually take into account stakeholders outside the organization, such as customers, suppliers and the community. In this sense, De Hoogh and Den Harog (2009) emphasize that ethical leadership should also encompass all aspects of corporate social responsibility. Another difficulty in discussing ethical leadership is measurement (Resick et al., 2006). Because ethical leadership is a highly socially desirable construct, it is difficult to measure it by asking leaders direct questions, but should be measured from a more descriptive perspective by analyzing how leaders act and the impact they have on followers, the organization as a whole, and stakeholders. Resick et al (2006) identify a number of key behaviors associated with ethical leadership: Integrity, ethical awareness, orientation towards others, motivational skills and accountability. Other authors (Banks et al. 2020) argue that ethical leadership can be perceived through moral emotions such as compassion, moral outrage or justice. These signals help followers decipher the authenticity and consistency of the leader. In this sense, ethical leadership cannot be understood as a list of good intentions or values, but as a dynamic process that involves an interaction between the leader, the organization and the stakeholders.

By examining the different aspects from which leadership has been analyzed (characteristics of the leader, behavior of the leader, relationship with followers and the environment), some concepts that characterize ethical leadership can be identified:

- Individual characteristics. Traits such as honesty, empathy, justice and high emotional intelligence are closely related to a leader's ethical perception (Den Hartog, 2015). However, ethical leadership is not an innate trait, but can be learned and developed through training and mentoring programs (Brown & Treviño, 2006).
- Behavior of the leader. Behavior is observable and consistent, is also reinforced by the expression of emotions, ethical behavior is legible and persuasive (Judge & Piccolo, 2004).
- Context. Ethical leadership changes according to industry, culture and stakeholder composition (Alkhadra, et al. 2023). In terms of organizational context, other research (Resick et al. 2006) highlights the extent to which internal policies and supervisor behavior influence the possibility of ethical leaders emerging. In other words, for a leader's ethics to develop, it needs fertile ground.
- Relationships. Through transparent behavior, the ethical leader encourages others to do the same. This creates authentic relationships that encourage feedback and create a cycle of information and growth (Kalshoven & Den Hartog, 2013).

Ethical leadership has numerous benefits for the organization at various levels. First, it has been shown to be effective in improving human capital by creating a positive work environment through employee engagement and satisfaction (Brown et al. 2006); it increases employee retention and productivity. Secondly, it strengthens corporate social responsibility as a concrete and strategic practice. This is because ethical leadership becomes a driving force in creating a corporate culture based on shared values and promotes coherence between mission and operational behavior (Kalshoven & Den Hartog, 2013). The ethical leader becomes a direct facilitator of CSR practices by ensuring their consistency and sustainability over time, mitigating external pressures and aligning social and environmental practices with strategic objectives. In this sense, ethical leadership and CSR together represent a powerful combination to consolidate stakeholder trust and attract ethically sensitive investments. In this way, ethical leadership helps organizations to manage and mitigate reputational risk, making them crisis resilient. In particular, an authentic relationship with stakeholders and a solid ethical culture help organizations to face crises with credibility (Resick et al. 2006).

Ethical Leadership as a Driver of Responsible Innovation

trainer of digital skills. Imran et al. (2016) particularly emphasize the role of the manager in interpreting data and making data-driven decisions, while Darics (2020) includes mastery of social media and collaborative platforms among the skills. Another recurring theme concerns relational and emotional skills. Shamim et al. (2017) speak of 'authentic' leadership based on transparency, listening and trust, while Alawamleh et al. (2025) emphasize the importance of emotional intelligence and constructive feedback. Finally, Kane et al. (2019) point to leadership that is focused on supporting and developing employees.

To summarize, talk of innovation necessarily involves the introduction of change, of something new. Innovation also means accepting the idea of failing many times before arriving at a solution. In addition, innovation, especially in modern contexts, requires different and overlapping skills (Conrow, 2011). It is precisely because of these characteristics that innovation cannot develop in an organizational climate characterized by fear or individualism. Instead, it is necessary to promote collaboration and a transparent communication style enriched by feedback (Williams & Seaman, 2016). In this context, ethical leadership becomes a necessary prerequisite for the responsible management of change precisely because of the characteristics described above. Ethical leadership is seen as an approach that provides a forward-looking vision of the company, is a guarantor of the organization's values and implements attitudes and behaviors that guarantee integrity, efficiency and justice. In addition, ethical leadership is able to increase the commitment and cohesion of the team thanks to an open communication style based on feedback. In this sense, ethical leadership seems to be an advantageous solution for highly technology-oriented organizations. Ethical leadership, based on mutual respect and shared values and enabling a collaborative dynamic, proves to be an ideal leadership style to foster innovation (Sacavém et al., 2019).

A study on the impact of ethical leadership on innovation comes from Lin et al. (2020), who propose an in-depth analysis of this interaction, focusing on a sample of companies operating in the B2B IT services sector. The authors state that ethical leadership, understood as a leader's ability to demonstrate appropriate behavior through their behavior and the propensity to create interpersonal relationships, is a crucial element to manage the adoption and implementation of innovative technologies in an efficient and responsible manner. In this sense, the ethical leader becomes a truly strategic factor since, on the one hand, it can influence technological progress that has a positive impact on business performance (Mohav, 2023) and, on the other hand, it positively moderates the relationship by reinforcing the impact of innovation on performance. Indeed, the study shows that high ethical leadership enhances the positive impact of innovation on performance. In particular, the effect of innovation is significantly stronger in companies with high ethical leadership scores. This finding suggests that ethical leadership can be seen as a catalyst for effective innovation, as it strengthens the trust of internal and external stakeholders and encourages creative behavior among employees thanks to a corporate culture that favors change. In summary, the work of Lin et al. (2020) represents an important reflection on the role that ethical values and social responsibility can play in bringing out the benefits of technological innovation.

A particular perspective, but one that confirms the findings of the aforementioned studies, is provided by Gloor et al. (2022), whose work identifies three types of leaders who influence innovation in different ways. Using a metaphor based on the animal kingdom, the author describes bee leaders who have universal ethics, are guided by values such as altruism, benevolence and the common good, promote an inclusive work environment and serve as inspiration for their teams. He then introduces leech leaders, who embody opportunistic leaders who only act in their own interests. They are therefore manipulative and can therefore often achieve quick wins, but their impact on the team and the organization is detrimental in the long term. Finally, ants are leaders who focus on following the common rules within their reference group. The author defines them as moral, but not necessarily ethical, leaders. These three types of leaders have different effects on innovation. Their focus on personal visibility at the expense of pursuing common goals reduces the group's ability to innovate and learn. On the other hand, ant leaders do not seem to influence the propensity to innovate either positively or negatively. Finally, teams led by bees showed better performance on innovation-related tasks and problem-solving skills. In particular, some attitudes of API leaders seem to have a positive impact on a team's ability to innovate: openness to risk and novelty; they are excellent motivators for the group by encouraging collaboration and the exploration of creative solutions; thanks to inclusive communication, bees are often a central part of the communication flow that connects people and facilitates the dissemination of knowledge. The last point in particular is seen by the various stakeholders as a fundamental contribution to promoting innovation.

Conclusions From a Literature Review

Faced with these challenges, science has been thinking about possible solutions that could combine technological development and humanity. One of the answers to enable a positive development of these technologies has been seen in ethical leaders who are able to combine strategic vision, usefulness for technological development, social sensitivity and personal integrity (Williams & Seaman, 2016). In particular, the ethical leader is seen as having the ability to act for the long term, characterized by a willingness to invest in solutions that create sustainable value. An approach that can be described as future-oriented and is essential for the introduction of AI. Technological solutions may appear efficient in the short term, but can cause systemic damage over a longer time horizon. Another recognized value of the ethical leader is the ability to build trust. In an environment where technology can instill fear, leaders must be able to communicate authentically and transparently, explaining technology decisions to all stakeholders. Furthermore, an ethical leader acts on the basis of morals that are committed to universal values. In a context where technology is evolving faster than the regulatory environment designed to protect its use, the presence of a person who makes the right decision is essential. Transformative accountability (Al-Omari & Al-Omari, 2006) is also important in this context. In other words, leaders must not only be accountable for the decisions they make, but also set the stage for the organization as a whole to make decisions that are consistent with and responsive to corporate social responsibility.

As Tagscherer and Carbon (2023) stated, “digital transformation is not just a technical matter: it is a matter of culture, vision and leadership. Ethical leadership, rooted in values and consciousness, is now the necessary condition to prevent AI from becoming a tool of inequality and control, rather than a catalyst for freedom, justice and collective well-being.

3. EXPLORING LEADERSHIP & RESPONSIBLE DATA USE: METHODS, RESULTS, AND INTERPRETIVE INSIGHTS

The aim of the study is to investigate the relationships between personal values, ethical behavior and processes of technological change in organizations. To achieve this goal, a mixed-methods approach was used to explore, on the one hand, what leaders' most important needs are and, on the other hand, how a leader's perceived ethics might influence the propensity to use technology.

The methodology therefore includes quantitative data collected through questionnaires and qualitative insights gained through focus groups. The questionnaire provided the basis for a more specific focus on the concept of technological development in order to give the study a concrete value. The qualitative part, on the other hand, allowed us to explore how managerial behavior and organizational culture can influence digital innovation processes. The approach aims to paint a complex picture that provides useful insights for strategic considerations in the management field.

The questionnaire was answered by 113 people who have a leadership role in their company and at the same time perform other tasks. The sample was balanced in terms of gender (57% men; 43% women) and age (between 30 and 55 years). The majority (68%) of the sample resided in countries belonging to the European Community, while the remaining part (32%) resided in non-EU countries. From a sectoral perspective, different macro sectors such as industry and manufacturing, financial services, technology, healthcare, consumer goods and other specialized sectors can be distinguished.

The questionnaire was divided into 4 sections:

- Personal data and working methods
- Sector and organizational context
- Perceived challenges and organizational context.
- Perceived ethical aspects

In addition to this questionnaire, we conducted 4 focus groups, in order to explore in greater depth the issues that emerged from the questionnaire. Participants were selected based on three main criteria:

1. sector they belong to
2. role they hold
3. characteristics that emerged in the questionnaire (e.g. experience of ethical leadership, perceived critical issues, level of use of data).

The focus groups followed a semi-structured scheme that built on the conceptual areas explored in the questionnaires and was supplemented with ideas from the literature on participatory qualitative research to create an authentic and reflective space. The aim of the focus group was to stimulate further reflection from the participants that could provide a relational and contextualized picture of the phenomena under investigation. In particular, a qualitative method was chosen, as there are many references in the literature to a business's "readiness" for technological change (e.g. Conrow, 2011; Salvador-Carulla, et al 2024), but no specific references to data culture. Therefore, it was decided to explore this topic through a qualitative analysis to find emerging themes and overarching categories, as well as dissonance and divergence. The focus groups were recorded and then transcribed and coded using qualitative analysis software.

After creating the questionnaire to collect quantitative data, the qualitative approach was explored using the focus group methodology, which allowed for an in-depth exploration of the context in relation to the topics of ethical leadership, data culture in organizations and their integration. The focus groups provided valuable information such as the thoughts, experiences and behaviors of the participants, enriching the understanding of the phenomena under investigation. Thus, the decision to integrate this qualitative part has two fundamental aspects. The first is that the reading reveals the limitations of leadership assessment questionnaires (e.g. Riggio et al. 2010); in this sense, the qualitative interview helps to get a more accurate idea of the situation. On the other hand, the topic of data culture is still in an exploratory phase in the literature; for this reason, the qualitative approach was essential to gain insights on this topic.

The discussion threads followed a common structure that was in line with the research objectives, while maintaining the flexibility of these tools that allows them to be adapted to the participants' way of thinking and acting, thus promoting an authentic exchange.

All content that emerged in all phases of the research was collected and transformed into thematic insights. The findings obtained were interpreted and processed in the form of narrative evidence that provides a variety of perspectives on the role of ethical leadership and the use of data to support strategic business decisions.

The results of the analysis are described below to highlight repetitions, dissonances and meanings that participants attributed to the items in this research.

3.1 Leadership

The data collected confirms what is emphasized in the literature described at the beginning of the chapter: Leadership is a daily practice of consistency and the ability to navigate complex contexts. In particular, in phrases such as “it's not just about making good decisions, but remembering every day why we do what we do”, participants recognize the heart of an ethical perceived leader in the alignment between stated values and behavior. Another element that emerged clearly is that of justice and respect for situations or people: “His decisions reflect fairness and respect, not just convenience”. These two elements, fairness and respect, together with transparency in communication, are perceived as indicators of integrity. A cross-cutting theme concerns the difficulty for leaders to maintain integrity in difficult situations.

Sentences such as "our leader talks about respect, but then he interrupts everyone in meetings and pushes through his ideas" or "we have to do it this way to get by" underline that the gap between words and actions creates mistrust and organizational passivity. On the other hand, leaders who are recognized as "moral role models" are the ones who act in accordance with their own values, even in difficult situations. Remaining present even in difficult situations has a multiplier effect: it stimulates virtuous behavior, creates trust and promotes a sense of belonging to a group that is guided by this type. On the contrary, inconsistency creates confusion and ambiguity. Phrases like "when he knows what to do and acts in accordance with what he has always preached, even in moments when everything goes dark, he pushes us to do more and in a way reminds us why it is worthwhile to be involved".

A recurring narrative is the difficulty faced by those who find themselves in an intermediate position, i.e. a position where they are called upon to set an example to a team on the one hand and accountable to a management team on the other, who often have high expectations of the team's immediate results. In this case, the manager may find themselves faced with moral dilemmas and unable to resolve them because they lack the space to reflect on these issues.

3.2 Business Data Driven: A Culture to be Cultivated

The second aspect examined concerns the introduction of a data culture. According to the participants, data enables clear decisions, reduces uncertainty and increases the transparency of the organization. In this sense, the systematic and integrated use of data is considered to have high strategic potential, even if in daily practice the use of data is not so cross-cutting.

One of the skills associated with data use by the participants is the ability to use analytical systems. Phrases like "we have the data, we have the tools... we just need the context to use them continuously" suggest, however, that these capabilities need fertile ground in which to grow if they are to reach their full potential. In other words, the availability of these capabilities faces cultural and organizational barriers: "We have the numbers, but no one discusses them: they stay on the board's slides.

Furthermore, data is often used in a timely manner, for example for performance monitoring, operational planning and strategic decisions. However, there is often a lack of structured governance, i.e. it is not clear who is responsible for the quality, dissemination and valorization of the data. This lack of clarity often slows down the use and availability of data that could prove valuable for strategic decisions. In contexts with more limited governance, data use is fragmented and poorly integrated into organizational processes; moreover, data use is limited to individual initiatives or specific functions. In this sense, the difference with more structured contexts is clear; in these cases, the use of data is at a systemic level and integrated into all decision-making processes.

In the participants' discussions, leadership emerges as an important turning point. It is up to leaders to actively promote a data culture, share information and improve the use of analytics tools, including by investing in training. Where this does not happen, resistance and a negative perception of data develops, as shown by phrases such as "in our company, data is seen as a control tool and not as a means of improvement" or "the weekly report is only used to find out who made a mistake". As with the "ethics" dimension, management also plays a supporting role in this case.

In light of this analysis, it was possible to understand which organizational characteristics limit the spread of a data-driven culture. The most common obstacles are:

1. a lack of integration of data in operational flows
2. limited access or difficult-to-use tools
3. lack of training and updating
4. organizational culture that uses data as a punitive tool.

In general, it is clear that to develop a data-based culture, on the one hand, adequate tools and training are needed, and on the other, a change in mentality. In this scenario, leadership becomes a facilitator of these practices, acting as an example for its team and for the entire organization.

3.3 Results Integration and Final Considerations

The integration of data from questionnaires and focus groups provided an overview of the changes in organizations. In particular, it was possible to examine ethical leadership and technological advancement, which in this text are expressed through an organization's ability to create a data-driven organizational culture. The intersection between these two areas shows that ethical leadership is a key element in the development of data-driven policies and practices. On the one hand, the study confirms the growing importance of data and its use in all business processes. However, this awareness comes up against real limitations - some structural, some cultural - that hinder this dissemination and thus promote uncertainty, mistrust and ambiguity. On the other hand, there is a growing awareness of the central role of leaders who must translate stated values into effective practices. Moral integrity, respect and transparency as well as a sense of responsibility create the conditions for a solid, widespread and functioning data culture. The trust that develops thanks to exemplary leadership leads to a greater willingness of the team to use analytics tools, share results and put the information received into action. The data-driven approach is not created by the mere implementation of tools, but by the coherent behavior of leaders. Without ethical leadership, data is often seen as a control tool that causes additional stress or serves as a weapon to justify decisions already made instinctively. The introduction of analytics tools is therefore often accompanied by mistrust, especially if there is no transparent narrative linking the data to a clear governance and value system. In other cases, the data remains in management silos, is only accessible to smaller groups and is not discussed collectively. In this case, data is no longer a lever for greater awareness and organizational justice, but a source of opacity and control at the decision-making level. In this context, the concept of ethics as a framework for data is particularly relevant - a foundation for creating the right environment for a truly data-driven culture. The analysis also repeatedly showed that both the data and the resulting ethical dilemmas need to be discussed. The goal is therefore a reflective governance that combines data and values. Here too, leadership plays a decisive role in creating, legitimizing and controlling these spaces.

In light of these considerations, the implications for management are manifold. First of all, ethical and coherent leadership that promotes virtuous behavior and creates a climate of trust proves to be an important element for the conscious introduction of a data culture. It is therefore essential to build ethical leadership that combines integrity and competence, empathy and vision. At the same time, it is important to strengthen digital skills - not only in the technical field, but also in interpretation and decision-making. To promote this, a supportive structure with clear roles, broad access to data and investment in training and integrative processes is essential. On the other hand, it is advisable to accompany the practice of comprehensive responsibility: People with analytical and interpretative skills can interact cross-functionally and make decisions faster and more responsibly. Leadership must therefore act as a visible and credible sponsor of technological projects, capable of linking operational processes to a long-term strategic vision. Finally, an ethical organizational culture proves to be central to building a value-based ecosystem that guides individual and collective responses to change.

In summary, the results of the study suggest that technological change not only concerns technical aspects but also requires reflection on values. In this context, ethical leadership serves as a model for establishing a culture of conscious data and for shaping the future in a visionary, prudent and courageous way.

Ethical Leadership: transformative leadership style that integrates values such as integrity, justice, transparency and responsibility with consistent behavior that sets an example for other members of the organization (Brown & Treviño, 2006; Resick et al., 2006; Den Hartog, 2015).

Data Culture: set of skills, attitudes and values that promote the strategic and conscious use of data at all decision-making levels of the organization. (Kitchin, 2014; Davenport & Harris, 2017; Wamba et al., 2017).

Decision: a process that allows organizations to adapt and integrate with the evolution of society. (Luhmann, 2018).

Ethical Organizational Culture: an organizational culture that promotes values such as integrity, organizational justice and responsibility in all decisions and processes. (Kalshoven & Den Hartog, 2013); Williams & Seaman, 2016).

Algorithmic Bias: distortion in decisions generated by algorithms derived from historical data or learning models influenced by biases. (Jobin et al., 2019; Al-Kfairy et al., 2024).

Decision transparency: the possibility of understanding, tracing and justifying the choices made through the use of automated systems. (Muneeza & Kunhibava, 2024; Saxena, 2024).

Data Governance: a set of rules, roles and processes aimed at guaranteeing the quality, security and ethical use of company data. (Al-Ruithe et al., 2019; Janssen et al., 2020).

REFERENCES

Ahani, A., Nilashi, M., Ibrahim, O., Sanzogni, L., & Weaven, S. (2019). Market segmentation and travel choice prediction in Spa hotels through TripAdvisor's online reviews. *International Journal of Hospitality Management, 80*, 52–77. DOI: 10.1016/j.ijhm.2019.01.003

Al-kfairy, M., Mustafa, D., Kshetri, N., Insiew, M., & Alfandi, O. (2024). Ethical challenges and solutions of generative AI: An interdisciplinary perspective. *Informatics (MDPI), 11*(58), 58. DOI: 10.3390/informatics11030058

Al-Omari, A., & Al-Omari, H. (2006). E-government readiness assessment model. *Journal of Computational Science, 2*(11), 841–845. DOI: 10.3844/jcssp.2006.841.845

Al-Ruithe, M., Benkhelifa, E., & Hameed, K. (2019). A systematic literature review of data governance and cloud data governance. *Personal and Ubiquitous Computing, 23*(5-6), 839–859. DOI: 10.1007/s00779-017-1104-3

Alawamleh, H. K., Alkayed, I. Y., Albdour, A. W. M., & Shatnawi, H. A. (2025). The E-leadership transformation in corporate environment: A bibliometric study. *Human Systems Management, 44*(2), 249–267.

Alkhadra, W. A., Khawaldeh, S., & Aldehayyat, J. (2023). Relationship of ethical leadership, organizational culture, corporate social responsibility and organizational performance: A test of two mediation models. *International Journal of Ethics and Systems, 39*(4), 737–760. DOI: 10.1108/IJOES-05-2022-0092

Banks, G. C., Fischer, T., Gooty, J., & Stock, G. (2020). Ethical leadership: Mapping the terrain for concept cleanup and a future research agenda. *The Leadership Quarterly, 31*(6), 101471.

Bass, B. M. (1995). Theory of transformational leadership redux. *The Leadership Quarterly, 6*(4), 463–478. DOI: 10.1016/1048-9843(95)90021-7

Brown, M. E., & Treviño, L. K. (2006). Ethical leadership: A review and future directions. *The Leadership Quarterly, 17*(6), 595–616. DOI: 10.1016/j.leaqua.2006.10.004

Conrow, E. H. (2011). Estimating technology readiness level coefficients. *Journal of Spacecraft and Rockets, 48*(1), 146–152. DOI: 10.2514/1.46753

Darics, E. (2020). E-leadership or "how to be boss in instant messaging?" The role of nonverbal communication. *International Journal of Business Communication, 57*(1), 3–29. DOI: 10.1177/2329488416685068

Davenport, T., & Harris, J. (2017). *Competing on analytics: Updated, with a new introduction: The new science of winning*. Harvard Business Press.

De Hoogh, A. H., & Den Harog, D. N. (2009). Neuroticism and locus of control as moderators of the relationships of charismatic and autocratic leadership with burnout. *The Journal of Applied Psychology*, *94*(4), 1058–1067. DOI: 10.1037/a0016253 PMID: 19594244

Deluga, R. J. (2001). American presidential Machiavellianism: Implications for charismatic leadership and rated performance. *The Leadership Quarterly*, *12*(3), 339–363. DOI: 10.1016/S1048-9843(01)00082-0

Den Hartog, D. N. (2015). Ethical leadership. *Annual Review of Organizational Psychology and Organizational Behavior, 2*, 4.1–4.26.

Donkers, T., Loepp, B., & Ziegler, J. (2017, August). Sequential user-based recurrent neural network recommendations. In *Proceedings of the eleventh ACM conference on recommender systems* (pp. 152-160). DOI: 10.1145/3109859.3109877

Gloor, P., Fronzetti Colladon, A., & Grippa, F. (2022). Measuring ethical behavior with AI and natural language processing to assess business success. *Scientific Reports*, *12*(1), 10228. DOI: 10.1038/s41598-022-14101-4 PMID: 35715458

House, R. J. (1977). A 1976 theory of charismatic leadership. In Hunt, J. G., & Larson, L. L. (Eds.), *Leadership: the cutting edge* (pp. 189–207). Southern Illinois Univ. Press.

Imran, M. K., Ilyas, M., Aslam, U., & Ubaid-Ur-Rahman, U.-U.-R. (2016). Organizational learning through transformational leadership. *The Learning Organization*, *23*(4), 232–248. DOI: 10.1108/TLO-09-2015-0053

Janssen, M., Brous, P., Estevez, E., Barbosa, L. S., & Janowski, T. (2020). Data governance: Organizing data for trustworthy Artificial Intelligence. *Government Information Quarterly*, *37*(3), 101493. DOI: 10.1016/j.giq.2020.101493

Jeeva, M., Leelavathi, R., Philip, B., Kalaivani, S., & Raj, R. R. (2024). A Study on Technological Revolutions in Dynamic Educational Sector Post-covid-19. In *Artificial Intelligence (AI) and Customer Social Responsibility (CSR)* (pp. 591–601). Springer Nature Switzerland. DOI: 10.1007/978-3-031-50939-1_45

Jobin, A., Ienca, M., & Vayena, E. (2019). *Artificial intelligence: The global landscape of ethics guidelines. Preprint version. Health Ethics & Policy Lab*. ETH Zurich.

Judge, T. A., & Piccolo, R. F. (2004). Transformational and transactional leadership: A meta-analytic test of their relative validity. *The Journal of Applied Psychology*, *89*(5), 755–768. DOI: 10.1037/0021-9010.89.5.755 PMID: 15506858

Kalshoven, K. A. R. I. A. N. N. E., & Den Hartog, D. (2013). Ethical and unethical leader behaviors and their impact on individual well-being and deviance. *Handbook of unethical work behavior: Implications for individual well-being*, 140-154.

Kane, G. C., Nguyen Phillips, A., Copulsky, J., & Andrus, G. (2019). How digital leadership is(n't) different. *MIT Sloan Management Review*, *60*(3), 34–39.

Karatzoglou, A., Amatriain, X., Baltrunas, L., & Oliver, N. (2010, September). Multiverse recommendation: n-dimensional tensor factorization for context-aware collaborative filtering. In *Proceedings of the fourth ACM conference on Recommender systems* (pp. 79-86). DOI: 10.1145/1864708.1864727

Kitchin, R. (2014). The data revolution: Big data, open data, data infrastructures and their consequences. *Sage (Atlanta, Ga.)*. Advance online publication. DOI: 10.4135/9781473909472

Latonero, M. (2018). Governing artificial intelligence: Upholding human rights & dignity. *Data & Society, 38.*

Lin, W. L., Yip, N., Ho, J. A., & Sambasivan, M. (2020). The adoption of technological innovations in a B2B context and its impact on firm performance: An ethical leadership perspective. *Industrial Marketing Management*, *90*, 320–329. DOI: 10.1016/j.indmarman.2019.12.009

Luhmann, N. (2018). *Organization and decision*. Cambridge University Press. DOI: 10.1017/9781108560672

Mathur, S.(2024) Digital Sovereignty: Balancing Security, Identity And Global Hegemony. *Navigation the digital frontiers: new paradigms of technology and society*, 19.

Mohav, Y. (2023). Ethical leadership in AI-driven organizations: Balancing innovation and responsibility. *International Journal of Advanced Engineering Technologies and Innovations*, *1*(4), 204–210.

Muneeza, A., & Kunhibava, S. (2024). Empowering Sustainable Livelihoods: The Ayady Social Kafalah Platform as a Solution to Socioeconomic Challenges. In *Artificial Intelligence (AI) and Customer Social Responsibility (CSR)* (pp. 135–144). Springer Nature Switzerland. DOI: 10.1007/978-3-031-50939-1_11

Northouse, P. G. (2025). *Leadership: Theory and practice*. Sage publications.

Otto, B. (2011). A morphology of the organisation of data governance.

Posner, B. Z., & Kouzes, J. M. (1988). Relating leadership and credibility. *Psychological Reports*, *63*(2), 527–530. DOI: 10.2466/pr0.1988.63.2.527

Resick, C. J., Hanges, P. J., Dickson, M. W., & Mitchelson, J. K. (2006). A cross-cultural examination of the endorsement of ethical leadership. *Journal of Business Ethics*, *63*(4), 345–359. DOI: 10.1007/s10551-005-3242-1

Riggio, R. E., Zhu, W., Reina, C., & Maroosis, J. A. (2010). Virtue-based measurement of ethical leadership: The leadership virtues questionnaire. *Consulting Psychology Journal*, *62*(4), 235–250. DOI: 10.1037/a0022286

Robinson, G. M., Magnusen, M., & Kim, J. W. (2019). The socially effective leader: Exploring the relationship between athletic director political skill and coach commitment and job satisfaction. *International Journal of Sports Science & Coaching*, *14*(2), 197–204. DOI: 10.1177/1747954119834118

Sacavém, A., Cruz, R. N., Sousa, M. J., & Rosário, A. M. (2019). An integrative literature review on leadership models for innovative organizations. *International Journal of Innovation and Economic Development*, *5*(6), 43–53.

Salvador-Carulla, L., Woods, C., de Miquel, C., & Lukersmith, S. (2024). Adaptation of the technology readiness levels for impact assessment in implementation sciences: The TRL-IS checklist. *Heliyon*, *10*(9), e29930. DOI: 10.1016/j.heliyon.2024.e29930 PMID: 38726201

Saxena, R. (2024). Artificial intelligence and sustainable social development. In Jorasia, A., & Kumar, R. (Eds.), *Navigation the digital frontiers: New paradigms of technology and society* (pp. 1–8). Career Point University.

Shamim, S., Cang, S., & Yu, H. (2017). Supervisory orientation, employee goal orientation, and knowledge management among front line hotel employees. *International Journal of Hospitality Management*, *62*, 21–32. DOI: 10.1016/j.ijhm.2016.11.013

Shoker, A. (2022). Digital sovereignty strategies for every nation. *Applied Cybersecurity & Internet Governance*, *1*(1), 1–17. DOI: 10.5604/01.3001.0016.0943

Squires, V. (2018). Northouse, PG (2016). Leadership: Theory and practice. Thousand Oaks, CA: Sage. Pages: 494. *Canadian Journal of Educational Administration and Policy*, •••, 185.

Stogdill, R. M. (1948). Personal factors associated with leadership: A survey of the literature. *The Journal of Psychology*, *25*(1), 35–71. DOI: 10.1080/00223980.1948.9917362 PMID: 18901913

Tagscherer, F., & Carbon, C.-C. (2023). Leadership for successful digitalization: A literature review on companies' internal and external aspects of digitalization. *Sustainable Technology and Entrepreneurship*, *2*(2), 100039. DOI: 10.1016/j.stae.2023.100039

Vaswani, G. (2024). Dawn of The Digital Era. *NAVIGATION THE DIGITAL FRONTIERS: NEW PARADIGMS OF TECHNOLOGY AND SOCIETY*, 9.

Wamba, S. F., Gunasekaran, A., Akter, S., Ren, S. J. F., Dubey, R., & Childe, S. J. (2017). Big data analytics and firm performance: Effects of dynamic capabilities. *Journal of Business Research*, *70*, 356–365. DOI: 10.1016/j.jbusres.2016.08.009

Williams, J. J., & Seaman, A. E. (2016). The influence of ethical leadership on managerial performance: Mediating effects of mindfulness and corporate social responsibility. *Journal of Applied Business Research*, *32*(3), 815–828. DOI: 10.19030/jabr.v32i3.9659

Winston, M. D. (2001). The importance of leadership diversity: The relationship between diversity and organizational success in the academic environment. *College & Research Libraries*, *62*(6), 517–526. DOI: 10.5860/crl.62.6.517

Wu, Y. (2014). Protecting personal data in E-government: A cross-country study. *Government Information Quarterly*, *31*(1), 150–159. DOI: 10.1016/j.giq.2013.07.003

Chapter 2
AI, Ethics, and Accountability:
The Role of Corporate Social Responsibility in Shaping Ethical Leadership

Mehak Jonjua
http://orcid.org/0000-0003-0123-8355
Sharda University, India

ABSTRACT

Artificial Intelligence (AI) keeps on changing the business topic. The integration of AI ethics into Corporate Social Responsibility has become a very important area of concern. This research work investigates how organizations operationalize ethical principles within AI development and deployment influenced by responsible leadership. Research uses case-study of even expert interviews- to understand the changing role of leadership in embedding ethical AI practices within CSR programs. Results show that ethical AI is no longer situated in an ivory tower but is being increasingly represented in organizational policies and practices. Leadership is the main driving force for this transformation because it encourages transparency, accountability, and fairness in the development and use of AI systems. This paper contributes to the discourse on responsible AI.

INTRODUCTION

As we enter the 21st century, the convergence of AI technology, business ethics and corporate social responsibility has become one of the most pressing governance

DOI: 10.4018/979-8-3693-4099-8.ch002

issues of this time. Companies are increasingly using AI systems to help them make decisions in their businesses today, whether it is for example to make hiring decisions, score credit worthiness or diagnose medical problems using AI systems or even to use AI systems for surveillance purposes. Companies must now start to ask questions of accountability, transparency, algorithmic fairness and moral governance as well as have them move from an abstract philosophical question to a practical necessity (Kandasamy, 2024). With AI systems arriving at an accelerating pace organisations face an opportunity paradox, i.e., although AI technology can deliver unprecedented operational efficiency, predictive insight and competitive advantage, they will also create a range of complex ethical dilemmas that intersect with long-established societal values about the intrinsic worth of every human being, privacy, equality and democracy.

Operating within this environment corporate leaders will be required to perform the dual roles of developing AI capabilities as quickly as possible to serve their customers and their shareholders, while also ensuring that AI technology is being developed in compliance with the ethical standards and social values of respect, fairness and human flourishing (Mathipurani & Narayanaswamy, 2024). This conflict between operational velocity and ethical deliberation becomes the primary governance challenge that modern organisations now face. The implications of this challenge are larger than merely reputational harm or potential for being fined by their respective regulators; they have the potential to challenge the fundamental societal contract between corporations and the societies they serve.

Corporate Social Responsibility offers an established institution-based framework for managing this complexity for organisations. Corporate Social Responsibility started out with principles such as environmental stewardship and stakeholder engagement, transparency, and social impacts (Camilleri, 2024). CSR has long been an ethical framework that functions as a guide for how organizations function beyond profit maximization. The application of CSR ethics to Corporate AI governance is a logical progression of how CSR has evolved over time. It is also a response to the realities that organization face in the digital economy today. By embedding social responsibility into AI development and implementation, organizations are able to create technology systems that not only deliver in terms of performance but also meet the ethical expectations of stakeholders over the long term.

The evolution of ethical governance for Corporate AI can be seen through the maturity of technology companies and the acknowledgement of success and challenges encountered. The development of Microsoft's Office of Responsible AI in 2019, following public pressure related to facial recognition technologies and disproportionate levels of surveillance and review on communities of colour, is a landmark innovation in how companies have developed governance frameworks around AI (Ferrell & Ferrell, 2024). Microsoft established and communicated that it would be using its governance frameworks to establish industry-wide innovation standards and demonstrate its commitment to responsible innovation through ethical reviews and publishing transparency reports.

The evolution of Google's Corporate AI ethics story is much more complicated and illustrates the complexity of turning ethics into action. Google created formal AI Principles and created the Advanced Technology External Advisory Council in 2016 in response to internal dissent and public controversy over Project Maven (a Pentagon contracted initiative to use AI to analyze drone footage). The departure in late 2020 of Timnit Gebru, a high-profile researcher in AI ethics, amid allegations of suppression of critical ethical research due to corporate interests demonstrates that formal ethics frameworks, while important, are not sufficient in and of themselves without true organizational culture change and structural protections for ethical advocacy, when they come into conflict with organizational power relations.

IBM's governance model for AI ethics creates another useful example. IBM provides centralized oversight of the implementation of ethics principles via its AI Ethics Board and has developed an open-source tool, AI Fairness 360, which allows organizations to detect and reduce the impact of algorithmic bias. These two separate efforts create a means for companies to operationalize responsible AI practices that are not confined to an organization's boundaries but also benefit the overall technology ecosystem. By advocating for precision-targeted regulation of AI as opposed to broad prohibitive regulation, IBM also demonstrates how companies can help policymakers create governance frameworks that simultaneously encourage innovation by companies while also providing necessary protections to the general public.

Corporate responsibility for AI ethics therefore goes beyond just protecting a particular organization from reputational damage and/or following the law.The manner in which large companies regulate the creation/implementation of artificial intelligence is affecting how the public views these systems for years to come. This means that AI's ability to help solve some of the biggest issues facing humanity - including climate change, drug development, education, and economics - will be influenced by the way big businesses develop and deploy AI in the present day (Camilleri, 2024). Ethical leadership from companies producing AI technologies will help support not just their long-term viability in the marketplace but also to the overall vision of developing new technologies that enhance human life as opposed to degrading it.

Governance Models must take into account how the industry has progressed historically to deliver the type of Public Trust that is essential for Governance Models to succeed in delivering on the substantial ethical challenges posed by the rapid progression of AI Technologies, particularly in Generative AI and Large Foundation Models (learning systems). By evaluating today's AI Governance issues within the historical context of the development of Corporate Ethics, we hope to clarify both the successes that have been achieved and the continuing need to build AI Governance Models that are worthy of obtaining Public Trust in AI Technologies.

LITERATURE REVIEW

Discourse on the Origins of AI Ethics

Long before the first commercial applications of Artificial Intelligence were developed and distributed to retailers, and long before there was widespread academic scholarship about the ethical and moral implications of that technology, AI was the subject of ethical and moral intellectual inquiries. The conceptual basis for thinking about machine ethics can be traced back to the 1942 short story "Runaround" by the science fiction author Isaac Asimov, which introduced his "Three Laws of Robotics." These laws outline a hierarchy of obligations for robots, including a prohibition against harming humans, obedience to human orders, and self-preservation. They also provide an early example of how to establish behavioral constraints on autonomous artificial agents (Lapatoura, 2025). Despite the extensive critique and limitations of Asimov's three laws, including that they are logically self-contradictory under certain conditions and insufficient to account for the realities of ethical dilemmas humans face every day, there continues to be a contemporary discourse of AI ethics rooted in the same project—defining the ethical constraints of artificial agents. That Asimov's framework continues to be the foundation for current discussions about ethics supports the idea that it will be 80 years later and still be relevant to today's questions about machines.

The Dartmouth Conference of 1956 was the first organized academic conference on artificial intelligence. At that time, eminent computer scientists such as Alan Turing, John McCarthy, and Marvin Minsky gathered to identify opportunities to create machine intelligence (Ferrell & Ferrell, 2024). This gathering established the foundation for both a new scientific discipline and a series of philosophical inquiries surrounding machine consciousness, moral responsibility and social responsibility, which have run parallel to technological developments over time. Turing laid the foundation for future philosophical provocations that have shaped the evolution of AI ethics, particularly the "Turing Test," which tested whether a machine could demonstrate human-like intelligent behaviour. The question at the centre of these philosophical discussions was: If a machine can demonstrate intelligent behaviour indistinguishable from that of a human, what are the implications for assigning moral and ethical status to that machine?

The early philosophical discussions began the development of ethical frameworks that stayed mainly in academic and speculative communities during the mid-twentieth century until the corporate AI ethical frameworks began to emerge over the next several decades. The concept vocabulary developed in this period — including autonomy, responsibility, transparency and alignment with human values — is the foundation of today's AI governance discussions and demonstrates the deep intellectual history associated with what might seem to be new policy developments at the corporate level.

Early Corporate Computing Ethics

The formal codification of professional computing ethics occurred before the current AI ethics movement and created institutional precedents which have evolved to now cover AI issues. The Association for Computing Machinery (ACM) first published its Code of Ethics in 1972, addressing professional issues in computer science and engineering and later extending those responsibilities to address AI as the technology has progressed (Herath & Herath, 2024). The professional ethics framework at this time showed that computers provide computing professionals significant power to manipulate information systems that have a social effect and, therefore, also impose the same ethical obligations.

By the end of the 1980s or the beginning of 1990s, several large technology companies (IBM, Microsoft) developed internal ethics committees for their internal corporate computing ethics; however, they primarily focused on privacy, data security, and intellectual property rather than on fairness algorithms and accountability for autonomous systems, issues that have defined AI ethics more recently. While limited in scope, the establishment of early institutional ethics committees set an example for developing internal corporate governance mechanisms that have since been expanded upon over the following decades as AI technologies advanced and their social ramifications became more apparent.

The development of corporate computing ethics has mirrored changing regulatory conditions and public expectations about technology. Increasing concern about database privacy, unauthorized access, and the social impact of computerized decision-making have led regulators to implement regulations (e.g., Computer Fraud and Abuse Act of 1986, USA) that establish and hold corporations accountable for their ethics initiatives. The relationship between corporate self-regulatory governance and regulatory external pressure has been established as a continuing interaction pattern for the governance of AI today.

The Rise of Corporate Social Responsibility (1990s–2000s)

Mainstreaming CSR as Organizational Practice

Throughout the early decades of the 21st century (i.e., the early 2000s through the mid-2010s) we saw a tremendous shift towards a more developed understanding of Corporate Social Responsibility (CSR)—both as a widely accepted business practice and a critical aspect of global corporate strategy. One key force behind this trend was John Elkington's popularization of the "triple bottom line" in 1994. The idea of balancing the three traditional business metrics of profit (the "bottom line") with social responsibility (people) and environmental responsibility (the planet) established a conceptual scaffolding around the understanding that all businesses have social and environmental obligations (Baba, 2024). Additionally, Elkington's framework of CSR as a necessity to create success in the long-run was further supported by the growing body of literature finding long-term financial success of a business is positively correlated with strong social and environmental practices. Elkington's work challenged conventional notions of "philanthropy" or "charitable donations" as being the primary method for corporations to fulfill their social and environmental obligations and instead positioned CSR as a developmental component of their strategic success.

Another key milestone in the establishment of CSR as a legitimate global business "norm" was the United Nations Global Compact, which was launched in 1999. The purpose of the Compact was to promote global corporate responsibility through adherence to a set of sustainability-based principles. By encouraging multinational corporations to adopt policies related to CSR and sustainability across their global operations, the UN Global Compact proved to be a crucial catalyst for the "institutionalization" of CSR at the international level. As of the early 2000s, CSR had gained such a sufficient level of global acceptance that corporations listed in the Fortune 500 maintained both a publicly available list of corporate values and formal CSR programs (Aljarah et al., 2024). These developments created a significant organizational infrastructure necessary to effectively manage CSR initiatives, including establishing ethics committees for determining the appropriateness of proposed CSR initiatives, engaging stakeholders in the appropriate oversight of social impacts associated with operational decisions, and using metrics to quantify and report an organization's social impact. The ability to create this infrastructure will be necessary to develop appropriate governance frameworks to address the unique challenges posed by the use of Artificial Intelligence (AI)-operated systems.

The concurrent development of global reporting standards supportive of social responsibility (i.e., the Global Reporting Initiative's Sustainability Reporting Standards) and the development of socially responsible investment criteria further supported the establishment of organizational CSR as the basis for a global financial industry. These reporting standards established a long-term expectation for transparency and accountability, which ultimately will provide the basis for establishing a similar expectation related to the development and use of AI systems.

Early AI Applications and Limited Ethical Frameworks

AI at that time was purpose-built with a limited number of capabilities based on unambiguous rules and was implemented in limited case-specific areas like medical diagnosis, banking and manufacturing (Akinsola, 2025). As these first AI systems operated within a defined set of predictable parameters, they generally posed ethical dilemmas that primarily centre around their overall reliability and appropriateness of use rather than the broader social issues that would later be debated in relation to AI ethics. Because the rules-driven systems operated under objective, predictable rules, the reasoning behind them was easily interpreted by humans, thereby limiting the broader issues of opacity and algorithmic accountability that would later become challenges due to the introduction of machine learning.

The defeat of world chess champion Garry Kasparov by IBM's Deep Blue in 1997 became an important moment in cultures for bringing into the public consciousness questions around how AI compares to human capabilities and the possibility of them competing against one another (Pai & Chandra, 2022). While this spectacle captured significant attention from the media and generated some controversy around competing between machine-based systems and human-based systems, there was not yet an infrastructure within the corporate community for addressing the ethical issues associated with developing AI. Technology companies tended to address ethics associated with AI through already-established regulatory and quality control procedures as opposed to creating separate regulatory structures for AI, suggesting to technology companies that their existing governance systems would be sufficient to manage the risk of these types of systems.

Emergence of Modern AI Ethics (2010–2016)

The Machine Learning Revolution and Its Ethical Implications

Machine learning techniques developed rapidly in the 2010s as a result of improved deep learning technologies, allowing for the capacity for complex pattern recognition by artificial intelligence systems at near or above human level across many additional field(s). Major milestones occurred in this decade (for example: IBM Watson winning Jeopardy! in 2011 and AlphaGo beating World Go Champion Lee Sedol in 2016), which significantly raised public awareness of what AI could accomplish, while simultaneously spurring $ billions of new investment into AI solutions and applications across multiple industries (Du & Sen, 2023).

The spread of machine learning across high-stakes social contexts (for example; criminal justice, credit scoring, employment screening, and medical diagnosis) created the first systematic evidence of the societal harm that AI systems with inadequate oversight could cause. (Ozkan, 2024). For example, the research conducted by Latanya Sweeney in 2013 demonstrated that online advertising systems had a significant racial bias towards the names presented in searches for criminal records. This clearly indicated that algorithms may propagate and amplify existing social inequality through their operation.

A landmark ProPublica investigative report published in 2016 highlighted the differentiated accuracy between racial groups within justice-based risk assessment tools (in this case COMPAS), potentially leading to millions of dollars of harm to both black and white defendants because of the way the system falsely identified black defendants with criminal implications and consequence biases. This report gained immediate attention by both the public and academia, raising the issue of bias within algorithms and bringing AI ethics into mainstream policy discussions.

Prior to this evidence, there was a techno-optimism amongst many researchers and policymakers that algorithmic decisions were inherently more objective and fair than those made by humans because they were based on data; this evidence disproved that assumption through the identification of systematic bias within algorithmic systems and the consequences that arise from these biases embedded in both the training data for the model and the design of the system itself. AI ethics have evolved into an impending civil rights / social justice issue from a dystopian science fiction concern raised through these revelations.

Formation of Industry Consortia and Self-Regulatory Initiatives

Amidst growing awareness of the societal implications of more powerful AI systems, technology companies created industry-wide collaborative governance initiatives during this time. The Partnership on AI, which was established in 2014 by such companies as Amazon, Facebook, Google, DeepMind, Microsoft and IBM, created a significant industry-led project for developing best practices in AI development through educating the public and multi-stakeholder dialogue among industry leaders (Du & Sen, 2023). While the implementation of this voluntary consortium remains a topic of debate within experienced academia, the formation of the partnership reflects an industry-wide commitment from leading technology companies that AI governance cannot be solely dealt with at an individual organisation and therefore required a coordinated industry-wide response.

During this time, individual companies also began creating their own proprietary ethical guidelines and internal review channels. In 2014, when Google acquired DeepMind, a corporate AI ethics board was developed, although the board's membership and deliberations were addressed privately, thus limiting the access and accountability of the ethics board. In 2016, Microsoft formed the Aether Committee (AI, Ethics, and Effects in Engineering and Research) to assist with company-wide governance decisions regarding emerging ethical dilemmas and served as a first example of the formalised ethics advisory structure that would become commonplace within large technology corporations in the following years.

During this time, many academic institutions will develop conceptual and methodical foundations for the study of AI Ethics through research groups studying this discipline. Institutions such as the Future of Life Institute (2014) and the NYU AI Now Institute (2017) created research infrastructures to examine the social implications of AI systems and train future scholars and practitioners in the ethical implications of AI. The establishment of dedicated research groups for AI ethics as a field of academic study, with and their own journals, conferences, and established methodology convention, produced an academic body of knowledge that corporate ethics professionals have access to in the development of their own internal governance frameworks.

Institutionalizing AI Ethics in Corporate Governance (2017–2019)

High-Profile Controversies and Accelerated Corporate Response

Between 2017 and 2019, a number of high-profile incidents greatly boosted the institutionalization of AI ethics into corporate governance structures. The Cambridge Analytica scandal (2018) raised huge alarms about algorithmic manipulation, the ethics of data, and social media AI and their political impact, as billions of personal data of those using Facebook were harvested improperly (Hamdan & Buallay, 2024). It became highly visible that AI systems were being used on a large scale to influence the democratic process, which incited calls for regulatory action and put immense pressure on technology companies to provide more robust ethical governance.

Amazon's internal findings that their AI recruitment platform systematically devalued resumes submitted by women (due to the training of the AI on historical hiring data that was already biased against women) offered a tangible example of how algorithmic bias can perpetuate discrimination without any intentional discrimination on the part of the users of the AI. This scenario became widely cited in academic literature and among the corporate sector as a cautionary tale on the need for bias testing and how diverse development teams are required in developing AI systems. The public disclosure of this mistake placed significant reputational pressure on other companies to create stronger bias detection and mitigation practices for themselves.

Google's conflict with its employees over Project Maven (AI technology to review data from drone surveillance footage to assist the U.S. Department of Defense) was a watershed from the perspective of technology employees, corporate ethics, and AI governance. The internal petition (signed by many thousands of Google employees) against the contract, which contributed to the company not renewing the contract, demonstrated that AI ethics commitments can create considerable internal organizational dynamics that corporate leadership must manage (Fernandes et al., 2024). In establishing its seven AI Principles in June of 2018 in response to this controversy, Google formalized its ethical framework to limit the applications for which it would participate in the development of AI technologies—specifically excluding autonomous weapons systems from AI technologies developed by the company.

Formalization of Corporate AI Ethics Frameworks

From 2018 to 2019, many of the world's largest technology firms created formal frameworks for AI ethics that were innovative and unprecedented. For example, Microsoft published its six principles for responsible AI — fairness; reliability and safety; privacy and security; inclusiveness; transparency; and accountability — in 2018. This set forth a comprehensive normative framework that would guide Microsoft's governance initiatives. IBM published its Principles for Trust and Transparency in the same year, while Salesforce established its Office of Ethical & Humane Use of Technology and Intel published an AI Ethics Policy in 2019 (Fioravante, 2024).

A scholarly analysis of the proliferating corporate frameworks for AI ethics shows that while there is significant convergence on the core principles included in them, they employ widely differing methods of implementation. While nearly all companies developing such frameworks included some form of each of these foundational ethical requirements — fairness, transparency, privacy protection, and human oversight — the operationalization of these ethical requirements varied to a significant degree, as did the accountability structures designed to accomplish compliance (Ozkan,2024). In part, the differences among the various corporate frameworks reflect the legitimate differences in organizational culture and technology context between companies, however, many critics have charged that these differences are also reflective of a strategic ambiguity that enables companies to assert ethical commitments, but without subjecting themselves to any binding standards or independent verification.

The development of international AI ethical frameworks by standardization organizations began during this period, providing external reference points to potentially complement or discipline corporate self-governance initiatives. The IEEE launched its Global Initiative on Ethics of Autonomous and Intelligent Systems in 2016, and the first version of the IEEE's Ethically Aligned Design document was published in 2019; ISO and IEC established a joint technical committee (ISO/IEC JTC 1/SC 42) to develop international standards for AI ethics and governance. Together, these standardization efforts laid the foundation for the more comprehensive certification frameworks that are expected to emerge over the coming years.

Integration of AI Ethics With CSR (2019–2021)

From Principles to Practice: Operationalizing Ethical Commitments

In 2019, the number of corporate AI ethics statements increased rapidly and attention shifted to implementation of these ethical policies (Fioravante, 2024). The gap between what was declared ethically and what actually happened was documented during this same time frame—this has been called 'ethics washing' or 'AI ethics theatre' and raised concerns regarding whether the frameworks provided for corporate ethics were actually serving any real governance purposes or if they were just a way to perform public relations activity.

Leading companies responded to these criticisms by building more comprehensive governance systems to oversee implementation of ethics within their organisation. For example, Microsoft created its Office of Responsible AI in 2019 which has cross-functional authority and resource dedicated to the implementation of responsible AI principles across all products sold by the company. IBM appointed its first Chief Ethical Officer for AI in 2019 and also established an AI Ethical Governance Board, both of which will provide governance over ethical implementation within the organisation. These structural investments are a significant change from the past where companies would only create policy around corporate ethics, but no oversight or accountability for implementation of those policies (Soubhari et al., 2025).

The departure of Timnit Gebru from Google's ethical AI team at the end of 2020 after conflicts regarding a research paper that examined risk of large language models and other concerns surrounding the independence of internal ethics research caused much controversy due to the exacerbated structural tensions between corporate interests versus ethical AI advocacy (Fernandes et al., 2024). The situation created substantial discussion regarding whether or not internal ethics teams could remain truly independent from commercial pressures and whether or not external mechanisms (such as independent ethical audits of corporations and minimal regulations) were needed to ensure that corporations' commitments to AI ethics were adequately integrated into their business practices, rather than simply managed as an afterthought.

Stakeholder Capitalism and the Broadening of AI Ethics Accountability

The creation of Corporate AI Ethics was altered in 2019 when the 181 CEOs of the Business Roundtable stated the purpose of a corporation to include all stakeholders as well as shareholders. With this declaration, the Business Roundtable established the normative framework for businesses to explore AI Ethics in light of their wider obligations to stakeholders, and that spending on AI governance would be viewed as a primary expression of a corporation's purpose rather than just protecting businesses from risk (Khan et al., 2024).

In Larry Fink's letter to corporate leaders in 2020, he suggested technology governance was important to sustainable long-term value creation, and therefore, Institutional Investors were beginning to consider AI Ethics in their evaluation of companies' sustainability and long-term value. This was reflected in that companies began including discussions about AI Ethics in their Sustainability Reports and CSR reports, defining responsible AI as a key element of their social impact story (Khan et al., 2024). By integrating AI Ethics into ESG (Environmental, Social, Governance) frameworks, businesses moved AI Governance closer to the existing reporting infrastructure for Sustainability and Investor Relations.

The Regulatory Landscape has also changed during this time frame, with the EU AI Act being introduced in 2021 as the most comprehensive attempt yet to create binding legal requirements for AI Governance. The EU AI Act creates a Risk-based Framework, with increased requirements for AI systems based on their relative risk of causing harm; where the most rigorous compliance requirements are for "high-risk" applications in employment, education and law enforcement—creating regulatory markers that will drive companies to improve their internal governance in preparation for compliance (Selvaraj, 2024). Binding Regulation creates an impetus for strategic governance investments that would not have otherwise existed with just voluntary frameworks.

Maturation and Standardization (2022–2024)

Integration With ESG Reporting Frameworks

AI governance has matured and grown beyond simply being a reputational and risk management concern into being part of mainstream corporate accountability infrastructure; therefore, there is growing interest in ensuring that there is an efficient framework for comparing AI governance across organizations. Comparability of governance allows for investors to make comparative assessments of AI governance practices, thus establishing competitive incentives for improvements to governance and an overall framework around the responsible investment thesis for AI among institutional investors. Emerging research is beginning to document a correlation between robust AI governance and financial performance, providing empirical support for the business cases for investing in responsible AI (Gupta et al., 2025).

Generative AI and Novel Ethical Challenges

The launch of DALL-E 2 in April 2022 and ChatGPT in November 2022 marked the beginning of generative AI's capabilities, both bringing forth unique ethical challenges that required immediate changes in how we govern.

The ability for large language models and image generation systems to create vast amounts of very realistic synthetic content raised many immediate concerns: misinformation, copyright violations, unsafe content, and job impacts across not only creative but also knowledge-based industries (Pathania & Srivastava, 2025). These concerns required a governing response not fully covered by existing frameworks; traditional governance structures had been designed primarily around the issues of discriminatory algorithmic decision-making.

Corporate governance systems developed a response to generative AI under extreme time pressure; the rapid acceleration of consumers' use of generative AI systems coupled with growing demands for safety and accountability led to an urgent need for corporate governance systems to provide adequate responses. OpenAI created a separate Safety and Security team, published risk mitigation documents, and developed other accountability frameworks. Microsoft generated the Microsoft Responsible AI Standard, which addressed generative AI, and subsequently integrated its responsible AI requirements into its third-party developer agreements. Google implemented principles to govern responsible development of generative AI; Adobe developed the Content Authenticity Initiative in response to the need for means of attributing AI-generated media (Aljarah et al., 2024). The totality of these responses shows the adaptability of corporate AI ethics infrastructure that existed in prior years, as well as the ongoing challenge of ensuring that corporate governance frameworks remain current due to the velocity of technological evolution.

Standardization and Certification Frameworks

During the time frame between the years 2023 and 2024, there was great advancement in creating global standardized frameworks that would offer stronger and more consistent bases for the way corporations govern AI systems. In January

2023, NIST (National Institute of Standards and Technology) published its Framework for Managing AI Risk, which outlines specific instructions for organizations to use to locate, identify, assess, and manage risks related to AI in an organized and repeatable way. Additionally, as of early 2024, ISO/IEC 42001 will become the first standard published for corporate AI Management Systems, including a certification framework similar to those used by other well-established management systems, i.e., ISO 9001 for Quality Management Systems or ISO 27001 for Information Security Management Systems, so organizations can acquire independent verification of their AI governance procedures (Soubhari et al., 2025).

These initiatives and associated standards created a qualitative leap forward regarding the maturity level of organizations' capabilities to manage the ethical aspects of AI by incorporating ethical considerations into existing governance frameworks instead of creating new ones. Organizations that earn third-party certification of compliance to these standards can transparently demonstrate to their customers, investors, regulators, and others their commitment to governing AI using independent credentials rather than relying on self-reported evidence. Leading organizations are already pursuing this type of recognition as indicators of their enhanced commitment to responsible AI governance practices (Kaleem et al., 2025).

Contemporary Landscape and Persistent Challenges

Mature Corporate Accountability Mechanisms

By 2024, the AI ethics of leading organizations had developed a comprehensive system of governance much beyond the policy declarations that created earlier phases of development. Most governance frameworks incorporate a dedicated ethics board or committee with representation from multiple disciplines (technical experts, legal & privacy professionals, accessibility specialists, and business representatives) to ensure that all points of view are considered before making decisions about AI governance and before escalating them to senior management levels (Pathania & Srivastava, 2025). It is now also common for organizations to have established formal processes for reviewing high risk AI applications through the use of multi-tiered assessment frameworks, which determine how in-depth an evaluation will be based on the potential impact of a system being reviewed. Evaluation steps usually include algorithm impact assessments, data audits, and fairness assessments prior to making deployment decisions.

The technological tools available to detect bias, assess explainability, and ensure safety have improved, with many organizations creating internal tools that provide their engineers with the means to evaluate their models using these criteria during the development process, not solely at the time of deployment (Pathania & Srivastava, 2025). Employee training has matured from providing frontline employees with awareness training to providing role-based training curricula for engineers on how to implement fairness in AI systems, product managers on how to identify ethical issues in the planning phase of a project, and executives through scenario planning for the consequences of making certain decisions with respect to high risk AI systems. Engaging stakeholders has become much more systematic, with leading organizations developing structured programs for community engagement, using independent advisory boards, and conducting comprehensive user experience studies to assess how their AI systems have a different impact on various demographic groups.

Unresolved Tensions and Emerging Challenges

Even with all that progress, the AI ethics field has to deal with many basic tensions that do not lend themselves to an easy resolution. The competitive dynamics of AI markets continue to place pressure on companies to cut the timeline for ethical assessments. As such, companies often rush to market in order to capture the first-mover advantage, oftentimes at a speed that is inconsistent with the time-intensive process of conducting a thorough ethical review of their product's safety (Selvaraj, 2024). Organizations routinely must also deal with the complexity of operating internationally and therefore must navigate the nuances of different jurisdictions, the most significant of which is the EU's expansive binding regulatory structure versus the patchwork of regulation governing companies in various other parts of the world. Because of this, organizations must develop complex compliance strategies and sometimes make very difficult decisions about whether to participate in a particular market and how to differentiate their products in that market.

At the same time, the concentration of advanced AI capabilities among a small group of large corporations leads to some fundamental questions about corporate governance and public accountability that the current corporate ethics frameworks do not answer (Zhou, et al., 2024). Once a corporation's decision about whether to develop and/or deploy AI has ramifications for a broad societal impact, then serious questions are raised regarding whether the self-governance structures that corporations are currently using are capable of providing sufficient accountability to the greater public good. These concerns have initiated current conversations regarding the appropriate breadth and structure of the regulatory oversight of corporate conduct regarding AI, the role that civil society plays in the governance of AI, and what limitations there should be placed on a corporation's authority over a technology that will have a significant impact on society.

Measurement continues to pose a considerable challenge to demonstrating that AI ethics governance functions properly and is effective, rather than merely complying with governance processes. While organizations can easily document the existence of training programs, review processes and any meetings of ethics boards, it continues to be difficult on a methodological basis to determine whether those mechanisms are actually preventing harms from being caused by AI systems as intended (Kaleem et al., 2025). In addition, due to the lack of any established metrics to evaluate the effectiveness of AI ethics—similar to those used for financial performance or environmental impacts—it has created barriers to measuring the effectiveness of different methods of governance, and limits the ability to be held accountable for the ultimate outcome of a governance process versus the process of complying with those governance processes. Accordingly, there is a need to develop robust measurement frameworks for determining the effectiveness of AI ethics in order to advance scholarship and practical innovation.

The relationship between AI's advance and the assurance of safety/goodness presents a continuing governance challenge, particularly as generative AI systems gain in power and versatility. The technical complexity of large-scale AI systems has made testing for safety across the totality of that system increasingly difficult. At the same time, given the competitive dynamics, companies have an incentive to deploy their new AI system as quickly as possible, creating the potential for that system to fail before the company has a good understanding of when (and why) it might fail. This challenge is particularly acute with respect to frontier AI models, for which their associated capabilities often do not become apparent until the models are sufficiently large and trained. Scholars throughout the world continue to agree that reconciling the tension between developing advanced capabilities and providing for sufficient verification of the safety of the AI systems to provide assurance of their goodness will comprise the most significant governance challenge facing the world in the next decade (Kaleem et al., 2025).

Synthesis and Future Directions

The development of corporate AI ethics has had an evolution from a philosophical perspective to an establishment of ethics and principles to a more institutionalized governance system through the use of existing infrastructure for accountability. Evidence shows that these developments have been influenced by the interactions of many different drivers; high-profile controversies illustrating the harms caused by unregulated AI; increasing regulatory pressure (especially within the European Union) and changing investor expectations through the use of ESG frameworks; as well as the ethical leadership of individuals within organizations who are invested in developing ethical technology (Zhou et al., 2024).

Embedding AI ethics within the CSR framework is one of the most important developments thus far, embedding AI governance into organizations' established accountability structures and connecting them to other commitments to stakeholders.

This shift has allowed for AI ethics to become part of the mainstream strategy and operations of organizations, their investor relations and external accountability, which was difficult to predict when company discussions were strictly philosophical. At the same time, the continued tension points noted through this review demonstrate that while institutional progress consists of developing solutions for ethical issues, and will always have time to develop further solutions for these issues in new organizational environments.

Future research in this area of study would benefit by placing a greater emphasis on empirical testing of the success of AI governance policies to identify if governance mechanisms are having a positive impact on reducing harm or if they are just creating documentation of compliance. A more extensive examination of how governance affects organizations through comparative studies will provide insight on how context shapes governance outcomes as well as under which circumstances governance tools are most effective. In addition to comparative studies, longitudinal tracking of organizations' trajectories in developing and evolving AI ethics governance control systems will provide valuable insight on how governance systems evolve as a function of technological advances, regulatory developments and the accumulation of an organization's experience. The completion of these research priorities will improve the academic foundations for developing successful AI governance in an era where the decisions made today will ultimately shape the outcomes of artificial intelligence in society for generations.

RESEARCH OBJECTIVES

This research looks into how the relationship between artificial intelligence ethics and the different corporate social responsibility frameworks are changing, especially under the ingress of true leaders who are integrating ethical considerations into the governance structures for AI. The study then looks into the ways in which ethical AI governance has developed from aspirational principles to operational mechanisms in organizational contexts through analyses of various corporate practices, regulatory developments, and emerging industry standards.

RESEARCH METHODOLOGY

This study adopts an overarching research design characterized as mixed methods, combining qualitative case studies and quantitative measures of the application of AI ethics across organizations. The methodological linchpin is centered on in-depth case studies of 12 organizations chosen to reflect diverse industry sectors (technology, financial services, healthcare, and manufacturing) and organizational characteristics (from Fortune 100 corporations to mid-sized companies with 500-5,000 employees). For each case study, semi-structured interviews are conducted with key stakeholders across the AI ethics governance ecosystem: Chief Ethics Officers; AI product managers; data scientists; legal counsel; and executive leadership responsible for AI strategy. The interview protocol evaluates both formal governance structure and informal organizational practices, with emphasis on how ethical considerations are integrated into everyday decision-making. About 72 interviews (approximately six for each organization) deliver sufficient depth to triangulate perspectives while capturing variance across organizational roles. These interviews are supplemented by document analysis of public-facing ethics statements, internal review protocols (when permitted), and published transparency reports to examine alignment between stated policies and actual practices. A standardized assessment tool is further administered to 200 AI practitioners from 50 organizations to quantitatively evaluate the maturity of AI ethics implementation in seven dimensions that our theoretical framework identifies. This methodological approach thus produces rich contextual knowledge of organizational dynamics squared against a comparative analysis of implementation patterns across the corporate arena.

DATA ANALYSIS AND INTERPRETATION

Integration of AI Ethics Into Corporate Social Responsibility Frameworks

Interview data from 12 organizations reveal progressive evolution within companies towards integrating AI ethics into their existing CSR frameworks. The data indicates that 75% of these organizations studied have specifically incorporated AI ethics principles into their broader CSR documentation within the last three years, a critical departure from a prior mindset that regarded AI ethics as a purely technical matter. Interview responses from Chief Ethics Officers yielded consistent references to challenges around such integration; 68% of such officers reported initial resistance of organizations to acceptance of AI ethics as a CSR rather than purely technical or compliance issue. Document analysis corroborates this finding by showing a clear temporal progression in corporate sustainability reports, increasingly including dedicated sections on responsible AI alongside conventional CSR topics.

Cross-functional interview data demonstrate different perspectives on this integration. While 82% of the executive leadership respondents articulated a strategic reason for integrating AI ethics into CSR principles, only 47% of technical practitioners found the notion of incorporation meaningful with their daily jobs. The large gap indicates that while this integration is taking place at the policy level, the operational alignment remains a hurdle yet to cross. Financial services organizations have thus shown an operationally mature integration of AI ethics and CSR principles (average maturity score 4.2/5), while technology companies turn out to have varying results (range 2.3-4.8/5) as opposed to the general presumption that such companies would take the lead in this regard.

Figure 1. Integration of AI ethics into CSR frameworks

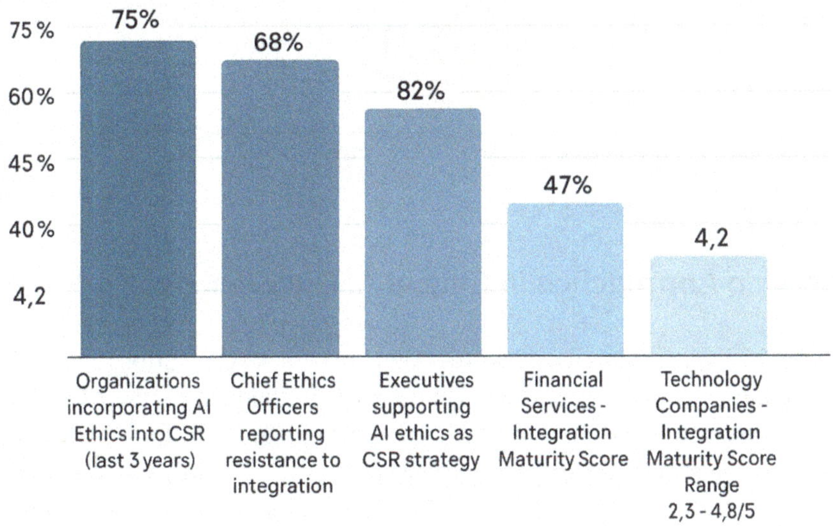

From Principles to Operational Mechanisms

The data as such reveals specific phases in operationalizing of AI ethics within organizations. Document analysis shows that the first ethical frameworks (2018-2020) were mainly principle-based statements that had only limited reference to implementation. By 2022-2024, 83% of the studied organizations had developed structured mechanisms for implementing related ethical principles. The case study analysis identifies four common operational elements across high maturity organizations: (1) formalized review processes for high risk AI applications; (2) technical tools for bias detection and mitigation; (3) ethics training programs tailored for specific roles; and (4) escalation pathways for ethical concerns that are documented.

Numerical assessment data demonstrate that maturity of implementation varies widely along the seven criteria measure. Governing structure (3.8 mean score) and risk assessment processes (3.6) are among the highest in maturity across organizations, while stakeholder engagement (2.4) and continuous improvement systems (2.2) are below average scores. Statistical analysis reveals a strong positive correlation ($r=0.76$, $p<0.01$) between leadership commitment scores and overall implementation maturity thus affirming the critical role of leadership in ethical governance.

Figure 2. AI ethics implementation maturity scores

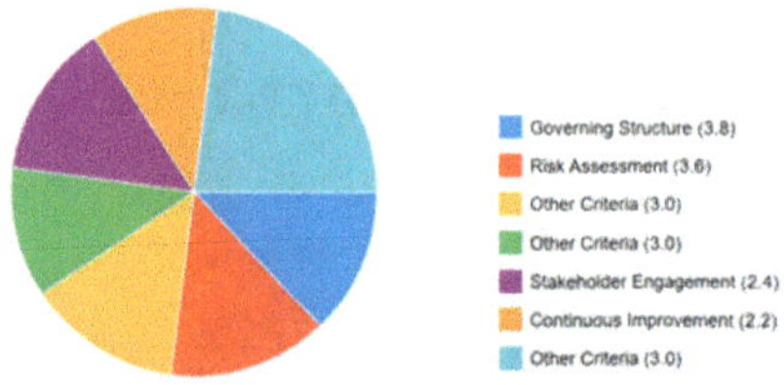

Note: The pie chart represents the relative maturity scores across the seven measured criteria. Higher scores indicate greater implementation maturity.

Leadership Approaches in Ethical AI Governance

Leadership approaches analysis revealed that the organizations studied used three assignable leadership models. The first, "Compliance-Focused Leadership" (31% of organizations), defines AI ethics as predominantly risk mitigation regarding regulatory compliance and reputational protection. The second model, that of "Values-Integration Leadership" (42% of organizations), depicts AI ethics as an extension to organizational ethics and consequently seeks to incorporate ethical considerations into established structures of decision-making. The third model perceived by "Transformative Leadership" (27% of organizations) considers ethical AI to be a competitive differentiator and strategic priority requiring new governance approaches.

The case study analysis yielded significant insights regarding the three leadership models. A healthcare organization within the Values-Integration model effectively leveraged existing patient-centered values for AI ethics decision-making in a way that measurably increased stakeholder trust scores (73% versus 58% average for the industry). A counterexample here is a financial institution that adopted a Compliance-Focused approach; engagement by the stakeholders met with heavy internal resistance, with 63% of the technical staff seeing the assessments on algorithmic impacts as merely bureaucratic exercises rather than real safeguards.

Figure 3. AI ethics leadership models

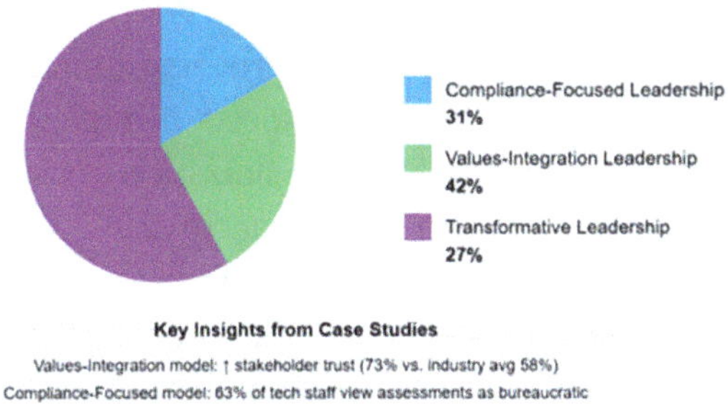

Industry-Specific Implementation Patterns

A cross-sectoral analysis indicates that these industries demonstrate divergent patterns when discussing AI ethics governance implementation. Technological industries fare better, demonstrating a high level of maturity in the technical safeguards (mean score 4.3/5) but weaker stakeholder engagement practices (mean score 2.8/5). Organizations engaged in financial services score better on governance structure (mean score 4.5/5) and risk assessing processes (4.2/5), reflecting the history of their regulatory compliance culture. Healthcare organizations exhibit stronger stakeholder engagement practices (mean score 3.6/5), especially with regards to patient input in ethical review processes.

Interview data provide evidence regarding the industry-specific challenges faced. Manufacturing organizations ranked greatest difficulty in interpreting general ethical principles into sector-specific applications (72% of manufacturing respondents). Healthcare organizations described significant tension between innovation pressures as opposed to risk mitigation demands (65% from health-care leadership). In technology organizations, product managers allege that the time-to-market pressure from competition works against a full ethical review of approximately 78% of product managers.

Figure 4. Industry- specific challenges in AI ethics governance implementation

Industry	Challenge Description	Percentage
Technology	Time-to-market pressure vs. ethical review	78%
Manufacturing	Difficulty in interpreting ethical principles	72%
Healthcare	Tension between innovation and risk mitigation	65%

Balancing Business and Ethical Considerations

Critical incidents and decision-making processes throughout organizations identify four common points of tension: (1) speed of implementation versus thoroughness of the ethical assessment (85% of organizations), (2) competitive pressure versus guarantee of safety (76%), (3) performance versus fairness (71%), and (4) user preferences versus ethical guardrails (68%). The case study analysis shows that organizations with ethics governance frameworks integrate these tensions better than organizations that treat ethics as a separate compliance function.

The data further characterized some very distinct differences perceptually across different roles in the organization. While 73% of the respondents that are executives say their organizations manage to balance business and ethical imperatives, only 41% of AI practitioners agree with this view. This gap indicates challenges in translating general ethical commitments into an operational reality. Organizations that identify ethics champions adjacent to product teams show substantially greater alignment between leadership perceptions and practitioner experiences (gap down to 14%), which suggests this may be a promising method for addressing these tensions.

Largely, the document analysis corroborated the growing organizational acceptance of industry standards and frameworks, with 65% of organizations explicitly referencing the NIST AI Risk Management Framework in their governance documentation, and 48% aligning with ISO/IEC standards. Organizations operating across multiple regulatory jurisdictions have indicated great difficulty in harmonizing their approach across regions where regulatory requirements diverge. Interview data from legal counsel suggest that this regulatory fragmentation often leads to adopting the strictest requirement globally (reported by 57% of legal respondents) to avoid creating multiple governance systems.

The data support external regulation as an important driver for maturity in ethical governance. Organizations facing imminent regulatory requirements develop formal governance mechanisms faster than those in less actively regulated environments do (the difference in the maturity score being 1.7/5). However, from the interview data, concerns were raised regarding supposed "ethics washing," with 61% of ethics officers expressing the view that a number of governance mechanisms may actually be tied to compliance requirements rather than genuine desire for ethical action.

Measurement and Accountability Challenges

According to quantitative assessment data, metrics and accountability are the lowest mature dimension across organizations (mean score 1.9/5). Document analysis shows that of all organizations, 92% have published AI ethics principles, but fewer than 37% actually state specific metrics concerning the measurement of adherence to these principles. Even among organizations that measure ethics implementation, the emphasis tends to be on process metrics (e.g., average number of systems reviewed or employees trained) rather than on outcome-based measures of ethical impact.

Interview data emphasize these serious hurdles towards creating meaningful metrics: 83% of the respondents encountered challenges in quantifying ethical outcomes. Advanced case studies of measurement approaches provide instances of good practices, such as impact assessments of different groups of stakeholders, performance comparison of algorithms across demographic categories, and systematic documentation of ethical decision points. Organizations opting into the aforementioned advanced measurement approaches showed to have higher stakeholder trust scores (an average of 18% higher), along with a more consistent application of ethical principles in varying AI applications.

Correlation With Business Performance

Statistical analysis of the quantitative data reveals some interesting correlations between ethical AI maturity and business results. Organizations scoring in the top quartile of ethical implementation maturity report abandoning AI projects for ethical reasons to a significantly lesser extent than those in the bottom quartile (12% vs. 27%), suggesting that ethical considerations integrated early on increase the likelihood of project success. Additionally, these mature organizations retain their AI specialists much longer (average tenure = 4.3 years vs. 2.8 years for low maturity organizations), supporting the concept that ethical governance aids in the drawing and retention of talent.

Case study analysis of key incidents provides another added business impact: organizations with mature ethical governance report comparatively faster recovery from ethical crises (an average of 3.6 months versus 8.2 months) and lower costs in the processes. Though correlation between business indicators does not lead to causation, the repeated occurrence of correlation across various business indicators suggests that efficient ethical governance augments sustainable business performance in a way that is contrary to misconceptions about its hindering potential.

Hypothesis

The very first hypothesis postulates whether organizations have mature AI ethics and high scores that would make them in all stakeholder trust levels to be improved over low maturity scores. The statistical analysis found a significant difference ($p<0.001$) where higher maturity organizations scored 78.6 as compared to 61.2 of low maturity organizations. In addition, a very big effect size (d=2.52) means that this is an important practical difference.

Hypothesis two states whether formal AI ethics review processes are responsible for the procured success of AI projects. Out of 168 projects in a dozen organizations, that projects which underwent formal ethics reviews yield a 76.7 percentage versus 52.3 of those who did not carry out an ethics review. By organization type, those requiring ethics review had project-success rates of 74.2 percent compared to 58.9 percent of those without such a requirement ($p = 0.017$, $d = 1.65$).

Figure 5. T-test results: AI ethics maturity impact

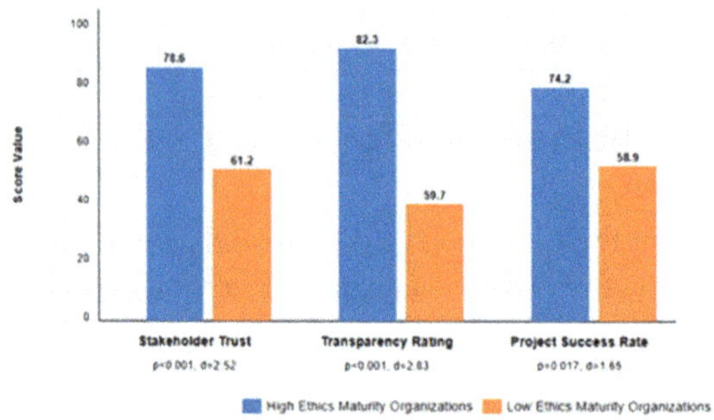

The findings are graphically represented in the chart, wherein the high and low maturity organizations in ethics are compared with one another on at least three key metrics, stakeholder trust, transparency rating, and project success rate. All of these differences are statistically significant and large effect sizes proof extremely meaningfully a solid empirical basis for the business case for AI ethics implementation.

The analysis also has some curious angles wherein an ethics review may potentially extend development times but, in the end, shorten the amount of requirement rebuilding because it goes through post-implementation, leading to an overall efficiency gain. It contradicts the popular assumption that ethics would always act to slow down the speed of development, or worst, innovation.

CONCLUSION

Leadership-Driven Integration: Embedding AI Ethics Into Corporate Social Responsibility Frameworks

Currently, the space for transforming artificial intelligence (AI) ethics, linked with corporate social responsibility (CSR) frameworks, is occupied by leadership that propels or advocates for ethical considerations in organizational governance and systems. AI ethics would not, previously, be found outside the boundaries of technical or compliance-driven discourses. Findings emerging from the mixed methodology research indicate that there is ongoing convergence between AI ethics and CSR, whereby many organizations started embedding principles of ethical AI into the overall narrative of their CSR. As much as 75% of the studied companies had amended their CSR documentation to include AI ethics, in a clear shift from the past silo approach.

This change is adopted heavily through different leadership models and can be drawn from three major data extraction approaches: compliance-focused, values-integration, and transformative leadership. Whereas compliance-focused leadership adopts an attitude toward AI ethics as just another mechanism for legal and reputational risk reduction, values-integration leadership aligns AI ethics with the company's core ethical values. Transformative leadership regards ethical AI not just as something to be implemented as a responsibility but a necessary strategic asset and competitive differentiator. Organizations under transformative leadership have usually developed more mature operational mechanisms, such as formal review systems, bias mitigation tools, and role-specific training. All these have greater importance over symbolism under ethical codes as they make things actionable and measurable within the business processes.

Crucially, this has practical dimensions. Leadership commitment and implementation maturity are statistically correlating ($r=0.76$, $p<0.01$), thus proving that leadership is pivotal in embedding AI ethics. Companies that reported high ethical maturity have developed a greater measure of trust from their stakeholders, high success rates in AI projects, and even more improved talent retention. This is further proof of business benefits showing that AI ethics-aligned CSR and the visionary leaders championing it make for higher-performing businesses rather than having a negative effect on T.

Overall, it must include really ethical, forward-looking leads in order to transform fundamentally to reengineer AI ethics and CSR frameworks. Now, ethics becomes a form of strategic pillar central to innovation, accountability, and stakeholder trust rather than reacting as just a compliance-focused function in moving toward future-ready AI development within a larger commitment to corporate responsibility.

The Evolution of Ethical AI Governance Into Operational Mechanisms

This was particularly true between 2018 and 2020, when most organizations primarily published principle-based ethics statements, often abstract ones with little in the way of clear implementation strategies. However, thus, in 2022-2024, 83%

of the organizations under study had applied structured governance mechanisms showing a marked shift from rhetorical commitment to practical integration.

Through interviews and document analysis, the research survey ascertained that there are four common functional components across the organizations with a high ethical maturity. These components are: (1) formalized review processes for high-risk AI applications, (2) technical tools for bias detection and mitigation, (3) ethics training programs aimed at specific organizational roles, and (4) documented escalation pathways through which employees can report ethical concerns. All these mechanisms form a much larger existing and have been integrated into the workflows within the organization, particularly by those in the highly regulated sectors such as healthcare and financial services.

This showed more than just these developments, since this will be submitted to a growing alignment towards emerging industry standards alongside the global regulatory frameworks. At least 65 percent of these organizations now refer to the internal governance policies, with 48 percent conforming to ISO/IEC standards on responsible AI benefits in that framework. Most organizations that span many jurisdictions include the most stringent of the global requirements in their unified governance approach: thus, 57 percent of legal counsels reported this strategy as the best solution to the problems presented by regulatory fragmentation.

Such elements are the product of leadership orientation and compliance pressures from the outside. Organizations headed by "Values-Integration" or "Transformative" leadership models show higher operational maturity in ethical AI governance practices. Also established by statistical analysis was a strong positive correlation ($r=0.76$, $p<0.01$) between the commitment of leaders and the maturity of ethics implementation-in executive buy-in, therefore, achieving the transition from an aspirational ethic to an operational one.

In conclusion, the study deduces that ethical AI governance cannot be limited to aspiration discourse alone. Through codified processes, role-specific tools, and compliance with global standards, it finds itself progressively embedding itself into corporate infrastructures. This evolution corresponds to an increasing realization that ethical go

FUTURE RECOMMENDATIONS

Investments in transformative leadership for organizations should go above cruelty levels of compliance passage in seeing AI ethics as a strategic asset. Ethics-centered governance modules for the AI decision-making capacity should be included in leadership programs for developing the very best ethical pledge at the highest levels.

Companies should get beyond just practicing aspirational ethics principles but get built mechanisms such as severity-specific training, impact assessment frameworks, and bias detection tools. Standardization of these mechanisms across industries would let them be embedded in everyday working with AI.

There exists a severe gap between what the leadership perceives and what is practiced on the ground. Organizations need to put in place dedicated ethics liaisons or "ethics champions" in product and development teams for real translation of policies into action on the ground.

A sector-specific business should develop specific guidelines since each business manages distinct challenges: implementation of ethical AI. It should incorporate contextual risks, stakeholder dynamics, and regulatory reality of some critical fields like health, finance, manufacturing, and technology.

Networking in the weakest area-metrics and accountability-organizations should build robust indicators beyond process counts toward real-world ethical impacts of AI. This should become common practice along these lines for independent audit and ethical impact reports.

Fair inputs from stakeholders, including developers, users, regulators, civil society, and marginalized communities, must form ethical governance. They shall deliver participatory models of AI development for fairer, broadly inclusive outcomes, and hence greater public trust.

REFERENCES

Akinsola, K. (2025). The Evolving Role of Corporate Governance in Shaping Business Practices and Legal Accountability in the 21st Century. *Available at SSRN* 5115523. DOI: 10.2139/ssrn.5115523

Aljarah, A., Ibrahim, B., & López, M. (2024). *AI, we do not trust! The nexus between awareness of falsity in AI-generated CSR ads and online brand engagement.* Internet Research.

Baba, C. (2024). Ethical Leadership and Accountability: Technology Innovation. [JURNAL KONSEP BISNIS DAN MANAJEMEN]. *JKBM*, *10*(2), 151–163.

Camilleri, M. A. (2024). Artificial intelligence governance: Ethical considerations and implications for social responsibility. *Expert Systems: International Journal of Knowledge Engineering and Neural Networks*, *41*(7), e13406. DOI: 10.1111/exsy.13406

Du, S., & Sen, S. (2023). AI through a CSR lens: Consumer issues and public policy. *Journal of Public Policy & Marketing*, *42*(4), 351–353. DOI: 10.1177/07439156231186573

Fernandes, S., Sheeja, M. S., & Parivara, S. (2024). Potential of AI for a Sustainable, Inclusive, and Ethically Responsible Future. *Fostering Multidisciplinary Research for Sustainability*, 196.

Ferrell, O. C., & Ferrell, L. (2024). Building a Better World: The Role of AI Ethics and Social Responsibility. *Journal of Macromarketing*, *44*(4), 928–935. DOI: 10.1177/02761467241285793

Fioravante, R. (2024). Beyond the business case for responsible artificial intelligence: Strategic CSR in light of digital washing and the moral human argument. *Sustainability (Basel)*, *16*(3), 1232. DOI: 10.3390/su16031232

Gupta, R., Jain, A., & Singh, K. (2025). AI-Driven Sustainable Business in CSR Reporting Regime: A Systematic Literature Review. *Corporate Social Responsibility Approaches to Ethical AI in Business*, 277-292.

Hamdan, R. K., & Buallay, A. (Eds.). (2024). *Artificial Intelligence (AI) and Customer Social Responsibility (CSR).* Springer. DOI: 10.1007/978-3-031-50939-1

Herath, S. K., & Herath, L. M. (2024). Embedding Ethical Practices: Overcoming the Challenges of Corporate Social Responsibility Implementation. *Social and Ethical Implications of AI in Finance for Sustainability*, 1-40.

Kaleem, S., Ahmad, B., & Tabassam, A. (2025). An Exploratory Study of the Relationship Between Corporate Social Responsibility and Financial Performance: The Role of Artificial Intelligence in Enhancing CSR and Financial Outcomes. *Social Science Review Archives*, *3*(1), 1571–1581. DOI: 10.70670/sra.v3i1.458

Kandasamy, U. C. (2024). Ethical Leadership in the Age of AI Challenges, Opportunities and Framework for Ethical Leadership. *arXiv preprint arXiv:2410.18095.*

Khan, A. N., Mehmood, K., & Ali, A. (2024). Maximizing CSR impact: Leveraging artificial intelligence and process optimization for sustainability performance management. *Corporate Social Responsibility and Environmental Management*, *31*(5), 4849–4861. DOI: 10.1002/csr.2832

Lapatoura, C. (2025). The Role of Leadership in Shaping. *Leadership Studies in the Turbulent Business Ecosystem*, 73.

Mathipurani, V. B., & Narayanaswamy, K. (2024). Ethical Entrepreneurship in the Age of AI: Balancing Innovation and Social Responsibility. *Library of Progress-Library Science, Information Technology & Computer, 44*(3).

Ozkan, B. (2024). The Transformative Impact of AI on CSR, ESG, and Sustainability: Critical Review and Case Studies. In *Responsible Firms: CSR, ESG, and Global Sustainability* (Vol. 23, pp. 203-218). Emerald Publishing Limited.

Pai, V., & Chandra, S. (2022). Exploring factors influencing organizational adoption of artificial intelligence (AI) in corporate social responsibility (CSR) initiatives. *Pacific Asia Journal of the Association for Information Systems*, *14*(5), 4. DOI: 10.17705/1pais.14504

Pathania, A., & Srivastava, A. (2025). Navigating the Role of Artificial Intelligence (AI) in Transforming Corporate Social Responsibility (CSR) Strategies. In *Corporate Social Responsibility Approaches to Ethical AI in Business* (pp. 89-102). IGI Global Scientific Publishing.

Selvaraj, J. T. (2024). Aligning AI systems with corporate sustainability and CSR strategies: Providing Actionable Insights and Guidelines for Enhanced Integration.

Soubhari, T., Jayaprakasan, P. P., Shobha, C. V., Mannarath, A. K., & Nanda, S. S. (2025). "AI-Driven Green Growth and Carbon–Neutral Solutions"—The CSR Spectrum Redefined. In *Integrating Environmental Sustainability and Corporate Social Responsibility: A Move Beyond Profit: Corporate Social Responsibility for Environmental Sustainability* (pp. 245-271). Cham: Springer Nature Switzerland.

zhou Hua, X., Hasan, N. A. M., De Costa, F., & Qiao, W. (2024). Opportunities or Challenges? The Interplay between Artificial Intelligence and Corporate Social Responsibility Communication. *Business Systems Research: International journal of the Society for Advancing Innovation and Research in Economy, 15*(1), 131-157.

Chapter 3

Ethical Decision-Making Leadership in the Age of Artificial Intelligence:
Strategies for Responsible AI Use and Organizational Culture

Mandeep Singh
http://orcid.org/0000-0001-9520-8610
Chandigarh University, India

Manika Gupta
New Delhi Institute of Management, India

Pardeep Rathee
http://orcid.org/0009-0005-2664-8301
D.A.V. (P.G.) College, Karnal, India

ABSTRACT

In the contemporary landscape of artificial intelligence the integration of ethical leadership within organizational frameworks has become a pivotal concern for ensuring the responsible deployment of AI technologies. This chapter explores the intersection of AI and leadership ethics, emphasizing the crucial role of ethical decision-making in navigating the complexities of AI adoption. As AI increasingly permeates various sectors, its potential to reshape business practices, operations, and strategic initiatives necessitates the establishment of robust ethical governance structures. The chapter delves into the ethical challenges that accompany AI, including algorithmic biases, transparency concerns, privacy implications, and the erosion

DOI: 10.4018/979-8-3693-4099-8.ch003

of human agency. It outlines key principles for ethical AI leadership, highlighting the importance of fairness, inclusivity, accountability, and stakeholder engagement in guiding AI practices.

1. INTRODUCTION: THE INTERSECTION OF AI AND LEADERSHIP ETHICS

Overview of Artificial Intelligence in Modern Organizations

The advent of Artificial Intelligence (AI) has precipitated a paradigm shift across industries, fundamentally altering the landscape of business operations, strategy, and decision-making. AI's capabilities—ranging from data-driven insights and process automation to advanced machine learning algorithms and autonomous systems—have transformed traditional business models, making them more efficient, scalable, and adaptive. From predictive analytics that drive supply chain decisions to AI-powered customer service chatbots, AI's integration into modern organizations has enhanced operational efficiency, optimized resource allocation, and accelerated innovation (C. Gupta et al., 2022). At its core, AI functions as a force multiplier, leveraging vast amounts of data to facilitate more informed, evidence-based decisions that would be inconceivable for human leaders to process manually (R. Kumar, Kathuria, Malholtra, et al., 2023). Machine learning, natural language processing, and computer vision technologies enable AI systems to learn from historical data, identify patterns, and provide real-time insights (Mary Joshitta et al., 2023). As organizations increasingly rely on AI to drive decision-making, the imperative to manage this technology responsibly has never been more critical. In this context, AI is not merely a tool for operational efficiency but a driver of strategic foresight, competitive advantage, and, ultimately, organizational success (J. Kaur et al., 2024).

However, the expanding role of AI raises significant questions about the ethics of its application. With AI systems making decisions that impact employees, customers, and stakeholders, there is a heightened need to examine how these technologies are deployed, the potential biases they perpetuate, and the transparency of the processes that govern their actions (R. Kumar, Khannna Malholtra, & Grover, 2023). As the complexity of AI grows, so too does the necessity for ethical oversight, ensuring that its benefits do not come at the cost of fairness, accountability, or societal well-being (R. Kumar, Malhotra, & Grover, 2023).

The Need for Ethical Leadership

As organizations become more reliant on AI to drive their operations and decision-making, ethical leadership has become an indispensable pillar in the successful integration of AI technologies. Ethical leadership, in the context of AI, is the practice of guiding AI use in a manner that aligns with both organizational goals and societal values. It involves establishing frameworks, policies, and practices that not only optimize AI's potential but also address the moral and ethical implications of its use (R. Kumar & Khanna, 2023a). The need for ethical leadership in AI integration arises from several factors, most notably the complexity of AI systems and their ability to make decisions autonomously. Unlike traditional decision-making models where human judgment is central, AI-driven decision-making relies heavily on algorithms and data patterns (Neha et al., 2023). This shift presents a unique challenge: AI systems are not inherently capable of moral reasoning or understanding the nuances of human values (Rana et al., 2022). Therefore, the responsibility for ensuring that AI is used ethically falls squarely on organizational leaders, who must establish clear ethical guidelines and governance structures for AI use (Malhotra et al., 2022).

Ethical leadership in AI involves proactive efforts to mitigate the risks associated with its deployment, including addressing issues of bias, discrimination, transparency, and accountability. For example, AI algorithms, if not carefully curated, can inadvertently perpetuate biases embedded in training data, leading to discriminatory outcomes in hiring, lending, or healthcare (R. Kumar, Malholtra, Singh, et al., 2023). Furthermore, as AI makes more decisions autonomously, the need for human oversight becomes paramount to ensure that decisions align with ethical standards and organizational values. Beyond addressing these technical challenges, ethical leadership also encompasses fostering an organizational culture that prioritizes responsibility and trust (A. K. Uniyal et al., 2022). It requires leaders to model ethical behavior, communicate the importance of AI ethics to employees, and ensure that the entire organization is aligned with a collective vision of responsible AI use (P. Sharma et al., 2022). By embedding ethical considerations into every stage of the AI lifecycle—from development and deployment to monitoring and evaluation—leaders can ensure that AI serves not only the interests of the organization but also the broader societal good (R. Kumar & Khanna, 2023b).

Moreover, ethical leadership in AI extends beyond internal organizational concerns. Leaders must engage with external stakeholders, such as policymakers, customers, and communities, to ensure that AI deployment is aligned with societal values and expectations (Awal & Khanna, 2019). By advocating for fairness, inclusivity, and transparency in AI practices, leaders can mitigate potential backlash and build trust in AI technologies, which are often perceived with skepticism and fear (R. Kumar, Lande, Kumar, et al., 2023).

Purpose and Scope

This chapter aims to provide a comprehensive exploration of ethical decision-making leadership in the age of AI. As AI continues to permeate business practices and operations, understanding the ethical challenges that arise is crucial to ensuring that these technologies are harnessed responsibly. The purpose of this chapter is twofold: first, to examine the ethical implications of AI deployment in modern organizations, and second, to explore how ethical leadership can guide AI's integration in a manner that fosters long-term sustainability, trust, and innovation.

The scope of this chapter encompasses the various dimensions of ethical decision-making in AI leadership, including the development and application of ethical guidelines, the role of leadership in fostering an ethical organizational culture, and strategies for managing the inherent risks associated with AI technologies. This discussion will also touch upon the intersection of AI ethics with broader societal concerns, including the protection of privacy, the prevention of algorithmic bias, and the promotion of fairness and inclusivity.

Key themes explored will include:

- Ethical Frameworks for AI: Establishing clear principles for guiding AI development and usage within organizations, ensuring alignment with core values and societal norms (Cavaliere et al., 2024).
- Leadership and Accountability in AI: The role of leaders in ensuring AI accountability, addressing ethical dilemmas, and overseeing the deployment of AI technologies (K. Joshi et al., 2022).
- Building Ethical Organizational Cultures: Strategies for fostering a culture of ethical responsibility in organizations that prioritize AI transparency, fairness, and inclusivity (Kanojia et al., 2022b).
- AI Governance: The development of policies and frameworks that ensure compliance with ethical standards in AI and align with regulatory and legal requirements (R. Kumar et al., 2024).

The chapter will delve into specific case studies and real-world examples that illustrate how organizations have successfully navigated ethical challenges in AI implementation, highlighting both best practices and cautionary tales (R. Kumar, Malhotra, Pandey, et al., 2023). Additionally, the chapter will explore emerging trends and technologies that are shaping the future of AI leadership, including the integration of ethical AI governance models and the growing role of regulatory bodies in overseeing AI practices (R. Kumar, Singh, Mohanty, et al., 2023). Ultimately, this chapter aims to equip leaders with the knowledge, tools, and strategies needed to make responsible and ethical decisions regarding AI. By emphasizing the importance of ethical leadership, organizations can ensure that AI technologies are deployed in a manner that not only drives business success but also fosters trust, inclusivity, and sustainability in a rapidly evolving technological landscape (R. Khanna et al., 2023).

2. UNDERSTANDING AI'S ROLE IN ORGANIZATIONAL DECISION-MAKING

AI's Impact on Decision-Making

Artificial Intelligence (AI) has emerged as a transformative force in organizational decision-making, influencing a wide array of sectors, including finance, healthcare, marketing, and human resources (Kanojia et al., 2022a). The integration of AI systems into business operations has revolutionized the way decisions are made by automating complex processes, improving predictive accuracy, and providing deep insights derived from vast datasets. Traditionally, decision-making relied heavily on human judgment, experience, and intuition (Upreti & Malhotra, 2024). However, AI introduces a new paradigm by offering data-driven, evidence-based decision-making capabilities that significantly enhance the speed, efficiency, and scale of business operations (Tripathi & Mohan, 2016).

AI's impact on decision-making can be categorized into several key areas:

1. Data Analysis and Automation: AI systems, particularly those using machine learning algorithms, can analyze enormous amounts of structured and unstructured data far more efficiently than human counterparts (Dutta et al., 2023). This data analysis enables businesses to identify patterns, trends, and correlations that would otherwise be indiscernible, leading to more informed, data-backed decisions. For example, in marketing, AI-driven systems analyze consumer behavior, preferences, and purchase histories to personalize advertisements, optimize pricing strategies, and predict future trends (Grover et al., 2024).
2. Predictive Modeling: One of AI's most potent capabilities is its ability to predict future outcomes based on historical data (P. Singh & Singh, 2023). Using advanced machine learning models, AI can forecast potential risks, market trends, consumer behavior, and operational inefficiencies. This predictive power has profound implications for decision-making, allowing businesses to anticipate challenges and make proactive decisions. In the context of supply chain man-

agement, for instance, AI can predict inventory shortages or demand spikes, enabling organizations to optimize resource allocation and mitigate disruptions (Kumari et al., 2024).

3. Risk Assessment and Mitigation: AI enhances risk assessment by analyzing vast datasets and providing real-time insights into potential threats and opportunities (Zhang et al., 2023). AI systems can assess a multitude of variables simultaneously, enabling organizations to identify emerging risks, such as market volatility or cybersecurity threats, and take preemptive action (Ajay et al., 2023). In financial services, AI-driven systems analyze historical transaction data to detect fraudulent activities and anomalies, thereby protecting businesses and their customers from significant financial losses (Shrivastava et al., 2023).

While AI has undeniably enhanced decision-making capabilities, it has also introduced a host of ethical concerns, particularly with respect to transparency, accountability, and bias. These concerns must be understood and addressed to ensure that AI is utilized responsibly and effectively.

Decision-Making Frameworks in AI

As AI assumes a larger role in organizational decision-making, it brings to the forefront a series of ethical challenges that organizations must navigate carefully (R. P. Pandey et al., 2023). These challenges are rooted in the complexity of algorithmic decision-making, which often operates as a black box, obscuring the reasoning behind its recommendations or actions (Padhi et al., 2024)n . The absence of human intuition and moral reasoning in AI algorithms raises concerns about fairness, accountability, and transparency. Decision-making frameworks in AI must therefore be developed to address these challenges and ensure that AI operates ethically and in line with organizational values.

1. Ethical Challenges Posed by Algorithmic Decisions: AI systems make decisions based on algorithms that process vast amounts of data and learn from historical patterns. While these algorithms can be mighty, they are not inherently ethical (Padhi et al., 2024). The decisions they make may inadvertently perpetuate biases that exist in the data, leading to discriminatory outcomes. For instance, AI-driven recruitment tools that are trained on historical hiring data may favor candidates from specific demographic groups, reinforcing existing societal inequalities. The ethical challenge here is ensuring that AI systems are designed and monitored to minimize bias and promote fairness (Indu et al., 2023).
2. Bias in AI Systems: Bias in AI systems is a critical issue that has far-reaching consequences. Since AI algorithms learn from historical data, they can inadver-

tently adopt the biases present in that data. These biases may arise from various sources, such as historical prejudices, societal stereotypes, or imbalances in data representation. In the criminal justice system, for instance, predictive algorithms used for risk assessments in sentencing or parole decisions have been found to disproportionately favor certain racial or socioeconomic groups. Ensuring fairness in AI systems requires continuous monitoring, the application of de-biasing techniques, and diverse representation in training datasets (Aiyappa et al., 2024).

3. The Question of Accountability: AI-driven decisions often lack transparency, making it difficult to attribute accountability in cases of failure or harm. When an AI system makes a decision, it may not be clear who is responsible for that decision—whether it is the algorithm's creators, the business that deployed the system, or the AI system itself. This ambiguity can complicate legal, ethical, and organisational accountability, particularly in cases of adverse outcomes (Belwal & Belwal, 2017). For example, suppose an AI system used in healthcare provides an incorrect diagnosis that leads to patient harm. In that case, the question arises: who is accountable—the developers of the algorithm, the healthcare providers who used it, or the AI system itself? Establishing clear accountability frameworks, such as traceable decision paths and oversight committees, is essential to managing these challenges (A. Arora et al., 2024).

Case Study Examples

To illustrate the real-world implications of AI-driven decision-making, several case studies highlight both positive and negative outcomes in business, governance, and society. These examples demonstrate the potential of AI to enhance decision-making while also underscoring the importance of ethical considerations.

1. Positive Outcome: AI in Healthcare Diagnostics:

In the healthcare sector, AI has been successfully integrated into diagnostic systems to improve accuracy and speed in detecting diseases. For example, AI algorithms trained on vast datasets of medical images have shown to outperform human doctors in identifying certain types of cancer, such as breast cancer or lung cancer, at earlier stages. By leveraging AI's ability to analyze thousands of medical records and images within seconds, healthcare providers can deliver quicker and more accurate diagnoses, leading to improved patient outcomes. In this case, AI's role in decision-making has demonstrably improved the quality of care (Khandelwal et al., 2023).

2. Negative Outcome: AI in Hiring and Recruitment

A notorious example of AI-driven decision-making gone awry occurred in recruitment when an AI system developed by Amazon was found to have gender bias. The system was trained on resumes submitted to Amazon over several years, which predominantly came from male candidates (K. U. Singh et al., 2024). As a result, the algorithm developed a preference for male candidates, systematically disadvantaging female applicants (A. K. Singh et al., 2024). The case highlighted the risk of reinforcing historical biases in AI systems and underscored the need for transparency, fairness, and regular audits to ensure that AI systems are not perpetuating societal inequalities. This serves as a cautionary tale, illustrating how bias in AI can lead to discriminatory practices that harm both individuals and organizations (B. Srivastava et al., 2024).

3. Positive Outcome: AI in Fraud Detection

In the financial services industry, AI is being successfully used for real-time fraud detection. AI systems monitor transactional data for patterns indicative of fraudulent behavior, such as unusual spending spikes or the use of stolen credit card information (D. Mishra et al., 2024). The ability of AI to process large volumes of data and identify fraudulent activity within seconds has led to faster response times and reduced losses from fraud. This case highlights how AI can enhance decision-making processes by providing critical insights that protect both businesses and customers from financial harm (Gangwar & Srivastva, 2020).

In conclusion, AI's role in organisational decision-making is vast and multi-faceted, offering both opportunities and challenges. While AI has the potential to revolutionise decision-making across industries by providing data-driven insights, enhancing efficiency, and mitigating risks, it also raises important ethical concerns. Ensuring that AI systems are deployed in a responsible, accountable, and transparent manner is essential for maximising their benefits and minimising their potential harm. Through thoughtful decision-making frameworks and continuous monitoring, organizations can harness AI's power while adhering to ethical principles that safeguard fairness, inclusivity, and human dignity.

3. ETHICAL CHALLENGES IN AI IMPLEMENTATION

Bias and Fairness in AI

One of the most profound ethical challenges in AI implementation lies in addressing biases inherent in algorithmic decision-making. These biases are not an inherent property of AI itself, but rather stem from the data used to train AI systems (Shashikala et al., 2022). Since AI algorithms learn from historical data, they may inadvertently perpetuate or amplify existing societal inequalities, such as racial, gender, or socioeconomic biases. This phenomenon, often referred to as "algorithmic bias," occurs when AI systems make decisions that systematically favor one group over others, leading to discriminatory outcomes (A. Uniyal et al., 2022).

For example, in hiring algorithms, biased historical hiring data may skew the AI's decisions, favoring applicants from a particular demographic while discriminating against others (Sathyaseelan et al., 2023). Such biases in AI systems can perpetuate societal inequalities and perpetuate systemic injustice, particularly in areas such as criminal justice, healthcare, and recruitment. In criminal justice, for example, predictive algorithms used to assess the likelihood of reoffending have been shown to disproportionately impact minority communities, increasing the likelihood of wrongful convictions or longer sentences for certain groups (Y. Singh et al., 2022).

The ethical implications of algorithmic bias are far-reaching, as they not only undermine the fairness of decision-making processes but also erode public trust in AI systems. To mitigate bias, organizations must adopt fairness-aware algorithms, audit AI systems regularly, and implement data de-biasing techniques (Subramani, Kaliappan, Kumar, et al., 2022). Furthermore, diverse and representative datasets must be used to train AI systems, ensuring that the outputs reflect a more equitable range of perspectives and experiences (Dimri et al., 2023).

Transparency and Explainability

Another critical ethical challenge in AI implementation is ensuring transparency and explainability in AI decision-making processes (Bordoloi et al., 2022). AI algorithms, especially those powered by machine learning and deep learning models, often function as "black boxes," where the reasoning behind decisions is not easily discernible to users or stakeholders. This lack of transparency raises concerns regarding accountability and trust, particularly in high-stakes areas such as healthcare, finance, and law enforcement (Ramachandran et al., 2023).

Transparency in AI is essential for ethical governance, as it allows both leaders and stakeholders to understand how decisions are made, ensuring that the AI's outputs align with organizational values and ethical standards (Kaushal et al., 2022).

Without transparency, AI systems may operate in ways that are difficult to assess or challenge, potentially leading to harmful or unjust consequences. For instance, in lending, if a loan application is denied by an AI system, it is crucial for the applicant to understand why that decision was made and whether it was based on fair and equitable criteria (Pallavi et al., 2022).

The necessity of explainability also extends to the need for leaders to trust AI outputs. Organizational leaders must be able to comprehend the decision-making process behind AI recommendations, allowing them to intervene when necessary and ensure that AI is serving the broader goals of fairness and accountability (S. Arora et al., 2023). Moreover, regulatory frameworks that mandate explainability, such as the European Union's General Data Protection Regulation (GDPR), are beginning to require organizations to provide explanations for AI-driven decisions, especially when these decisions affect individuals' rights or livelihoods (N. M. Kumar, Islam, Podder, et al., 2023).

Privacy and Data Ethics

The vast amounts of data required to train AI systems raise significant ethical concerns regarding user privacy and data ethics. AI systems, particularly those powered by machine learning, rely on large-scale data collection and processing to make accurate predictions and decisions (K. D. Singh et al., 2022). This data often includes sensitive personal information, such as medical records, financial details, or behavioral patterns, raising the question of how to balance the utility of AI with the protection of individual privacy (Pande et al., 2023).

In an era of data-driven AI, ensuring user privacy becomes paramount. Ethical data collection involves obtaining explicit consent from users, clearly communicating how their data will be used, and safeguarding that data from unauthorized access (Ram & Xing, 2023). However, the challenge lies in the fact that AI systems often require extensive datasets, which may include sensitive personal information (Nethravathi et al., 2022). The temptation to use data indiscriminately—sometimes without proper consent or transparency—can lead to violations of privacy and the exploitation of vulnerable individuals (M. Gupta, Verma, et al., 2023).

Furthermore, the ethical use of data extends to how it is stored, shared, and utilized by AI systems. The advent of techniques like data anonymization and encryption has allowed for more secure handling of personal data, but questions remain about how much data is ethically justifiable for AI purposes (A. Srivastava et al., 2022). Should AI systems be allowed to collect data on individuals' behaviors, emotions, or even subconscious reactions? These concerns underscore the need for robust data ethics frameworks that prioritize transparency, security, and user autonomy (Manjunatha et al., 2023).

Autonomy vs. Human Agency

The increasing reliance on AI systems raises a critical ethical debate about the autonomy of AI and the erosion of human agency. As AI systems become more sophisticated, they begin to assume decision-making roles that were traditionally handled by human leaders (A. Gupta & Kumar, 2022). In many cases, AI has the potential to outperform humans in certain tasks, such as predicting market trends, diagnosing diseases, or optimizing supply chains. However, this raises important questions about the extent to which we should allow AI to make decisions without human oversight (Kukreti et al., 2023).

One of the core ethical concerns is the potential erosion of human agency in critical decision-making processes (Ahmed et al., 2022). When AI systems are given unchecked autonomy, they may make decisions that are misaligned with human values, leading to unforeseen or undesirable outcomes. In the context of autonomous vehicles, for example, AI systems must make split-second decisions in life-and-death situations, such as how to prioritize the safety of the vehicle's occupants versus pedestrians. Such moral dilemmas challenge the notion of human agency, as they raise the question of whether we are willing to cede life-altering decisions to machines (S. Joshi & Sharma, 2022).

Moreover, the delegation of decision-making to AI can lead to a loss of accountability. If an AI system makes a harmful decision—such as a medical misdiagnosis or an unfair hiring recommendation—who is responsible? Is it the developer who created the algorithm, the organization that deployed the system, or the AI itself? These questions underscore the need to carefully navigate the balance between human agency and AI autonomy (Eswar et al., 2023; S. Joshi & Sharma, 2023; Reddy et al., 2023).

The debate between autonomy and human agency is also pertinent in sectors like military and defense, where AI systems may be tasked with making strategic decisions that could impact national security (Aggarwal & Sharma, 2022; Gururani et al., 2022). This raises concerns about the ethical implications of delegating life-and-death decisions to machines and the potential for AI systems to act in ways that are not fully aligned with human ethical standards (S. Joshi et al., 2023).

The implementation of AI in organizational decision-making introduces profound ethical challenges that require thoughtful consideration and careful management. These challenges span issues of bias and fairness, transparency and explainability, privacy and data ethics, and the balance between AI autonomy and human agency (Maurya et al., 2022). Addressing these concerns is not only crucial for the responsible use of AI but also essential for maintaining public trust, organizational integrity, and the ethical alignment of technology with human values. As AI continues to evolve and shape organizational practices, it is imperative for leaders to establish robust ethical frameworks that guide AI implementation, ensuring that AI serves as a tool for enhancing decision-making while respecting individual rights, promoting fairness, and upholding accountability (Agarwal & Sharma, 2023; Ahmad et al., 2023; R. K. Bisht et al., 2022).

4. PRINCIPLES OF ETHICAL DECISION-MAKING IN AI LEADERSHIP

Responsibility and Accountability

In the realm of AI leadership, the concepts of responsibility and accountability are paramount. As AI systems are increasingly integrated into organizational decision-making processes, it is crucial to delineate clear lines of accountability for the decisions made by these systems (Salama et al., 2023). Ethical decision-making in AI is not solely the responsibility of the algorithm or the AI itself but is a shared responsibility between developers, organizational leaders, and stakeholders (Hajoary et al., 2023; H. Sharma et al., 2023).

Leadership plays a critical role in overseeing AI ethics, ensuring that AI systems are deployed in a manner that aligns with organizational values and societal norms. The absence of clear accountability can lead to unethical outcomes, as it becomes difficult to attribute responsibility for actions taken by AI systems (P. K. Juneja et al., 2022; Pai et al., 2022; Sen Thapa et al., 2022). This can be particularly problematic in high-stakes environments, such as healthcare, criminal justice, or autonomous vehicles, where AI-driven decisions directly impact human lives. For instance, if an AI system erroneously diagnoses a patient or makes an unjust recommendation in the context of criminal sentencing, it is imperative that leadership holds itself accountable for ensuring that such outcomes are prevented (Akberdina et al., 2023).

To ensure accountability, organizational leaders must establish clear frameworks for auditing AI systems, implement oversight mechanisms, and provide avenues for transparency in decision-making processes (P. J. Juneja et al., 2020; Masal et al., 2022; K. Sharma et al., 2022). These frameworks should outline who is responsible for designing, training, and deploying AI systems, as well as who will be held accountable in the event of an unethical outcome. Furthermore, leadership must prioritize continuous monitoring and adaptation of AI systems to rectify potential ethical pitfalls, fostering a culture of accountability that extends to all stages of the AI lifecycle (Chandna, 2022; Lokanadham et al., 2022).

Fairness and Inclusivity

AI systems have the potential to either perpetuate or alleviate societal inequalities. To mitigate risks of bias and discrimination, leaders must prioritize fairness and inclusivity in the design and deployment of AI solutions (M. A. Kumar et al., 2022). This involves ensuring that AI technologies do not disproportionately benefit one group while marginalizing others, particularly vulnerable or historically disadvantaged groups (Ahmed et al., 2022).

Fairness in AI is multifaceted, encompassing both procedural fairness (ensuring that AI systems are developed and implemented through equitable processes) and distributive fairness (ensuring that AI outcomes do not exacerbate societal inequalities). For example, in the realm of hiring, an AI system trained on historical data may inherit biases from past discriminatory practices, resulting in biased hiring decisions (P. Verma, Kumar, et al., 2022). To mitigate such risks, ethical leadership must ensure that AI systems are designed to be inclusive, using diverse and representative datasets and implementing fairness-enhancing algorithms that reduce the potential for bias (A. Kumar, Saxena, Sastry, et al., 2023).

Inclusivity, on the other hand, requires a commitment to ensuring that AI solutions are accessible and equitable for all stakeholders, regardless of their socioeconomic status, race, gender, or other characteristics. Inclusivity should extend beyond the development phase, encompassing the deployment and operational stages as well (Chandran et al., 2022). Leadership must actively engage with marginalized groups to understand their unique needs and ensure that AI technologies do not unintentionally perpetuate inequities. This may involve designing AI systems that accommodate the needs of persons with disabilities, language minorities, or economically disadvantaged populations (M. Verma et al., 2022).

A commitment to fairness and inclusivity in AI not only aligns with ethical principles but also enhances the long-term success of AI deployments by fostering broader acceptance and trust among diverse stakeholders (Chandna et al., 2022).

Ethical Leadership Models

Ethical leadership in the age of AI requires the adoption of leadership models that prioritize moral responsibility and the welfare of stakeholders. Three prominent models of ethical leadership are particularly relevant in the context of AI decision-making: servant leadership, transformational leadership, and ethical stewardship (S. Uniyal et al., 2022).

- Servant Leadership: This model places the leader in the role of a servant to their followers, prioritizing the well-being and development of those they lead. In the context of AI, servant leaders would ensure that AI systems are designed and deployed in ways that serve the needs and interests of all stakeholders. This involves being attuned to the potential ethical implications of AI and making decisions that prioritize the welfare of individuals, especially those who might be adversely impacted by AI technologies (Jayadeva et al., 2023; MITRA et al., 2022).

- Transformational Leadership: Transformational leaders inspire and motivate their teams to achieve higher levels of performance, often through a shared vision of innovation and change (R. Kumar, Kandpal, & Ahmad, 2023). In AI leadership, this model emphasizes the importance of fostering innovation while remaining committed to ethical principles. Transformational leaders would advocate for the responsible use of AI, encouraging the development of AI systems that not only drive organizational success but also promote social good and align with ethical norms (Shah et al., 2023; S. Sharma et al., 2023).
- Ethical Stewardship: Ethical stewardship involves leaders acting as caretakers of the organization's values, ensuring that ethical principles guide decision-making and organizational practices (N. K. Singh et al., 2023). In the context of AI, ethical stewardship means ensuring that AI technologies are deployed with a strong commitment to social responsibility. Ethical stewards would ensure that AI systems are transparent, accountable, and aligned with the broader goal of societal well-being, rather than simply optimizing for profit or efficiency (Mehershilpa et al., 2023).

By applying these leadership models, AI decision-makers can ensure that ethical considerations remain at the forefront of AI implementation and that AI technologies are developed in alignment with moral principles that benefit society as a whole.

Stakeholder Engagement

Ethical decision-making in AI is not a solitary endeavor but one that requires active engagement with a wide range of stakeholders. These stakeholders include employees, customers, regulators, and the broader public, all of whom are impacted by the ethical ramifications of AI deployment (Ram & Xing, 2023). Engaging stakeholders in discussions about AI use ensures that diverse perspectives are considered, promoting greater transparency and trust in AI systems.

- Employees are critical stakeholders who may be directly impacted by AI-driven changes in the workplace, such as automation or algorithmic performance evaluations. Leaders must engage employees in conversations about the ethical implications of AI in their roles, ensuring that AI technologies are introduced in a manner that respects human dignity and promotes worker welfare.

- Customers are the ultimate beneficiaries of AI technologies, and their trust is essential for the widespread adoption of AI systems (K. Pandey et al., 2022). Engaging customers in discussions about the ethical use of their data, the transparency of AI systems, and the fairness of AI-driven decisions builds trust and ensures that organizations are held accountable to their customers' interests (Venkatesh et al., 2023).
- Regulators play a vital role in establishing legal frameworks and ethical guidelines for AI use. Collaboration with regulators helps organizations navigate the complex ethical and legal challenges associated with AI and ensures compliance with regulations such as the GDPR or the AI Ethics Guidelines proposed by various international bodies (Diddi et al., 2022).
- The broader public is also a key stakeholder in AI ethics, as the implications of AI technologies extend far beyond organizational borders. Public engagement ensures that AI technologies are developed in ways that align with societal values, promoting the collective good while minimizing harm (Gaurav et al., 2023).

By engaging stakeholders in a continuous dialogue around AI ethics, leaders can ensure that their AI systems are both effective and aligned with the ethical principles that govern their industries. This collaborative approach fosters greater accountability, transparency, and trust, which are essential for the ethical implementation of AI (Ansari & Afzal, 2022; Rajbalaji et al., 2023).

The principles of ethical decision-making in AI leadership require a nuanced and holistic approach that encompasses responsibility and accountability, fairness and inclusivity, ethical leadership models, and stakeholder engagement (Kowsalya et al., 2023). By adhering to these principles, leaders can ensure that AI technologies are developed and deployed in a manner that aligns with ethical norms, promotes social responsibility, and fosters trust among all stakeholders. As AI continues to shape organizational decision-making, ethical leadership will be critical in guiding its use for the betterment of society (R. Arora et al., 2022).

5. AI GOVERNANCE AND REGULATION

Establishing AI Governance Structures

In the age of artificial intelligence, the necessity for robust governance frameworks to manage AI systems within organizations has never been more pronounced. Effective AI governance structures ensure that AI technologies are deployed in a responsible, ethical, and transparent manner (Subramani, Kaliappan, Sekar, et al., 2022). These frameworks must provide comprehensive oversight over all AI-related processes, from design and deployment to monitoring and post-deployment evaluation, with an emphasis on accountability and ethical compliance. Governance structures should include cross-disciplinary teams of experts, including ethicists, data scientists, legal professionals, and business leaders, to collaborate on establishing standards that mitigate the risks associated with AI while fostering innovation (R. Kumar & Khanna, 2023b).

One of the central aspects of AI governance is ensuring that AI decision-making processes are transparent, auditable, and accountable (Komkowski et al., 2023a). AI systems must be able to explain the rationale behind their outputs, especially in high-stakes domains such as healthcare, finance, or law enforcement. A well-defined governance structure ensures that leadership is empowered to oversee AI activities, mitigate potential risks, and guarantee that AI technologies align with an organization's ethical and business objectives. Furthermore, organizations should invest in continuous governance assessments to ensure that evolving technological developments are aligned with their ethical standards (Kohli et al., 2022).

The governance structure also includes the allocation of resources for ongoing monitoring of AI systems' impact, ensuring that they operate within legal and moral boundaries. This process also involves keeping abreast of technological advancements, regulatory changes, and public expectations to anticipate challenges before they arise (E. Sharma et al., 2023).

Ethical Codes of Conduct

As AI technologies permeate various sectors, the need for ethical codes of conduct becomes crucial to guide their development and application (Gonfa et al., 2023). These ethical guidelines ensure that organizations adhere to fundamental ethical principles, such as fairness, accountability, transparency, and privacy, in their AI-driven processes (Hajoary et al., 2023). Establishing clear and robust ethical codes of conduct serves as the foundation for responsible AI practices, providing employees and stakeholders with a shared understanding of the ethical boundaries within which AI systems must operate (S. Sharma et al., 2023).

AI ethics codes address a broad array of concerns, including bias mitigation, transparency in AI decision-making, data privacy, and the responsible use of AI in sensitive areas such as employment, healthcare, and criminal justice (Ram et al., 2022). These codes should be tailored to the specific needs and contexts of the organization, while still aligning with broader global ethical principles. For instance, an ethical code may include guidelines on ensuring that AI systems are designed to eliminate algorithmic biases, that data used to train AI models are ethically sourced, and that AI outcomes are interpretable and understandable to end-users (Johri et al., 2023).

The creation of an AI ethics code must be a collaborative process, involving diverse stakeholders, including technical teams, legal advisors, and external ethicists (Behera & Singh Rawat, 2023). This ensures that all relevant perspectives are considered, and that the ethical guidelines reflect both the practical realities of AI development and the moral imperatives of responsible innovation. A successful AI ethics code should also be adaptive and capable of evolving in response to new ethical challenges posed by emerging technologies (S. Sharma & Bhadula, 2023).

Global AI Regulation

The global regulatory landscape for artificial intelligence is still in its infancy, with disparate approaches being adopted by different countries and regions (Kamra et al., 2023). Nevertheless, there is growing momentum towards the establishment of international AI regulations aimed at ensuring that AI technologies are developed and deployed ethically, safely, and responsibly (S. P. Singh et al., 2023).

In Europe, the General Data Protection Regulation (GDPR) has set a precedent for AI governance, particularly in areas related to privacy and data protection. Additionally, the European Commission has proposed the Artificial Intelligence Act, a comprehensive framework aimed at regulating high-risk AI systems. This act emphasizes transparency, accountability, and risk management and is a significant step toward the regulation of AI technologies within the EU (Rajeswari et al., 2022). Similarly, other regions such as the United States and China are making strides to regulate AI, albeit with differing focuses. While the U.S. is more oriented toward innovation and market-driven regulation, China has a more state-centric approach, particularly focused on controlling the development and use of AI technologies for societal stability (Uike et al., 2022).

International bodies such as the OECD (Organisation for Economic Co-operation and Development) and the United Nations are playing a crucial role in shaping global AI guidelines (Krishna et al., 2022). The OECD has released recommendations for trustworthy AI, which emphasize the importance of inclusivity, transparency, and fairness. These guidelines provide a foundation for international collaboration and set a standard for nations and industries looking to adopt AI technologies responsibly (P. Verma, Chaudhari, et al., 2022).

While the regulatory landscape is evolving, the complexity of AI systems and their global reach presents significant challenges in creating universally applicable regulations (S. Bansal et al., 2023). As AI technologies transcend borders, global cooperation and standardized frameworks will be essential in ensuring that AI remains a force for good across cultures and regions (Pandya et al., 2023). Coordination between governments, regulatory bodies, industry leaders, and civil society is paramount to ensuring the responsible development and deployment of AI (Caiado et al., 2023).

Challenges in Regulatory Compliance

As the pace of AI development accelerates, organizations face significant challenges in staying compliant with evolving regulatory standards. One of the main obstacles is the dynamic nature of AI technologies, which often outpaces the speed at which traditional regulatory frameworks are updated (Umamaheswaran et al., 2023). Many regulations are still in the early stages of development, and existing laws often fail to address the nuances and complexities inherent in AI systems. The rapid growth of machine learning algorithms, deep learning models, and autonomous systems makes it difficult for regulatory bodies to keep pace with the latest developments, leaving gaps in governance that could result in the misuse of AI (Abdullah et al., 2023).

For instance, regulatory authorities may struggle to create rules that govern AI in contexts where human involvement is minimal, such as in autonomous vehicles or fully automated financial trading systems. In such scenarios, it becomes difficult to determine who is legally responsible when something goes wrong—whether it is the AI system itself, the developers, or the organizations that deployed the system.

Moreover, companies operating across borders must navigate different regulatory regimes with potentially conflicting requirements, adding complexity to global compliance efforts (Jindal et al., 2022). A company that deploys AI-driven systems in the European Union, the United States, and Asia may need to adhere to vastly different regulations concerning data privacy, algorithmic transparency, or liability, creating an additional layer of regulatory burden (Gopal et al., 2023).

To mitigate these challenges, organizations must invest in comprehensive compliance strategies that monitor and adapt to changing regulatory requirements. This may involve engaging legal and policy experts, forming partnerships with industry groups, and staying updated on emerging regulations at both the national and international levels. Proactive efforts to engage with regulators and policymakers will also be crucial in shaping future regulations that are practical, effective, and aligned with technological advancements (A. S. Kumar & Desi, 2023).

In conclusion, AI governance and regulation are crucial to ensuring that AI technologies are deployed responsibly, ethically, and in a manner that benefits society at large (Rana et al., 2022). Establishing clear governance structures, ethical codes, and participating in global regulatory efforts are all key components of this process (Medhi et al., 2023). However, the dynamic and complex nature of AI technologies poses significant challenges to regulatory compliance, underscoring the need for continuous adaptation and international collaboration. Only through responsible AI governance can organizations navigate the ethical and legal complexities of AI and harness its potential for positive societal impact (S. S. Rawat et al., 2022).

6. BUILDING AN ETHICAL AI CULTURE WITHIN ORGANIZATIONS

Organizational Culture and AI Ethics

Organizational culture profoundly influences the ethical use of artificial intelligence (AI) within any enterprise. At its core, culture refers to the shared values, beliefs, norms, and behaviors that define how an organization functions and how its employees interact with one another and with external stakeholders (V. Kumar & Korovin, 2023). In the context of AI, the organizational culture can act as a pivotal force in determining how AI technologies are designed, implemented, and monitored to ensure ethical outcomes (Singla et al., 2023). A culture that prioritizes transparency, accountability, and fairness will inspire AI practitioners to develop systems that align with these values. Conversely, a culture that tolerates or overlooks unethical practices, such as bias or lack of transparency, can inadvertently lead to harmful AI outcomes (V. Kumar & Korovin, 2023).

The integration of AI into organizational operations demands an ongoing commitment to aligning its deployment with the organization's ethical principles. This alignment requires that AI-related decisions, from algorithm development to implementation, are made with a clear understanding of how they impact both internal stakeholders and society at large (N. K. Pandey et al., 2023). When AI is embedded into an organization's core values and ethical frameworks, it promotes responsible decision-making at every stage of the AI lifecycle (Gonfa et al., 2023).

A positive organizational culture that fosters ethical AI practices encourages employees to raise concerns, share best practices, and hold one another accountable for the responsible development and use of AI (Kaliappan et al., 2023). Additionally, an ethical AI culture nurtures an environment where both AI technologies and their creators are scrutinized, ensuring that the organization remains vigilant in preventing discrimination, bias, and other negative societal impacts that may arise from AI applications (B. Bisht et al., 2023).

Leadership's Role in Shaping Culture

Leadership plays a central role in cultivating an ethical AI culture within an organization. As the architects of the organization's values and vision, leaders must lead by example, demonstrating a commitment to responsible AI practices (Nadeem et al., 2023). Ethical leadership involves not only adhering to ethical guidelines but also actively promoting these values to foster a culture of ethical responsibility. Leaders must set the tone for the organization by making ethical decision-making a core principle in the AI development process (Rakhra et al., 2022).

One of the primary ways leaders influence the ethical use of AI is by modeling behaviors that prioritize ethical considerations (Sahu & Rawat, 2023). This includes demonstrating openness to ethical discussions, actively addressing concerns raised by employees or stakeholders, and being transparent about the decision-making processes (Lade et al., 2023). By prioritizing transparency, accountability, and ethical practices, leaders signal to employees and other organizational stakeholders that ethics is not just a peripheral concern but a fundamental aspect of AI development (Mehershilpa et al., 2023).

Moreover, leadership's role extends beyond merely setting the example—it involves creating policies and structures that encourage ethical behavior (Ekren et al., 2023). This may include integrating ethical AI considerations into hiring practices, performance evaluations, and decision-making frameworks (Bist et al., 2022). Leaders must also advocate for the establishment of ethics committees, whose role it is to oversee AI projects, assess potential risks, and ensure that ethical standards are upheld. In doing so, leaders create a formalized structure that reinforces ethical values and integrates them into organizational decision-making processes (Medhi et al., 2023).

Training and Education

Training and education are crucial components of fostering an ethical AI culture within organizations. As AI technologies continue to evolve rapidly, both employees and leaders must receive ongoing education on ethical principles related to AI development and use (K. Pandey et al., 2020). A well-structured training program should encompass key topics such as algorithmic fairness, data privacy, bias detection, transparency, and the social implications of AI systems. Employees across all levels of the organization—ranging from AI developers to business leaders—must be equipped with the knowledge and tools necessary to make ethically sound decisions regarding AI (H. Kaur et al., 2023).

Training also facilitates the development of critical thinking skills in employees, enabling them to evaluate AI systems from an ethical standpoint. Rather than passively following instructions or adhering to technical specifications, employees must be able to ask probing questions, such as: "What impact will this AI model have on marginalized communities?" or "How transparent are the decision-making processes of this AI system?" In fostering a culture of continuous learning, organizations create an environment in which ethical awareness becomes ingrained in the fabric of the organization, leading to more responsible AI development and deployment (Dixit et al., 2022).

In addition to training, organizations should establish formalized mechanisms for employees to voice concerns related to AI ethics. This can include ethics hotlines, anonymous reporting systems, or regular ethical audits of AI projects. By empowering employees to raise ethical issues, organizations signal that ethical responsibility is a shared duty, not just the responsibility of leadership or AI experts.

Cross-Department Collaboration

The integration of AI ethics within an organization requires cross-departmental collaboration, particularly between AI specialists, ethicists, legal experts, and leadership. AI development is a multifaceted process that necessitates input from diverse expertise to ensure that the technology meets ethical standards. The involvement of ethicists and legal teams ensures that AI systems align with relevant ethical guidelines, laws, and regulations, such as data protection laws and fairness standards. By working together, these departments can identify potential ethical risks early in the AI development process, ensuring that solutions are designed with inclusivity and fairness at their core.

One of the most important outcomes of cross-departmental collaboration is the creation of a holistic approach to AI development. AI specialists focus on the technical aspects, but it is the collaboration with ethicists and legal experts that provides a more comprehensive understanding of how AI technologies impact society and individuals. For instance, ethicists can advise on how to mitigate algorithmic bias, while legal teams can ensure that data privacy laws are adhered to. Through such collaborations, organizations can create AI systems that are not only technically proficient but also ethically sound.

Furthermore, leadership must facilitate these collaborations by fostering an environment where open communication and cooperation are prioritized. This involves breaking down silos between departments and encouraging the sharing of ideas and best practices. Regular discussions and workshops between AI specialists and ethics experts can provide valuable opportunities for both parties to learn from each other and align their objectives. By promoting collaboration, organizations can ensure that AI practices are more than just technically efficient—they are also ethically responsible, inclusive, and transparent (Goswami & Sharma, 2022; Jena & Gairola, 2022; Mohd et al., 2023; Raja et al., 2022).

Building an ethical AI culture within an organization is essential for ensuring the responsible development and deployment of AI technologies. The influence of organizational culture on ethical AI practices cannot be overstated, as it shapes the behavior of AI practitioners and decision-makers. Leadership plays a critical role in setting the ethical tone for the organization, promoting ethical behaviors, and fostering a culture of accountability and transparency. Training and education are indispensable in ensuring that both employees and leaders are equipped with the knowledge necessary to navigate the complex ethical challenges of AI. Cross-departmental collaboration between AI specialists, ethicists, and legal teams ensures that AI practices align with organizational values and external regulatory requirements. By establishing a strong ethical foundation and continuously engaging in ethical decision-making, organizations can harness the power of AI for the benefit of society while minimizing its potential risks (Bhamangol et al., 2022; A. K. Mishra & Wazid, 2023; K. D. Singh et al., 2023; Trache et al., 2022).

7. STRATEGIES FOR RESPONSIBLE AI USE

Designing Ethical AI Solutions

Designing ethical AI solutions requires a deliberate and thoughtful approach to the development and deployment of artificial intelligence. Central to this process is the commitment to principles of fairness, transparency, and privacy. Fairness entails ensuring that AI systems do not reinforce or perpetuate biases, particularly those related to race, gender, or socioeconomic status. Designers must consider the diverse implications of their algorithms, conducting rigorous testing to ensure that AI systems treat all demographic groups equitably, without discrimination or skewed outcomes. This can be achieved through methods such as bias mitigation algorithms, which actively adjust outputs to minimize disparities (Chahar et al., 2022; T. Pandey et al., 2023; Sunori et al., 2023).

Transparency in AI is equally vital. For AI systems to be ethically responsible, their decision-making processes must be understandable and explainable to all stakeholders, including end-users, regulators, and even developers (Das et al., 2023; Singamaneni et al., 2022). Transparent AI design involves providing clear explanations of how algorithms arrive at specific outcomes, which can be achieved by implementing explainable AI (XAI) methodologies. These techniques make it possible for users to comprehend AI's rationale, even when its operations are complex, thus enhancing trust and facilitating informed decisions (Josphineleela, Siva Reddy, et al., 2023).

Privacy concerns, particularly in the realm of data collection, storage, and processing, are paramount when designing ethical AI systems. Given the massive volumes of personal and sensitive data involved in AI-driven operations, developers must ensure compliance with data protection regulations, such as the GDPR or CCPA. Employing techniques like differential privacy, which allows for data analysis without exposing individual details, can mitigate privacy risks. The design process must also prioritize data anonymization to protect users' identities and prevent unauthorized surveillance (Negi et al., 2021; Raman et al., 2023; R. C. Sharma et al., 2023).

AI Risk Management Frameworks

Effective risk management is a cornerstone of responsible AI deployment. Organizations must implement robust AI risk management frameworks that proactively address ethical, operational, and technological risks throughout the AI lifecycle—from conceptualization to deployment and ongoing monitoring. A comprehensive risk management strategy begins with an assessment of potential risks at the inception phase, where AI models are first conceptualized and their societal and environmental impacts are evaluated (Akana et al., 2023; Josphineleela, Jyothi, et al., 2023; L. S. Khanna et al., 2023).

One of the most critical aspects of an AI risk management framework is the identification of ethical risks such as bias, transparency issues, and violations of privacy. This requires conducting thorough impact assessments that evaluate the broader societal consequences of deploying AI solutions. Additionally, organizations must integrate safeguards that ensure AI does not inadvertently exacerbate existing inequalities or discrimination (Begum et al., 2022).

At the deployment stage, frameworks should incorporate real-time monitoring to ensure the AI's performance aligns with ethical expectations (H. Gupta et al., 2023; Kathir et al., 2022; Raju et al., 2022). Regular audit trails must be established to track AI decisions and ensure they remain aligned with organizational values and ethical standards. Periodic evaluations also allow organizations to adjust and fine-tune AI systems to prevent ethical breaches, ensuring continuous compliance with legal standards.

Furthermore, risk mitigation strategies must address potential failures in algorithmic models or biases in AI-driven decision-making. This can be achieved by creating mechanisms for human intervention—such as supervisory decision-makers who can override AI actions when necessary. Establishing clear escalation protocols ensures that ethical risks are flagged and rectified promptly, minimizing harm to stakeholders (Davuluri et al., 2023; R. Kumar, Saxena, & Singh, 2023; Manjunatha et al., 2023).

Ensuring Algorithmic Accountability

Algorithmic accountability is critical in ensuring that AI systems remain trustworthy, fair, and transparent. To ensure that AI systems are consistently performing ethically, regular auditing and monitoring must be integrated into the design and operation of AI models. Audits should focus on three key factors: fairness, accuracy, and bias (Davuluri et al., 2023; Unhelkar et al., 2022; Yeruva et al., 2022). Fairness audits assess whether AI outcomes disproportionately disadvantage certain groups. This can be done through the use of disparate impact analysis, a technique that compares the outcomes for different demographic groups and identifies any discrepancies (Godbole et al., 2023; K. Joshi et al., 2023; R. Rawat et al., 2023).

Accuracy audits involve evaluating the precision of AI models by comparing predicted outcomes against actual results, ensuring that the AI's decisions are both reliable and valid. These audits help identify areas where AI systems may need recalibration or adjustments to improve decision-making. Finally, bias audits examine the extent to which AI models may perpetuate prejudices based on flawed data. Algorithms can be tested for discriminatory bias and adjusted to ensure that they are inclusive and equitable (K. Kumar, Chaudhary, Anandaram, et al., 2023; R. Kumar, Kandpal, & Ahmad, 2023; S. K. Singh et al., 2023).

The concept of algorithmic accountability also necessitates the establishment of mechanisms for correcting flawed outcomes. This includes the ability to trace AI decisions back to their source and identify the specific factors that led to a particular outcome. One promising approach to improving accountability is the creation of AI ethics boards or oversight committees within organizations. These bodies would be responsible for monitoring AI models' performance, reviewing ethical risks, and ensuring corrective actions are taken when necessary (Akberdina et al., 2023; Komkowski et al., 2023b).

Moreover, AI liability frameworks should be developed to assign responsibility when AI systems cause harm. Such frameworks would clarify the roles of various stakeholders, including developers, companies, and regulatory bodies, ensuring that those responsible for deploying AI systems are held accountable for any adverse consequences of their use (S. Bansal et al., 2023; Bhatt & Ghuman, 2022; Luthra et al., 2022).

Responsible Innovation

Fostering responsible innovation in AI involves developing technologies with a balanced focus on both technological advancement and ethical considerations. In the rush to innovate and harness the full potential of AI, it is easy to overlook the ethical implications of deploying such technologies. Responsible innovation necessitates that AI developers and business leaders adopt an ethical lens when making decisions about the scope and direction of AI projects (Kannan et al., 2022; Shabbiruddin et al., 2023; M. Sharma et al., 2022).

A key aspect of responsible innovation is the idea of human-centered AI, which emphasizes the well-being and dignity of individuals over purely technological progress. AI systems must be developed with the intention of enhancing human life, addressing societal challenges, and respecting fundamental rights. To achieve this, AI solutions should be aligned with long-term societal goals, such as sustainable development, equity, and inclusion, rather than being driven solely by immediate profit maximization.

Organizations must encourage an innovation environment that balances risk-taking with a keen awareness of ethical boundaries. This can be achieved through the implementation of innovation ethics guidelines, which set out clear parameters for ethical decision-making in the AI development process. Furthermore, encouraging cross-disciplinary collaboration between technologists, ethicists, social scientists, and other relevant stakeholders is essential to ensuring that innovation occurs within a framework that safeguards public welfare and fosters ethical responsibility.

Organizations should also adopt ethical foresight practices, which involve proactively identifying potential ethical challenges in emerging AI technologies. This foresight approach enables companies to anticipate and mitigate ethical risks before they become ingrained in the AI deployment process.

In summary, responsible AI use requires an integrated approach that combines ethical design, risk management, algorithmic accountability, and a commitment to responsible innovation. By prioritizing fairness, transparency, privacy, and inclusivity in AI systems, organizations can build solutions that benefit society while minimizing potential harms. Through continuous monitoring, audits, and corrective measures, AI can be deployed in a manner that fosters trust, accountability, and social good. Responsible innovation ensures that technological advancements do not come at the cost of ethical considerations, and instead promote a future where AI serves humanity in a manner that is both progressive and principled.

8. REAL-WORLD APPLICATIONS AND CASE STUDIES

Case Study 1: AI in Hiring and Recruitment

AI-driven recruitment systems have transformed the hiring landscape, offering organizations efficiencies in sourcing, screening, and selecting candidates. However, these systems raise significant ethical challenges, particularly in terms of bias and fairness. AI models are often trained on historical data that may reflect existing societal biases. For example, if past hiring decisions favored certain demographic groups, AI systems could inadvertently replicate these biases, leading to discriminatory outcomes in hiring practices. This bias can manifest in various forms, including gender, racial, and socioeconomic biases, which perpetuate inequality in the workforce.

To mitigate these challenges, organizations must implement responsible AI practices such as regular bias audits and the development of diverse training datasets. Bias audits can identify and address disparities in the outcomes produced by AI systems, ensuring that they are fair and equitable. Organizations should also invest in transparent algorithms, where the decision-making processes are explainable and understandable to human decision-makers. This transparency allows for greater scrutiny and accountability, ensuring that recruitment processes are based on merit rather than historical biases.

Leadership plays a crucial role in this context by establishing ethical recruitment guidelines and promoting diversity and inclusion in AI model design. By fostering a culture of fairness and transparency, organizations can mitigate the risk of biased AI systems and ensure that recruitment decisions are just, equitable, and aligned with ethical standards.

Case Study 2: AI in Healthcare Decision-Making

AI applications in healthcare have grown rapidly, particularly in the areas of diagnostic tools and treatment recommendations. AI models have demonstrated the potential to assist healthcare providers in diagnosing diseases, recommending personalized treatment plans, and even predicting patient outcomes. However, the use of AI in healthcare also introduces a host of ethical concerns, primarily around patient autonomy, informed consent, and data privacy.

One of the most pressing ethical dilemmas in healthcare AI is ensuring that AI-driven diagnostics do not compromise the doctor-patient relationship. Patients have the right to know and understand how AI systems inform medical decisions. Informed consent becomes especially critical when AI is used in diagnostics, as patients should be made aware of the AI's role in the decision-making process and its potential limitations. Healthcare professionals must also be transparent about the extent to which AI systems influence the final diagnosis or treatment plan, allowing patients to make informed decisions about their care.

Moreover, data privacy is a critical issue, as AI systems require vast amounts of sensitive medical data to function effectively. The ethical leadership in healthcare organizations must ensure that patient data is stored securely and used only with explicit consent, complying with stringent data protection regulations like HIPAA in the U.S. or GDPR in the European Union. Ethical leaders must prioritize the safeguarding of patient confidentiality, ensuring that AI applications are deployed in ways that protect individuals' privacy rights.

To ensure the responsible use of AI in healthcare, ethical leadership should champion the development of robust AI ethics frameworks that prioritize patient welfare. Furthermore, continuous training for healthcare professionals on AI ethics and the implications of AI in medical decision-making is crucial for maintaining high ethical standards in practice.

Case Study 3: AI in Autonomous Vehicles

The advent of autonomous vehicles (AVs) has revolutionized the transportation industry, promising to reduce traffic accidents, improve road safety, and enhance transportation efficiency. However, the integration of AI into self-driving cars has raised profound ethical dilemmas, particularly in life-and-death scenarios. One of the most debated ethical issues is the trolley problem, which poses a scenario where an autonomous vehicle must decide between harming one individual to save several others or avoiding the harm but causing more significant consequences. For example, if a self-driving car must choose between hitting a pedestrian or swerving into a wall, leading to the potential injury of its passengers, what decision should the car make?

The responsibility of leadership in autonomous vehicle development is to ensure that AI systems are programmed with transparent ethical decision-making frameworks that reflect society's values. Ethical leaders must engage in public consultations, involving diverse stakeholders—such as ethicists, legal experts, engineers, and the general public—to create ethical guidelines for AV decision-making processes. These guidelines must be based on collective moral principles, taking into account considerations such as minimizing harm, equity, and justice.

Moreover, accountability for decisions made by autonomous vehicles remains a critical issue. As these vehicles operate without human intervention, the question arises: who is liable in the event of an accident? Should the manufacturer, software developers, or the passengers be held responsible? Ethical leadership in the automotive and tech industries must advocate for clear liability frameworks that delineate responsibility and ensure that victims of AV-related accidents are compensated fairly. Additionally, transparent algorithms in AVs are essential to ensure that the decision-making processes behind critical moments, like those involving pedestrian safety, are understandable and auditable.

In conclusion, the ethical challenges posed by AI in recruitment, healthcare, and autonomous vehicles highlight the importance of integrating ethical leadership and responsible practices across sectors. In each case study, leaders must prioritize fairness, accountability, transparency, and human dignity to ensure that AI technologies are deployed in ways that benefit society while mitigating potential harms. Through the proactive establishment of ethical guidelines, continuous stakeholder engagement, and rigorous monitoring, AI can be harnessed for the greater good, creating innovative solutions that are not only technologically advanced but also ethically sound.

9. THE ROLE OF ETHICS IN AI ADOPTION AND STAKEHOLDER TRUST

Trust and AI

Ethical AI practices serve as the cornerstone for fostering trust among key stakeholders—consumers, employees, and the public. Trust is foundational to the successful integration of AI into any organization, as stakeholders are increasingly scrutinizing how AI systems affect their lives, rights, and privacy. The primary ethical principles that contribute to trust-building include transparency, accountability, and fairness. Transparency ensures that AI algorithms are comprehensible and their decision-making processes are understandable, allowing individuals to trust that they are being treated equitably and not subject to arbitrary or discriminatory decisions. When AI is deployed in a manner that is transparent, stakeholders can gain confidence that they are being respected and valued (Dangwal et al., 2022; M. Gupta, Arora, et al., 2023; Taneja & Özen, 2023; Taneja & Sharma, 2023).

Accountability in AI practices further amplifies trust, as it ensures that when AI systems make decisions that affect individuals or groups, there is a clear responsibility framework in place. Ethical AI practices must involve mechanisms to audit, monitor, and correct AI behavior to ensure its decisions are fair and aligned with societal values. Lastly, fairness plays a crucial role in AI adoption—organizations must ensure that their systems are designed to be inclusive, free from bias, and aligned with ethical guidelines that protect marginalized and vulnerable populations. By adhering to these principles, organizations can cultivate an environment where AI is perceived not as a threat but as a trustworthy, reliable tool that benefits all stakeholders (N. Bansal et al., 2023; Dahiya & Taneja, 2023; Reepu et al., 2023; Taneja, Gupta, Bhushan, Bhatnagar, et al., 2023).

Organizational Reputation and Brand Value

The adoption of ethical AI practices has a profound impact on an organization's reputation, brand value, and long-term sustainability. In an era where public scrutiny is magnified by social media and global connectivity, companies are under immense pressure to uphold ethical standards not only in their products and services but also in their internal operations and technological innovations. Organizations that integrate AI in an ethical manner contribute to a positive societal perception, enhancing their reputation as responsible, transparent, and trustworthy entities (Kour et al., 2025; A. Singh et al., 2024; Taneja, Gupta, Singh, Bhatnagar, et al., 2023; TANEJA et al., 2024).

A reputation for ethical AI usage can provide a significant competitive advantage. In a market where consumers and investors are increasingly prioritizing corporate social responsibility (CSR), businesses that adopt ethical AI solutions position themselves as leaders in their industries. Ethical AI adoption signals to customers and stakeholders that the company is committed to integrity, sustainability, and human well-being, all of which bolster brand loyalty and consumer trust. Companies that operate with a clear ethical framework not only attract conscientious consumers but also forge stronger, more resilient relationships with employees, regulators, and other key stakeholders (Bhatnagar, Rajaram, et al., 2024; Taneja, Bhatnagar, Kumar, & Rupeika-apoga, 2023).

In terms of long-term sustainability, ethical AI ensures that an organization is future-proofed against the evolving landscape of regulatory scrutiny and market expectations. By implementing responsible AI strategies, organizations can avoid the risks associated with legal penalties, reputational damage, or public backlash, positioning themselves for sustained growth and innovation (A. Kaur et al., 2023; P. Sharma et al., 2024).

Consumer and Public Expectations

As AI technologies become more pervasive, consumer and public expectations regarding ethical usage are evolving at an unprecedented pace. Consumers now demand more transparency in the technologies they use, with a particular emphasis on how their personal data is handled and how AI systems make decisions (Bhatnagar, Kumar, et al., 2024). Public consciousness around issues such as data privacy, algorithmic fairness, and autonomy is rising, with increasing calls for organizations to be held accountable for the ethical implications of their AI systems (Bhatnagar, Taneja, et al., 2024).

Ethical leadership is essential in responding to these rising expectations. Leaders must not only comply with existing regulations but also proactively engage with stakeholders to anticipate and address emerging concerns. This involves establishing a clear ethical vision for AI adoption, ensuring that all AI-related practices align with broader social and moral values. Ethical leaders should foster a culture of continuous dialogue and feedback, keeping the public, consumers, and employees informed about how AI is being used, what safeguards are in place, and how the organization is working to prevent harm or discrimination (Bhatnagar et al., 2023; P. Kumar, Verma, Bhatnagar, et al., 2023; Taneja, Bhatnagar, Kumar, & Grima, 2023).

In meeting these expectations, organizations should integrate inclusive design principles that cater to the diverse needs of their user base, ensuring that AI systems are accessible, non-discriminatory, and equitable. By actively demonstrating their commitment to ethical AI practices, organizations can reassure the public that their AI systems serve not only commercial interests but also contribute to broader societal well-being (P. Kumar, Reepu, et al., 2024).

Moreover, ethical leadership in AI can also serve as a differentiator in a crowded marketplace, offering organizations a way to distinguish themselves based on their commitment to responsible AI practices. In this respect, ethical AI adoption is not merely a regulatory or compliance requirement but a critical strategic lever that shapes organizational reputation and long-term success.

In conclusion, the role of ethics in AI adoption cannot be overstated. Ethical AI practices build trust among stakeholders, enhance organizational reputation, and align business practices with the evolving expectations of consumers and the public. Leaders who prioritize transparency, accountability, and fairness in their AI initiatives set their organizations on a path toward long-term success, fostering stakeholder trust, improving brand loyalty, and safeguarding against reputational and regulatory risks. As AI continues to reshape industries, ethical leadership will be the key differentiator in navigating the complexities of AI adoption and ensuring that technological advancements benefit both organizations and society at large (P. Kumar, Taneja, et al., 2024).

10. CONCLUSION: THE FUTURE OF ETHICAL AI LEADERSHIP

Balancing Innovation with Ethical Responsibility

As we advance into an era increasingly dominated by artificial intelligence, the imperative to balance innovation with ethical responsibility becomes ever more critical. The rapid pace of AI development presents a unique challenge for leaders who must reconcile the drive for technological progress with the potential societal, economic, and environmental consequences of such advancements. AI holds transformative potential across myriad sectors, from healthcare to finance, manufacturing to transportation, and yet its deployment is fraught with ethical dilemmas that demand meticulous attention.

In this context, ethical responsibility must be viewed not as an impediment to progress, but as a fundamental pillar that supports sustainable and beneficial AI development. Leaders must forge an equilibrium that enables continuous innovation while ensuring that the technology serves the common good, respects human dignity, and operates within established moral frameworks. This involves recognizing that the benefits of AI, if not properly governed, can be easily overshadowed by unintended harmful consequences, such as algorithmic bias, privacy violations, and economic displacement. Striking this balance is essential for ensuring that AI remains a tool for societal benefit rather than exacerbating inequities or eroding trust in technological systems.

Ongoing Challenges in Ethical Leadership

Despite the increasing integration of AI across organizational frameworks, ethical leadership in AI remains a dynamic and ongoing challenge. The evolving nature of AI technology presents continuous ethical dilemmas that require adaptive leadership and the ability to pivot in response to new ethical considerations. As AI systems grow more autonomous, opaque, and complex, leaders must ensure that their organizations stay ahead of emerging risks, maintain accountability, and ensure that AI-driven decisions align with ethical norms.

The very nature of AI presents novel challenges that transcend traditional leadership models. For example, as AI systems become more capable of autonomous decision-making, the question of responsibility becomes less clear. Who is held accountable when an AI system makes a discriminatory decision, or when its operation inadvertently causes harm? How can leaders ensure that AI algorithms are continually audited for fairness, transparency, and bias? These are questions that demand proactive engagement, continuous oversight, and the implementation of ethical AI frameworks that are flexible enough to adapt to technological innovations.

Furthermore, ethical AI leadership is not solely the responsibility of those in charge of AI departments. It is a shared obligation across all levels of the organization, from frontline practitioners to executive leadership, as well as external stakeholders like regulators, ethicists, and consumers. As such, organizations must cultivate an organizational culture that integrates ethical decision-making into every phase of the AI lifecycle, from development to deployment.

Call to Action for Leaders

The future of AI leadership lies in the hands of those who are willing to champion ethical AI practices and integrate AI ethics into the core of their organizational strategies. Leaders must transcend the traditional confines of technological stewardship and actively embrace their role as ethical stewards—not only safeguarding the integrity of AI systems but ensuring that they serve the broader social good. This requires leaders to foster a culture of responsible innovation, where AI technologies are developed with a deep commitment to equity, fairness, transparency, and accountability.

Moreover, the call to action is not just for organizations but for industries as a whole. The complexity and scale of AI's potential for disruption necessitate a collaborative approach to ethical governance, involving policymakers, thought leaders, academic researchers, and corporate entities. It is only through this multifaceted collaboration that we can cultivate a future where AI operates in alignment with human values and societal principles. Leaders must prioritize continuous education and awareness on the ethical implications of AI, encouraging open discussions around responsible AI usage and shared ethical frameworks.

In conclusion, the future of ethical AI leadership is inherently linked to the ability of leaders to navigate the fine line between fostering innovation and upholding ethical integrity. As AI continues to evolve, the role of leadership will be pivotal in shaping a future where AI is not only a tool for technological progress but a force for societal good. By embracing ethical decision-making, inclusive practices, and proactive engagement, leaders can ensure that AI serves the collective interests of humanity and advances us toward a more equitable, transparent, and sustainable world.

REFERENCES

Abdullah, K. H., Abd Aziz, F. S., Dani, R., Hammood, W. A., & Setiawan, E. (2023). Urban Pollution: A Bibliometric Review. *ASM Science Journal, 18*, 1–16. DOI: 10.32802/asmscj.2023.1440

Agarwal, P., & Sharma, S. (2023). Smart Urban Traffic Management System using Energy Efficient Optimized Path Discovery. *Proceedings of the 3rd International Conference on Artificial Intelligence and Smart Energy, ICAIS 2023*, 858 – 863. DOI: 10.1109/ICAIS56108.2023.10073840

Aggarwal, S., & Sharma, S. (2022). Voice Based Secured Smart Lock Design for Internet of Medical Things: An Artificial Intelligence Approach. *2022 International Conference on Wireless Communications, Signal Processing and Networking, WiSPNET 2022*, 1 – 9. DOI: 10.1109/WiSPNET54241.2022.9767113

Ahmad, I., Sharma, S., Kumar, R., Dhyani, S., & Dumka, A. (2023). Data Analytics of Online Education during Pandemic Health Crisis: A Case Study. *2nd Edition of IEEE Delhi Section Owned Conference, DELCON 2023 - Proceedings*. DOI: 10.1109/DELCON57910.2023.10127423

Ahmed, R., Das Gupta, A., Krishnamurthy, R. M., Goyal, M., Kumar, K. S., & Gangodkar, D. (2022). The Role of Smart Grid Data Analytics in Enhancing the Paradigm of Energy Management for Sustainable Development. *2022 2nd International Conference on Advance Computing and Innovative Technologies in Engineering, ICACITE 2022*, 198 – 201. DOI: 10.1109/ICACITE53722.2022.9823542

Aiyappa, S., Kodikal, R., & Rahiman, H. U. (2024). Accelerating Gender Equality for Sustainable Development: A Case Study of Dakshina Kannada District, India. *Technical and Vocational Education and Training, 38*, 335–349. DOI: 10.1007/978-981-99-6909-8_30

Ajay, D., Sharad, K., Singh, K. P., & Sharma, S. (2023). Impact of Prolonged Mental Torture on Housewives in Middle Class Families. *Journal for ReAttach Therapy and Developmental Diversities, 6*(4), 1–7.

Akana, C. M. V. S., Kumar, A., Tiwari, M., Yunus, A. Z., Vijayakumar, E., & Singh, M. (2023). An Optimized DDoS Attack Detection Using Deep Convolutional Generative Adversarial Networks. *Proceedings of the 5th International Conference on Inventive Research in Computing Applications, ICIRCA 2023*, 668 – 673. DOI: 10.1109/ICIRCA57980.2023.10220745

Akberdina, V., Kumar, V., Kyriakopoulos, G. L., & Kuzmin, E. (2023). Editorial: What Does Industry's Digital Transition Hold in the Uncertainty Context? In K. V., K. G.L., A. V., & K. E. (Eds.), *Lecture Notes in Information Systems and Organisation: Vol. 61 LNISO* (pp. 1 – 4). Springer Science and Business Media Deutschland GmbH. DOI: 10.1007/978-3-031-30351-7_1

Ansari, M. F., & Afzal, A. (2022). Sensitivity and Performance Analysis of 10 MW Solar Power Plant Using MPPT Technique. *Lecture Notes in Electrical Engineering, 894 LNEE*, 512–518. DOI: 10.1007/978-981-19-1677-9_46

Arora, A., Singh, R., Malik, K., & Kestwal, U. (2024). Association of sexual performance and intimacy with satisfaction in life in head and neck cancer patients: A review. *Oral Oncology Reports, 11*, 100563. Advance online publication. DOI: 10.1016/j.oor.2024.100563

Arora, R., Singh, A. P., Sharma, R., & Chauhan, A. (2022). A remanufacturing inventory model to control the carbon emission using cap-and-trade regulation with the hexagonal fuzzy number. *Benchmarking, 29*(7), 2202–2230. DOI: 10.1108/BIJ-05-2021-0254

Arora, S., Pargaien, S., Khan, F., Misra, A., Gambhir, A., & Verma, D. (2023). Smart Parking Allocation Using Raspberry Pi based IoT System. *Proceedings of the 5th International Conference on Inventive Research in Computing Applications, ICIRCA 2023*, 1457 – 1461. DOI: 10.1109/ICIRCA57980.2023.10220619

Awal, G., & Khanna, R. (2019). Determinants of millennial online consumer behavior and prospective purchase decisions. *International Journal of Advanced Science and Technology, 28*(18), 366–378.

Bansal, N., Bhatnagar, M., & Taneja, S. (2023). Balancing priorities through green optimism: A study elucidating initiatives, approaches, and strategies for sustainable supply chain management. In *Handbook of Research on Designing Sustainable Supply Chains to Achieve a Circular Economy*. IGI Global., DOI: 10.4018/978-1-6684-7664-2.ch004

Bansal, S., Kumar, V., Kumari, A., & Kuzmin, E. (2023). Understanding the Role of Digital Technologies in Supply Chain Management of SMEs. In K. V., K. G.L., A. V., & K. E. (Eds.), *Lecture Notes in Information Systems and Organisation: Vol. 61 LNISO* (pp. 195 – 205). Springer Science and Business Media Deutschland GmbH. DOI: 10.1007/978-3-031-30351-7_16

Begum, S. J. P., Pratibha, S., Rawat, J. M., Venugopal, D., Sahu, P., Gowda, A., Qureshi, K. A., & Jaremko, M. (2022). Recent Advances in Green Synthesis, Characterization, and Applications of Bioactive Metallic Nanoparticles. *Pharmaceuticals (Basel, Switzerland), 15*(4), 455. Advance online publication. DOI: 10.3390/ph15040455 PMID: 35455452

Behera, A., & Singh Rawat, K. (2023). A brief review paper on mining subsidence and its geo-environmental impact. *Materials Today: Proceedings*. Advance online publication. DOI: 10.1016/j.matpr.2023.04.183

Belwal, R., & Belwal, S. (2017). Employers' perception of women workers in Oman and the challenges they face. *Employee Relations, 39*(7), 1048–1065. DOI: 10.1108/ER-09-2016-0183

Bhamangol, B., Kaiwade, A., Pant, B., Rana, A., Kaiwade, A., & Shaikh, A. (2022). An Artificial Intelligence based Design and Implementation for classifying the Missing Data in IoT Applications. *Proceedings of 5th International Conference on Contemporary Computing and Informatics, IC3I 2022*, 1376 – 1382. DOI: 10.1109/IC3I56241.2022.10072634

Bhatnagar, M., Kumar, P., Taneja, S., Sood, K., & Grima, S. (2024). From digital overload to trading Zen: The role of digital detox in enhancing intraday trading performance. In *Business Drivers in Promoting Digital Detoxification*. IGI Global., DOI: 10.4018/979-8-3693-1107-3.ch010

Bhatnagar, M., Rajaram, R., Taneja, S., & Kumar, P. (2024). Balancing acts: The Yin and Yang of debit and credit on the stage of financial well-being. In *Emerging Perspectives on Financial Well-Being*. IGI Global., DOI: 10.4018/979-8-3693-1750-1.ch002

Bhatnagar, M., Taneja, S., & Kumar, P. (2023). The Effectiveness of Carbon Pricing Mechanism in Steering Financial Flows Toward Sustainable Projects. *International Journal of Environmental Impacts, 6*(4), 183–196. DOI: 10.18280/ijei.060403

Bhatnagar, M., Taneja, S., Kumar, P., & Özen, E. (2024). Does financial education act as a catalyst for SME competitiveness? *International Journal of Education Economics and Development, 15*(3), 377–393. DOI: 10.1504/IJEED.2024.139306

Bhatt, Y., & Ghuman, K. (2022). Managerial cognition and environmental behavioral intentions: A behavioral reasoning theory perspective. *Corporate Social Responsibility and Environmental Management, 29*(5), 1315–1329. DOI: 10.1002/csr.2271

Bisht, B., Gururani, P., Aman, J., Vlaskin, M. S., Anna, I. K., Irina, A. A., Joshi, S., Kumar, S., & Kumar, V. (2023). A review on holistic approaches for fruits and vegetables biowastes valorization. *Materials Today: Proceedings*, *73*, 54–63. DOI: 10.1016/j.matpr.2022.09.168

Bisht, R. K., Bisht, I. P., & Joshi, B. C. (2022). Growth of Micro, Small and Medium Enterprises (MSMEs) in Uttarakhand (India). In D. N. & C. A. (Eds.), *AIP Conference Proceedings* (Vol. 2481). American Institute of Physics Inc. DOI: 10.1063/5.0103881

Bist, A., Dobriyal, R., Gwalwanshi, M., & Avikal, S. (2022). Influence of Layer Height and Print Speed on the Mechanical Properties of 3D-Printed ABS. In D. N. & C. A. (Eds.), *AIP Conference Proceedings* (Vol. 2481). American Institute of Physics Inc. DOI: 10.1063/5.0107304

Bordoloi, D., Singh, V., Sanober, S., Buhari, S. M., Ujjan, J. A., & Boddu, R. (2022). Deep Learning in Healthcare System for Quality of Service. *Journal of Healthcare Engineering*, *2022*, 1–11. Advance online publication. DOI: 10.1155/2022/8169203 PMID: 35281541

Caiado, R. G. G., Scavarda, L. F., Vidal, G., de Mattos Nascimento, D. L., & Garza-Reyes, J. A. (2023). A taxonomy of critical factors towards sustainable operations and supply chain management 4.0 in developing countries. *Operations Management Research*. DOI: 10.1007/s12063-023-00430-8

Cavaliere, L. P. L., Byloppilly, R., Khan, S. D., Othman, B. A., Muda, I., & Malhotra, R. K. (2024). Acceptance and effectiveness of Industry 4.0 internal and external organisational initiatives in Malaysian firms. *International Journal of Management and Enterprise Development*, *23*(1), 1–25. DOI: 10.1504/IJMED.2024.138422

Chahar, A., & Christobel, Y. A. Ritika, Adakane, P. K., Sonal, D., & Tripathi, V. (2022). The Implementation of Big Data With Cloud and Edge Computing in Enhancing the Smart Grid Information Processes Through Sem Model. *2022 2nd International Conference on Advance Computing and Innovative Technologies in Engineering, ICACITE 2022*, 608 – 611. DOI: 10.1109/ICACITE53722.2022.9823896

Chandna, R. (2022). Selecting the most agile manufacturing system with respect to agile attribute-technology-fuzzy AHP approach. *International Journal of Operations Research*, *43*(4), 512–532. DOI: 10.1504/IJOR.2022.122812

Chandna, R., Saini, S., & Kumar, S. (2022). Selecting the Most Agile Manufacturing System with Respect to Agile Attribute-Technology: Fuzzy AHP Approach. In D. N. & C. A. (Eds.), *AIP Conference Proceedings* (Vol. 2481). American Institute of Physics Inc. DOI: 10.1063/5.0103804

Chandran, G. C., Synthia Regis Prabha, D. M. M., Malathi, P., Kapila, D., Arunkumar, M. S., Verma, D., & Teressa, D. M. (2022). Built-In Calibration Standard and Decision Support System for Controlling Structured Data Storage Systems Using Soft Computing Techniques. *Computational Intelligence and Neuroscience*, *2022*, 1–7. Advance online publication. DOI: 10.1155/2022/3476004 PMID: 36065369

Dahiya, K., & Taneja, S. (2023). To Analyse the Impact of Multi-Media Technology on the Rural Entrepreneurship Development. In *Contemporary Studies of Risks in Emerging Technology* (pp. 221–240). DOI: 10.1108/978-1-80455-562-020231015

Dangwal, A., Kaur, S., Taneja, S., & Ozen, E. (2022). A bibliometric analysis of green tourism based on the scopus platform. In *Developing Relationships, Personalization, and Data Herald in Marketing 5.0*. IGI Global., DOI: 10.4018/978-1-6684-4496-2.ch015

Das, T., Thakur, R., Dhua, S., Teixeira-Costa, B. E., Beber Rodrigues, M., Pereira, M. M., Mishra, P., & Gupta, A. K. (2023). Processing of Cereals. In *Cereal Grains: Composition, Nutritional Attributes, and Potential Applications*. CRC Press., DOI: 10.1201/9781003252023-10

Davuluri, S. K., Alvi, S. A. M., Aeri, M., Agarwal, A., Serajuddin, M., & Hasan, Z. (2023). A Security Model for Perceptive 5G-Powered BC IoT Associated Deep Learning. *6th International Conference on Inventive Computation Technologies, ICICT 2023 - Proceedings*, 118 – 125. DOI: 10.1109/ICICT57646.2023.10134487

Diddi, P. K., Sharma, P. K., Srivastava, A., Madduru, S. R. C., & Reddy, E. S. (2022). Sustainable Fast Setting Early Strength Self Compacting Concrete(FSESSCC) Using Metakaolin. *IOP Conference Series. Earth and Environmental Science*, *1077*(1), 012009. Advance online publication. DOI: 10.1088/1755-1315/1077/1/012009

Dimri, R., Mall, S., Sinha, S., Joshi, N. C., Bhatnagar, P., Sharma, R., Kumar, V., & Gururani, P. (2023). Role of microalgae as a sustainable alternative of biopolymers and its application in industries. *Plant Science Today*, *10*, 8–18. DOI: 10.14719/pst.2460

Dixit, A. K., Kumar, T. V., Joshi, A., Bedi, H. S., Chakravarthi, M. K., & Singh, D. P. (2022). Trends in Robotics and Computer Integrated Manufacturing. *Proceedings of 5th International Conference on Contemporary Computing and Informatics, IC3I 2022*, 212 – 216. DOI: 10.1109/IC3I56241.2022.10072745

Dutta, A., Singh, P., Dobhal, A., Mannan, D., Singh, J., & Goswami, P. (2023). Entrepreneurial Aptitude of Women of an Aspirational District of Uttarakhand. *Indian Journal of Extension Education*, *59*(2), 103–107. DOI: 10.48165/IJEE.2023.59222

Ekren, B. Y., Stylos, N., Zwiegelaar, J., Turhanlar, E. E., & Kumar, V. (2023). Additive manufacturing integration in E-commerce supply chain network to improve resilience and competitiveness. *Simulation Modelling Practice and Theory, 122*, 102676. Advance online publication. DOI: 10.1016/j.simpat.2022.102676

Eswar, K. N. D. V. S., Doss, M. A. N., Vishnuram, P., Selim, A., Bajaj, M., Kotb, H., & Kamel, S. (2023). Comprehensive Study on Reduced DC Source Count: Multilevel Inverters and Its Design Topologies. *Energies, 16*(1), 18. Advance online publication. DOI: 10.3390/en16010018

Gangwar, V. P., & Srivastva, S. P. (2020). Impact of micro finance in poverty eradication via SHGs: A study of selected districts in U.P. *International Journal of Advanced Science and Technology, 29*(2), 3818–3829.

Gaurav, G., Singh, A. B., Khandelwal, C., Gupta, S., Kumar, S., Meena, M. L., & Dangayach, G. S. (2023). Global Development on LCA Research: A Bibliometric Analysis From 2010 to 2021. *International Journal of Social Ecology and Sustainable Development, 14*(1), 1–19. Advance online publication. DOI: 10.4018/IJSESD.327791

Godbole, V., Kukrety, S., Gautam, P., Bisht, M., & Pal, M. K. (2023). Bioleaching for Heavy Metal Extraction from E-waste: A Sustainable Approach. In *Microbial Technology for Sustainable E-waste Management*. Springer International Publishing., DOI: 10.1007/978-3-031-25678-3_4

Gonfa, Y. H., Tessema, F. B., Tadesse, M. G., Bachheti, A., & Bachheti, R. K. (2023). Medicinally Important Plant Roots and Their Role in Nanoparticles Synthesis and Applications. In *Secondary Metabolites from Medicinal Plants: Nanoparticles Synthesis and their Applications*. CRC Press., DOI: 10.1201/9781003213727-11

Gopal, S., Gupta, P., & Minocha, A. (2023). Advancements in Fin-Tech and Security Challenges of Banking Industry. *4th International Conference on Intelligent Engineering and Management, ICIEM 2023*. DOI: 10.1109/ICIEM59379.2023.10165876

Goswami, S., & Sharma, S. (2022). Industry 4.0 Enabled Molecular Imaging Using Artificial Intelligence Technique. *2022 1st International Conference on Computational Science and Technology, ICCST 2022 - Proceedings*, 455–460. DOI: 10.1109/ICCST55948.2022.10040406

Grover, D., Sharma, S., Kaur, P., Mittal, A., & Sharma, P. K. (2024). Societal Elements that Impact the Performance of Women Entrepreneurs in Tier-II Cities: A Study of Rohilkhand Region of Uttar Pradesh. *2024 IEEE Zooming Innovation in Consumer Technologies Conference. ZINC, 2024*, 114–117. DOI: 10.1109/ZINC61849.2024.10579316

Gupta, A., & Kumar, H. (2022). Multi-dimensional perspectives on electric vehicles design: A mind map approach. *Cleaner Engineering and Technology*, *8*, 100483. Advance online publication. DOI: 10.1016/j.clet.2022.100483

Gupta, C., Jindal, P., & Malhotra, R. K. (2022). A Study of Increasing Adoption Trends of Digital Technologies - An Evidence from Indian Banking. In D. N. & C. A. (Eds.), *AIP Conference Proceedings* (Vol. 2481). American Institute of Physics Inc. DOI: 10.1063/5.0104572

Gupta, H., Taluja, R., Shaw, S., Chari, S. L., Deepak, A., & Rana, A. (2023). Internet of Things Based Reduction of Electricity Theft in Urban Areas. *Proceedings of International Conference on Contemporary Computing and Informatics, IC3I 2023*, 2642 – 2645. DOI: 10.1109/IC3I59117.2023.10397868

Gupta, M., Arora, K., & Taneja, S. (2023). Bibliometric analysis on employee engagement and human resource management. In *Enhancing Customer Engagement Through Location-Based Marketing*. IGI Global., DOI: 10.4018/978-1-6684-8177-6.ch013

Gupta, M., Verma, P. K., Verma, R., & Upadhyay, D. K. (2023). Applications of Computational Intelligence Techniques in Communications. In *Applications of Computational Intelligence Techniques in Communications*. CRC Press., DOI: 10.1201/9781003452645

Gururani, P., Bhatnagar, P., Bisht, B., Jaiswal, K. K., Kumar, V., Kumar, S., Vlaskin, M. S., Grigorenko, A. V., & Rindin, K. G. (2022). Recent advances and viability in sustainable thermochemical conversion of sludge to bio-fuel production. *Fuel*, *316*, 123351. Advance online publication. DOI: 10.1016/j.fuel.2022.123351

Hajoary, P. K., Balachandra, P., & Garza-Reyes, J. A. (2023). Industry 4.0 maturity and readiness assessment: An empirical validation using Confirmatory Composite Analysis. *Production Planning and Control*. Advance online publication. DOI: 10.1080/09537287.2023.2210545

Indu, R., Dimri, S. C., & Kumar, B. (2023). Identification of Location for Police Headquarters to Deal with Crime Against Women in India Using Clustering Based on K-Means Algorithm. *International Journal of Computing and Digital Systems*, *14*(1), 965–974. DOI: 10.12785/ijcds/140175

Jayadeva, S. M., Prasad Krishnam, N., Raja Mannar, B., Prakash Dabral, A., Buddhi, D., & Garg, N. (2023). An Investigation of IOT-Based Consumer Analytics to Assist Consumer Engagement Strategies in Evolving Markets. *2023 3rd International Conference on Advance Computing and Innovative Technologies in Engineering, ICACITE 2023*, 487 – 491. DOI: 10.1109/ICACITE57410.2023.10183310

Jena, S., & Gairola, A. (2022). Numerical Method to Generate and Evaluate Environmental Wind Over Hills: Comparison of Pedestrian Winds Over Hills and Plains. *CFD Letters*, *14*(10), 56–67. DOI: 10.37934/cfdl.14.10.5667

Jindal, T., Sheoliha, N., Kishore, K., Uike, D., Khurana, S., & Verma, D. (2022). A Conceptual Analysis on the Impact of Internet of Things (IOT) Towards on Digital Marketing Transformation. *2022 2nd International Conference on Advance Computing and Innovative Technologies in Engineering, ICACITE 2022*, 1943 – 1947. DOI: 10.1109/ICACITE53722.2022.9823714

Johri, S., Singh Sidhu, K., Jafersadhiq, A., Mannar, B. R., Gehlot, A., & Goyal, H. R. (2023). An investigation of the effects of the global epidemic on Crypto Currency returns and volatility. *2023 3rd International Conference on Advance Computing and Innovative Technologies in Engineering, ICACITE 2023*, 345 – 348. DOI: 10.1109/ICACITE57410.2023.10182988

Joshi, K., Patil, S., Gupta, S., & Khanna, R. (2022). Role of Pranayma in emotional maturity for improving health. *Journal of Medical Pharmaceutical and Allied Sciences*, *11*(2), 4569–4573. DOI: 10.55522/jmpas.V11I2.2033

Joshi, K., Sharma, R., Singh, N., & Sharma, B. (2023). Digital World of Cloud Computing and Wireless Networking: Challenges and Risks. In *Applications of Artificial Intelligence in Wireless Communication Systems*. IGI Global., DOI: 10.4018/978-1-6684-7348-1.ch003

Joshi, S., & Sharma, M. (2022). Sustainable Performance through Digital Supply Chains in Industry 4.0 Era: Amidst the Pandemic Experience. *Sustainability (Basel)*, *14*(24), 16726. Advance online publication. DOI: 10.3390/su142416726

Joshi, S., & Sharma, M. (2023). Strategic challenges of deploying LARG approach for sustainable manufacturing: Research implications from Indian SMEs. *International Journal of Internet Manufacturing and Services*, *9*(2–3), 373–397. DOI: 10.1504/IJIMS.2023.132791

Joshi, S., Sharma, M., & Barve, A. (2023). Implementation challenges of blockchain technology in closed-loop supply chain: A Waste Electrical and Electronic Equipment (WEEE) management perspective in developing countries. *Supply Chain Forum*, *24*(1), 59 – 80. DOI: 10.1080/16258312.2022.2135972

Josphineleela, R., Jyothi, M., Natrayan, L., Kaviarasu, A., & Sharma, M. (2023). Development of IoT based Health Monitoring System for Disables using Microcontroller. *Proceedings - 7th International Conference on Computing Methodologies and Communication, ICCMC 2023*, 1380 – 1384. DOI: 10.1109/ICCMC56507.2023.10084026

Josphineleela, R., Siva Reddy, K. V., Reddy, M. V. S. S., & Rawat, R. S. (2023). Design and Development of a Smart Sprinkler Device for IoT-Integrated Plants Irrigation. *Proceedings of the 2023 2nd International Conference on Electronics and Renewable Systems, ICEARS 2023*, 498 – 501. DOI: 10.1109/ICEARS56392.2023.10084960

Juneja, P. J., Sunori, S., Sharma, A., Sharma, A., & Joshi, V. (2020). Modeling, Control and Instrumentation of Lime Kiln Process: A Review. In S. S. & D. P. (Eds.), *Proceedings - 2020 International Conference on Advances in Computing, Communication and Materials, ICACCM 2020* (pp. 399 – 403). Institute of Electrical and Electronics Engineers Inc. DOI: 10.1109/ICACCM50413.2020.9212948

Juneja, P. K., Kumar Sunori, S., Manu, M., Joshi, P., Sharma, S., Garia, P., & Mittal, A. (2022). Potential Applications of Fuzzy Logic Controller in the Pulp and Paper Industry - A Review. *5th International Conference on Inventive Computation Technologies, ICICT 2022 - Proceedings*, 399 – 401. DOI: 10.1109/ICICT54344.2022.9850626

Kaliappan, S., Natrayan, L., & Garg, N. (2023). Checking and Supervisory System for Calculation of Industrial Constraints using Embedded System. *Proceedings of the 4th International Conference on Smart Electronics and Communication, ICOSEC 2023*, 87 – 90. DOI: 10.1109/ICOSEC58147.2023.10275952

Kamra, J., Mani, A. P., & Tripathi, V. M. (2023). Decarbonization Trajectory in Cement Industry. In S. P., N. S., R. J.J.P.C., R. J.J.P.C., R. J.J.P.C., L.-I. G.-A. D., P. T., C. L., & P. L. (Eds.), *2023 8th International Conference on Smart and Sustainable Technologies, SpliTech 2023*. Institute of Electrical and Electronics Engineers Inc. DOI: 10.23919/SpliTech58164.2023.10193682

Kannan, P. R., Periasamy, K., Pravin, P., & Vinod Kumaar, J. R. (2022). An experimental investigation of wire breakage and performance optimisation of WEDM process on machining of recycled aluminium alloy metal matrix composite. *Materials Science Poland*, *40*(3), 12–26. DOI: 10.2478/msp-2022-0030

Kanojia, P., Malhotra, R. K., & Uniyal, A. K. (2022a). Impact of Organizational Commitment Components on the Teachers of Higher Education in Uttarakhand: An Emperical Analysis. *Proceedings - 2022 International Conference on Recent Trends in Microelectronics, Automation, Computing and Communications Systems, ICMACC 2022*, 360–364. DOI: 10.1109/ICMACC54824.2022.10093606

Kanojia, P., Malhotra, R. K., & Uniyal, A. K. (2022b). Organizational Commitment and the Academic Staff in HEI's in North West India. *Proceedings - 2022 International Conference on Recent Trends in Microelectronics, Automation, Computing and Communications Systems, ICMACC 2022*, 365–370. DOI: 10.1109/ICMACC54824.2022.10093347

Kathir, I., Haribabu, K., Kumar, A., Kaliappan, S., Patil, P. P., Dhanalakshmi, C. S., Madhu, P., & Birhanu, H. A. (2022). Utilization of Tea Industrial Waste for Low-Grade Energy Recovery: Optimization of Liquid Oil Production and Its Characterization. *Advances in Materials Science and Engineering, 2022*, 1–9. Advance online publication. DOI: 10.1155/2022/7852046

Kaur, A., Kumar, P., Taneja, S., & Ozen, E. (2023). Fintech emergence – an opportunity or threat to banking. *International Journal of Electronic Finance, 13*(1), 1–19. DOI: 10.1504/IJEF.2024.135163

Kaur, H., Thacker, C., Singh, V. K., Sivashankar, D., Patil, P. P., & Gill, K. S. (2023). An implementation of virtual instruments for industries for the standardization. *2023 International Conference on Artificial Intelligence and Smart Communication, AISC 2023*, 1110 – 1113. DOI: 10.1109/AISC56616.2023.10085547

Kaur, J., Khanna, R., Kumar, R., & Sunil, G. (2024). Role of Blockchain Technologies in Goods and Services Tax. *Proceedings - 2024 3rd International Conference on Sentiment Analysis and Deep Learning, ICSADL 2024*, 607–612. DOI: 10.1109/ICSADL61749.2024.00104

Kaushal, D., Kumar, S., Raj, R., & Negi, A. (2022). Understanding the effect of entrepreneurial orientation, innovation capability and differentiation strategy on firm performance: A study on small and medium enterprises. *International Journal of Business and Globalisation, 30*(1), 57–80. DOI: 10.1504/IJBG.2022.122280

Khandelwal, C., Kumar, S., Tripathi, V., & Madhavan, V. (2023). Joint impact of corporate governance and risk disclosures on firm value: Evidence from emerging markets. *Research in International Business and Finance, 66*, 102022. Advance online publication. DOI: 10.1016/j.ribaf.2023.102022

Khanna, L. S., Yadav, P. S., Maurya, S., & Vimal, V. (2023). Integral Role of Data Science in Startup Evolution. *Proceedings - 2023 15th IEEE International Conference on Computational Intelligence and Communication Networks, CICN 2023*, 720 – 726. DOI: 10.1109/CICN59264.2023.10402129

Khanna, R., Jindal, P., & Noja, G. G. (2023). Blockchain technologies, a catalyst for insurance sector. In *The Application of Emerging Technology and Blockchain in the Insurance Industry*. DOI: 10.1201/9781032630946-19

Kohli, P., Sharma, S., & Matta, P. (2022). Secured Privacy Preserving Techniques Analysis of 6G Driven Vehicular Communication Network in Industry 5.0 Internet-of-Everything (IoE) Applications. *2022 International Conference on Smart Generation Computing, Communication and Networking, SMART GENCON 2022*. DOI: 10.1109/SMARTGENCON56628.2022.10084289

Komkowski, T., Antony, J., Garza-Reyes, J. A., Tortorella, G. L., & Pongboonchai-Empl, T. (2023a). A systematic review of the integration of Industry 4.0 with quality-related operational excellence methodologies. *The Quality Management Journal, 30*(1), 3–15. DOI: 10.1080/10686967.2022.2144783

Komkowski, T., Antony, J., Garza-Reyes, J. A., Tortorella, G. L., & Pongboonchai-Empl, T. (2023b). Integrating Lean Management with Industry 4.0: An explorative Dynamic Capabilities theory perspective. *Production Planning and Control*. Advance online publication. DOI: 10.1080/09537287.2023.2294297

Kour, M., Taneja, S., Özen, E., Sood, K., & Grima, S. (2025). *Financial Landscape Transformation Technological Disruptions*.

Kowsalya, K., & Rani, R. P. J. Ritu, Bhiyana, M., Saini, M., & Patil, P. P. (2023). Blockchain-Internet of things-Machine Learning: Development of Traceable System for Multi Purposes. *2023 3rd International Conference on Advance Computing and Innovative Technologies in Engineering, ICACITE 2023*, 1112 – 1115. DOI: 10.1109/ICACITE57410.2023.10183065

Krishna, S. H., Upadhyay, A., Tewari, M., Gehlot, A., Girimurugan, B., & Pundir, S. (2022). Empirical investigation of the key machine learning elements promoting e-business using an SEM framework. *Proceedings of 5th International Conference on Contemporary Computing and Informatics, IC3I 2022*, 1960 – 1964. DOI: 10.1109/IC3I56241.2022.10072712

Kukreti, A., Shriyal, A., Sharma, S., & Bhadula, S. (2023). Internet-of-Things Enabled Smart and Portable Terrace Garden Protection Shed. *2023 4th IEEE Global Conference for Advancement in Technology, GCAT 2023*. DOI: 10.1109/GCAT59970.2023.10353281

Kumari, J., Singh, P., Mishra, A. K., Singh Meena, B. P., Singh, A., & Ojha, M. (2024). Challenges Hindering Women's Involvement in the Hospitality Industry as Entrepreneurs in the Era of Digital Economy. In *Revolutionizing the AI-Digital Landscape: A Guide to Sustainable Emerging Technologies for Marketing Professionals*. Taylor and Francis., DOI: 10.4324/9781032688305-9

Lade, J., Mohammed, K. A., Singh, D., Prasad Verma, R., Math, P., Saraswat, M., & Raj Gupta, L. (2023). A critical review of fabrication routes and their effects on mechanical properties of AMMCs. *Materials Today: Proceedings*. Advance online publication. DOI: 10.1016/j.matpr.2023.03.041

Lokanadham, D., Sharma, R. C., Palli, S., & Bhardawaj, S. (2022). Wear Rate Modelling and Analysis of Limestone Slurry Particulate Composites Using the Fuzzy Method. *International Journal on Recent and Innovation Trends in Computing and Communication, 10*(1), 133–143. DOI: 10.17762/ijritcc.v10i1s.5818

Luthra, S., Sharma, M., Kumar, A., Joshi, S., Collins, E., & Mangla, S. (2022). Overcoming barriers to cross-sector collaboration in circular supply chain management: A multi-method approach. *Transportation Research Part E, Logistics and Transportation Review, 157*, 102582. Advance online publication. DOI: 10.1016/j.tre.2021.102582

Malhotra, R. K., Gupta, C., & Jindal, P. (2022). Blockchain and Smart Contracts for Insurance Industry. In *Blockchain Technology in Corporate Governance*. Transforming Business and Industries., DOI: 10.1002/9781119865247.ch11

Manjunatha, B. N., Chandan, M., Kottu, S., Rappai, S., Hema, P. K., Singh Rawat, K., & Sarkar, S. (2023). A Successful Spam Detection Technique for Industrial IoT Devices based on Machine Learning Techniques. *Proceedings of the 2nd International Conference on Applied Artificial Intelligence and Computing, ICAAIC 2023*, 363 – 369. DOI: 10.1109/ICAAIC56838.2023.10141275

Mary Joshitta, S., & Sunil, M. P. Badriasulaimanalfurhood, Bodhankar, A., Ch.Sreedevi, & Khanna, R. (2023). The Integration of Machine Learning Technique with the Existing System to Predict the Flight Prices. *2023 3rd International Conference on Advance Computing and Innovative Technologies in Engineering, ICACITE 2023*, 398–402. DOI: 10.1109/ICACITE57410.2023.10182539

Masal, V., Pavithra, P., Tiwari, S. K., Singh, R., Panduro-Ramirez, J., & Gangodkar, D. (2022). Deep Learning Applications for Blockchain in Industrial IoT. *Proceedings of 5th International Conference on Contemporary Computing and Informatics, IC3I 2022*, 276 – 281. DOI: 10.1109/IC3I56241.2022.10073357

Maurya, S. K., Ghosal, A., & Manna, A. (2022). Experimental investigations during fabrication and electrical discharge machining of hybrid Al/(SiC+ZrO2+NiTi) MMC. *International Journal of Machining and Machinability of Materials, 24*(3–4), 215–230. DOI: 10.1504/IJMMM.2022.125195

Medhi, M. K., Ambust, S., Kumar, R., & Das, A. J. (2023). Characterization and Purification of Biosurfactants. In *Advancements in Biosurfactants Research*. Springer International Publishing., DOI: 10.1007/978-3-031-21682-4_4

Mehershilpa, G., Prasad, D., Sai Kiran, C., Shaikh, A., Jayashree, K., & Socrates, S. (2023). EDM machining of Ti6Al4V alloy using colloidal biosilica. *Materials Today: Proceedings*. Advance online publication. DOI: 10.1016/j.matpr.2023.02.443

Mishra, A. K., & Wazid, M. (2023). Design of a cloud-based security mechanism for Industry 4.0 communication. *ICSCCC 2023 - 3rd International Conference on Secure Cyber Computing and Communications*, 337 – 343. DOI: 10.1109/ICSCCC58608.2023.10176702

Mishra, D., Kandpal, V., Agarwal, N., & Srivastava, B. (2024). Financial Inclusion and Its Ripple Effects on Socio-Economic Development: A Comprehensive Review. *Journal of Risk and Financial Management, 17*(3), 105. Advance online publication. DOI: 10.3390/jrfm17030105

Mitra, D., Mondal, R., Khoshru, B., Senapati, A., Radha, T. K., Mahakur, B., Uniyal, N., Myo, E. M., Boutaj, H., Sierra, B. E. G. U. E. R. R. A., Panneerselvam, P., Ganeshamurthy, A. N., Elković, S. A. N. Đ. J., Vasić, T., Rani, A., Dutta, S., & Mohapatra, P. K. D. A. S.MITRA. (2022). Actinobacteria-enhanced plant growth, nutrient acquisition, and crop protection: Advances in soil, plant, and microbial multifactorial interactions. *Pedosphere, 32*(1), 149–170. DOI: 10.1016/S1002-0160(21)60042-5

Mohd, N., Kumar, I., & Khurshid, A. A. (2023). Changing Roles of Intelligent Robotics and Machinery Control Systems as Cyber-Physical Systems (CPS) in the Industry 4.0 Framework. *2023 International Conference on Communication, Security and Artificial Intelligence, ICCSAI 2023*, 647 – 651. DOI: 10.1109/ICCSAI59793.2023.10421085

Nadeem, S. P., Garza-Reyes, J. A., & Anosike, A. I. (2023). A C-Lean framework for deploying Circular Economy in manufacturing SMEs. *Production Planning and Control*. Advance online publication. DOI: 10.1080/09537287.2023.2294307

Negi, D., Sah, A., Rawat, S., Choudhury, T., & Khanna, A. (2021). Block Chain Platforms and Smart Contracts. *EAI/Springer Innovations in Communication and Computing*, 65 – 76. DOI: 10.1007/978-3-030-65691-1_5

Neha, M., S., Alfurhood, B. S., Bakhare, R., Poongavanam, S., & Khanna, R. (2023). The Role and Impact of Artificial Intelligence on Retail Business and its Developments. *2023 International Conference on Artificial Intelligence and Smart Communication, AISC 2023*, 1098–1101. DOI: 10.1109/AISC56616.2023.10085624

Nethravathi, K., Tiwari, A., Uike, D., Jaiswal, R., & Pant, K. (2022). Applications of Artificial Intelligence and Blockchain Technology in Improved Supply Chain Financial Risk Management. *Proceedings of 5th International Conference on Contemporary Computing and Informatics, IC3I 2022*, 242 – 246. DOI: 10.1109/IC3I56241.2022.10072787

Padhi, B. K., Singh, S., Gaidhane, A. M., Abu Serhan, H., Khatib, M. N., Zahiruddin, Q. S., Rustagi, S., Sharma, R. K., Sharma, D., Arora, M., & Satapathy, P. (2024). Inequalities in cardiovascular disease among elderly Indians: A gender perspective analysis using LASI wave-I (2017-18). *Current Problems in Cardiology*, *49*(7), 102605. Advance online publication. DOI: 10.1016/j.cpcardiol.2024.102605 PMID: 38692448

Pai, H. A., Almuzaini, K. K., Ali, L., Javeed, A., Pant, B., Pareek, P. K., & Akwafo, R. (2022). Delay-Driven Opportunistic Routing with Multichannel Cooperative Neighbor Discovery for Industry 4.0 Wireless Networks Based on Power and Load Awareness. *Wireless Communications and Mobile Computing*, *2022*(1), 5256133. Advance online publication. DOI: 10.1155/2022/5256133

Pallavi, B., Othman, B., Trivedi, G., Manan, N., Pawar, R. S., & Singh, D. P. (2022). The Application of the Internet of Things (IoT) to establish a technologically advanced Industry 4.0 for long-term growth and development. *2022 2nd International Conference on Advance Computing and Innovative Technologies in Engineering, ICACITE 2022*, 1927 – 1932. DOI: 10.1109/ICACITE53722.2022.9823481

Pande, S. D., Bhatt, A., Chamoli, S., Saini, D. K. J. B., Kute, U. T., & Ahammad, S. H. (2023). Design of Atmel PLC and its Application as Automation of Coal Handling Plant. *2023 International Conference on Sustainable Emerging Innovations in Engineering and Technology, ICSEIET 2023*, 178 – 183. DOI: 10.1109/ICSEIET58677.2023.10303627

Pandey, K., Joshi, H., Paliwal, S., Pawar, S., & Kumar, N. (2020). Technology transfer: An overview of process transfer from development to commercialization. *International Journal of Current Research and Review*, *12*(19), 188–192. DOI: 10.31782/IJCRR.2020.121913

Pandey, K., Paliwal, S., Joshi, H., Bisht, N., & Kumar, N. (2022). A review on change control: A critical process of the pharmaceutical industry. *Journal of Medical Pharmaceutical and Allied Sciences*, *11*(2), 4588–4592. DOI: 10.55522/jmpas.V11I2.2077

Pandey, N. K., Kashyap, S., Sharma, A., & Diwakar, M. (2023). Contribution of Cloud-Based Services in Post-Pandemic Technology Sustainability and Challenges: A Future Direction. In *Evolving Networking Technologies: Developments and Future Directions*. wiley. DOI: 10.1002/9781119836667.ch4

Raja, S., Agrawal, A. P. P., Patil, P., Thimothy, P., Capangpangan, R. Y., Singhal, P., & Wotango, M. T. (2022). Optimization of 3D Printing Process Parameters of Polylactic Acid Filament Based on the Mechanical Test. *International Journal of Chemical Engineering*, *2022*(1), 5830869. Advance online publication. DOI: 10.1155/2022/5830869

Rajbalaji, S., Raman, R., Pant, B., Rathour, N., Rajagopa, B. R., & Prasad, C. R. (2023). Design of deep learning models for the identifications of harmful attack activities in IIOT. *2023 International Conference on Artificial Intelligence and Smart Communication, AISC 2023*, 609 – 613. DOI: 10.1109/AISC56616.2023.10085088

Rajeswari, M., Kumar, N., Raman, P., Patjoshi, P. K., Singh, V., & Pundir, S. (2022). Optimal Analysis for Enterprise Financial Management Based on Artificial Intelligence and Parallel Computing Method. *Proceedings of 5th International Conference on Contemporary Computing and Informatics, IC3I 2022*, 2081 – 2086. DOI: 10.1109/IC3I56241.2022.10072851

Raju, K., Balakrishnan, M., Prasad, D. V. S. S. S. V., Nagalakshmi, V., Patil, P. P., Kaliappan, S., Arulmurugan, B., Radhakrishnan, K., Velusamy, B., Paramasivam, P., & El-Denglawey, A. (2022). Optimization of WEDM Process Parameters in Al2024-Li-Si3N4MMC. *Journal of Nanomaterials*, *2022*(1), 2903385. Advance online publication. DOI: 10.1155/2022/2903385

Rakhra, M., Bhargava, A., Bhargava, D., Singh, R., Bhanot, A., & Rahmani, A. W. (2022). Implementing Machine Learning for Supply-Demand Shifts and Price Impacts in Farmer Market for Tool and Equipment Sharing. *Journal of Food Quality*, *2022*, 1–19. Advance online publication. DOI: 10.1155/2022/4496449

Ram, M., Negi, G., Goyal, N., & Kumar, A. (2022). Analysis of a Stochastic Model with Rework System. *Journal of Reliability and Statistical Studies*, *15*(2), 553–582. DOI: 10.13052/jrss0974-8024.1527

Ram, M., & Xing, L. (2023). Reliability Modeling in Industry 4.0. In *Reliability Modeling in Industry 4.0*. Elsevier., DOI: 10.1016/C2021-0-01679-5

Ramachandran, K. K., Lamba, F. L. R., Rawat, R., Gehlot, A., Raju, A. M., & Ponnusamy, R. (2023). An Investigation of Block Chains for Attaining Sustainable Society. *2023 3rd International Conference on Advance Computing and Innovative Technologies in Engineering, ICACITE 2023*, 1069 – 1076. DOI: 10.1109/ICACITE57410.2023.10182462

Raman, R., Kumar, R., Ghai, S., Gehlot, A., Raju, A. M., & Barve, A. (2023). A New Method of Optical Spectrum Analysis for Advanced Wireless Communications. *2023 3rd International Conference on Advance Computing and Innovative Technologies in Engineering, ICACITE 2023*, 1719 – 1723. DOI: 10.1109/ICACITE57410.2023.10182414

Rana, M. S., Cavaliere, L. P. L., Mishra, A. B., Padhye, P., Singh, R. R., & Khanna, R. (2022). Internet of Things (IOT) Based Assessment for Effective Monitoring Data Against Malicious Attacks on Financial Collectors. *2022 2nd International Conference on Advance Computing and Innovative Technologies in Engineering, ICACITE 2022*, 177–181. DOI: 10.1109/ICACITE53722.2022.9823612

Rawat, R., Sharma, S., & Goyal, H. R. (2023). Intelligent Digital Financial Inclusion System Architectures for Industry 5.0 Enabled Digital Society. *Winter Summit on Smart Computing and Networks. WiSSCoN, 2023*, 1–5. Advance online publication. DOI: 10.1109/WiSSCoN56857.2023.10133858

Rawat, S. S., Pant, S., Kumar, A., Ram, M., Sharma, H. K., & Kumar, A. (2022). A State-of-the-Art Survey on Analytical Hierarchy Process Applications in Sustainable Development. *International Journal of Mathematical. Engineering and Management Sciences*, *7*(6), 883–917. DOI: 10.33889/IJMEMS.2022.7.6.056

Reddy, P. N., Umaeswari, P., Natrayan, L., & Choudhary, A. (2023). Development of Programmed Autonomous Electric Heavy Vehicle: An Application of IoT. *Proceedings of the 2023 2nd International Conference on Electronics and Renewable Systems, ICEARS 2023*, 506 – 510. DOI: 10.1109/ICEARS56392.2023.10085492

Reepu, R., Taneja, S., Ozen, E., & Singh, A. (2023). A globetrotter to the future of marketing: Metaverse. In *Cultural Marketing and Metaverse for Consumer Engagement*. IGI Global., DOI: 10.4018/978-1-6684-8312-1.ch001

Sahu, S. R., & Rawat, K. S. (2023). Analysis of Land subsidencein coastal and urban areas by using various techniques– Literature Review. *The Indonesian Journal of Geography*, *55*(3), 488–495. DOI: 10.22146/ijg.83675

Salama, R., Al-Turjman, F., Bordoloi, D., & Yadav, S. P. (2023). Wireless Sensor Networks and Green Networking for 6G communication- An Overview. *2023 International Conference on Computational Intelligence, Communication Technology and Networking, CICTN 2023*, 830 – 834. DOI: 10.1109/CICTN57981.2023.10141262

Sathyaseelan, K., Vyas, T., Madala, R., Chamundeeswari, V., Rai Goyal, H., & Jayaraman, R. (2023). Blockchain Enabled Intelligent Surveillance System Model with AI and IoT. *Proceedings of 8th IEEE International Conference on Science, Technology, Engineering and Mathematics, ICONSTEM 2023*. DOI: 10.1109/ICONSTEM56934.2023.10142303

Sen Thapa, B., Pandit, S., Patwardhan, S. B., Tripathi, S., Mathuriya, A. S., Gupta, P. K., Lal, R. B., & Tusher, T. R. (2022). Application of Microbial Fuel Cell (MFC) for Pharmaceutical Wastewater Treatment: An Overview and Future Perspectives. *Sustainability (Basel)*, *14*(14), 8379. Advance online publication. DOI: 10.3390/su14148379

Shabbiruddin, Kanwar, N., Jadoun, V. K., Jayalakshmi, N. S. J., Afthanorhan, A., Fatema, N., Malik, H., & Hossaini, M. A. (2023). Industry - Challenge to Pro-Environmental Manufacturing of Goods Replacing Single-Use Plastic by Indian Industry: A Study Toward Failing Ban on Single-Use Plastic Access. *IEEE Access : Practical Innovations, Open Solutions*, *11*, 77336–77346. DOI: 10.1109/ACCESS.2023.3296097

Shah, J. K., Sharma, R., Misra, A., Sharma, M., Joshi, S., Kaushal, D., & Bafila, S. (2023). Industry 4.0 Enabled Smart Manufacturing: Unleashing the Power of Artificial Intelligence and Blockchain. *2023 1st DMIHER International Conference on Artificial Intelligence in Education and Industry 4.0, IDICAIEI 2023*. DOI: 10.1109/IDICAIEI58380.2023.10406671

Sharma, E., Rana, S., Sharma, I., Sati, P., & Dhyani, P. (2023). Organic polymers for CO2 capture and conversion. In *CO2-Philic Polymers, Nanocomposites and Solvents: Capture, Conversion and Industrial Products*. Elsevier., DOI: 10.1016/B978-0-323-85777-2.00002-0

Sharma, H., Verma, D., Rana, A., Chari, S. L., Kumar, R., & Kumar, N. (2023). Enhancing Network Security in IoT Using Machine Learning- Based Anomaly Detection. *Proceedings of International Conference on Contemporary Computing and Informatics, IC3I 2023*, 2650 – 2654. DOI: 10.1109/IC3I59117.2023.10397636

Sharma, K., Pandit, S., Sen Thapa, B., & Pant, M. (2022). Biodegradation of Congo Red Using Co-Culture Anode Inoculum in a Microbial Fuel Cell. *Catalysts*, *12*(10), 1219. Advance online publication. DOI: 10.3390/catal12101219

Sharma, M., Hagar, A. A., Krishna Murthy, G. R., Beyane, K., Gawali, B. W., & Pant, B. (2022). A Study on Recognising the Application of Multiple Big Data Technologies and its Related Issues, Difficulties and Opportunities. *2022 2nd International Conference on Advance Computing and Innovative Technologies in Engineering, ICACITE 2022*, 341 – 344. DOI: 10.1109/ICACITE53722.2022.9823623

Sharma, P., Malhotra, R. K., Ojha, M. K., & Gupta, S. (2022). Impact of meditation on mental & physical health and thereby on academic performance of students: A study of higher educational institutions of Uttarakhand. *Journal of Medical Pharmaceutical and Allied Sciences*, *11*(2), 4641–4644. DOI: 10.55522/jmpas.V11I2.2309

Sharma, P., Taneja, S., Kumar, P., Özen, E., & Singh, A. (2024). Application of the UTAUT model toward individual acceptance: Emerging trends in artificial intelligence-based banking services. *International Journal of Electronic Finance*, *13*(3), 352–366. DOI: 10.1504/IJEF.2024.139584

Sharma, R. C., Palli, S., & Sharma, S. K. (2023). Ride analysis of railway vehicle considering rigidity and flexibility of the carbody. *Zhongguo Gongcheng Xuekan*, *46*(4), 355–366. DOI: 10.1080/02533839.2023.2194918

Sharma, S., & Bhadula, S. (2023). Secure Federated Learning for Intelligent Industry 4.0 IoT Enabled Self Skin Care Application System. *Proceedings of the 2nd International Conference on Applied Artificial Intelligence and Computing, ICAAIC 2023*, 1164 – 1170. DOI: 10.1109/ICAAIC56838.2023.10141028

Sharma, S., Gupta, A., & Tyagi, R. (2023). Sustainable Natural Resources Utilization Decision System for Better Society Using Vedic Scripture, Cloud Computing, and IoT. In B. R.C., S. K.M., & D. M. (Eds.), *Proceedings of IEEE 2023 5th International Conference on Advances in Electronics, Computers and Communications, ICAECC 2023*. Institute of Electrical and Electronics Engineers Inc. DOI: 10.1109/ICAECC59324.2023.10560335

Shashikala, R., Singh, B. P., Azam, M., & Magesh, C. R. Rajat, & Singh, D. P. (2022). IoT Engineering Nanomaterial's Approach To Sustainable Advance Crop Production Management. *2022 2nd International Conference on Advance Computing and Innovative Technologies in Engineering, ICACITE 2022*, 2284 – 2288. DOI: 10.1109/ICACITE53722.2022.9823573

Shrivastava, A., Usha, R., Kukreti, R., Sharma, G., Srivastava, A. P., & Khan, A. K. (2023). Women Safety Precaution. *2023 1st International Conference on Circuits, Power, and Intelligent Systems, CCPIS 2023*. DOI: 10.1109/CCPIS59145.2023.10291594

Singamaneni, K. K., Dhiman, G., Juneja, S., Muhammad, G., AlQahtani, S. A., & Zaki, J. (2022). A Novel QKD Approach to Enhance IIOT Privacy and Computational Knacks. *Sensors (Basel), 22*(18), 6741. Advance online publication. DOI: 10.3390/s22186741 PMID: 36146089

Singh, A. K., Singh, R., & Singh, S. (2024). A review on factors affecting and performance of nutritional security of women and children in India. In *Impact of Women in Food and Agricultural Development.* IGI Global., DOI: 10.4018/979-8-3693-3037-1.ch019

Singh, K. D., Singh, P., Chhabra, R., Kaur, G., Bansal, A., & Tripathi, V. (2023). Cyber-Physical Systems for Smart City Applications: A Comparative Study. In K. R., K. R., G. M., G. M., S. R., & S. R. (Eds.), *2023 International Conference on Advancement in Computation and Computer Technologies, InCACCT 2023* (pp. 871 – 876). Institute of Electrical and Electronics Engineers Inc. DOI: 10.1109/InCACCT57535.2023.10141719

Singh, K. D., Singh, P., Tripathi, V., & Khullar, V. (2022). A Novel and Secure Framework to Detect Unauthorized Access to an Optical Fog-Cloud Computing Network. In R. H.S., B. R., G. P.K., & S. V.K. (Eds.), *PDGC 2022 - 2022 7th International Conference on Parallel, Distributed and Grid Computing* (pp. 618 – 622). Institute of Electrical and Electronics Engineers Inc. DOI: 10.1109/PDGC56933.2022.10053223

Singh, P., & Singh, K. D. (2023). Fog-Centric Intelligent Surveillance System: A Novel Approach for Effective and Efficient Surveillance. In K. R., K. R., G. M., G. M., S. R., & S. R. (Eds.), *2023 International Conference on Advancement in Computation and Computer Technologies, InCACCT 2023* (pp. 762 – 766). Institute of Electrical and Electronics Engineers Inc. DOI: 10.1109/InCACCT57535.2023.10141802

Srivastava, A., Jawaid, S., Singh, R., Gehlot, A., Akram, S. V., Priyadarshi, N., & Khan, B. (2022). Imperative Role of Technology Intervention and Implementation for Automation in the Construction Industry. *Advances in Civil Engineering, 2022*(1), 6716987. Advance online publication. DOI: 10.1155/2022/6716987

Srivastava, B., Kandpal, V., & Jain, A. K. (2024). Financial well-being of women self-help group members: A qualitative study. *Environment, Development and Sustainability, 27*(12), 29471–29492. Advance online publication. DOI: 10.1007/s10668-024-04879-w

Subramani, R., Kaliappan, S., Kumar, P. V. A., Sekar, S., De Poures, M. V., Patil, P. P., & Raj, E. S. E. (2022). A Recent Trend on Additive Manufacturing Sustainability with Supply Chain Management Concept, Multicriteria Decision Making Techniques. *Advances in Materials Science and Engineering, 2022*, 1–12. Advance online publication. DOI: 10.1155/2022/9151839

Subramani, R., Kaliappan, S., Sekar, S., Patil, P. P., Usha, R., Manasa, N., & Esakkiraj, E. S. (2022). Polymer Filament Process Parameter Optimization with Mechanical Test and Morphology Analysis. *Advances in Materials Science and Engineering, 2022*, 1–8. Advance online publication. DOI: 10.1155/2022/8259804

Sunori, S. K., Kant, S., Agarwal, P., & Juneja, P. (2023). Development of Rainfall Prediction Models using Linear and Non-linear Regression Techniques. *2023 4th IEEE Global Conference for Advancement in Technology, GCAT 2023*. DOI: 10.1109/GCAT59970.2023.10353508

TANEJA. S., KUMAR, P., REEPU, KUKRETI, M., & OZEN, E. ¨. (2024). *Data Alchemy in the Insurance Industry*. Emerald Publishing Limited. https://doi.org/https://doi.org/10.1108/978-1-83608-582-920241033

Taneja, S., Bhatnagar, M., Kumar, P., & Grima, S. (2023). A Panel Analysis of the Effectiveness of the Asset Management in Indian Agricultural Companies. *International Journal of Sustainable Development and Planning, 18*(3), 653–660. DOI: 10.18280/ijsdp.180301

Taneja, S., Bhatnagar, M., Kumar, P., & Rupeika-apoga, R. (2023). India ' s Total Natural Resource Rents (NRR) and GDP : An Augmented Autoregressive Distributed Lag (ARDL) Bound Test. *Journal of Risk and Financial Management, 16*(2), 91. https://doi.org/doi.org/10.3390/jrfm16020091. DOI: 10.3390/jrfm16020091

Taneja, S., Gupta, M., Bhushan, P., Bhatnagar, M., & Singh, A. (2023). Cultural marketing in the digital era. In *Cultural Marketing and Metaverse for Consumer Engagement*. IGI Global., DOI: 10.4018/978-1-6684-8312-1.ch008

Taneja, S., Gupta, S., Singh, A., Bhatnagar, M., & Gaur, A. (2023). Green management - A new paradigm in the world of business. *Green Management - A New Paradigm in the World of Business*, 1–230. DOI: 10.52305/DLIH6622

Taneja, S., & Özen, E. (2023). To analyse the relationship between bank's green financing and environmental performance. *International Journal of Electronic Finance, 12*(2), 163–175. DOI: 10.1504/IJEF.2023.129919

Taneja, S., & Sharma, V. (2023). Role of beaconing marketing in improving customer buying experience. In *Enhancing Customer Engagement Through Location-Based Marketing*. IGI Global., DOI: 10.4018/978-1-6684-8177-6.ch012

Trache, D., Tarchoun, A. F., Abdelaziz, A., Bessa, W., Hussin, M. H., Brosse, N., & Thakur, V. K. (2022). Cellulose nanofibrils-graphene hybrids: Recent advances in fabrication, properties, and applications. *Nanoscale, 14*(35), 12515–12546. DOI: 10.1039/D2NR01967A PMID: 35983896

Tripathi, V. M., & Mohan, A. (2016). Microfinance and empowering rural women in the Terai, Uttarakhand, India. *International Journal of Agricultural and Statistics Sciences, 12*(2), 523–530.

Uike, D., Agarwalla, S., Bansal, V., Chakravarthi, M. K., Singh, R., & Singh, P. (2022). Investigating the Role of Block Chain to Secure Identity in IoT for Industrial Automation. In D. R.K., S. A.Kr., K. G., & B. S. (Eds.), *Proceedings of the 2022 11th International Conference on System Modeling and Advancement in Research Trends, SMART 2022* (pp. 837 – 841). Institute of Electrical and Electronics Engineers Inc. DOI: 10.1109/SMART55829.2022.10047385

Umamaheswaran, S. K., Singh, G., Dixit, A. K., Mc, S. C., Chakravarthi, M. K., & Singh, D. P. (2023). IOT-Based Analysis for Effective Continuous Monitoring Prevent Fraudulent Intrusions in Finance and Banking. *2023 International Conference on Artificial Intelligence and Smart Communication, AISC 2023*, 548 – 552. DOI: 10.1109/AISC56616.2023.10084920

Unhelkar, B., Joshi, S., Sharma, M., Prakash, S., Mani, A. K., & Prasad, M. (2022). Enhancing supply chain performance using RFID technology and decision support systems in the industry 4.0–A systematic literature review. *International Journal of Information Management Data Insights*, *2*(2), 100084. Advance online publication. DOI: 10.1016/j.jjimei.2022.100084

Uniyal, A., Prajapati, Y. K., Ranakoti, L., Bhandari, P., Singh, T., Gangil, B., Sharma, S., Upadhyay, V. V., & Eldin, S. M. (2022). Recent Advancements in Evacuated Tube Solar Water Heaters: A Critical Review of the Integration of Phase Change Materials and Nanofluids with ETCs. *Energies, 15*(23), 8999. Advance online publication. DOI: 10.3390/en15238999

Uniyal, A. K., Kanojia, P., Khanna, R., & Dixit, A. K. (2022). Quantitative Analysis of the Impact of Demography and Job Profile on the Organizational Commitment of the Faculty Members in the HEI'S of Uttarakhand. *Communications in Computer and Information Science, 1742 CCIS*, 24–35. DOI: 10.1007/978-3-031-23647-1_3

Uniyal, S., Sarma, P. R. S., Kumar Mangla, S., Tseng, M.-L., & Patil, P. (2022). ICT as "Knowledge Management" for Assessing Sustainable Consumption and Production in Supply Chains. In *Research Anthology on Measuring and Achieving Sustainable Development Goals* (Vol. 3). IGI Global. DOI: 10.4018/978-1-6684-3885-5.ch048

Upreti, H., & Malhotra, R. K. (2024). Bridging The Urban-Rural Education Gap In India Through CSR (Corporate Social Responsibility) Initiatives: A Conceptual Study With Special Reference To Sustainable Development Goal 4 (Quality Education). In P. P.K. (Ed.), *E3S Web of Conferences* (Vol. 556). EDP Sciences. DOI: 10.1051/e3sconf/202455601032

Venkatesh, J., Shukla, P. K., Ahanger, T. A., Maheshwari, M., Pant, B., Hemamalini, R. R., & Halifa, A. (2023). A Complex Brain Learning Skeleton Comprising Enriched Pattern Neural Network System for Next Era Internet of Things. *Journal of Healthcare Engineering*, *2023*(1), 2506144. Advance online publication. DOI: 10.1155/2023/2506144

Verma, M., Ahmad, W., Park, J.-H., Kumar, V., Vlaskin, M. S., Vaya, D., & Kim, H. (2022). One-step functionalization of chitosan using EDTA: Kinetics and isotherms modeling for multiple heavy metals adsorption and their mechanism. *Journal of Water Process Engineering*, *49*, 102989. Advance online publication. DOI: 10.1016/j.jwpe.2022.102989

Verma, P., Chaudhari, V., Dumka, A., & Singh, R. P. (2022). A Meta-Analytical Review of Deep Learning Prediction Models for Big Data. In *Encyclopedia of Data Science and Machine Learning*. IGI Global., DOI: 10.4018/978-1-7998-9220-5.ch023

Verma, P., Kumar, V., Daim, T., Sharma, N. K., & Mittal, A. (2022). Identifying and prioritizing impediments of industry 4.0 to sustainable digital manufacturing: A mixed method approach. *Journal of Cleaner Production*, *356*, 131639. Advance online publication. DOI: 10.1016/j.jclepro.2022.131639

Yeruva, A. R., Vijaya Durga, C. S. L., Gokulavasan, B., Pant, K., Chaturvedi, P., & Srivastava, A. P. (2022). A Smart Healthcare Monitoring System Based on Fog Computing Architecture. *Proceedings of International Conference on Technological Advancements in Computational Sciences, ICTACS 2022*, 904 – 909. DOI: 10.1109/ICTACS56270.2022.9987881

Zhang, Y., Cao, C., Gu, J., & Garg, H. (2023). The Impact of Top Management Team Characteristics on the Risk Taking of Chinese Private Construction Enterprises. *Systems*, *11*(2), 67. Advance online publication. DOI: 10.3390/systems11020067

Chapter 4
Cross-Cultural Considerations in AI Ethics and Leadership

Mustafa Kayyali
http://orcid.org/0000-0003-3300-262X
Maaref University of Applied Sciences, Syria

ABSTRACT

As artificial intelligence becomes embedded in the decision-making processes of global organizations, its ethical implications can no longer be approached from a singular cultural lens. This chapter explores the nuanced interplay between AI ethics and cross-cultural leadership, examining how diverse moral frameworks shape expectations, responses, and resistance to AI technologies across the world. Drawing on interdisciplinary insights—from moral philosophy and cultural psychology to organizational behavior and global governance—it argues that ethical leadership in the AI era must go beyond compliance checklists. It must foster genuine intercultural sensitivity and moral imagination. Case examples from Asia, the Middle East, Europe, and Africa highlight how cultural contexts alter the interpretation of fairness, privacy, accountability, and human dignity in AI systems. In a world where digital systems transcend borders but human values remain grounded in place, leaders must learn to navigate with both moral compass and cultural empathy.

INTRODUCTION

There was once a time when technological advancement was largely a matter of engineering prowess—when the morality of a machine was measured solely by its efficiency, reliability, and capacity to outpace human limitations. But in the

DOI: 10.4018/979-8-3693-4099-8.ch004

age of artificial intelligence, something fundamental has shifted. The questions we now face are no longer about what machines can do, but what they should do—and more importantly, who gets to decide. At the heart of this paradigm shift lies an often-overlooked complexity: ethics are not universal in practice, even when they are in principle. While we may all agree on the abstract importance of fairness, accountability, and human dignity, the meanings and manifestations of these values diverge dramatically across cultures. What one society sees as ethical transparency, another may perceive as a breach of trust or an erosion of authority. What one leadership model deems inclusive, another may find destabilizing (Simmons & Yawson, 2022). In AI ethics, these differences matter—not as footnotes or complications, but as central forces shaping both technological deployment and its moral legitimacy. Artificial intelligence is not an apolitical force. It is embedded in human intent, organizational culture, economic strategy, and social history. When AI enters a new environment—be it a healthcare system in Rwanda, a banking network in Japan, or a smart-city initiative in the Gulf—it does not simply "adapt." It interacts, disrupts, and in some cases, collides with deeply held cultural values, social expectations, and traditional modes of leadership. Yet far too often, AI governance frameworks are modeled on Western-centric ethical templates, assuming that concepts such as autonomy, transparency, and individual rights will carry the same weight and connotation in every society. This assumption is not only flawed; it is dangerous. It risks ethical imperialism in a world that is crying out for mutual understanding and moral plurality.

Leadership, too, finds itself at an inflection point (Duggan, 2023). Traditional models of ethical leadership, grounded in stable hierarchies and clear moral codes, are increasingly tested by AI systems that operate at scales and speeds beyond human intuition. Leaders are no longer just decision-makers—they are mediators between machine logic and human values, between algorithmic recommendations and cultural resonance. Their role is not simply to enforce regulations but to foster environments where moral reflection is possible, where the design and deployment of AI tools are not seen as isolated technical decisions but as deeply human choices. Cross-cultural perspectives in AI ethics are not only an academic concern; they are a lived reality. In the boardrooms of multinational corporations, in policy circles drafting regional AI guidelines, in classrooms where future technologists are trained, the question remains: how do we lead ethically in a world where moral norms are multiple, overlapping, and sometimes conflicting? How do we ensure that AI systems respect not just the laws of a land but the moral landscapes of its people? And how do we cultivate ethical leaders who are not merely well-intentioned, but culturally literate and globally responsive?

This chapter aims to confront these questions head-on. Through a multi-disciplinary lens, it explores the intersections of artificial intelligence, ethical leadership, and cultural diversity. It brings to light the tensions and opportunities that emerge when global technologies meet local values. It examines case studies where well-meaning AI initiatives faltered due to cultural misalignment—and others where sensitive leadership turned ethical dilemmas into moments of transformation. Ultimately, it argues for a more pluralistic and dialogical approach to AI ethics—one that embraces the richness of human culture not as a barrier to innovation but as its most important context. As we stand at the crossroads of ethics, technology, and global leadership, this chapter does not pretend to offer a one-size-fits-all solution. Instead, it offers a framework for rethinking AI ethics as a shared human responsibility—one that begins not in code, but in culture; not in programming languages, but in the stories, rituals, and values that shape how we live, lead, and imagine what it means to be human in a world increasingly run by machines.

FRAMING ETHICS IN A GLOBAL AI LANDSCAPE: WHY CULTURE MATTERS

Ethics is often spoken of in absolutes (Sidgwick, 2022). In boardrooms and policy circles, one frequently hears words like *universal principles*, *global standards*, or *fundamental rights* tossed around with the assumption that they mean the same thing to everyone. But when it comes to artificial intelligence—a technology now reaching into every facet of life, from employment and education to medicine, governance, and beyond—these concepts begin to show their seams. The ethical frameworks that guide AI development and implementation are not suspended in some objective ether. They are built, brick by brick, from the cultural soil in which they are conceived. This is where the conversation must begin: with the honest recognition that ethics, while aspiring to universality, is always interpreted through a cultural lens.

In many ways, the AI revolution is a global one. Algorithms designed in Silicon Valley are deployed in Nairobi, Shanghai, São Paulo, and Riyadh (Arora, 2019). Facial recognition tools developed in the United States are now used to monitor crowds in London and train surveillance systems in the Middle East. Predictive policing software built on data from one population is repurposed in another, without fully accounting for its cultural, racial, or historical baggage. These systems move faster than regulations, often faster than understanding. And as they cross borders, they do more than adapt to new environments—they interact with, challenge, and sometimes clash with deeply rooted social values. What makes this collision so ethically volatile is that artificial intelligence, by its very architecture, carries embedded assumptions. Machine learning models, for instance, depend on datasets—often collected, labeled, and normalized in one sociopolitical context—being applied across others. Bias, long understood as a human flaw, is now encoded into algorithms that are treated as objective. But bias is not the only thing being transferred. Norms, definitions of justice, perceptions of harm, expectations of privacy—these too are baked into AI systems. A chatbot trained to communicate empathetically in English may falter in a culture where emotional restraint is the norm (Zhai et al, 2024). An AI hiring tool developed to prioritize individual achievements might overlook qualifications that emerge from collectivist societies where success is tied to group identity and relational harmony.

Cultural friction in AI ethics does not only exist at the level of design; it surfaces most profoundly in deployment (Luusua & Ylipulli, 2020). Consider the concept of privacy—a cornerstone of AI ethics in much of the Western world. In many European countries, shaped by a post-war sensitivity to state overreach, privacy is sacred, protected under law, and often tied to the concept of individual autonomy. But in parts of Asia, where Confucian or collectivist values hold sway, privacy may not be understood in strictly individualistic terms. The idea that one's data might be shared with family, community, or government in exchange for security or societal benefit may not seem invasive but rather expected. An AI system that strictly adheres to European privacy standards could, in such contexts, appear opaque or even antisocial. Similarly, facial recognition technologies that are fiercely contested in some Western democracies for infringing civil liberties are readily accepted in other cultures where public order and collective safety are paramount concerns. These divergences are not anomalies—they are structural. And they raise a critical question: whose ethics are we coding into our machines?

This question becomes even more urgent when we examine the institutions that govern AI ethics today. Most major AI ethics guidelines—whether from the OECD, UNESCO, the EU Commission, or the big tech giants—tend to emerge from a relatively narrow band of cultural experience (Lombana Diaz, 2025). They are often developed in English, built on Enlightenment-era philosophical traditions, and grounded in liberal democratic values. While these values—such as transparency, accountability, and fairness—are laudable and widely respected, they are not interpreted uniformly across the globe. To assume so is to replicate a subtle form of ethical colonialism, where one worldview dominates under the guise of neutrality. Let us take the value of *fairness*, a term that appears in almost every AI ethics framework. In Western contexts, fairness is often operationalized as statistical parity—ensuring that different demographic groups receive similar outcomes or opportunities. But fairness, in other parts of the world, may hinge on very different considerations: historical injustice, social cohesion, or even spiritual balance. In some Indigenous cultures, fairness is not just about humans—it includes the environment, ancestors, and future generations. How can an AI system designed to optimize present-day outcomes reflect such a worldview? And more importantly, how can leaders ensure that these worldviews are not erased in the name of scalability or efficiency?

Leadership, then, becomes not just about setting technical standards or compliance protocols, but about holding space for cultural narratives that may not be immediately legible to a globalized tech industry (Zahari et al, 2024). It requires a shift from ethical universalism to ethical pluralism—not as a surrender to relativism, but as a mature acknowledgment that moral truth is often multifaceted. This kind of leadership asks different questions: Who is missing from the table where decisions are made? Whose voices are not being heard in data collection, in algorithm design, in ethical audits? How can AI systems reflect not just diversity of users, but diversity of values?

A practical example might help here. In a multinational AI project aiming to improve agricultural decision-making across Sub-Saharan Africa, the Western team initially proposed drone surveillance and satellite-driven yield optimization as their core innovation. On paper, it was a brilliant model. But on the ground, it faced immediate resistance. Local communities—many of which had been historically marginalized—viewed the overhead surveillance not as innovation, but as intrusion. Traditional farming methods, rooted in ancestral knowledge and seasonal intuition, were not seen as inferior but sacred (Ihuah, 2024). It was only when the project team invited local elders and spiritual leaders into the design process—acknowledging not just their data, but their wisdom—that trust began to build. The end product was not just a "better algorithm" but a richer, more respectful process. And that made all the difference. Stories like this are instructive because they illustrate what is often missing in global AI ethics discourse: listening. Not just consultation or public comment periods, but deep, sustained, reciprocal listening. Leadership in the AI age must be dialogical (Kergel et al, 2022). It must be patient with ambiguity, comfortable with contradiction, and open to perspectives that do not fit neatly into PowerPoint slides or ethics checklists. What emerges from this approach is a deeper understanding of what ethical AI can truly mean. Not merely compliance with codes, but alignment with human meaning. Not just prediction and optimization, but cultural resonance. This is especially vital in regions of the world that are not major AI producers but are increasingly its consumers. Ethical leadership cannot be unidirectional. It must include the perspectives of communities who have little control over how AI is made but live every day with its consequences.

This brings us to a final, sobering insight. As we speak about AI ethics, we must remember that ethics itself is not static. It evolves. It is contested. It grows in conversation, in disagreement, in contradiction. In some cases, it even grows through conflict. But only if we allow that conflict to be visible, to be spoken aloud rather than hidden beneath layers of consensus-driven policy language. Only if we are willing to admit that there is no single ethical horizon toward which all cultures are marching—but rather many ethical constellations, illuminating different paths toward justice, dignity, and flourishing. So when we ask "Why does culture matter in AI ethics?", the answer is not simply because it influences public acceptance or user trust—though it does. It matters because ethics without culture is abstraction, and abstraction cannot lead. Culture brings ethics down from the clouds into the soil of human experience. It is what turns algorithms into stories, data points into decisions, and systems into relationships. In a world where artificial intelligence is poised to shape the very fabric of society, that grounding is not optional—it is essential. And so, framing ethics in a global AI landscape requires us to do more than write guidelines. It asks us to reimagine the foundation of ethical thought itself—not as a fixed doctrine, but as a living, breathing conversation among cultures, disciplines, and worldviews. It is in this conversation—not in any single answer—that we may find the most human way forward.

WESTERN VS. NON-WESTERN MORAL FRAMEWORKS IN AI DEPLOYMENT

Artificial Intelligence, by its very design, is often imagined as neutral—an elegant convergence of data, mathematics, and code. Yet this perception crumbles when we ask a deceptively simple question: *What is "right" or "wrong" for a machine to do?* The answer to that question is never just technical. It is, and always has been, profoundly moral—and morality, like culture, is never one-size-fits-all. As AI systems are developed, deployed, and embedded into everyday life across continents, they inevitably carry with them the ethical assumptions of their creators. In most cases, these systems are born within Western contexts—primarily North America and Western Europe—where certain philosophical traditions, institutional logics, and moral norms guide the design and governance of technology. The problem arises when these systems travel, often uncritically, into cultures whose ethical frameworks are built on fundamentally different understandings of selfhood, duty, responsibility, and justice. To say that Western and Non-Western moral systems differ is not to draw a sharp line between them, nor to reduce either to monoliths (Acharya, 2020). Rather, it is to acknowledge that beneath the surface of shared human values lie distinct interpretive traditions—formed over centuries by religion, philosophy, language, history, and ways of life. These traditions don't merely shape how people live; they shape how people *ought* to live. And when technologies like AI become arbiters of fairness, gatekeepers of opportunity, or mediators of trust, these ethical undercurrents become more than abstract—they become decisive.

The Western moral tradition, particularly in the realm of ethics, is heavily informed by Enlightenment thinking. It centers the individual as an autonomous agent, capable of rational thought and moral choice. Foundational concepts like individual rights, privacy, liberty, and justice often draw from the works of Kant, Locke,

Mill, and later, Rawls. These ideas have profoundly shaped how Western societies think about law, governance, and technology. In AI, this often translates to a strong emphasis on *individual autonomy*, *consent*, *transparency*, and *fairness as equality of opportunity*. Bias in an algorithm, for example, is framed as a violation of an individual's right to be treated equally—something that must be audited, corrected, and disclosed to the user (Shen et al, 2021). It is a deeply procedural ethic, focusing on systems, fairness in process, and accountability through visibility. Contrast this with many Non-Western frameworks, where the individual is not the central unit of moral consideration. In many African, Asian, Indigenous, and Middle Eastern philosophies, the self is deeply relational. Moral worth is often measured not by what one chooses for oneself, but by one's responsibilities to others—family, community, ancestors, nature, or divine law. In Confucian ethics, for instance, moral conduct is rooted in harmony, hierarchy, and role-based obligations. Ethics is not about asserting one's rights but fulfilling one's duties in accordance with one's place in society. In many Islamic traditions, ethics is grounded in divine revelation, with right and wrong framed less as social contracts and more as spiritual imperatives. In Ubuntu philosophy, prevalent in parts of Sub-Saharan Africa, the phrase "I am because we are" captures the idea that personhood itself is relational and communal. These traditions prioritize different virtues—*respect, harmony, piety, loyalty, collective well-being, humility*—which may clash with, or at least complicate, Western assumptions about what an "ethical AI" should prioritize.

The implications of these differing moral foundations become particularly vivid when we look at real-world AI deployments. Take the example of biometric surveillance technologies. In Western liberal democracies, such technologies are often criticized for violating individual privacy and enabling state overreach. But in some East Asian societies, particularly those influenced by Confucian values, such surveillance may be viewed less critically—especially when it is perceived as enhancing public safety, maintaining social order, or enabling collective prosperity. In such contexts, the moral calculus shifts. Transparency and individual consent may matter less than the perceived social benefits. The ethical question becomes not "Did I agree to this?" but "Does this help the community function better?" Or consider AI in healthcare. In the United States, AI tools used in predictive diagnostics must be rigorously tested for bias to ensure individual patients are treated equitably (Hanna et al, 2024). The emphasis is on *informed consent*, *data privacy*, and *individual risk minimization*. But in parts of India or Thailand, where health is often understood as a collective family matter, AI recommendations might be interpreted or overridden by family elders, religious advisors, or community health workers. Consent becomes a shared process, not an individual declaration. Trust is not built solely through technical transparency but through relational credibility—who is recommending the AI, and do they hold moral authority?

Even in workplace settings, AI's ethical footprint varies by culture. In many Western contexts, algorithmic monitoring of employee productivity is viewed with suspicion, often equated with coercion or an infringement of autonomy. But in parts of East Asia, such monitoring may be accepted—or at least tolerated—within a broader ethic of collective effort and respect for hierarchical leadership (Kayyali, 2025 A). Here, the focus may not be on protecting individual liberties but on preserving harmony and organizational discipline. What appears ethically invasive from one perspective may be seen as ethically responsible from another. These differences are not trivial. They matter because they influence how people experience AI systems, how they resist or embrace them, and how they interpret the intentions behind them. An AI that "works" in one context may backfire in another, not because of technical failure, but because of cultural dissonance. The machine may function perfectly, but its moral grammar is foreign. This is why culturally responsive leadership is so critical in AI ethics. It is not enough to export Western ethical frameworks and hope they hold. Nor is it sufficient to translate policy documents into local languages without reexamining the moral assumptions embedded within them. True ethical leadership in AI means being attuned to local narratives of right and wrong, listening to culturally situated voices, and building AI systems that are *locally legible* as well as globally responsible.

Such leadership demands a kind of ethical humility—a willingness to admit that our own frameworks are limited, that what we consider "best practices" may not be best for everyone. It calls for collaboration with local ethicists, anthropologists, community leaders, and religious scholars. It may mean designing AI systems that are flexible by default—modular, interpretable, and adaptable to moral variation. It may mean embracing slower development cycles in favor of deeper engagement, more conversation, more contradiction. And it will certainly mean discomfort—because listening across cultures always disrupts the illusion of moral certainty. At the same time, we must avoid the trap of cultural relativism. Not all practices justified by culture are ethically defensible. Harm is still harm, even if it is culturally sanctioned. The point is not to surrender to pluralism, but to wrestle with it. To build ethical AI that does not flatten moral diversity in the name of efficiency, but navigates it with care, with conflict, and with constant moral reflection (Bayan, 2024). Universal values may exist—but their expressions are always situated. And perhaps this is where the true power of AI ethics lies: not in setting fixed rules, but in cultivating the conditions for ongoing dialogue. AI can be a catalyst for cross-cultural ethical engagement—not just a source of division, but a reason to ask harder questions about what it means to be human, to lead, and to live together in an increasingly algorithmic world.

When leaders understand that AI ethics is not just a matter of code but of culture, they begin to lead differently. They stop looking for consensus and start creating coalitions. They stop imposing and start listening. They move from command-and-control models to facilitative leadership—one that creates room for ambiguity, for silence, for stories that don't fit neatly into bullet points. And in that shift, a new kind of ethical intelligence begins to emerge. Not artificial. Not even entirely human. But something forged between us—something that respects the many ways we make meaning, and the many worlds we are trying to protect. This, then, is the task ahead—not to choose between Western and Non-Western ethics, but to hold them in tension. To let their differences sharpen our sense of justice rather than divide us. To build AI systems—and more importantly, AI cultures—that are not only technically sophisticated, but morally awake.

LEADERSHIP AT THE INTERSECTION OF AI GOVERNANCE AND CULTURAL INTEGRITY

There's something quietly radical about ethical leadership in the age of artificial intelligence—particularly when that leadership is asked to navigate the treacherous terrain between rapidly evolving technologies and the deeply rooted values of diverse communities. At this intersection, where code meets custom and governance meets tradition, leadership is no longer about commanding authority or enforcing policy. It becomes something more fragile, more human, and more difficult: holding space for nuance, dissent, cultural memory, and moral responsibility in a world that increasingly prizes speed, scale, and uniformity.

Artificial intelligence is changing how decisions are made (Barnea, 2020). From resource allocation in hospitals to risk assessments in criminal justice systems, from recruitment tools in multinational corporations to recommendation engines in education, AI systems are increasingly acting as decision-support—or even decision-making—tools. But unlike traditional bureaucracies or leadership hierarchies, these systems often lack a face, a voice, a moral compass that can be interrogated or reasoned with. They are fast, quiet, and often invisible in their operations. This invisibility makes them powerful, and also dangerous—especially when deployed without deep consideration of the cultural contexts they enter. Leadership at this moment cannot be about technological literacy alone. It must be about ethical fluency—an ability to understand not just what AI can do, but what it *should* do in relation to the people and cultures it touches. This is especially critical in culturally heterogeneous environments where values are not monolithic, and where communities may hold different—sometimes conflicting—visions of what constitutes dignity, justice, or progress. The challenge is not merely technical, nor is it simply procedural. It is moral, and it is cultural. And it demands a kind of leadership that is rare in contemporary organizations: one that is not afraid of ethical tension, that does not rush to resolve complexity, but instead recognizes that meaningful governance in the age of AI begins where certainty ends.

To lead at the intersection of AI governance and cultural integrity is to refuse the illusion of neutrality. It is to acknowledge that no AI system is value-free, and that no leadership decision is made in a vacuum. Every algorithm is shaped by assumptions. Every deployment reflects a set of priorities. Every metric that is chosen—accuracy, efficiency, optimization—comes at the cost of something else, often something less measurable but equally vital: trust, belonging, identity, memory. Ethical leadership, then, begins with awareness. But it cannot end there. It must evolve into something more active, more relational (Nicholson & Kurucz, 2019). Leaders must become translators—not just of code or strategy, but of moral meaning across cultural boundaries. They must be able to listen with humility to perspectives that challenge their own frameworks. They must be able to stand in the discomfort of conflicting value systems and resist the urge to flatten that tension into consensus too quickly. They must know when to pause, when to consult, when to yield. And they must do all of this not as a sign of weakness, but as an act of integrity. Cultural integrity in this context is not about preserving tradition for tradition's sake. It is about honoring the moral architectures that communities have built over time—through rituals, stories, faith, struggle, and survival. It is about refusing to allow AI systems, however advanced, to erase or overwrite those architectures in the name of innovation. It is about asking not just *what works*, but *for whom*, *why*, and *at what cost*.

In many parts of the world, especially in the Global South, AI is arriving as part of a broader package—tied to development aid, foreign investment, global partnerships, and infrastructure modernization. These relationships are not neutral. They are shaped by histories of colonialism, economic dependency, and unequal power. In such contexts, ethical leadership must also be decolonial. It must resist the tendency to see AI as a gift from the "developed" world to the "developing" one, and instead reframe it as a shared challenge that requires mutual learning and respect. This means involving local voices—not just as end-users or beneficiaries, but as co-creators and co-governors. It means building ethical review processes that are not just modeled after Silicon Valley best practices but are rooted in local norms of deliberation and accountability. It means allowing space for spiritual leaders, cultural historians, community elders, and youth activists to shape the future of AI—not because they are "experts" in the conventional sense, but because they hold essential forms of knowledge that no algorithm can replicate.

Such leadership is slow. It is messy. It is often inefficient by the standards of quarterly reports and product roadmaps. But it is precisely this slowness, this messiness, that allows for deeper trust, richer dialogue, and more just outcomes. In a world obsessed with scale, ethical leadership reminds us of the value of specificity, of place, of people whose lives do not fit easily into datasets but who must live with the consequences of decisions made far from them. And make no mistake: the stakes are high. Without culturally anchored ethical leadership, AI systems risk becoming tools of cultural erasure or moral homogenization (Bello, 2023). They risk replacing local problem-solving mechanisms with external ones that may be technically superior but ethically discordant. They risk amplifying the voices of the powerful while silencing the wisdom of the marginalized. But with the right kind of leadership—patient, dialogical, morally awake—AI can become something else. It can become a bridge, a mirror, a tool for reflection and renewal. It can help communities articulate their values more clearly, test their assumptions more rigorously, and imagine futures that are both technologically advanced and ethically rooted.

This kind of leadership does not require one to be a philosopher or an engineer (Kayyali, 2025 B). It requires one to be human, to care deeply about the consequences of one's choices, to be willing to hold the tension between progress and preservation, between innovation and tradition. It requires the courage to say *no* when a system does not serve the people it claims to help. And perhaps most of all, it requires the wisdom to know that leadership is not about control, but about stewardship—about tending to the fragile relationships that make ethical governance possible. In practice, this might mean rethinking how organizations design their AI ethics committees. Are they diverse not only in terms of demographics, but in terms of worldview? Do they include people who understand the cultural contexts in which AI systems will be deployed? Do they meet in formats that allow for genuine listening, not just reporting? Are their findings acted upon, or merely archived? It might also mean rethinking how success is measured. Is a high-performing AI system one that optimizes revenue, or one that preserves cultural dignity? Can we design metrics that account for ethical nuance, for community feedback, for long-term trust? These are not technical questions. They are leadership questions. And they require leaders who are willing to expand the very definition of what it means to lead. This is the work. Not glamorous. Not easy. But essential.

For the world we are moving into is not only one shaped by data and code—it is one that will be remembered by how we chose to lead. Did we lead with humility or hubris? Did we listen more than we spoke? Did we honor the stories that shaped the people behind the statistics? Did we create space for disagreement, for culture, for the sacred? If we did, then perhaps we will look back not just on the rise of artificial intelligence, but on the rise of a more human kind of leadership—one that stood at the intersection of governance and integrity, and chose to protect the fragile beauty of difference, even as the machines raced ahead.

TOWARDS A PLURALISTIC AI FUTURE: BRIDGING CULTURES, ALIGNING VALUES

If the age of artificial intelligence has taught us anything so far, it is that there is no such thing as a neutral system (Fjelland, 2020). Behind every model, every algorithm, every line of code, there are choices—conscious or not. And behind those choices are values. Some are visible. Many are not. They are shaped by language, history, culture, religion, power, pain, and hope. They determine who is seen, who is heard, who is protected, and who is left vulnerable. As AI systems continue to shape the architecture of modern life, from the intimate to the institutional, we must confront a pressing truth: if we are to build a future that is both technologically advanced and ethically grounded, we must embrace a pluralistic vision of AI—one that actively bridges cultures and aligns values without flattening their diversity.

Pluralism is not simply a philosophical idea; it is a moral and political necessity. In a world composed of over 190 nations, thousands of languages, and countless cultural identities, the dream of a single ethical framework governing all AI systems is as dangerous as it is naïve. Ethical pluralism acknowledges that different societies will—and should—approach moral questions in ways that reflect their own traditions, beliefs, and lived experiences (Nardin & Mapel, 2021). But it also insists that diversity of values does not mean the absence of shared responsibility. Pluralism is not relativism. It is not the abdication of truth, but the recognition that truth is often multifaceted. And when it comes to the deployment of AI, this recognition is our only path to legitimacy. To move toward a pluralistic AI future, we must begin by abandoning the comfort of universality as a blanket solution. So many global AI frameworks, even those produced with the best of intentions, operate from a place of ethical certainty. They offer lists—transparency, fairness, accountability, explainability—without interrogating what these terms mean in different cultural registers. They presume alignment where there may be none. They assume that values are easily translatable when, in reality, they are deeply rooted in context. Take, for example, the value of *autonomy*. In many Western societies, autonomy is framed as individual freedom—the right to choose, to consent, to dissent. In AI ethics, this becomes the foundation for user control, opt-in systems, and informed consent protocols. But in many non-Western societies, autonomy is relational. It is not the right to separate, but the responsibility to remain connected. Decision-making may involve elders, families, spiritual leaders. Consent may not be an individual matter, but a communal one. Designing AI systems that only recognize individual autonomy risks alienating the very communities they aim to empower. A pluralistic AI future does not erase these differences; it designs for them.

Designing for pluralism means reimagining the development lifecycle of AI systems from the ground up (Giaccardi & Bendor, 2024). It means involving diverse communities not as passive users but as co-authors. It means embedding cultural interpreters, ethicists, anthropologists, and community leaders into design teams—not as consultants after the fact, but as equal partners from the start. It means translating not only languages, but worldviews. And most importantly, it means being willing to slow down, to revise, to reflect, and to say *no* when a system is not ethically sound, even if it is technically impressive. This vision of pluralism also demands something rare in the tech world: humility. Not performative humility, but the kind that knows how to listen. The kind that can sit in the discomfort of contradiction without rushing to resolve it. The kind that recognizes that a rural teacher in Bangladesh or a tribal elder in the Amazon may have ethical insights about technology that a Silicon Valley engineer has never considered. True pluralism honors the wisdom of the margins. It believes that power and insight are not the same thing. Of course, pluralism is not easy. It requires that we tolerate, even embrace, ethical friction. It requires that we design systems that are more adaptable, more layered, less rigid. It requires that we build mechanisms for negotiation—not just between users and systems, but between values themselves. It asks us to see difference not as an obstacle, but as a generative force. This does not mean we must give up on shared principles. But it does mean that shared principles must be the result of dialogue, not imposition. What does justice look like in an AI system that operates across borders? It cannot simply be the export of Western legalism. Nor can it rest solely on local customs if those customs perpetuate harm. Justice, in a pluralistic AI future, is a process—not a destination. It is shaped through conversation, through conflict, through co-creation.

Imagine an AI system for hiring that operates in both Brazil and South Korea. In Brazil, personal charisma and creative thinking may be seen as indicators of leadership potential. In South Korea, humility and deference to hierarchy may be valued more highly. A universal algorithm that scores candidates the same way across both cultures will fail to recognize either set of values (Shin et al., 2022). But a pluralistic system—one that allows for cultural parameters, ethical flexibility, and localized weighting—has a better chance at not only fairness, but resonance. Or consider a facial recognition system deployed in a multicultural city. In one community, face-covering may be a religious expression. In another, it may be associated with protest and anonymity. In a third, it may be a response to past trauma with surveillance. A single policy about facial visibility cannot ethically encompass all three. A pluralistic approach requires that we think beyond enforcement toward empathy. It requires that we ask what people are protecting when they resist visibility—and how systems might honor that without compromising safety or equity. Pluralism is not about fragmentation. It is about depth. It is about building systems that do not just *function* across cultures, but that make sense within them. It is about aligning values not by erasing difference, but by elevating dialogue. This work is slow. It is messy. It is often at odds with the speed and efficiency worshipped in most AI organizations. But it is also the only work that builds systems people can truly trust.

This future cannot be built by technologists alone. It requires philosophers, artists, linguists, elders, youth, and everyone in between. It requires that AI governance structures become as diverse and porous as the communities they impact. It requires regional councils, ethics assemblies, localized protocols, cultural audits—not as side projects, but as core components of responsible design. And while global institutions have a role to play, the most transformative work may happen at the local level. In cities, in cooperatives, in tribal nations, in spiritual communities—where people are already thinking deeply about what it means to live well with technology, even if they don't call it AI ethics. These grassroots insights must not be mined and exported. They must be supported, protected, resourced, and respected. The journey toward a pluralistic AI future is not a clean arc. It will involve false starts, failed partnerships, difficult conversations (Haque, 2024). But it is a journey worth making. Because at its heart, this future is not just about machines. It is about us—about whether we are willing to lead with humility, to design with care, and to imagine a world where the dignity of difference is not just tolerated, but celebrated. In such a future, AI will not be a force that flattens culture, but one that reflects it—beautifully, complexly, imperfectly. It will not demand that we all think the same, act the same, live the same. It will remind us, again and again, that we are many—and that being many is not our weakness, but our greatest strength. And in that future, the question will no longer be whether AI is ethical enough. The question will be whether *we* are courageous enough to create the ethical world it deserves to serve.

CONCLUSION

There is a quiet but urgent truth that runs through every discussion about artificial intelligence and ethics: no technology, however advanced, is culturally neutral. Algorithms may calculate with precision, but they do not operate in vacuums. They reflect the values of their designers, the assumptions of their users, and the historical and cultural patterns of the societies they seek to serve. In a world as diverse as ours, this reality presents both a profound challenge and a unique opportunity. Throughout this chapter, we have journeyed through the layered complexities of cross-cultural ethics in AI and the evolving role of leadership in navigating these waters. We have seen how Western ethical frameworks, though often globalized in intent, can falter in contexts where values like communal well-being, spiritual cohesion, or deference to authority take precedence over individual autonomy or radical transparency. We have explored the nuanced ways in which leadership must shift—not merely to accommodate cultural differences, but to honor them, to integrate them meaningfully into organizational strategy and technological design. The conclusion, however, is not a fixed point. It is an opening—an invitation to move away from binary thinking and toward a richer ethical tapestry, one that recognizes moral diversity not as a threat but as a foundation for innovation. AI does not need to flatten cultural landscapes to function effectively. On the contrary, its most meaningful potential lies in its ability to adapt, to learn, and to respond to the distinct moral ecosystems in which it operates.

Leadership in this context cannot be reactive or regulatory alone. It must be visionary, culturally attuned, and ethically courageous. It requires leaders who are not only fluent in the language of data and strategy but who can listen across difference, who understand that the future of AI is not only shaped in research labs or boardrooms but in village councils, religious communities, family structures, and indigenous worldviews. It calls for an ethic of humility—an acknowledgment that no single cultural framework holds the monopoly on wisdom, and that moral legitimacy is something to be earned, not assumed. This is not an easy path. Cultural pluralism introduces tension. It slows decision-making. It complicates compliance. But it also deepens trust, strengthens resilience, and builds systems that are truly rooted in the people they are meant to serve. If AI is to fulfill its promise—not just as a tool of efficiency, but as a force for collective flourishing—it must be guided by leadership that is as diverse, dynamic, and deeply human as the world itself. In the end, the ethical success of AI will not be judged solely by its outputs or accuracy, but by the quality of relationships it enables—between people, between cultures, and between the systems we build and the values we hold. Cross-cultural ethical leadership is not a soft skill; it is the backbone of sustainable AI governance. It is the bridge between innovation and justice, between global ambition and local wisdom. And so, we must ask ourselves—not just as technologists or policymakers, but as citizens of an interconnected world: What kind of future are we designing? And who do we become when we choose to lead, not with domination or certainty, but with dialogue, curiosity, and care?

REFERENCES

Acharya, A. (2020). The myth of the "civilization state": Rising powers and the cultural challenge to world order. *Ethics & International Affairs*, *34*(2), 139–156. DOI: 10.1017/S0892679420000192

Arora, P. (2019). *The next billion users: Digital life beyond the West.* Harvard University Press. DOI: 10.4159/9780674238879

Barnea, A. (2020). How will AI change intelligence and decision-making? *Journal of Intelligence Studies in Business*, *10*(1), 75–80. DOI: 10.37380/jisib.v10i1.564

Bayan, F. M. H. (2024). The Ethics of AI: Navigating the Moral dilemmas of Artificial Intelligence. Arab Journal for Scientific Publishing (AJSP). *ISSN*, *2663*, 5798.

Bello, E. D. (2023). *Empowering Leaders: NAVIGATING CULTURE, COMMUNICATION, AND AI ETHICS IN NEGOTIATION.* BoD–Books on Demand.

Duggan, T. J. (2023). Inflection Points and Forming a Leadership Identity: The Identity Work of Women Leaders in Organizations (Doctoral dissertation, Fielding Graduate University).

Fjelland, R. (2020). Why general artificial intelligence will not be realized. *Humanities & Social Sciences Communications*, *7*(1), 1–9. DOI: 10.1057/s41599-020-0494-4

Giaccardi, E., & Bendor, R. (2024). Rethink design: a vocabulary for designing with AI.

Hanna, M., Pantanowitz, L., Jackson, B., Palmer, O., Visweswaran, S., Pantanowitz, J., & Rashidi, H. (2024). Ethical and Bias considerations in artificial intelligence (AI)/machine learning. *Modern Pathology*, , 100686. PMID: 39694331

Haque, E. (2024). *AI Horizons: Shaping a Better Future Through Responsible Innovation and Human Collaboration.* Walter de Gruyter GmbH & Co KG. DOI: 10.1515/9781501518430

Ihuah, A. S. (2024). African endogenous knowledge and sustainable development: Evolving an African agrarian philosophy. In *African agrarian philosophy* (pp. 287–310). Springer International Publishing.

Kayyali, M. (2025a). Leadership's Role in Fostering a Resilient Organizational Culture. In *Enhancing Resilience in Business Continuity Management* (pp. 267–294). IGI Global Scientific Publishing. DOI: 10.4018/979-8-3693-8809-9.ch009

Kayyali, M. (2025b). The Role of Leadership in Promoting Workplace Happiness. In *Insights on Wellbeing and Happiness in the Workplace* (pp. 233–254). IGI Global Scientific Publishing. DOI: 10.4018/979-8-3693-2939-9.ch012

Kergel, D., Heidkamp-Kergel, B., Nørreklit, H., & Paulsen, M. (Eds.). (2022). *Agile Learning and Management in a Digital Age: Dialogic Leadership*. Taylor & Francis. DOI: 10.4324/9781003188728

Lombana Diaz, C. (2025). AI Ethics. In *Human-Centered AI: An Illustrated Scientific Quest* (pp. 439–474). Springer Nature Switzerland. DOI: 10.1007/978-3-031-61375-3_5

Luusua, A., & Ylipulli, J. (2020, July). Artificial intelligence and risk in design. In *Proceedings of the 2020 ACM designing interactive systems conference* (pp. 1235-1244). DOI: 10.1145/3357236.3395491

Nardin, T., & Mapel, D. R. (2021). International Society: Diverse. *Ethical Perspectives*.

Nicholson, J., & Kurucz, E. (2019). Relational leadership for sustainability: Building an ethical framework from the moral theory of 'ethics of care'. *Journal of Business Ethics*, *156*(1), 25–43. DOI: 10.1007/s10551-017-3593-4

Shen, H., DeVos, A., Eslami, M., & Holstein, K. (2021). Everyday algorithm auditing: Understanding the power of everyday users in surfacing harmful algorithmic behaviors. Proceedings of the ACM on Human-Computer Interaction, 5(CSCW2), 1-29.

Shin, D., Chotiyaputta, V., & Zaid, B. (2022). The effects of cultural dimensions on algorithmic news: How do cultural value orientations affect how people perceive algorithms? *Computers in Human Behavior*, *126*, 107007. DOI: 10.1016/j.chb.2021.107007

Sidgwick, H. (2022). *The methods of ethics*. DigiCat.

Simmons, S. V., & Yawson, R. M. (2022). Developing leaders for disruptive change: An inclusive leadership approach. *Advances in Developing Human Resources*, *24*(4), 242–262. DOI: 10.1177/15234223221114359

Zahari, A. I., Said, J., Muhamad, N., & Ramly, S. M. (2024). Ethical culture and leadership for sustainability and governance in public sector organisations within the ESG framework. *Journal of Open Innovation*, *10*(1), 100219. DOI: 10.1016/j.joitmc.2024.100219

Zhai, C., Wibowo, S., & Li, L. D. (2024). Evaluating the AI dialogue System's intercultural, humorous, and empathetic dimensions in English language learning: A case study. *Computers and Education: Artificial Intelligence*, *7*, 100262. DOI: 10.1016/j.caeai.2024.100262

Chapter 5
Human Resource Management and Artificial Intelligence

Uğur Berdibek
http://orcid.org/0000-0003-3202-8342
Bingöl Üniversitesi, Turkey

Koray Gündüz
http://orcid.org/0000-0002-9734-3290
Bingöl Üniversitesi, Turkey

ABSTRACT

In today's world, digitization, global competition, and evolving employee expectations have continuously heightened the demand for more strategic, rapid, and analytical approaches in the field of Human Resources Management (HRM) (Dulebohn & Johnson, 2021). At this juncture, artificial intelligence (AI) technologies, with their data processing, machine learning, and predictive analytics capabilities, play a pivotal role in shaping the future of HRM. In conclusion, the application of AI-driven solutions in HRM goes beyond merely expediting routine tasks. By fostering a data-oriented decision-making culture, AI contributes to a more strategic and agile HRM framework. Moreover, one must remember that the human element remains central to all HRM functions. AI outputs achieve their greatest impact when they are integrated with managerial expertise and the organization's core values (Eren, 2022). Consequently, the implementation of planned, ethical, and sustainable digital transformation strategies stands out as a comprehensive approach illuminating the future of HRM.

DOI: 10.4018/979-8-3693-4099-8.ch005

INTRODUCTION

In recent years, digital transformation, globalization and rapid changes in the expectations of the workforce have reshaped the human resource management (HRM) practices of businesses. In particular, the development of artificial intelligence (AI) technologies leads to significant transformations in HRM processes and enables these processes to become more strategic, fast and analytical (Dulebohn & Johnson, 2013, p. 74). The data processing, machine learning and predictive analytics capabilities offered by AI have the potential to improve the effectiveness of core HRM functions such as recruitment, performance evaluation, talent management and training (Sharma & Sharma, 2017, p. 687).

In this chapter, the main dimensions of the integration of AI into HRM processes will be discussed and issues such as strategic planning, data management, recruitment and selection, performance evaluation, compensation, talent management, training and development, organizational culture and change management, ethical and legal dimensions, and leadership support will be examined. Thus, the advantages and potential risks of integrating AI applications into HRM processes will be discussed in a comprehensive manner.

1. STRATEGIC PLANNING AND ARTIFICIAL INTELLIGENCE

The rapid spread of AI technologies in today's business world significantly affects the strategic planning processes of businesses. Strategic planning is a process in which businesses determine their long-term goals and systematically plan the necessary resources and methods to achieve these goals (Brynjolfsson & Mcafee, 2017, p. 1). The integration of AI into these processes helps businesses gain competitive advantage and achieve sustainable growth.

The integration of AI technologies into strategic planning processes primarily increases the effectiveness of decision-making processes. By analyzing large data sets thanks to AI algorithms, businesses can make more accurate predictions for the future and base their strategic decisions on more solid foundations. For example, analyzing complex data such as customer behavior, market trends, and competitive conditions enables businesses to create more realistic and feasible plans when setting strategic goals (Shrestha et al., 2019, p. 68-70).

Another important contribution of AI to strategic planning processes is risk management and uncertainty reduction. By using AI-based forecasting models, businesses can better predict the risks they may face in the future and take proactive measures against these risks. In this context, AI systems enable businesses to develop more reliable and sustainable strategies by reducing uncertainties in strategic planning processes (Agrawal et al., 2019, p. 45-47).

Another dimension of using AI in strategic planning processes is the effective management and optimization of resources. Thanks to AI algorithms, businesses can use their existing resources more efficiently and reduce costs by optimizing resource allocation. For example, AI-based optimization systems used in production processes help businesses reduce production costs and make resource use more efficient (Brynjolfsson & Mcafee, 2017, p. 1-2).

The integration of AI technologies into strategic planning processes also contributes to increasing the innovation capacity of businesses. Thanks to AI systems, businesses can develop new business models and gain competitive advantage by differentiating in the market. In this context, AI technologies enable businesses to adopt innovative approaches in their strategic planning processes and provide sustainable competitive advantage (Iansiti & Lakhani, 2020, p. 62-64).

As a result, top management support and leadership commitment are critical for the successful integration of AI technologies into strategic planning processes. Top management's explicit support for AI applications positively affects employees' attitudes towards these technologies and increases the success of strategic planning processes (Fountaine et al., 2019, p. 66). Therefore, in order for businesses to use AI technologies effectively in their strategic planning processes, it is important for them to provide leadership support from senior management and develop employees' digital competencies. The integration of AI technologies into strategic planning processes improves the decision-making processes of businesses, reduces risks, optimizes resource use, and increases their innovation capacity. In order for businesses to use these technologies effectively, the support of senior management and the development of employees' digital competencies are critical.

2. DATA MANAGEMENT AND ARTIFICIAL INTELLIGENCE

The effective use of AI technologies in businesses depends to a large extent on the availability of accurate, reliable and high quality data. In this context, the concept of data management emerges as one of the key elements that determine the success of AI applications. Data management is defined as a systematic approach covering the processes of collecting, storing, processing and analyzing data and plays a critical role in the strategic decision-making processes of businesses (Wang & Hajli, 2017, p. 289).

The effectiveness of AI applications is directly related to the quality and accuracy of the data used. Quality data is defined as data that contains accurate, up-to-date, complete and consistent information and is important for algorithms to produce accurate results (Lee et al., 2019, p. 3). High-quality data is needed for AI systems, especially in HRM processes, to make the right decisions in critical areas such as employee performance evaluations, recruitment processes and career planning (Black & van Esch, 2021, p. 217). Therefore, businesses need to standardize data collection processes and regularly check the accuracy of data to improve data quality.

Another important dimension of data management is ensuring data security and confidentiality. Most of the data used in AI applications contain personal and sensitive information, and the protection of this data is critical in legal and ethical terms (Kaplan & Haenlein, 2020, p. 42). Regulations such as the European Union's General Data Protection Regulation (GDPR) and Turkey's Personal Data Protection Law clearly define the rules that businesses must comply with in the processes of collecting, processing and storing personal data (Voigt & Von dem Bussche, 2017, p. 23). In this context, it is important for businesses to rigorously implement data security policies in data management processes and take necessary measures to protect employees' personal data.

The effectiveness of data management in AI applications is also related to the integration and accessibility of data. Integrating data from different departments and systems in businesses enables AI algorithms to make more comprehensive and accurate analyzes (Wang & Hajli, 2017, p. 292). For example, integrating data from different sources such as employee performance data, training records and career development information in HRM processes enables a more accurate assessment of employees' talents and potentials (Lee et al., 2019, p. 5). Therefore, businesses need to create the technical infrastructure to ensure data integration in data management processes and increase the accessibility of data across departments.

AI tools used in data management include techniques such as big data analytics, machine learning algorithms and natural language processing. The effective use of these tools depends on ensuring data quality and security (Davenport & Ronanki, 2018, p. 78). Moreover, international regulations such as the GDPR set the legal framework for AI applications in data management, requiring businesses to be more careful about data privacy and security (European Commission, 2023).

As a result, adopting transparency and accountability principles in data management processes increases the reliability of AI applications. The fact that businesses openly share with employees how the data used in AI systems are collected, processed and analyzed strengthens employees' trust in these systems (Floridi & Cowls, 2019, p. 9). In addition, regular auditing of data management processes and the establishment of independent audit mechanisms are important factors that increase the effectiveness and reliability of data management (Kaplan & Haenlein, 2020, p. 44). In order for AI technologies to be used effectively and sustainably in businesses, data management processes should be handled meticulously. Improving data quality, ensuring data security and confidentiality, realizing data integration and acting in accordance with the principles of transparency stand out as the main factors that determine the success of AI applications.

3. USING ARTIFICIAL INTELLIGENCE IN RECRUITMENT AND SELECTION PROCESSES

Recruitment and selection processes are recognized as one of the most critical functions of HRM. The effectiveness of these processes plays an important role in helping organizations gain competitive advantage and achieve sustainable success. In recent years, the integration of AI technologies into recruitment processes has brought significant innovations in candidate evaluation and selection processes (Black & van Esch, 2021, p. 215). Especially in large-scale organizations, the high number of candidates in recruitment processes makes it difficult and costly in terms of time to evaluate candidates with traditional methods. In this context, the use of AI-based systems increases the speed and efficiency of recruitment processes, allowing human resources professionals to focus on more strategic tasks (Albert, 2019, p. 218).

AI technologies can automate processes such as screening candidates' CVs, analyzing their competencies and assessing their suitability for the position. These systems can analyze various criteria such as candidates' educational background, work experience, competencies and personality traits to identify the most suitable candidates for the position (Hmoud & Laszlo, 2019, p. 24). For example, natural language processing (NLP) algorithms can analyze candidates' CVs and application forms and calculate the match rates with the criteria specified in the job advertisement. Thus, human resources professionals can narrow down the candidate pool more quickly and objectively (Black & van Esch, 2021, p. 217).

However, the use of AI systems in recruitment processes brings with it some ethical and legal risks. In particular, the quality and diversity of the data used by algorithms can increase the risk of discrimination and bias in recruitment processes (Köchling & Wehner, 2020, p. 780). For example, if the data used in the training of algorithms contains biases related to factors such as gender, age, ethnicity, or university of graduation, discriminatory results may occur in recruitment processes. Therefore, during the use of AI systems in recruitment processes, algorithms should be constantly audited and the data used should be evaluated in terms of diversity and inclusion (Raghavan et al., 2020, p. 3).

AI tools used in recruitment processes include natural language processing algorithms that analyze candidates' CVs and sentiment analysis systems that evaluate video interviews (Chamorro-Premuzic et al., 2019, p. 89).

As a result, while the use of AI technologies in recruitment and selection processes offers significant advantages for businesses, the ethical and legal dimensions of these technologies should also be taken into account. While integrating AI systems into recruitment processes, it is important for businesses to pay attention to issues such as transparency of algorithms, data quality and diversity, and to provide training for human resources professionals on the use of these systems.

4. USING ARTIFICIAL INTELLIGENCE IN PERFORMANCE APPRAISAL SYSTEMS

Performance appraisal systems are recognized as one of the main functions of HRM to measure employees' job performance, provide feedback and support their career development. Traditional performance appraisal methods are often based on subjective evaluations of managers, which can lead to a weakened perception of fairness among employees (Cappelli et al., 2019, p. 24). In recent years, the development of AI technologies has enabled the emergence of more objective, data-driven and comprehensive evaluation methods in performance evaluation processes (Tambe et al., 2019, p. 15).

AI-based performance appraisal systems can make more comprehensive and objective evaluations by using various data sources to measure employee performance. For example, different data sources such as employee email communications, project management tools, customer feedback, and work results can be analyzed by AI algorithms to provide a more holistic assessment of employee performance. These systems can also evaluate dimensions of employee performance that are difficult to measure with traditional methods, such as collaboration, innovation, flexibility and contribution to teamwork (Cheng & Hackett, 2021, p. 6-8).

However, the use of AI systems in performance appraisal processes brings some risks. In particular, the quality and accuracy of the data used by the algorithms directly affect the reliability of the evaluation results. Moreover, evaluating the performance of employees based only on quantitative data can negatively affect employee motivation and job satisfaction. Therefore, it is important to use AI-based performance appraisal systems together with human managers' appraisals and to continuously review the results of the algorithms (Köchling et al., 2025, p. 1207-1209).

Although the integration of AI systems into performance appraisal processes enables more objective and comprehensive evaluations of employee performance, the ethical and legal aspects of these systems should also be considered. In particular, it is important that data security and privacy policies are meticulously implemented during the use of AI systems in order to protect employees' personal data and privacy rights (Tambe et al., 2019, p. 17).

AI systems used in performance appraisal processes include machine learning algorithms that analyze employee performance data and systems that provide real-time feedback (Cappelli & Tavis, 2016, p. 102).

As a result, the use of AI technologies in performance appraisal processes offers significant advantages for organizations and contributes to the creation of more objective appraisal processes. However, in order to use these technologies effectively, issues such as transparency of algorithms, data quality and privacy rights of employees need to be carefully addressed. In this context, the integration of AI-based performance appraisal systems into HRM processes should be supported by the expertise and experience of human managers.

5. USE OF ARTIFICIAL INTELLIGENCE IN REMUNERATION AND REWARDING PROCESSES

As one of the core functions of HRM, compensation and reward processes are critical for increasing employee motivation, retaining talent, and supporting the achievement of the strategic goals of the organization. Traditional compensation methods are often based on market research and subjective evaluations of managers, which can lead to a weakened perception of fairness among employees and loss of motivation (Bussin & Christos, 2022, p. 42). In recent years, the development of AI technologies has enabled the creation of more objective, data-driven and fair systems in compensation and reward processes (Cheng & Hackett, 2021, p. 7).

AI-based systems can simultaneously analyze market data, employee performance metrics and internal compensation structures to ensure internal and external pay equity in compensation processes (Bussin & Christos, 2022, p. 42). By taking into account various criteria such as employees' competencies, experience and performance, these systems help to create more consistent and fair compensation policies. For example, AI algorithms can detect wage inequalities by comparing the wages of individuals working in similar positions and provide recommendations to eliminate these inequalities (Cheng & Hackett, 2021, p. 9).

In rewarding processes, AI technologies can evaluate the individual performance of employees and their contributions to the organization more objectively. By analyzing the performance data of employees, these systems allow more accurate and fair decisions to be made regarding which employees should be rewarded. Moreover, AI-based systems can provide personalized reward recommendations to increase employee motivation and thus strengthen employee loyalty to the organization (Köchling et al., 2025, p. 1206-1208).

However, the use of AI systems in compensation and reward processes brings some ethical and legal risks. In particular, the quality and diversity of the data used by algorithms may increase the risk of discrimination and bias in remuneration and reward processes. For example, if there are biases in the data used in the training of algorithms regarding factors such as gender, age or ethnicity, discriminatory results may occur in compensation and reward processes. Therefore, during the use of AI systems in remuneration and reward processes, the algorithms should be constantly audited and the data used should be evaluated in terms of diversity and inclusion (Raisch & Krakowski, 2021, p. 195-197).

AI systems used in compensation processes aim to create fair and competitive compensation policies by analyzing market data (Lawler & Boudreau, 2009, p. 134). However, it is stated that algorithms carry the risk of increasing wage inequality and therefore it is critical to ensure algorithmic transparency and fairness. Businesses are recommended to regularly review the compensation decisions of AI systems and be transparent with employees (Manyika et al., 2017, p. 88).

In conclusion, the use of AI technologies in compensation and reward processes offers significant advantages for businesses and contributes to the creation of more objective, fair and data-driven systems. However, in order to use these technologies effectively, issues such as transparency of algorithms, data quality and privacy rights of employees need to be carefully addressed. In this context, the integration of AI-based compensation and reward systems into HRM processes should be supported by the expertise and experience of human managers.

6. USING ARTIFICIAL INTELLIGENCE IN TALENT MANAGEMENT AND CAREER DEVELOPMENT

In today's business world, talent management and career development are critical for businesses to gain competitive advantage and achieve sustainable success. Talent management is a comprehensive process that involves identifying and developing employees' competencies and aligning them with organizational goals (Collings et al., 2019, p. 543). Career development, on the other hand, includes activities carried out to align individual goals with organizational needs and to maximize the potential of employees (De Vos, Jacobs & Verbruggen, 2021, p. 3). The development of AI technologies in recent years offers significant innovations and opportunities in talent management and career development processes.

AI-based systems enable more effective management of the talent pool within the organization by analyzing the competencies, performance and career goals of employees in talent management processes (Collings et al., 2019, p. 545). These systems use big data analytics and machine learning algorithms to assess employees' current competencies and future potential. For example, by analyzing information such as employees' past performance data, training records and career preferences, employees' strengths and weaknesses can be identified and personalized career development plans can be created (De Vos et al., 2021, p. 5).

AI technologies also offer significant advantages in matching the individual career goals of employees with the strategic needs of the organization in career development processes. By analyzing employees' career expectations and competencies, these systems can identify suitable positions or projects within the organization and offer personalized career recommendations to employees. Thus, employees' career satisfaction and motivation increase, and businesses can reduce their dependence on external resources by using the internal talent pool more effectively (Stahl et al., 2020, p. 8-10).

However, the use of AI systems in talent management and career development processes brings some ethical and legal risks. In particular, the quality and diversity of data used by algorithms can increase the risk of discrimination and bias in employees' access to career opportunities. For example, if the data used in the training of algorithms contains biases related to factors such as gender, age or ethnicity, inequalities may arise in the career development processes of employees. Therefore, during the use of AI systems in talent management and career development processes, the algorithms should be continuously audited and the data used should be evaluated for diversity and inclusion (Tambe et al., 2019, p. 23).

It is emphasized that these systems have positive effects on employee engagement and job satisfaction, but it is necessary to be sensitive about the protection of employees' personal data and privacy issues (Cascio & Boudreau, 2010, p. 92).

In conclusion, the use of AI technologies in talent management and career development processes offers significant advantages for organizations and contributes to the creation of more objective, fair and data-driven systems. However, in order to use these technologies effectively, issues such as transparency of algorithms, data quality and privacy rights of employees need to be carefully addressed. In this context, the integration of AI-based talent management and career development systems into HRM processes should be supported by the expertise and experience of human managers.

7. USING ARTIFICIAL INTELLIGENCE IN TRAINING AND DEVELOPMENT PROCESSES

Employee training and development processes are critical for organizations to gain competitive advantage and achieve sustainable success. Traditional training methods usually provide standardized content to all employees and fail to take individual differences into account. This reduces the effectiveness of training activities and can negatively affect employee motivation (Sousa & Rocha, 2019, p.

3). In recent years, the development of AI technologies has enabled the creation of personalized and more effective learning experiences in training and development processes (Holmes et al., 2019, p. 12).

AI-based training systems can offer personalized training programs by analyzing employees' current knowledge levels, learning speeds and individual career goals. These systems can continuously monitor employees' interactions with training content and adapt learning processes in real time (Sousa & Rocha, 2019, p. 5). For example, by identifying the topics that employees have difficulty with during training, additional content or different learning methods can be suggested for these topics. Thus, employees' learning processes become more efficient and the effectiveness of training activities increases (Holmes et al., 2019, p. 14).

AI technologies also offer significant advantages in terms of measuring employee performance in training and development processes and evaluating the effectiveness of training activities. These systems can measure the impact of training activities on employees' job performance by analyzing employees' performance data before and after training. In addition, AI-based analytical tools can be used to calculate the financial return on investment (ROI) of training activities. In this way, organizations can more accurately evaluate the effectiveness of their training investments and use their training budgets more efficiently (Chatterjee et al., 2021, p. 8-10).

However, the use of AI systems in training and development processes brings along some ethical and legal risks. Especially the privacy and security of employees' personal data collected in training processes is an important issue. Therefore, data security policies should be meticulously implemented during the use of AI-based training systems and necessary measures should be taken to protect the personal data of employees. In addition, the quality and diversity of the data used by algorithms in training processes directly affect the effectiveness of training activities. In this context, it is important to continuously audit algorithms and evaluate the data used in terms of diversity and inclusiveness (Kaplan & Haenlein, 2020, p. 40-42).

AI-supported learning platforms used in educational processes increase learning effectiveness by providing adaptive learning algorithms and personalized educational content (Noe & Kodwani, 2018, p. 167). It is stated that these systems positively affect employees' learning motivation and performance, but the quality of training content and the accuracy of algorithmic recommendations need to be continuously monitored (Kirkpatrick & Kirkpatrick, 2023, p. 78).

In conclusion, the use of AI technologies in training and development processes offers significant advantages for businesses and contributes to the creation of more personalized, effective and data-driven training systems. However, in order to use these technologies effectively, issues such as transparency of algorithms, data quality and privacy rights of employees need to be carefully addressed. In this context, the integration of AI-based training and development systems into HRM processes should be supported by the expertise and experience of human managers.

8. ARTIFICIAL INTELLIGENCE IN TERMS OF ORGANIZATIONAL CULTURE AND CHANGE MANAGEMENT

In today's business world, the adoption of AI technologies by businesses is considered not only as a technical transformation process, but also as an important transformation in terms of organizational culture and change management. Organizational culture is defined as a complex structure that includes values, norms and behavioral patterns shared by employees and plays a critical role in achieving the strategic goals of businesses (Grover et al., 2022, p. 180). The integration of AI into organizations brings about a comprehensive change process that requires the questioning of existing cultural structures and the adoption of new values.

The integration of AI technologies into organizational culture is significantly influenced by factors such as employees' attitudes towards technology, digital competencies and openness to change. In this context, in order for organizations to successfully adopt AI applications, employees' digital competencies should be developed and positive attitudes towards technology should be encouraged. In addition, it is important for top management to adopt open communication and transparency policies in order to shape employees' perceptions towards AI technologies in a positive way. In this process, informing employees about the purposes, scope and expected outcomes of AI applications will help to reduce resistance to change (Wilson & Daugherty, 2018, p. 116-118).

On the other hand, the integration of AI technologies into organizational culture may also bring some concerns in terms of job security and career prospects of employees. In particular, employees' fear of losing their jobs due to AI technologies may lead to increased resistance to change. Therefore, it is important for organizations to develop clear policies on job security and career development of employees in the process of adopting AI applications. In addition, increasing the competencies of employees to work with AI technologies and encouraging a culture of continuous learning will contribute to more effective management of the change process (Schneider & Leyer, 2019, p. 229-231).

In the process of integrating AI technologies into organizational culture, leadership support and top management commitment are critical. Top management's explicit support and commitment to AI applications positively affect employees' attitudes towards change and increase the success of organizational transformation (Grover et al., 2022, p. 182). In this context, top management should emphasize the strategic importance of AI applications and actively support employees in this process.

As a result, the integration of AI technologies into organizational culture is a comprehensive change process that requires reshaping organizational values, norms and behavior patterns rather than a technical transformation. In order to manage this process successfully, it is important to develop employees' digital competencies, promote a culture of continuous learning, adopt open communication policies and ensure strong support from top management.

9. ETHICAL AND LEGAL ASPECTS OF ARTIFICIAL INTELLIGENCE APPLICATIONS

Although the use of AI technologies in HRM processes provides significant advantages for businesses, it also brings along various ethical and legal debates. In particular, issues such as the protection of employees' personal data, algorithmic biases and transparency are the main elements that constitute the ethical and legal dimensions of AI applications (Floridi, 2019, p. 5).

Algorithmic biases and the risk of discrimination are at the top of the ethical dimensions in AI applications. Biases in the data sets on which algorithms are trained can lead to discriminatory results in processes such as recruitment, performance evaluation and remuneration (Raghavan et al., 2020, p. 470). For example, it is known that the AI-based system used by Amazon in its recruitment processes developed a systematic bias against female candidates and the company had to stop the application (Dastin, 2018, p. 2). In order to prevent such situations, the datasets on which algorithms are trained should be continuously audited for diversity and inclusiveness, and algorithmic decisions should be transparently explainable (Floridi, 2019, p. 186).

Another ethical dimension of AI applications is the privacy and data confidentiality rights of employees. For AI systems to work effectively, a large amount of personal data of employees needs to be collected and analyzed. This increases the risk of violating the protection of employees' personal data and privacy rights (Taddeo & Floridi, 2018, p. 751). Legal regulations such as the GDPR and Turkey's Personal Data Protection Law clearly define the rules that businesses must comply with in the processes of collecting, processing and storing employees' personal data (Voigt & Von dem Bussche, 2017, p. 23). In this context, it is important for businesses to rigorously implement data security policies in AI applications and take necessary measures to protect employees' personal data.

Another important issue in terms of legal aspects of AI applications is the transparency and accountability of algorithmic decisions. It is critical to make it clear how and according to which criteria the decisions made by AI systems are made so that employees can exercise their right to object to these decisions (Jobin et al., 2019,

p. 395). Within the scope of the European Union's AI regulations, transparency and explainability of algorithmic decisions are defined as a legal obligation (European Commission, 2021, p. 12). Therefore, businesses need to ensure the transparency of algorithmic decisions in AI applications and secure employees' right to information and appeal rights regarding these decisions.

As a result, the use of AI technologies in HRM processes brings with it important ethical and legal responsibilities. In order to use these technologies effectively and sustainably, organizations need to carefully address issues such as algorithmic biases, data privacy and transparency, and strictly comply with the relevant legal regulations. In this context, human resources professionals and managers have important roles in managing the ethical and legal dimensions of AI applications.

10. CONTINUOUS MONITORING AND IMPROVEMENT OF ARTIFICIAL INTELLIGENCE APPLICATIONS

Although the integration of AI technologies into HRM processes provides significant advantages for businesses, these technologies need to be continuously monitored and improved in order to sustain their effectiveness. Regular evaluation of the performance of AI systems is critical to ensure the accuracy and fairness of algorithmic decisions (Floridi & Cowls, 2019, p. 7). In this context, it is important for businesses to continuously monitor their AI applications, identify emerging problems and take necessary improvement steps.

Continuous monitoring of AI applications primarily involves evaluating the performance and decision quality of algorithms. It is known that the performance of algorithms may change over time, and systems with initially high accuracy rates may lose performance over time due to changes in data sets (Holm, 2019, p. 26). Therefore, it is necessary to measure the performance of algorithms at regular intervals and analyze the causes of performance decreases. For example, periodic evaluation of the accuracy rates of AI systems used in recruitment processes in candidate selection is important to maintain the effectiveness of the system (Black & van Esch, 2021, p. 220).

Another important issue that should be addressed within the scope of continuous monitoring of AI applications is the detection of algorithmic biases and discrimination risks. Biases in the data sets on which algorithms are trained can lead to systematic discrimination over time (Raghavan et al., 2020, p. 472). Therefore, businesses need to regularly audit the fairness of algorithmic decisions and take necessary measures to mitigate discrimination risks. In this process, it is important to continuously review the data sets used by algorithms in terms of diversity and inclusion (Floridi & Cowls, 2019, p. 9).

Continuous improvement of AI applications includes the activities carried out in order to eliminate the problems identified in the monitoring processes and to improve the performance of the algorithms. In this context, steps such as updating the data sets on which algorithms are trained, retraining algorithmic models, and improving systems in line with user feedback are taken (Holm, 2019, p. 26). For example, continuous updating of AI systems used in performance evaluation processes in line with employee and manager feedback increases the effectiveness of the system (Köchling et al., 2025, p. 1206).

In the processes of continuous monitoring and improvement of AI applications, it is important for businesses to act in accordance with the principles of transparency and accountability. Making it clear how algorithmic decisions are made and securing the rights of employees to obtain information and object to these decisions increase the acceptability of AI applications (Jobin et al., 2019, p. 396). In addition, establishing structures such as ethics committees or independent audit mechanisms in the monitoring and improvement processes of AI applications increases the reliability of the systems and the trust of employees (Floridi & Cowls, 2019, p. 11).

Methods used for continuous monitoring of AI systems include algorithmic auditing and regular monitoring of performance metrics (Raji et al., 2022, p. 33). These methods help to continuously improve the effectiveness and fairness of the systems.

As a result, AI technologies need to be continuously monitored and improved in order to be used effectively and sustainably in HRM processes. In order for businesses to manage these processes effectively, it is important to regularly evaluate algorithmic performance, identify and eliminate algorithmic biases, take user feedback into account and act in accordance with the principles of transparency.

11. LEADERSHIP SUPPORT AND SENIOR MANAGEMENT COMMITMENT IN ARTIFICIAL INTELLIGENCE APPLICATIONS

The successful implementation of AI technologies in organizations is not limited to the establishment of technical infrastructure and processes. The effective adoption and sustainability of these technologies largely depends on leadership support and top management commitment. Top management's explicit support for AI applications positively affects employees' attitudes towards these technologies and increases the success of organizational change (Brock & von Wangenheim, 2019, p. 118).

Top management's commitment to AI applications starts with determining the strategic vision and sharing this vision with employees. The adoption of AI technologies in organizations can often create uncertainty and resistance among employees. Therefore, it is important for top management to clearly and transparently articulate the objectives, expected benefits, and advantages of AI applications to employees

(Fountaine et al., 2019, p. 64). For example, if top management emphasizes that AI applications will reduce employees' workload, enable more objective decisions, and contribute to employees' career development, this will positively shape employees' attitudes towards these technologies (Fountaine et al., 2019, p. 66).

Another important dimension of leadership support is the provision of necessary resources for the realization of AI applications. Top management's provision of financial resources, technical infrastructure and human resources for AI projects is critical for the successful implementation of these projects. In addition, top management's setting clear performance indicators to measure the success of AI applications and regularly monitoring these indicators increases the effectiveness of the applications (Bughin et al., 2018, p. 12-14).

Top management's commitment to AI practices also includes leadership behaviors that support the transformation of organizational culture. In this context, it is important that top management fosters a culture of continuous learning and provides the necessary training and development opportunities for employees to develop their digital competencies. For example, organizing regular training programs to educate employees on AI technologies and developing incentive policies for employees to increase their competencies in these technologies will increase the success of organizational transformation (Wilson & Daugherty, 2018, p. 118-120). Leaders' attitudes towards AI applications directly affect employees' adaptation to these technologies. The explicit support and commitment of top management plays a critical role in the success of AI projects (Westerman et al., 2014, p. 98).

As a result, top management also needs to assume ethical and legal responsibilities for AI applications. Managing ethical issues and legal risks that may arise during the use of AI technologies is the responsibility of top management. Therefore, it is important for top management to continuously monitor the ethical and legal dimensions of AI applications and take necessary measures. Moreover, if top management establishes the necessary mechanisms to ensure transparency and accountability of AI applications, it will increase employees' trust in these technologies (Floridi & Cowls, 2019, p. 9-11). Leadership support and top management commitment are critical for the successful implementation of AI technologies in organizations. Top management's setting a strategic vision, providing the necessary resources, promoting a culture of continuous learning, and assuming ethical responsibilities are key elements that increase the effectiveness and sustainability of AI applications.

12. APPLICATION EXAMPLES IN THE WORLD

The use of AI technologies in HRM processes has been adopted by many organizations around the world and has become widespread with different application examples. In this section, the practical reflections of AI in HRM processes will be revealed by examining some examples of applications in the international literature that have attracted attention in recent years.

One of the most striking examples of the use of AI in recruitment processes is the digital recruitment system implemented by Unilever. Unilever uses the artificial intelligence-based HireVue platform to analyze video interviews of candidates in recruitment processes. This system analyzes candidates' facial expressions, tone of voice and word choices to assess their suitability for the position (Black & van Esch, 2021, p. 218). Thanks to this application, Unilever has saved time and cost in recruitment processes and made candidate evaluation processes more objective.

An example of the use of AI in performance evaluation processes is the Watson Analytics platform developed by IBM. IBM Watson analyzes employee performance data and provides managers with detailed reports on employees' strengths and weaknesses. This system evaluates the performance of employees according to objective criteria and provides managers with more fair and comprehensive evaluation opportunities (Köchling et al., 2025, p. 1204).

An important example of the use of AI in remuneration and reward processes is the wage analytics system implemented by Google. Google uses AI-supported analytical tools to determine employees' wages and ensure pay equity. This system analyzes employee performance data, market wages and internal wage balances, identifies wage inequalities and provides recommendations to managers (Bussin & Christos, 2022, p. 43). With this practice, Google has increased transparency in compensation processes and strengthened employees' perception of fairness.

An example of the use of AI in talent management and career development processes is the career planning system implemented by Amazon. Amazon uses artificial intelligence-based algorithms to create personalized career development plans by analyzing employees' career goals and competencies. This system evaluates the current competencies and future potential of employees and offers them appropriate career opportunities (De Vos et al., 2021, p. 7).

An important example of the use of AI in training and development processes is the personalized training platform implemented by Siemens. By analyzing the individual learning needs of employees, Siemens uses AI-supported learning systems to provide personalized training content. This system continuously monitors employees' interactions with training content and adapts learning processes in real time (Sousa & Rocha, 2019, p. 263). Thanks to this application, Siemens has increased the effectiveness of its training activities and strengthened employees' motivation to learn.

As a result, it is seen that businesses operating in different sectors around the world have achieved significant gains by integrating AI technologies into HRM processes. These application examples clearly demonstrate the potential of AI to increase efficiency, reduce costs and strengthen employee motivation in HRM processes. However, it should be kept in mind that ethical, legal and organizational dimensions should be carefully considered for the successful implementation of these technologies.

CONCLUSION AND EVALUATION

In light of the issues discussed in this chapter, it is seen that the integration of AI into HRM processes poses significant opportunities and challenges for businesses. It is understood that AI increases the effectiveness of basic HRM functions such as recruitment and selection, performance evaluation, compensation and reward, talent management, career development, training and development processes, organizational culture and change management, and makes processes more objective, fast and data-driven (Black & van Esch, 2021, p. 217; Cheng & Hackett, 2021, p. 9; Stahl et al., 2020, p. 10).

The integration of AI technologies into HRM processes saves time and cost in the evaluation and selection of candidates, especially in recruitment processes, and enables more objective and comprehensive evaluations in performance evaluation processes (Albert, 2019, p. 218; Köchling et al., 2025, p. 2208). In remuneration and rewarding processes, it offers significant advantages in terms of ensuring internal and external wage equality and increasing employee motivation (Bussin & Christos, 2022, p. 43). In addition, it enables the creation of personalized career plans by analyzing the competencies and career goals of employees in talent management and career development processes (De Vos et al., 2021, p. 5). In training and development processes, it contributes to the design of training programs suitable for the individual learning needs of employees and to increase the effectiveness of training activities (Sousa & Rocha, 2019, p. 262).

However, the integration of AI technologies into HRM processes brings along some ethical, legal and organizational risks. In particular, the quality and diversity of the data used by algorithms may increase the risk of discrimination and bias in recruitment, performance evaluation and compensation processes (Raghavan et al., 2020, p. 472; Raisch & Krakowski, 2021, p. 197). In addition, data security policies need to be meticulously implemented to protect employees' personal data and to ensure that their privacy rights are not violated (Kaplan & Haenlein, 2020, p. 42). In terms of organizational culture and change management, it is important to consider factors such as employees' attitudes towards AI technologies, digital competencies and job security concerns (Schneider & Leyer, 2019, p. 231).

In this context, in order to successfully integrate AI technologies into HRM processes, businesses need to pay attention to issues such as strategic planning, data management, ethical and legal compliance, continuous monitoring and evaluation. In addition, strong top management support and leadership commitment, developing employees' digital competencies, and fostering a culture of continuous learning stand out as critical factors that increase the success of AI applications (Grover et al., 2022, p. 182; Wilson & Daugherty, 2018, p. 118).

As a result, although the integration of AI technologies into HRM processes offers significant advantages for businesses, ethical, legal and organizational dimensions need to be carefully considered in order to use these technologies effectively and sustainably. In this process, the role of human resources professionals and managers is critical and it is important to manage AI applications with a people-oriented approach and continuous improvement approach.

REFERENCES

Agrawal, A., Gans, J., & Goldfarb, A. (2019). Artificial intelligence: The ambiguous labor market impact of automating prediction. *The Journal of Economic Perspectives*, *33*(2), 31–50. DOI: 10.1257/jep.33.2.31

Albert, E. T. (2019). AI in talent acquisition: A review of AI-applications used in recruitment and selection. *Strategic HR Review*, *18*(5), 215–221. DOI: 10.1108/SHR-04-2019-0024

Black, J. S., & van Esch, P. (2021). AI-enabled recruiting: What is it and how should a manager use it? *Business Horizons*, *64*(2), 215–226. https://doi.org/10.1016/j.bushor.2019.12.001DOI: 10.1016/j.bushor.2019.12.001

Brock, J. K. U., & von Wangenheim, F. (2019). Demystifying AI: What digital transformation leaders can teach you about realistic artificial intelligence. *California Management Review*, *61*(4), 110–134. DOI: 10.1177/1536504219865226

Brynjolfsson, E., & Mcafee, A. N. D. R. E. W. (2017). The business of artificial intelligence. *Harvard Business Review*, *7*(1).

Bughin, J., Seong, J., Manyika, J., Chui, M., & Joshi, R. (2018). Notes from the AI frontier: Modeling the impact of AI on the world economy. McKinsey Global Institute Discussion Paper, 1-48.

Bussin, M., & Christos, D. (2022). How to link TALENT MANAGEMENT and REMUNERATION. *HR Future*, (4), 42–44.

Cappelli, P., & Tavis, A. (2016). *Performance management revolution: The future of performance reviews*. Harvard Business Review Press.https://hbr.org/2016/10/the-performance-management-revolution

Cascio, W., & Boudreau, J. (2010). *Investing in people: Financial impact of human resource initiatives*. Ft Press.

Chamorro-Premuzic, T., Akhtar, R., & D'Annunzio, P. (2019). The Future of Work: AI in Recruitment and Selection. Psychology Today.

Chatterjee, S., Rana, N. P., Dwivedi, Y. K., & Baabdullah, A. M. (2021). Understanding AI adoption in manufacturing and production firms using an integrated TAM-TOE model. *Technological Forecasting and Social Change*, *170*, 120880. DOI: 10.1016/j.techfore.2021.120880

Cheng, M. M., & Hackett, R. D. (2021). A critical review of algorithms in HRM: Definition, theory, and practice. *Human Resource Management Review, 31*(1), 100698. DOI: 10.1016/j.hrmr.2019.100698

Collings, D. G., Mellahi, K., & Cascio, W. F. (2019). Global talent management and performance in multinational enterprises: A multilevel perspective. *Journal of Management, 45*(2), 540–566. DOI: 10.1177/0149206318757018

Dastin, J. (2018). Amazon scraps secret AI recruiting tool that showed bias against women. Reuters. https://www.reuters.com/article/us-amazon-com-jobs-automation-insight-idUSKCN1MK08G

Davenport, T. H., & Ronanki, R. (2018). Artificial intelligence for the real world. *HBR'S 10 MUST*, 67.

De Vos, A., Jacobs, S., & Verbruggen, M. (2021). Career transitions and employability. *Journal of Vocational Behavior, 126*, 1–13. DOI: 10.1016/j.jvb.2020.103475

Dulebohn, J. H., & Johnson, R. D. (2013). Human resource metrics and decision support: A classification framework. *Human Resource Management Review, 23*(1), 71–83. DOI: 10.1016/j.hrmr.2012.06.005

European Commission. (2021). Proposal for a regulation laying down harmonised rules on artificial intelligence (Artificial Intelligence Act). Brussels: European Commission. https://eur-lex.europa.eu/legal-content/EN/TXT/?uri=CELEX%3A52021PC0206

European Commission. (2023). *General Data Protection Regulation (GDPR): Official guidelines and regulations.* Retrieved from https://ec.europa.eu/info/law/law-topic/data-protection_en

Floridi, L. (2019). Establishing the rules for building trustworthy AI. *Nature Machine Intelligence, 1*(6), 185–186. DOI: 10.1038/s42256-019-0055-y

Floridi, L., & Cowls, J. (2019). A unified framework of five principles for AI in society. *Harvard Data Science Review, 1*(1), 1–15. DOI: 10.1162/99608f92.8cd550d1

Fountaine, T., McCarthy, B., & Saleh, T. (2019). Building the AI-powered organization. *Harvard Business Review, 97*(4), 62–73.

Grover, P., Kar, A. K., & Dwivedi, Y. K. (2022). Understanding artificial intelligence adoption in operations management: Insights from the review of academic literature and social media discussions. *Annals of Operations Research, 308*(1), 177–213. DOI: 10.1007/s10479-020-03683-9

Hmoud, B., & Laszlo, V. (2019). Will artificial intelligence take over human resources recruitment and selection? *Network Intelligence Studies, 7*(13), 21–30.

Holm, E. A. (2019). In defense of the black box. *Science, 364*(6435), 26–27. DOI: 10.1126/science.aax0162 PMID: 30948538

Holmes, W., Bialik, M., & Fadel, C. (2019). *Artificial intelligence in education: Promises and implications for teaching and learning*. Center for Curriculum Redesign.

Iansiti, M., & Lakhani, K. R. (2020). Competing in the age of AI: Strategy and leadership when algorithms and networks run the world. Harvard Business Review Press, 60-75.

Jobin, A., Ienca, M., & Vayena, E. (2019). The global landscape of AI ethics guidelines. *Nature Machine Intelligence, 1*(9), 389–399. DOI: 10.1038/s42256-019-0088-2

Kaplan, A., & Haenlein, M. (2020). Rulers of the world, unite! The challenges and opportunities of artificial intelligence. *Business Horizons, 63*(1), 37–50. DOI: 10.1016/j.bushor.2019.09.003

Kirkpatrick, J. D., & Kirkpatrick, W. K. (2023). *Kirkpatrick's four levels of training evaluation* (2nd ed.). ATD Press.

Köchling, A., & Wehner, M. C. (2020). Discriminated by an algorithm: A systematic review of discrimination and fairness by algorithmic decision-making in the context of HR recruitment and HR development. *Business Research, 13*(3), 795–848. DOI: 10.1007/s40685-020-00134-w

Köchling, A., Wehner, M. C., & Ruhle, S. A. (2025). This (AI) n't fair? Employee reactions to artificial intelligence (AI) in career development systems. *Review of Managerial Science, 19*(4), 1195–1228. DOI: 10.1007/s11846-024-00789-3

Lawler, E. E., & Boudreau, J. W. (2009). *Achieving excellence in human resources management: An assessment of human resource functions*. Stanford University Press.

Lee, C. K. H., Suh, A., Roy, D., & Baucus, M. (2019). Emerging technology and business model innovation: The case of artificial intelligence. *Journal of Open Innovation, 5*(3), 1–13. DOI: 10.3390/joitmc5030044

Manyika, J., Chui, M., Miremadi, M., Bughin, J., George, K., Willmott, P., & Dewhurst, M. (2017). *Harnessing automation for a future that works*. McKinsey Global Institute.

Noe, R. A., & Kodwani, A. D. (2018). *Employee training and development, 7e*. McGraw-Hill Education.

Raghavan, M., Barocas, S., Kleinberg, J., & Levy, K. (2020). Mitigating bias in algorithmic hiring: Evaluating claims and practices. Proceedings of the 2020 Conference on Fairness, Accountability, and Transparency (FAT* '20), 469-481. https://doi.org/DOI: 10.1145/3351095.3372828

Raisch, S., & Krakowski, S. (2021). Artificial intelligence and management: The automation–augmentation paradox. *Academy of Management Review*, *46*(1), 192–210. DOI: 10.5465/amr.2018.0072

Raji, I. D., Smart, A., White, R. N., Mitchell, M., Gebru, T., Hutchinson, B., & Smith-Loud, J. (2022). *Closing the AI accountability gap: Defining an end-to-end framework for internal algorithmic auditing. Proceedings of the 2022 ACM Conference on Fairness, Accountability, and Transparency*, 33-44.

Schneider, S., & Leyer, M. (2019). Me or information technology? Adoption of artificial intelligence in the delegation of personal strategic decisions. *MDE. Managerial and Decision Economics*, *40*(3), 223–231. DOI: 10.1002/mde.2982

Sharma, A., & Sharma, T. (2017). HR analytics and performance appraisal system: A conceptual framework for employee performance improvement. *Management Research Review*, *40*(6), 684–697. DOI: 10.1108/MRR-04-2016-0084

Shrestha, Y. R., Ben-Menahem, S. M., & von Krogh, G. (2019). Organizational decision-making structures in the age of artificial intelligence. *California Management Review*, *61*(4), 66–83. DOI: 10.1177/0008125619862257

Sousa, M. J., & Rocha, Á. (2019). Skills for disruptive digital business. *Journal of Business Research*, *94*, 257–263. DOI: 10.1016/j.jbusres.2017.12.051

Stahl, G. K., Brewster, C. J., Collings, D. G., & Hajro, A. (2020). Enhancing the role of human resource management in corporate sustainability and social responsibility: A multi-stakeholder, multidimensional approach to HRM. *Human Resource Management Review*, *30*(3), 1–16. DOI: 10.1016/j.hrmr.2019.100708

Taddeo, M., & Floridi, L. (2018). How AI can be a force for good. *Science*, *361*(6404), 751–752. DOI: 10.1126/science.aat5991 PMID: 30139858

Tambe, P., Cappelli, P., & Yakubovich, V. (2019). Artificial intelligence in human resources management: Challenges and a path forward. *California Management Review*, *61*(4), 15–42. DOI: 10.1177/0008125619867910

Voigt, P., & Von dem Bussche, A. (2017). *The EU General Data Protection Regulation (GDPR): A practical guide*. Springer International Publishing., DOI: 10.1007/978-3-319-57959-7

Wang, Y., & Hajli, N. (2017). Exploring the path to big data analytics success in healthcare. *Journal of Business Research, 70*, 287–299. DOI: 10.1016/j.jbusres.2016.08.002

Westerman, G., Bonnet, D., & McAfee, A. (2014). *Leading digital: Turning technology into business transformation*. Harvard Business Press.

Wilson, H. J., & Daugherty, P. R. (2018). Collaborative intelligence: Humans and AI are joining forces. *Harvard Business Review, 96*(4), 114–123.

Chapter 6
Bridging the Gap Through the Integration of AI and Emotional Intelligence to Enhance CSR Initiatives

Saadet Nur Karadenizli Sinap
http://orcid.org/0000-0002-2908-2172
Hacettepe University, Turkey

Vahid Sinap
http://orcid.org/0000-0002-8734-9509
Ufuk University, Turkey

ABSTRACT

This chapter explores the strategic integration of Artificial Intelligence (AI) and Emotional Intelligence (EI) within Corporate Social Responsibility (CSR) practices. While AI enhances efficiency through data-driven insights, it lacks emotional depth and ethical awareness. EI complements this gap by fostering empathy, ethical reflection, and stakeholder sensitivity. Grounded in stakeholder theory, institutional theory, and organizational learning, the chapter presents a framework where AI and EI operate in synergy to strengthen CSR's ethical foundation and relational impact. By illustrating how emotionally intelligent leadership and responsible innovation can align with technological advancement, this chapter contributes to both theoretical development and practical application in responsible business transformation.

DOI: 10.4018/979-8-3693-4099-8.ch006

INTRODUCTION

In the era of digital transformation, organizations are increasingly required to balance technological innovation with human-centered values. Within this evolving context, EI has emerged as a vital competency, enabling employees to navigate complex interpersonal dynamics, collaborate effectively across diverse teams, and make ethically grounded decisions. EI encompassing skills such as self-awareness, empathy, emotional regulation, and social awareness are no longer perceived merely as a personal trait but as a strategic organizational asset (Ikart, 2023; Ruisel, 1992). EI enhances leadership effectiveness, cultivates cohesive teamwork, and strengthens stakeholder trust while improving individual performance, a vital combination in contemporary business contexts where ethical practices and social responsibility shape organizational reputation. However, alongside the growing emphasis on EI, AI has rapidly advanced into key areas of organizational functioning, including talent management and CSR. AI excels at processing massive datasets, uncovering patterns, generating predictive insights, and automating routine or complex decision-making processes (Khan, 2024). These capabilities make it an attractive solution for organizations seeking efficiency, scalability, and evidence-based decision-making in their strategic and operational domains. Yet, herein lies a fundamental paradox: while AI can optimize processes and provide analytical precision, it lacks the emotional depth and ethical intuition that are central to meaningful human interaction and socially responsive leadership.

This paradox presents a profound organizational challenge. As CSR evolves from philanthropic gestures to a core strategic imperative, the role of EI becomes even more significant. CSR initiatives today are expected to be transparent, accountable, and inclusive, aiming to build long-term stakeholder relationships, address societal needs, and contribute to environmental sustainability (Ashurov et al., 2024; Wang et al., 2021). In this environment, emotionally intelligent employees and leaders demonstrate stronger capacity to interpret stakeholder needs, address societal issues compassionately, and develop CSR approaches that balance strategic rigor with emotional authenticity and ethical validity (Ahsan, 2023; Odame et al., 2020). Yet, the growing reliance on AI to enhance CSR practices introduces a critical limitation: AI systems, no matter how sophisticated, operate based on data-driven logic and computational models that lack the capacity to feel, intuit, or morally reflect. While AI tools can efficiently track sustainability metrics, forecast social risks, or automate CSR reporting, they are fundamentally incapable of understanding human emotions, engaging in authentic dialogue with communities, or making context-sensitive ethical judgments (Zhou, 2023). This technological limitation underscores a widening gap between the mechanical efficiency of AI and the human-centric essence of CSR. This tension raises important strategic questions for contemporary organizations:

How can AI be deployed without undermining the emotional and ethical qualities that are essential to CSR? Can technology and empathy coexist within the same decision-making frameworks? What happens when the emotional labor traditionally carried out by humans is replaced by algorithms that cannot experience emotion?

The core argument of this chapter is that organizations must not choose between AI and EI, but instead, seek a synergistic integration that allows both to complement each other. Rather than viewing AI as a substitute for human intelligence, it should be leveraged as a tool to enhance EI within the workforce by identifying EI gaps, personalizing training programs, and measuring the relational and social outcomes of CSR efforts. In doing so, companies can create organizational ecosystems that are both data-informed and emotionally intelligent, capable of achieving efficiency without compromising empathy, and pursuing innovation without losing sight of ethical responsibility.

Research Problem and Objectives

While AI is increasingly employed to enhance the efficiency and scalability of CSR efforts, the absence of EI in algorithmic decision-making poses critical limitations for stakeholder engagement, ethical alignment, and social impact. This chapter seeks to explore how AI and EI can be synergistically integrated to strengthen CSR outcomes. By doing so, it contributes to an emerging body of knowledge that emphasizes the importance of balancing technological capability with human sensibility in shaping the future of sustainable and responsible business practices.

The core objectives of this chapter are as follows:

- To explore the role of EI in sustaining the ethical and emotional integrity of CSR initiatives,
- To examine the ways in which AI can support CSR through enhanced data analysis, risk forecasting, and decision support,
- To analyze how organizations can strategically integrate AI and EI to foster more impactful, accountable, and stakeholder-responsive CSR strategies,
- To identify the ethical challenges, organizational tensions, and governance implications of AI-EI integration in CSR contexts.

In addressing these objectives, this chapter is structured into six main sections. Following the introduction, the second section traces the strategic evolution of CSR in organizational contexts, emphasizing its foundational role in promoting accountability and stakeholder engagement. The third section examines the expanding role of AI in CSR, supported by theoretical insights and empirical examples. The fourth section delves into the critical importance of EI in ensuring the effectiveness and ethical grounding of CSR activities. The fifth section offers a comprehensive framework for integrating AI and EI to optimize CSR outcomes. Finally, the concluding section synthesizes key findings and offers implications for both theory development and practical implementation. By examining the convergence of technology, emotion, and ethics, this chapter provides meaningful contributions to academic research while guiding organizations through the challenges of responsible innovation.

THE EVOLUTION AND STRATEGIC ROLE OF CSR IN CONTEMPORARY ORGANIZATIONS

CSR cannot be merely regarded as a philanthropic activity or a public relations strategy. Rather, CSR represents a strategic approach that shapes both societal development and the long-term success of organizations. In this context, social, environmental, and ethical issues have begun to take precedence over traditional economic objectives in today's business world. This shift is of vital importance not only for the sustainability of organizations but also for the well-being of societies and the future of the planet. As renowned management theorist Peter Drucker (1996) also noted, while economic factors have dominated the business agenda over the past 40–50 years, it is anticipated that social factors will play a much more decisive role in the future. Within this framework, CSR emerges as a multidimensional field of analysis at the theoretical level, and as an institutional obligation in practice, requiring organizations to integrate their social responsibilities into strategic decision-making processes.

Conceptual Foundations of CSR

The existence of various definitions of CSR in the literature reflects the multifaceted nature of the concept as well as the increasingly deep interaction between theory and practice (Arouri & Pijourlet, 2017). One of the earliest scholars to define CSR, Bowen (1953) argued that businesspeople should develop policies that align with societal values and expectations, framing this approach as the social responsibility of business. According to Bowen, CSR is shaped within a framework where organizations are expected to respond to economic goals, as well as social and ethical values. This definition establishes the core principle of CSR and emphasizes that corporate decisions should be based on economic rationale, ethical concerns, and social responsibilities. Kilcullen and Ohles Kooistra (1999), on the other hand, argue that CSR involves the entire business world, not just executives. Their perspective positions CSR as a societal obligation, underscoring that all actors within the business ecosystem must contribute to this responsibility. They highlight that CSR is a responsibility that applies to entire industries and society as a whole, beyond individual organizations. The World Business Council for Sustainable Development (2000) offers a more comprehensive definition of CSR. According to this view, CSR is presented as an ethical commitment that enhances the quality of life and contributes to development. This definition emphasizes that CSR involves fulfilling an organization's obligations to society, the environment, and its employees in a comprehensive way. CSR aims to foster positive change both in the business world and in society.

CSR represents a management approach that encompasses the relationships organizations build with all their stakeholders, ranging from customers and employees to suppliers, competitors, local communities, investors, and public authorities. Within this framework, the core components of CSR include initiatives focused on social benefit, practices that promote employment, the establishment of sustainable relationships with employees, environmental sensitivity, corporate governance processes, and financial responsibility (Khoury et al., 1999). These developments show that CSR has evolved from being merely an ethical obligation to becoming a legal requirement for organizations in fulfilling their societal responsibilities. Since the 1960s, particularly within the American business context, legal regulations aimed at protecting workers' rights and consumer safety have supported the evolution of CSR. Legislations such as the Fair Packaging and Labeling Act of 1960, the Equal Pay Act of 1963, the National Environmental Policy Act of 1969, and the Clean Air Act of 1970 have shaped organizational responsibilities toward society within a legal, rather than solely voluntary, framework (Moura-Leite & Padgett, 2011). Frederick (1960) emphasized the inadequacy of approaches that prioritize only the narrow interests of individuals or private organizations, arguing instead for the allocation of resources in alignment with broader societal goals. In line with this perspective, it is essential for organizations to maintain their operations, generate economic profit, and contribute to social stability, cohesion, and public trust (Drucker, 1954).

The Historical Development of CSR and Its Role in the Modern Business World

CSR is not a concept that emerged solely in the modern era; its historical roots can be traced back to ancient civilizations. Provisions related to labor rights in Sumerian tablets, the emphasis on commercial responsibilities in the Code of Hammurabi dating back to 1800 BCE, and Aristotle's reflections on business ethics laid the early foundations of CSR. These ancient texts reveal the initial traces of ethical responsibility in business, and over time, these responsibilities have evolved through broader social and economic interactions.

With the Industrial Revolution, the growth of large-scale industrial production and organizational expansion made it imperative to improve workers' living conditions. One of the prominent figures of this period, though not fully appreciated in his time, was Robert Owen. He initiated systematic efforts to enhance workers' living standards and is regarded as one of the early advocates of CSR. Owen made a significant moral contribution to CSR by arguing that employers have economic responsibilities and social obligations (Carrasco, 2007). By the late 19th century, business leaders such as Andrew Carnegie and John D. Rockefeller reinforced this understanding through philanthropy and social initiatives. Carnegie argued for the use of wealth in service of the public good, while Rockefeller contributed to society through his support for the fight against poverty and disease. These influential industrialists demonstrated that CSR could serve as a powerful force for societal welfare and progress (Bahri, 2023). However, in the aftermath of World War II, CSR had yet to become a strategic priority for many companies. In the 1950s, Frank Abrams, an executive at Standard Oil Company, asserted that businesses had an ethical responsibility toward society (Abrams, 1951). Nevertheless, in the 1970s, economist Milton Friedman famously contended that businesses were only responsible for maximizing shareholder value. Freeman's (1984) Stakeholder Theory later broadened this perspective by arguing that organizations should be accountable to shareholders, employees, customers, society, and the environment. These developments highlight that businesses should be evaluated based on their economic performance, ethical conduct, and level of social responsibility. As Farcane and Bureana (2015) emphasize, in modern society, it is crucial for organizations to act as "corporate citizens." Today, businesses are expected to go beyond profit maximization and adopt a structure that contributes to society, upholds environmental responsibility, and respects ethical values.

By the end of the 20th century, the rise of sustainability transformed CSR into a strategic orientation for businesses. Sustainability began to include environmental, social, and economic dimensions. In line with this understanding, the "Triple Bottom Line" (TBL) approach emerged, rejecting the notion that a business's success should be measured solely by its economic performance. Instead, it promotes a three-dimensional perspective in which organizations assess their environmental impact (planet), social contributions (people), and financial performance (profit). The TBL approach advocates that businesses should consider profit, as well as their contributions to society and the environment. This represents a significant strategic transformation that enables CSR to be implemented more systematically within organizations. Based on the triad of "Profit, People, Planet," this model encourages companies to operate in a more holistic manner. Organizations aim for economic success as well as environmentally and socially sustainable development. The adoption of the TBL framework has allowed CSR to be employed more broadly as a strategic tool. This strategy enables companies to evaluate their long-term success from a financial standpoint, along with social and environmental sustainability. Thus, CSR becomes a strategy that reinforces the sustainability of organizations, society, and the planet. Today, limited resources, ecological imbalances, and rising societal expectations have made sustainability a fundamental strategic objective for organizations. CSR is no longer merely an ethical obligation but is recognized as an integral part of long-term strategic planning. This transformation highlights the integration of CSR into organizational strategies and its role in gaining competitive advantage. Moreover, strong evidence suggests that CSR practices positively influence employee engagement. Participation in social responsibility projects enhances job satisfaction and organizational commitment (Silva et al., 2023). Research indicates that CSR initiatives strengthen employees' sense of belonging to their workplace, reducing their intention to leave (Yassin & Beckmann, 2024). Additionally, an effective CSR strategy increases organizational resilience during times of crisis. Strong ties with the community and adherence to ethical values enhance corporate reputation, securing stakeholder support in adverse situations, an essential factor for long-term sustainability.

In the current labor market, where talent has become scarce and highly valuable, organizations are compelled to integrate talent management with CSR strategies. Employees increasingly prefer to work in organizations that demonstrate social responsibility and uphold ethical values (Hsieh et al., 2022). This trend gives companies an advantage in attracting and retaining top talent. CSR practices contribute to the formation of high-performing teams by boosting organizational commitment and employee satisfaction (Mai et al., 2023). Furthermore, CSR significantly strengthens corporate brand image, thereby enhancing customer loyalty. Today's consumers are concerned with product quality and the socially responsible activities of brands. This shift in consumer behavior leads to a greater preference for socially conscious brands and a willingness to pay premium prices for their products (Shimul & Cheah, 2023). Moreover, effective CSR implementation enables companies to enhance their brand image and expand their market share. When companies align their actions with societal expectations, they foster stronger customer loyalty and cultivate a dedicated customer base, contributing to sustainable growth in the long run. In today's context, CSR is not just an ethical responsibility but a vital tool for achieving organizational strategic goals. From employee engagement to brand image, customer loyalty to corporate resilience, CSR generates positive outcomes across various domains, making it indispensable for long-term success. In this regard, adopting CSR as a strategic priority can enable organizations to achieve sustainable growth and development.

LEVERAGING AI IN CSR

The integration of AI into CSR reshapes how organizations pursue sustainability, equity, and profitability. Technologies such as machine learning, predictive analytics, natural language processing, and autonomous systems provide tools to strengthen CSR's strategic focus, ethical foundation, and societal contributions. By enabling precise data analysis, proactive governance, and efficient operations, AI redefines the ethical and strategic contours of responsible business practices. This section examines AI's role in CSR through a theoretical lens, grounding its impact in frameworks like stakeholder theory, shared value creation, institutional theory, and responsible innovation.

Stakeholder Theory and Data-Driven CSR

Stakeholder theory (Freeman, 1984) fundamentally reshapes corporate accountability by expanding organizational obligations beyond shareholders to encompass multiple constituencies from employees and communities to supply chains, consumers, and natural environments. This theory positions the firm as a socially embedded entity whose legitimacy and long-term success depend on its ability to manage interdependent relationships with these stakeholder groups. Rather than treating stakeholder engagement as a peripheral concern, stakeholder theory integrates it into the core strategic and ethical framework of the organization. Building on this foundation, Jones and Wicks (1999) propose a convergent stakeholder theory, aligning moral duties with practical gains, showing that responsible management of stakeholder ties fosters long-term competitive edge.

AI applied to stakeholder management marks a significant advancement in translating the principles of stakeholder theory into practical organizational action. AI technologies enable firms to analyze vast quantities of unstructured data, such as social media posts, online reviews, employee feedback, and community discourse. These technologies offer a level of analytic granularity and speed that traditional tools cannot match. By identifying patterns in stakeholder sentiment and behavior, AI allows organizations to understand evolving concerns with greater accuracy and responsiveness. This capability is particularly valuable in volatile environments where stakeholder expectations shift rapidly and demand real-time engagement.

The relevance of AI to stakeholder theory becomes more pronounced when viewed through the lens of stakeholder salience, a framework proposed by Mitchell, Agle, and Wood (1997), which suggests that stakeholders should be prioritized based on their possession of power, legitimacy, and urgency. AI systems can assist in mapping these dimensions by analyzing digital expressions of stakeholder activity such as the intensity of social media activism or the frequency of sustainability-related complaints, thereby informing managerial decisions on which issues require immediate attention. Importantly, this also enables the identification of marginalized stakeholders, such as small-scale suppliers or local environmental groups, whose voices are often underrepresented in traditional decision-making processes. By amplifying these perspectives, AI contributes to more inclusive CSR strategies, thereby advancing the moral imperatives of stakeholder theory.

Beyond fostering inclusive practices, AI's strategic role in CSR resonates with Porter and Kramer's (2011) shared value creation framework. Shared value refers to policies and operating practices that enhance the competitiveness of a company while simultaneously advancing the social and economic conditions of the communities in which it operates. AI contributes to this dual objective by facilitating the analysis of consumer preferences, sustainability trends, and societal needs. Predictive analytics, for instance, can guide the development of eco-friendly products that appeal to values-driven consumers, enhancing competitive advantage while generating societal benefits demonstrating AI's dual role as both a catalyst for principled business practices and strategic innovation.

Empirical evidence supports this synergy between AI-enabled analytics and stakeholder-centric CSR. Bechtsis et al. (2022) demonstrate that organizations leveraging data-driven stakeholder insights exhibit higher levels of stakeholder trust, brand equity, and reputational resilience. Integrating advanced analytics into CSR frameworks plays a critical role in strengthening stakeholder engagement and building durable organizational legitimacy over time. However, these advantages depend on AI systems being developed and implemented responsibly. Without proper safeguards, algorithmic bias can marginalize vulnerable groups, misrepresent stakeholder voices, and ultimately undermine the inclusive ethos promoted by stakeholder theory. This reinforces the imperative for governance mechanisms that ensure transparency, fairness, and accountability in AI applications principles that are essential to upholding Freeman's original vision of inclusive and ethically sound stakeholder capitalism.

Institutional Theory and Predictive CSR

Institutional theory offers a powerful lens for understanding how organizations align their structures and practices with the norms, values, and expectations of their broader social and regulatory environments. DiMaggio and Powell's (1983) institutional theory argues that organizations balance economic rationality with conformity to institutional norms when pursuing legitimacy. These pressures manifest through three mechanisms of isomorphism: coercive (legal and regulatory requirements), mimetic (imitation of industry peers in response to uncertainty), and normative (professional standards and cultural expectations). Such an approach positions CSR as an institutional obligation reflecting prevailing standards of appropriate corporate behavior, beyond being a matter of choice or conscience.

The integration of AI into CSR can be interpreted as a technologically mediated response to these institutional pressures. AI tools equip firms with the capability to anticipate and respond to emerging regulatory shifts, social norms, and stakeholder demands with greater agility. For example, machine learning models can simulate future policy developments in areas such as carbon emissions, labor rights, or supply chain transparency, enabling firms to preemptively adapt their CSR strategies. This approach enables organizations to meet current normative expectations while simultaneously establishing themselves as forward-looking, credible entities for key stakeholders including regulators, investors, and community members. Such AI-enabled foresight aligns with the concept of dynamic capabilities, an extension of the resource-based view, which refers to an organization's ability to integrate, build, and reconfigure internal and external resources to address rapidly changing environments (Teece et al., 1997). When applied to CSR, dynamic capabilities may involve redirecting investments toward renewable energy, optimizing logistics to reduce environmental impact, or realigning workforce development in response to shifting labor expectations. AI serves as a catalyst in this process by transforming vast datasets into actionable foresight, thus enhancing the organization's capacity to adapt to its CSR practices in a timely and informed manner.

The strategic value of aligning AI-based forecasting tools with corporate sustainability goals becomes evident in how these technologies enhance decision-making processes. By enabling scenario modeling and comprehensive risk assessments, such systems support more informed approaches to capital allocation and investment planning within CSR frameworks (Adekunle et al., 2023). These predictive capabilities allow organizations to anticipate environmental and social challenges, proactively adjust their strategies, and better align with long-term sustainability objectives such as carbon neutrality and resource efficiency. However, the effectiveness of these tools is inherently dependent on the quality of input data, the transparency of algorithmic processes, and the interpretability of model outcomes. Without these foundational elements, predictive systems risk generating misleading insights, thereby compromising the integrity and strategic coherence of CSR initiatives. Scott's (2014) analysis reveals that institutional legitimacy requires genuine congruence with societal expectations, transcending mere performative compliance. If AI systems are based on incomplete or biased data, they may lead organizations to pursue ill-informed or superficial CSR initiatives that ultimately erode trust and legitimacy rather than reinforce it. Thus, while institutional theory explains the why behind CSR adaptation, AI provides the how the technological infrastructure through which firms can operationalize institutional responsiveness. The combination of institutional sensitivity and algorithmic foresight creates new opportunities for responsible innovation but also raises new governance challenges. Firms must anticipate institutional transformations while rigorously examining the ethical and social consequences of the technologies driving these changes.

Automation and Sustainable Entrepreneurship

Automation within corporate operations constitutes a pivotal dimension of AI, carrying substantial implications for innovation and entrepreneurship aligned with sustainability goals. This growth parallels sustainable entrepreneurship theory, emphasizing business solutions that harmonize wealth creation with planetary and societal wellbeing (Schaltegger & Wagner, 2011). Unlike traditional entrepreneurial models that prioritize short-term profit maximization, sustainable entrepreneurship embraces a broader value proposition one that aligns business goals with long-term ecological and social well-being. This paradigm is closely related to Elkington's (1997) triple bottom line framework, which advocates for measuring organizational success across three dimensions: economic, environmental, and social performance. In this context, automation, manifested through autonomous systems, robotics, and AI-driven process optimization, plays a critical role in advancing sustainability objectives. In manufacturing and logistics, intelligent systems can dynamically adjust production volumes, streamline supply chains, and reduce energy consumption, thereby minimizing environmental externalities. These applications embody the principle of eco-efficiency, defined by Dyllick and Hockerts (2002) as the ability to deliver greater value with fewer ecological resources. Moreover, AI-powered automation supports the ethos of frugal innovation, which prioritizes cost-effective, resource-conserving solutions that are especially valuable in emerging markets or under resource constraints (Escudero-Cipriani et al., 2024).

Beyond operational efficiency, automation can also free up human labor from repetitive tasks, allowing organizations to reallocate talent toward higher-value activities such as community engagement, CSR program development, or social innovation initiatives. Automation functions as both an environmental safeguard and a catalyst for enhanced societal engagement. However, this dual benefit is not automatic. Drawing from the resource-based view (RBV) of the firm, automation yields competitive advantage only when it is embedded in complementary organizational resources such as human capital, absorptive capacity, and ethical leadership (Cohen & Levinthal, 1990). If introduced without adequate planning or consideration of social consequences, automation can lead to labor displacement, deepen inequalities, and generate new ethical dilemmas. This tension necessitates deliberate CSR interventions, particularly in the form of workforce reskilling, inclusive technology governance, and transparent stakeholder dialogue. Organizations that adopt proactive strategies for workforce reskilling and transition are more likely to sustain public trust and institutional legitimacy throughout digital transformation processes, as emphasized in recent reviews of local government technology adoption strategies (David et al., 2023). Furthermore, this aligns with Hart's (1995) natural-resource-based view, which argues that sustainable competitive advantage can arise from capabilities that address environmental and social imperatives. Automation, when guided by a principled commitment to sustainability and social justice, can serve as a transformative force within CSR. However, achieving these demands strong governance frameworks to prevent efficiency improvements from undermining fundamental human rights and social equity.

Responsible Innovation and Ethical Governance

The concept of responsible innovation provides a normative framework for aligning technological advancement with societal values, ethical principles, and democratic governance. Drawing from science and technology studies, responsible innovation emphasizes reflexive, inclusive, and anticipatory practices to align emerging technologies with both economic and societal value creation (Von Schomberg, 2013). Within the context of CSR, this framework urges firms to consider the broader implications of deploying AI, particularly its potential to affect issues such as equity, transparency, accountability, and human rights.

The ethical complexities associated with AI are manifold. The vast amounts of data processed by AI systems raise pressing concerns about privacy, surveillance, and consent, especially when stakeholder information is collected without clear guidelines or informed permissions. Furthermore, algorithmic bias can disproportionately harm marginalized populations, skew decision-making processes, and ultimately undermine the inclusive goals of CSR. These risks call for deliberate ethical oversight mechanisms within firms, including the development of AI ethics boards, transparency protocols, and multi-stakeholder review processes to assess the societal consequences of AI applications in CSR activities. This ethical imperative resonates with Carroll's (1991) CSR pyramid, which conceptualizes corporate responsibility as a multi-layered construct, encompassing economic, legal, ethical, and philanthropic dimensions. Responsible innovation particularly reinforces the ethical and philanthropic layers by advocating that firms go beyond compliance and profit-seeking behavior to actively promote social justice, inclusion, and environmental stewardship. This perspective requires AI to go beyond streamlining CSR operations. It must actively strengthen marginalized groups, ensure fair resource distribution, and protect democratic principles.

A critical extension of this discussion is the notion of corporate citizenship, as articulated by Matten and Crane (2005), which positions corporations as quasi-political actors with responsibilities akin to those of democratic institutions. In deploying

AI firms increasingly make decisions that affect civil rights, resource distribution, and public discourse. Therefore, corporate engagement in AI-driven CSR must incorporate deliberative accountability, where decisions are made transparently, in consultation with affected stakeholders, and in accordance with normative social contracts. Moreover, the environmental footprint of AI itself, particularly the high energy consumption associated with training large machine learning models, poses a paradox for sustainability-oriented CSR. As Strubell et al. (2019) highlight, the carbon emissions of AI systems can negate environmental gains achieved in other areas, unless mitigated through green computing practices and renewable energy sourcing. These findings advocate for circular CSR analysis, where technological interventions are appraised for their core functionality while mapping their network of ecological and social repercussions. Responsible innovation must be operationalized through governance structures that embed stakeholder participation, ensure algorithmic accountability, and foster a culture of ethical awareness within firms (Camilleri, 2024). Without such institutional scaffolding, the deployment of AI in CSR risks becoming performative rather than transformative. Thus, responsible innovation serves as both a theoretical foundation and a practical imperative for aligning technological progress with the evolving expectations of society, ensuring that AI becomes a vehicle for deep, systemic, and inclusive corporate responsibility.

Practical Manifestations of AI in CSR

The exploration of AI in CSR centers on theoretical inquiry, yet real-world applications illuminate how frameworks like stakeholder theory, shared value creation, institutional theory, sustainable entrepreneurship, and responsible innovation translate into measurable outcomes. From supply chain algorithms to smart energy systems, AI breathes life into theoretical models by harmonizing cutting-edge solutions with accountable stewardship and community impact. This section examines these examples to show how AI reshapes CSR, emphasizing the need for principled implementation to uphold its commitment to fairness and sustainability.

Sustainable Sourcing and Shared Value Creation

In practice, AI has played a pivotal role in transforming how companies manage sustainable sourcing across complex supply chains. For example, Nestlé has implemented AI-driven analytics platforms to monitor environmental and social indicators at various points in its cocoa and coffee supply networks. These systems process satellite imagery, local farm data, and third-party certification records to detect risks related to deforestation, child labor, and water scarcity. When irregularities are identified, such as sudden land use changes or yield anomalies, automated alerts are generated, prompting field-level audits or supplier engagement programs. This allows for rapid intervention before issues escalate, ensuring both compliance and continuity in ethically sensitive operations.

In another instance, Unilever has employed AI tools to optimize sourcing decisions for raw materials such as palm oil and soy. Through predictive modeling that incorporates climate data, geopolitical trends, and supplier performance histories, the company has been able to diversify its sourcing base and reduce reliance on high-risk regions. These technologies create a virtuous cycle environmental safeguards through spatial analytics translate into operational reliability and enhanced corporate standing. Smaller enterprises have also adopted AI-powered sourcing strategies. For example, some fashion brands now use natural language processing to assess supplier reputation based on open-source reports, social media content, and NGO publications. This digital vetting process helps these companies identify suppliers who align with their sustainability values, even in the absence of formal certifications. In turn, the visibility provided by such systems strengthens accountability and encourages continuous improvement among vendors striving to remain competitive within sustainability-conscious markets.

Predictive Modeling for Energy Transition and Institutional Legitimacy

In the renewable energy sector, predictive modeling serves as a manifestation of institutional theory, which posits that legitimacy is closely tied to societal expectations (DiMaggio & Powell, 1983). Companies in the energy sector, as analyzed in the International Energy Agency (IEA, 2025) report, use AI to forecast grid demands, optimize energy storage, and integrate renewable sources like solar and wind. These AI models anticipate consumption shifts, aligning production with net-zero goals and earning credibility with regulators and environmental advocates. This adaptability connects to dynamic capabilities, where firms reconfigure resources to navigate change (Teece et al., 1997). Companies like Ørsted are investing in battery storage technologies rather than fossil fuels, achieving a 15% reduction in emissions annually for certain grids, thus accelerating the global energy transition (Voldsgaard & Rüdiger, 2022). Nevertheless, the reliance on accurate data and clear forecasting methodologies is critical, as flawed predictions could waste resources and erode trust, a concern raised by Scott (2014) in institutional analysis.

Retail Automation and Sustainable Entrepreneurship

Retail automation, exemplified by Walmart's real-time inventory systems, reflects sustainable entrepreneurship, which merges profitability with ecological and societal objectives (Schaltegger & Wagner, 2011). AI in this context monitors stock levels, curbing overstocking and reducing waste from unsold perishables. Algorithms that analyze purchase trends and regional preferences optimize delivery routes, minimizing emissions while maintaining low operational costs. This illustrates eco-efficiency, which aims to deliver business value with minimal environmental impact (Dyllick & Hockerts, 2002), alongside frugal innovation, which scales resource-smart practices (Escudero-Cipriani et al., 2024). Furthermore, automation frees up staff to engage in community-driven initiatives, such as charity partnerships, enhancing the company's social contributions (Elkington, 1997).

Future Imperatives in AI-Driven CSR

The incorporation of AI into CSR signifies a transformative shift that transcends mere operational optimization, reaching into the strategic and moral foundations of business (Zhang & Yang, 2024). As AI systems increasingly guide decisions related to environmental impact, stakeholder engagement, and supply chain governance, organizations must ensure that these technologies are deployed within frameworks that prioritize transparency, inclusivity, and long-term societal alignment (Marchegiani, 2023). The imperative is no longer merely to adopt AI for CSR, but to do so in ways that reinforce trust, anticipate systemic risks, and avoid the unintended reproduction of bias or harm. These demands are transforming governance frameworks to ensure algorithmic transparency, participatory design methods that amplify underrepresented voices, and leadership that harmonizes technical expertise with moral foresight (Camilleri, 2024). Furthermore, as the environmental footprint of AI becomes more apparent, companies must embed ecological responsibility into digital strategies to preserve the integrity of their sustainability claims (Podile et al., 2024). Ultimately, the future of CSR in an AI-driven world hinges not on the sophistication of the tools themselves, but on the institutional courage and foresight with which they are governed. Yet AI's constraints in domains demand moral discernment, empathetic engagement, and human-centric judgment underscore the necessity for balancing competencies. Here, EI proves vital for enriching CSR's principled foundations, interpersonal dimensions, and transformative influence (Zhao & Gómez Fariñas, 2023).

EI AS A DRIVER OF CSR EFFECTIVENESS

CSR is a strategy for gaining competitive advantage, fulfilling social obligations, and carries an ethical dimension shaped by human values. At this point, the human factor, which constitutes the foundation of organizations comes to the forefront.

The level of EI possessed by individuals becomes a crucial element determining the quality and success of CSR practices. EI refers to an individual's ability to accurately perceive both their own emotions and those of others, manage these emotions effectively, and utilize them in decision-making processes (Bar-On, 1997; Mayer & Salovey, 1997). The presence of employees and managers with high EI is vital in implementing CSR initiatives through an empathetic and ethical approach. According to Goleman (1995), high EI enhances environmental awareness and social responsibility consciousness. The success of CSR practices depends less on mechanically following corporate strategies and more on enriching these strategies with a human-oriented perspective.

At this juncture, it is necessary to examine more closely the key components that constitute EI. EI is defined as a multidimensional set of competencies that individuals can develop through learning, and it is structured around five core elements: self-awareness, self-regulation, intrinsic motivation, empathy, and social skills (Goleman, 1995; Boyatzis & Sala, 2004). These elements support individuals' capacity development while also ensuring the effective implementation of CSR. Self-awareness refers to the ability of individuals to recognize their own emotions and understand how these emotions influence their behavior (Tamunomiebi & Owhorji, 2018). Individuals with high self-awareness are better able to align their personal values with organizational values, thereby internalizing CSR policies more quickly and sincerely. Self-regulation, on the other hand, entails the ability to control emotions and impulses, especially in high-pressure situations, and to make thoughtful and ethical decisions (Rojas-Saffie & García-Matte, 2024). This competence lays the foundation for behavioral consistency that ensures adherence to CSR principles even during times of crisis.

Intrinsic motivation refers to an individual's drive to act based on their internal values and search for meaning, without seeking external rewards (Fishbach & Woolley, 2022). As emphasized by Lievens and Chan (2017) and Pant and Yadav (2016), this type of internal drive fosters a high level of engagement and commitment, particularly in CSR initiatives aimed at generating social benefit. Such individuals approach social responsibility projects as a way of creating personal meaning and value, not just as a task. Similarly, the skill of empathy enables individuals to understand the emotions and needs of others and to develop appropriate and sensitive behaviors accordingly (Ratka, 2018). This competency enhances the social dimension of CSR by helping organizations that interact with the broader community to better understand their social stakeholders and to develop more responsive policies. Social skills, on the other hand, refer to the ability to communicate effectively in interpersonal contexts, demonstrate a collaborative attitude, and generate cooperative solutions in diverse social settings (Notari et al., 2014). These skills play a critical role in the sustainable execution of CSR initiatives involving both internal and external stakeholders. Employees with well-developed social skills contribute significantly to both the perceived and actual success of CSR by effectively managing internal coordination and external representation.

Theoretical Links Between EI and CSR

The relationship between EI and CSR behaviors is interpreted within the organizational behavior literature through various psychosocial theories, offering a theoretical framework for understanding this connection. In this context, Social Exchange Theory and Attachment Theory serve as an explanatory function in elucidating the link between individuals' levels of EI and their approach to CSR practices. According to Social Exchange Theory, individuals evaluate their social relationships and participation on the basis of mutual benefit (Homans, 1961). From this perspective, when employees perceive that their organization values them, acts with sensitivity, and adopts a socially responsible outlook, they tend to develop a sense of commitment and are more likely to engage willingly and voluntarily in CSR activities. Among individuals with high EI, this process tends to emerge more strongly and sustainably. Components of EI, such as empathy, self-awareness, and intrinsic motivation, shape the expectation of mutual benefit in both material and meaningful terms (Antonopoulou, 2024).

Complementing this theoretical framework, Attachment Theory explains the quality of emotional bonds that individuals form with their organizations, asserting that this bond directly influences their level of participation in CSR processes (Bowlby, 1982). Employees who build a trust-based relationship with their organization approach social responsibility projects with genuine commitment and make meaningful contributions that go beyond their formal job descriptions (Bulińska-Stangrecka & Bagieńska, 2021). These contributions go beyond professional responsibilities, encouraging employees to engage in volunteer activities within and outside the organization, take active roles in social initiatives that benefit society, and reflect the organization's ethical stance to external stakeholders. This situation also lays the groundwork for the proliferation of voluntary and supportive behaviors that fall under the scope of Organizational Citizenship Behavior (OCB). Employees with high EI integrate their sense of organizational belonging with commitment and social contribution awareness, thereby participating in CSR activities more sincerely and sustainably (Liu et al., 2024).

Emotional Factors in CSR Engagement

CSR initiatives inherently transcend formal job descriptions, requiring employees' voluntary contributions, emotional commitment, and intrinsic motivation. At this point, the impact of EI on CSR processes becomes more comprehensible, particularly within the framework of the concept of "emotional labor." Hochschild (1983) defines emotional labor as the effort to control, express, or suppress emotions within one's social or professional roles. In this context, individuals with high EI are better equipped to manage this process consciously and effectively, developing the ability to express emotions with genuine understanding and authenticity. When combined with the emotional behavior known as "deep acting," this competence facilitates participation in CSR projects with a true sense of belonging and responsibility, rather than for visibility (Khan et al., 2021).

Most CSR practices involve activities such as volunteering, donations, social aid, and environmental awareness domains that align closely with employees' personal values and require emotional engagement. The effectiveness of such initiatives depends on organizational planning and the EI levels of those involved in implementation (Najimi et al., 2021). Emotionally intelligent individuals demonstrate profound commitment to CSR projects. Alongside technical outcomes, they prioritize the human dimensions and ethical consistency inherent in the implementation phase. This multidimensional sensitivity enhances both the internal integrity of CSR and its perceived value among external stakeholders. Therefore, EI increases voluntary participation, strengthens the perceived effectiveness of CSR, and contributes significantly to organizational reputation.

Emotional and Digital Transformation in CSR

As the EI competencies of individuals increase at the organizational level, this individual capacity gradually evolves into a collective organizational competency (Kaur & Hirudayaraj, 2021). This transformation influences individual behavior and reshapes organizational decision-making processes, stakeholder relations, and the overall understanding of CSR. In organizations where emotionally intelligent individuals constitute the majority, empathy-based communication, ethical sensitivity, and social awareness become core elements of the organizational culture (Arghode et al., 2022). Within this context, the formation of a "high EI organization" allows for more sensitive, sustainable, and responsibility-driven decisions towards internal stakeholders, society, the environment, and other external stakeholders. Thus, EI transcends being merely an individual psychological competency, emerging as a strategic resource that enhances the organization's capacity to generate social value. Emotionally intelligent employees uphold ethical standards, promote teamwork, participate voluntarily in social projects, and lead the formation of an organizational climate that enhances corporate reputation.

A particularly noteworthy development in this context is the integration of EI with next-generation technologies such as AI. The unification of human-centered approaches with digital systems will expand the scope of CSR practices and foster more qualitative and empathetic environments for interaction. Especially in decision support systems, aligning human-centered empathetic perceptions with digital processes can promote ethical, transparent, and sustainable approaches within organizations. This integration is expected to go beyond data-driven methodologies and contribute to the development of value-oriented organizational structures, while simultaneously positioning EI as a strategic competitive factor in institutional systems. EI has become a core component of organizational sustainability, both in contemporary CSR practices and broader digital transformation processes, acting as an ethical compass for future developments.

SYNERGISTIC INTEGRATION OF AI AND EI IN ADVANCING CSR OUTCOMES

The use of AI-based systems in CSR practices is creating a significant transformation in data-driven decision-making processes. However, the ability of these systems to ensure corporate legitimacy and generate social impact is not limited to technical accuracy alone. Supporting AI's analytical capacity with an EI-focused approach is crucial in designing decision-making processes that prioritize empathetic communication, ethical evaluation, and consideration of social context (Ashkanasy et al., 2017). Integrating AI analysis with EI creates a powerful synergy enabling both systematic categorization of stakeholder input and nuanced interpretation of its emotional undertones. In this regard, for instance, an algorithm's analysis of environmental impact data, when complemented by an emotional interpretation of how communities experience and perceive these impacts, results in a multilayered corporate responsibility consciousness. Freeman's stakeholder theory reveals that effective engagement requires analyzing both stakeholder statements and their underlying emotional states (Freeman et al., 2010).

The bridge established between Goleman's EI components (self-awareness, social awareness, relationship management) and the outputs of algorithmic analyses creates a new intuitive layer in organizational learning processes. For CSR to achieve its goal of generating social value, this intuitive layer must guide technical outputs. Interpreting AI-identified trends through EI's relational literacy enables the development of reactive solutions as well as those that are proactive and contextual (Goleman, 1995). This integration also necessitates a restructuring of leadership practices. Managers equipped with EI can evaluate AI-generated insights as strategic resources that guide empathetic decision-making processes. Consequently, CSR transcends technical accuracy, evolving into a multidimensional governance model infused with societal sensitivity. The integrated use of AI and EI enhances CSR's accountability and offers new perspectives on social inclusivity, ethical awareness, and sustainable trust relationships. This approach redefines CSR, moving it beyond a data-centric strategy to a multifaceted platform for societal interaction.

The Transformative Potential of AI-EI Integration in CSR

The simultaneous and holistic integration of AI and EI into CSR processes significantly enhances organizations' capacity to transform their societal functions. This integration reshapes operational efficiency, data-driven predictive capabilities, and the sensitivity of corporate decisions to emotional contexts. In this regard, transformation can be theoretically evaluated through three main axes: the deepening of ethical interactions, the intuitive analysis of social complexity, and the reproduction of corporate social capital.

Firstly, AI's big data analytics enables the quantitative tracking and pattern recognition of stakeholder behaviors, while EI uncovers the emotional and cultural layers of meaning behind these patterns (Salovey & Mayer, 1990). In multi-stakeholder environments, such as global supply chains or multicultural workforces, analyzing both the content and the emotional tone of stakeholder responses significantly enhances the perceived legitimacy and social acceptance of CSR policies (Buhmann & Fieseler, 2021). EI helps make sense of quantitative data and enables the reflection of stakeholders' voices, sensitivities, and expectations in corporate strategies from a more holistic perspective. This contribution plays a decisive role in managing rapidly changing social demands and enhancing an organization's capacity to generate societal resonance. At this point, the concept of emotional value creation emerges, moving beyond the traditional notion of "shared value" creation (Porter & Kramer, 2011). Emotional value creation refers to a form of responsibility that addresses stakeholders' rational expectations, emotional connections to corporate processes, their sense of perceived justice, and their psychological sense of belonging. EI, positioned at the core of this process, ensures that CSR deepens in terms of social benefit production and in fostering emotional integrity and relational trust (Zhu, 2025).

The integration of AI and EI enables the addressing of societal issues at both a symptomatic level and in conjunction with their structural causes, thereby providing a deeper perspective on corporate responsibility. When considered within the framework of Parsons' social systems theory, which emphasizes the symbiotic relationship between institutions and their environments, AI facilitates the rapid processing of signals from societal systems, while EI allows these signals to be interpreted within their historical context and socio-cultural fabric (Parsons, 1951). For example, the analytical evaluation of carbon emission data, supported by the social empathy provided by EI, enables companies to structure both their environmental and societal responsibilities more coherently (Goleman et al., 2013). This multilayered analytical capability encourages the repositioning of CSR as not just a reputation strategy but as an integral part of organizational learning and social responsibility ethics.

The relationship management and social awareness dimensions of EI serve as a critical balancing factor, ensuring that AI-based decision systems operate in alignment with human-centered principles. Particularly when considering the impacts of automation and digitalization on the workforce, EI-supported governance models are indispensable in designing fair transition policies, reskilling strategies, and inclusive communication processes for employees. When evaluated within the framework of Hart's (1995) natural resource-based view of the firm, this highlights that sustainable competitive advantage is linked to both environmental factors and social responsibility capacity.

From an organizational theory perspective, the contribution of this integration to corporate social capital cannot be overlooked. In line with Coleman's (1988) social capital theory, the strengthening of mutual trust, normative alignment, and communication channels is made possible by activating EI within an organizational context. When the speed and scalability advantages offered by AI are combined with EI's empathetic interpretive capacity, organizations gain depth in their relationships with both external and internal stakeholders (employees, unions, community representatives). This enhances social impact and facilitates the dynamic reconstruction of corporate legitimacy.

The strategic and ethical integration of AI and EI transforms the role of CSR within organizational structures from a mere technical function into something far greater. This transformation enables organizations to become more responsive, inclusive, and accountable at both the systemic and emotional-cognitive levels. Consequently, it lays the groundwork for CSR to fulfill its mission of generating societal value in a more profound and sustainable manner.

Harmonized System Design and Ethical Algorithm Development

The effective and ethical use of AI systems in CSR depends on algorithmic accuracy, technical efficiency, and the extent to which these technologies are designed in alignment with organizational values, societal norms, and EI-supported ethical sensitivity. While integrating AI into decision-support processes provides organizations with advantages such as strategic foresight, large-scale analytical capabilities, and rapid adaptation, the responsible use of these advantages requires the presence of a specific ethical architecture. Therefore, ethical algorithm design should be approached as a multilayered process that includes technological, normative, managerial, and societal dimensions.

The development of ethical algorithms must first be grounded in a framework that addresses the questions of "whom they serve," "which values they prioritize," and "what kinds of outcomes they produce." In this context, Von Schomberg's (2013) concept of "responsible innovation" emphasizes the need to embed normative orientations in technological design processes. This approach suggests that AI systems should be evaluated for their contributions to long-term societal well-being, sense of justice, and democratic values, in addition to their technical success. In the context of CSR practices, such algorithms should respond to stakeholder demands while also being held accountable for avoiding the reproduction of societal inequalities, preventing the exclusion of vulnerable groups, and fostering greater inclusivity in decision-making processes (Stahl, 2021). At this point, the social awareness and empathy skills provided by EI play a complementary role in ensuring the ethical oversight of algorithmic systems. An EI-based approach enables a focus on the statistical accuracy of algorithmic outputs as well as the emotional and social experiences of individuals and communities affected by these outputs (Wong, 2020). Consequently, in applications such as performance analyses based on employee satisfaction or the classification of customer feedback, algorithms can be designed to produce decisions shaped by contextual sensitivities rather than superficial generalizations.

The design of ethical algorithms is directly linked to the principles of transparency, explainability, and accountability. The "AI ethical principles" proposed by Floridi and Cowls (2019), including responsibility, autonomy, harm minimization, and justice, serve as fundamental normative reference points that must be considered at every stage of system design. Systems aligned with these principles comply with regulations and foster the integration of an ethical governance culture into organizational practices. However, for these principles to be truly effective, the decision logic of algorithms must be structured in a traceable and explainable manner. Otherwise, the "black box" nature of algorithmic decisions can undermine the trust of internal stakeholders and lead to scrutiny of corporate legitimacy among external stakeholders (Mittelstadt et al., 2016). In this context, the ethical design process of AI systems necessitates a multidisciplinary organizational structure that includes technical experts, decision-makers equipped with EI, human resources professionals, legal experts, and stakeholder representatives. Such a structure ensures that algorithms are tested for technical accuracy as well as social sensitivity, thereby contributing to the formation of decision-making processes that are more socially acceptable (Jobin et al., 2019). Particularly in applications like CSR, which have a high public impact, the ability of algorithms to operate within ethical boundaries plays a decisive role in the sustainability of corporate responsibility.

Issues such as AI's energy consumption, data privacy violations, and algorithmic biases must also be evaluated within the framework of ethical system design. Bender et al. (2021) highlights the environmental footprint of large language models, revealing that AI's claims of environmental sustainability may contradict practical realities. These contradictions necessitate the structuring of CSR practices with a holistic perspective. Similarly, the risk of algorithmic biases reinforcing societal inequalities should be treated as an ethical responsibility domain, rather than merely a technical flaw (Crawford, 2021). The contribution of EI in this context lies in making the experiences of disadvantaged groups visible and ensuring their voices are considered in algorithm design.

In the context of CSR, harmonious system design requires a synthesis of technical expertise and ethical sensitivity, analytical inferences and empathetic intuition, and corporate strategy and societal values. This synthesis produces responsible algorithms and enables the reconstruction of organizations in the digital age based on trust, transparency, and accountability (Taddeo & Floridi, 2018). In this regard, ethical algorithm development should be reimagined as the technological embodiment of corporate conscience, instead of a tool in the future of CSR.

Organizational Learning, Leadership, and the Future of CSR

One of the core dynamics behind the transformative paradigm offered by the integration of AI and EI in the context of CSR is the effective embedding of these technological and emotional competencies into organizational learning processes. Argyris and Schön's (1997) double-loop learning framework posits that sustainable organizational change requires both policy evaluation and fundamental reassessment of the core beliefs shaping those policies. The integration of AI's data-driven analysis and EI's human-centric understanding creates an adaptive knowledge framework, allowing organizations to simultaneously reassess both operational ecosystems and institutional mindsets. This flexibility brings about a learning capacity that extends beyond mere technical innovations, reshaping corporate ethics, leadership approaches, and the culture of social responsibility.

In an organizational environment where AI and EI are jointly operationalized, the leadership approach also diverges from traditional norms, becoming more rooted in ethical intuition, empathy, and systemic thinking. Transformational leadership theory (Bass, 1985) frames leaders as both strategic architects and cultural catalysts who reshape organizational value systems. Transformational leaders, by integrating the data power provided by AI with the meaning and contextual insight offered by EI, can develop more inclusive and effective CSR policies that consider the emotional motivations, value orientations, and societal sensitivities of individuals within the organization. This leadership approach also elevates the "philanthropic responsibility" level at the top of Carroll's (1991) CSR pyramid to domains where technical and ethical decisions converge, transforming voluntary contributions into strategic and value-driven actions. However, organizational learning processes are not limited to leadership alone; they are multidimensional, drawing from interactions with all organizational stakeholders. When assessed within Nonaka and Takeuchi's (1996) knowledge creation model (SECI), the "externalization" phase involves the codification of technical knowledge through AI-based analyses, while the "internalization" phase integrates EI-driven empathetic awareness into individual sensemaking processes. This cyclical process influences both personal learning trajectories and collective institutional memory, fostering increasingly adaptive, coherent, and enduring CSR methodologies. Furthermore, in line with this knowledge creation model, collective learning mechanisms developed through the participation of employees and other internal stakeholders enable organizations to internalize social responsibility not as a "project" but as a "culture."

The synergy of AI and EI in organizational learning and leadership processes reduces resistance to corporate change and enables organizations to systematically enhance their performance based on environmental, social, and governance (ESG) indicators. The key point is that this integration supports data-driven decision-making while transforming the organizational value system by aligning decisions with their ethical, social, and emotional dimension. In the internalization of sustainable development goals by businesses, incorporating environmental and economic analyses, alongside social impact assessments and stakeholders' emotional responses, requires the strategic use of EI (Sachs, 2015).

The next-generation organizational learning processes and leadership styles shaped by the combined application of AI and EI ensure that CSR transcends being merely a corporate reflex responding to external demands. This transformation repositions CSR as a governance paradigm that both places it at the core of organizational identity and integrates societal benefit creation with strategic objectives (Elkington, 1997). Within this framework, the integrated CSR approach, shaped by the convergence of technology and emotion, data and intuition, and analysis and meaning, makes organizations more accountable, responsive, adaptable, and ethically grounded (Ocasio et al., 2018). The corporate future will secure its societal legitimacy and sustainability to the extent that it internalizes this integrated learning and leadership approach.

AI-EI Asymmetry: The Dialectic Between Technological Rationality and Human Judgment

The core tension between AI and EI in CSR practices stems from the ontological mismatch between the structural determinism of technological systems and the dialectical nature of social interactions (Tretter, 2024). This asymmetry deepens, particularly between AI's claim to data-driven objectivity and the complexity of the contextual and emotional variables required by EI, compelling organizations into a continuous search for balance between technological rationality and human intuition (Ghotbi, 2023). AI systems' pattern recognition and optimization solutions, based on large datasets, often fail to fully comprehend the multidimensional nature of social reality, which can lead to ethical dilemmas in critical areas such as supply chain management, customer relations, and employee policies (Sandel, 2020). For instance, a supply chain optimization algorithm focused on cost minimization may overlook the socio-economic structure of local communities, or automated customer service systems, while providing technically accurate responses, may damage brand reputation by failing to establish empathetic connections (Wu, 2024).

Overcoming this epistemological tension requires a transformation that goes beyond a mere technical optimization problem and demands a profound shift in organizational learning and governance paradigms. Incorporating EI components into AI system design is crucial for detecting algorithmic biases and systematically embedding human values in corporate decision-making mechanisms (Tretter, 2024). In this context, the synergy between AI and EI in CSR practices requires conceptualizing technological tools as "learning systems" adaptable to social contexts, supported by human-centered ethical frameworks (Partnership on AI, 2021). Particularly in stakeholder engagement processes, combining AI's data analytics with EI's capacity for contextual interpretation enables the development of holistic solutions that maintain operational efficiency while considering social sensitivity. Ultimately, managing this asymmetry becomes a critical measure of an organization's ability to balance technological capacity with social responsibility during digital transformation processes. In the absence of AI-EI alignment, CSR practices risk losing legitimacy and trust, even if they result in efficiency gains (Ghotbi, 2023; Wu, 2024). Therefore, the future of CSR largely lies in the hands of organizations capable of synthesizing these two forms of intelligence integrating technological progress with human values. The success of this synthesis hinges on strengthening technical infrastructure and transforming organizational cultures and leadership approaches to align with this holistic vision (Zhao & Gómez Fariñas, 2023).

CONCLUSIONS AND IMPLICATIONS FOR THEORY AND PRACTICE

This chapter has explored the intersection of AI, EI, and CSR as mutually influential components in contemporary organizational systems. It has been argued that while AI brings unprecedented analytical and operational capacities to CSR initiatives it lacks the capacity for empathy, ethical judgment, and emotionally nuanced engagement, which are essential to human-centered and socially impactful CSR practices. EI, conversely, fills this void by enabling employees and leaders to navigate the ethical complexities of stakeholder engagement, support inclusive decision-making, and foster socially responsible behavior.

The theoretical foundation of this analysis is grounded in socio-technical systems theory and augmented by stakeholder theory, both of which emphasize the dynamic interplay between technological advancement and human values. The 'Theoretical Model of AI, EI, and CSR Synergy' presented in Figure 1 developed in this chapter illustrates how organizations can orchestrate a symbiotic integration of AI and EI to enhance CSR performance. This model conceptualizes AI as a structural enabler and EI as a relational moderator, converging on CSR outcomes that are ethically grounded, emotionally resonant, and strategically effective.

Figure 1. Theoretical model of AI, EI, and CSR synergy

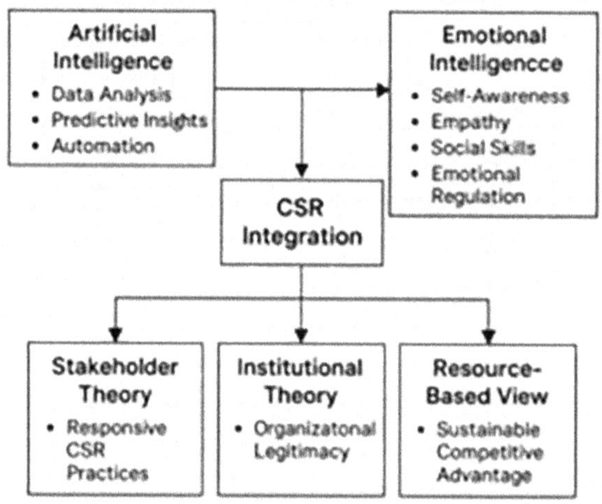

From a theoretical standpoint, the integration of AI and EI into CSR reflects a multidimensional alignment across stakeholder theory, institutional theory, the RBV, and organizational learning. Stakeholder theory (Freeman, 1984) highlights the ethical duty of firms toward diverse actors, and while AI enhances analytical precision in mapping stakeholder needs, it is EI that brings emotional depth and inclusivity to engagement, particularly by informing the legitimacy, urgency, and power dimensions outlined in the stakeholder salience model (Mitchell et al., 1997). Similarly, institutional theory (DiMaggio & Powell, 1983) underscores the importance of conforming to societal norms; here, AI enables real-time adaptation, but EI ensures authenticity and moral resonance, bridging the gap between symbolic compliance and substantive legitimacy (Scott, 2014). From the RBV and its natural-resource-based extension (Hart, 1995), AI becomes a competitive asset when complemented by EI-driven capabilities such as empathy, trust-building, and ethical reflection, enhancing absorptive capacity (Cohen & Levinthal, 1990) and fostering social capital (Coleman, 1988). These insights align with the framework of responsible innovation (Von Schomberg, 2013), which calls for ethically designed AI systems shaped by EI-informed leadership to avoid bias and ensure inclusivity. Finally, through the lens of double-loop learning (Argyris & Schön, 1997), AI provides analytical insights and predictive capabilities, while EI fosters reflective practice and ethical discourse together enabling organizations to evolve CSR strategies that balance data-driven rigor with human-centered values.

In practical terms, the integration of AI and EI into CSR practices opens actionable pathways for organizational leaders, policymakers, and practitioners seeking to create more inclusive, responsive, and ethically robust systems of social responsibility. Digital transformation initiatives must be approached holistically, where the development of AI tools is closely aligned with emotional and ethical learning processes. Stakeholder mapping technologies require co-design with emotionally intelligent practitioners, ensuring algorithmic models capture both quantitative salience metrics and the nuanced emotional needs of diverse stakeholder populations. Similarly, CSR performance systems should incorporate affective indicators such as trust, perceived fairness, and emotional engagement to evaluate the resonance of corporate initiatives beyond technical success metrics. The emotional blindness of AI systems, if left unaddressed, can reinforce social inequities and erode stakeholder trust. Therefore, the design of ethical algorithms must be informed by inclusive, participatory approaches that center EI as a mediating force between computational precision and human impact. Establishing interdisciplinary AI ethics committees that include technical experts, EI-aware managers, social scientists, and stakeholder representatives can help align algorithmic logic with broader justice and accountability frameworks. This convergence also calls for a transformation in leadership and organizational culture, where technical acumen is complemented by empathetic insight. Leaders must cultivate the ability to interpret AI-generated insights not as neutral outputs but as socially embedded signals, requiring reflection, deliberation, and contextual sensitivity. Embedding AI-EI synergy into organizational learning models, particularly those informed by double-loop learning can facilitate adaptive, resilient, and value-driven CSR strategies that evolve with shifting societal expectations. CSR must evolve beyond rigid compliance checklists and fragmented initiatives to become a living governance framework rooted in EI and adaptive responsiveness. When mediated through the dual lenses of technology and empathy, CSR becomes a living system of value co-creation, ethical innovation, and trust cultivation, positioning organizations as socially responsive institutions in an increasingly complex and interconnected world.

Managerial Implications and Recommendations

To translate the theoretical insights into actionable strategies, the following managerial recommendations are proposed:

- EI assessments and training modules should be integrated into leadership development, onboarding, and performance management systems. This ensures that CSR decision-makers possess the emotional competencies necessary for ethical judgment, stakeholder sensitivity, and value-driven engagement.
- Internal review boards or ethics committees should be established to evaluate AI algorithms used in CSR planning and reporting. These mechanisms should ensure transparency, accountability, and adherence to ethical standards, particularly when AI is used in interactions with vulnerable communities or sensitive social issues.
- Decision-making structures should be designed to intentionally combine AI-generated insights with human empathy and ethical reasoning. For example, while AI may suggest optimal CSR resource allocations, final decisions should be made by cross-functional teams trained in EI to ensure ethical soundness and stakeholder alignment.
- AI-based tools such as sentiment analysis, natural language processing, and behavioral analytics should be employed to detect potential EI deficiencies in teams responsible for CSR initiatives. The insights gained should be used to tailor development pathways and enhance emotional capacity in ethical leadership.
- In addition to quantitative KPIs (e.g., carbon emissions reduced, volunteer hours logged), qualitative indicators capturing stakeholder trust, emotional engagement, and community sentiment should be included. These EI-informed metrics can offer a more comprehensive view of CSR impact.
- Collaboration between AI developers, CSR strategists, and HR professionals should be encouraged to design systems that reflect both computational precision and human values. Such interdisciplinary collaboration can help ensure AI tools are contextually aware and emotionally intelligent.
- The role of AI in CSR should be revisited regularly to ensure alignment with evolving organizational values and societal expectations. Stakeholder feedback loops, emotional climate surveys, and ethical audits should inform continuous improvements in AI-supported CSR frameworks.

The convergence of AI and EI in CSR represents a paradigm shift redefining the very foundations of CSR for the digital age through both conceptual innovation and practical transformation. This synthesis provides a roadmap for a new generation of CSR practices that are technologically agile, ethically reflexive, emotionally grounded, and systemically inclusive. By situating this integration within robust theoretical foundations and aligning it with actionable organizational strategies, this chapter offers both a conceptual advancement and a practical guide for scholars and practitioners navigating the complexity of responsible business in the 21st century. The future of CSR will be shaped more by the EI and ethical leadership guiding algorithms than by their technical complexity alone.

REFERENCES

Abrams, F. W. (1951). Management's responsibilities in a complex world. *Harvard Business Review*, *29*(3), 29–34.

Adekunle, B. I., Chukwuma-Eke, E. C., Balogun, E. D., & Ogunsola, K. O. (2023). Integrating AI-driven risk assessment frameworks in financial operations: A model for enhanced corporate governance. *International Journal of Scientific Research in Computer Science. Engineering and Information Technology*, *9*(6), 445–464.

Antonopoulou, H. (2024). The value of emotional intelligence: Self-awareness, self-regulation, motivation, and empathy as key components. *Technium Education and Humanities*, *8*, 78–92. DOI: 10.47577/teh.v8i.9719

Arghode, V., Lathan, A., Alagaraja, M., Rajaram, K., & McLean, G. N. (2022). Empathic organizational culture and leadership: Conceptualizing the framework. *European Journal of Training and Development*, *46*(1/2), 239–256. DOI: 10.1108/EJTD-09-2020-0139

Argyris, C., & Schön, D. A. (1997). Organizational learning: A theory of action perspective. *Revista Española de Investigaciones Sociológicas*, (77/78), 345–348. DOI: 10.2307/40183951

Arouri, M., & Pijourlet, G. (2017). CSR performance and the value of cash holdings: International evidence. *Journal of Business Ethics*, *140*(2), 263–284. DOI: 10.1007/s10551-015-2658-5

Ashkanasy, N. M., Humphrey, R. H., & Huy, Q. N. (2017). Integrating emotions and affect in theories of management. *Academy of Management Review*, *42*(2), 175–189. DOI: 10.5465/amr.2016.0474

Ashurov, S., Musse, O. S. H., & Abdelhak, T. (2024). Evaluating corporate social responsibility in achieving sustainable development and social welfare. *BRICS Journal of Economics*, *5*(2), 77–102. DOI: 10.3897/brics-econ.5.e121429

Bahri, S. (2023). Long history of corporate social responsibility (CSR). In *Proceeding International Conference on Economics, Business Management, and Accounting (ICOEMA)*-2023 (Vol. 2, pp. 457–465).

Bar-On, R. (1997). *The Emotional Quotient Inventory (EQ-i): Technical manual.* Multi-Health Systems.

Bass, B. M. (1985). *Leadership and performance beyond expectations.* Free Press.

Bechtsis, D., Tsolakis, N., Iakovou, E., & Vlachos, D. (2022). Data-driven secure, resilient and sustainable supply chains: Gaps, opportunities, and a new generalised data sharing and data monetisation framework. *International Journal of Production Research, 60*(14), 4397–4417. DOI: 10.1080/00207543.2021.1957506

Bender, E. M., Gebru, T., McMillan-Major, A., & Shmitchell, S. (2021). On the dangers of stochastic parrots: Can language models be too big? *Proceedings of the 2021 ACM Conference on Fairness, Accountability, and Transparency*, 610–623. DOI: 10.1145/3442188.3445922DOI: 10.1145/3442188.3445922

Bowen, Z. (1953). *Bowen. HR,(1953), Social Responsibilities of the Businessman.* Harper & Row.

Bowlby, J. (1982). Attachment and loss: Vol. 1. *Attachment* (2nd ed.). Basic Books.

Boyatzis, R. E., & Sala, F. (2004). Assessing emotional intelligence competencies. In Geher, G. (Ed.), *The measurement of emotional intelligence: Common ground and controversy* (pp. 147–180). Nova Science.

Buhmann, A., & Fieseler, C. (2021). Towards a deliberative framework for responsible innovation in artificial intelligence. *Technology in Society, 64*, 101475. DOI: 10.1016/j.techsoc.2020.101475

Bulińska-Stangrecka, H., & Bagieńska, A. (2021). The impact of employee training and development on tacit knowledge transfer and the mediating role of trust. *International Journal of Learning and Change, 13*(4-5), 474–489. DOI: 10.1504/IJLC.2021.116668

Camilleri, M. A. (2024). Artificial intelligence governance: Ethical considerations and implications for social responsibility. *Expert Systems: International Journal of Knowledge Engineering and Neural Networks, 41*(7), e13406. DOI: 10.1111/exsy.13406

Carrasco, I. (2007). Corporate social responsibility, values, and cooperation. *International Advances in Economic Research, 13*(4), 454–460. DOI: 10.1007/s11294-007-9110-2

Carroll, A. B. (1991). The pyramid of corporate social responsibility: Toward the moral management of organizational stakeholders. *Business Horizons, 34*(4), 39–48. DOI: 10.1016/0007-6813(91)90005-G

Cohen, W. M., & Levinthal, D. A. (1990). Absorptive capacity: A new perspective on learning and innovation. *Administrative Science Quarterly, 35*(1), 128–152. DOI: 10.2307/2393553

Coleman, J. S. (1988). Social capital in the creation of human capital. *American Journal of Sociology*, *94*(Supplement), 95–120. DOI: 10.1086/228943

Crawford, K. (2021). *Atlas of AI: Power, politics, and the planetary costs of artificial intelligence*. Yale University Press., DOI: 10.2307/j.ctv1ghv45t

David, A., Yigitcanlar, T., Li, R. Y. M., Corchado, J. M., Cheong, P. H., Mossberger, K., & Mehmood, R. (2023). Understanding local government digital technology adoption strategies: A PRISMA review. *Sustainability (Basel)*, *15*(12), 9645. DOI: 10.3390/su15129645

DiMaggio, P. J., & Powell, W. W. (1983). The iron cage revisited: Institutional isomorphism and collective rationality in organizational fields. *American Sociological Review*, *48*(2), 147–160. DOI: 10.2307/2095101

Drucker, P. F. (1954). *The practice of management*. Collins. (Reprinted 2006)

Drucker, P. F. (1996). *Yönetim uygulaması* (Yarmalı, E. S., Trans.). İnkilap Kitabevi.

Dyllick, T., & Hockerts, K. (2002). Beyond the business case for corporate sustainability. *Business Strategy and the Environment*, *11*(2), 130–141. DOI: 10.1002/bse.323

Elkington, J. (1997). *Cannibals with forks: The triple bottom line of 21st century business*. Capstone., DOI: 10.1002/tqem.3310080106

Escudero-Cipriani, C., García-del Junco, J., Chafloque-Céspedes, R., & Alvarez-Risco, A. (2024). Frugal innovation in the business environment: A literature review and future perspectives. *Frontiers in Artificial Intelligence*, *7*, 1385522. DOI: 10.3389/frai.2024.1385522 PMID: 39712468

Farcane, N., & Bureana, E. (2015). History of corporate social responsibility concept. *Annales Universitatis Apulensis Series Oeconomica*, *17*(2), 31–48. DOI: 10.29302/oeconomica.2015.17.2.3

Fishbach, A., & Woolley, K. (2022). The structure of intrinsic motivation. *Annual Review of Organizational Psychology and Organizational Behavior*, *9*(1), 339–363. DOI: 10.1146/annurev-orgpsych-012420-091122

Floridi, L., & Cowls, J. (2019). A unified framework of five principles for AI in society. *Harvard Data Science Review*, *1*(1), 1–14. DOI: 10.1162/99608f92.8cd550d1

Frederick, W. C. (1960). The growing concern over business responsibility. *California Management Review*, *2*(4), 52–61. DOI: 10.2307/41165405

Freeman, R. E. (1984). *Strategic management: A stakeholder approach*. Cambridge University Press.

Freeman, R. E., Harrison, J. S., Wicks, A. C., Parmar, B. L., & De Colle, S. (2010). *Stakeholder theory: The state of the art*. Cambridge University Press., DOI: 10.1017/CBO9780511815768

Ghotbi, N. (2023). The ethics of emotional artificial intelligence: A mixed method analysis. *Asian Bioethics Review*, *15*(4), 417–430. DOI: 10.1007/s41649-022-00237-y PMID: 37808444

Goleman, D. (1995). *Emotional intelligence: Why it can matter more than IQ*. Bantam Books.

Goleman, D., Boyatzis, R. E., & McKee, A. (2013). *Primal leadership: Unleashing the power of emotional intelligence*. Harvard Business Press.

Hart, S. L. (1995). A natural-resource-based view of the firm. *Academy of Management Review*, *20*(4), 986–1014. DOI: 10.2307/258963

Homans, G. C. (1961). *Social behavior: Its elementary forms*. Harcourt, Brace & World.

Hsieh, Y. C., Weng, J., Pham, N. T., & Yi, L. H. (2022). What drives employees to participate in corporate social responsibility? A personal characteristics-CSR capacity-organizational reinforcing model of employees' motivation for voluntary CSR activities. *International Journal of Human Resource Management*, *33*(18), 3703–3735. DOI: 10.1080/09585192.2021.1967422

IEA. (2025). *World energy outlook 2025*. International Energy Agency.

Ikart, E. (2023). Emotional intelligence: Why it matters in change leadership and innovation in the 21st century styles of work. *International Journal of Business Innovation*, *2*, e34732.

Jobin, A., Ienca, M., & Vayena, E. (2019). The global landscape of AI ethics guidelines. *Nature Machine Intelligence*, *1*(9), 389–399. DOI: 10.1038/s42256-019-0088-2

Jones, T. M., & Wicks, A. C. (1999). Convergent stakeholder theory. *Academy of Management Review*, *24*(2), 206–221. DOI: 10.2307/259075

Kaur, N., & Hirudayaraj, M. (2021). The role of leader emotional intelligence in organizational learning: A literature review using 4I framework. *New Horizons in Adult Education and Human Resource Development*, *33*(1), 51–68. DOI: 10.1002/nha3.20305

Khan, M. A. S., Du, J., Anwar, F., Khan, H. S. U. D., Shahzad, F., & Qalati, S. A. (2021). Corporate social responsibility and the reciprocity between employee perception, perceived external prestige, and employees' emotional labor. *Psychology Research and Behavior Management*, *14*, 61–75. DOI: 10.2147/PRBM.S277850 PMID: 33500672

Khan, M. R. (2024). Application of artificial intelligence for talent management: Challenges and opportunities. *Intelligent Human Systems Integration (IHSI 2024). Integrating People and Intelligent Systems*, *119*, 324–329. DOI: 10.54941/ahfe1004496

Khoury, G., Rostami, J., & Turnbull, P. L. (1999). *Corporate social responsibility: Turning words into action*. Conference Board of Canada.

Kilcullen, M., & Ohles Kooistra, J. (1999). At least do no harm: Sources on the changing role of business ethics and corporate social responsibility. *RSR. Reference Services Review*, *27*(2), 158–178. DOI: 10.1108/00907329910275150

Lievens, F., & Chan, D. (2017). Practical intelligence, emotional intelligence, and social intelligence. In Farr, J. L., & Tippins, N. T. (Eds.), *Handbook of employee selection* (2nd ed., pp. 342–364). Routledge. DOI: 10.4324/9781315690193-15

Liu, S. C., Luu, T. T., Pham, N. T., & Tang, A. D. (2024). Internal CSR and work-family facilitation: A dual mechanism of organizational citizenship behaviors and moderating role of emotional intelligence. *Journal of Hospitality and Tourism Management*, *58*, 394–408. DOI: 10.1016/j.jhtm.2024.02.008

Mai, N. K., An Nguyen, K. T., Do, T. T., & Phan, L. N. (2023). Corporate social responsibility strategy practices, employee commitment, reputation as sources of competitive advantage. *SAGE Open*, *13*(4), 1–17. DOI: 10.1177/21582440231216248

Marchegiani, L. (2023). AI, corporate governance and sustainability. In Monteduro, M., Marchegiani, L., & Saraceno, F. (Eds.), *Digital economy, sustainability and international economic law* (pp. 65–88). Bentham Science Publishers. DOI: 10.2174/9789815124064123030006

Matten, D., & Crane, A. (2005). Corporate citizenship: Toward an extended theoretical conceptualization. *Academy of Management Review*, *30*(1), 166–179. DOI: 10.5465/amr.2005.15281448

Mayer, J. D., & Salovey, P. (1997). What is emotional intelligence? In Salovey, P., & Sluyter, D. (Eds.), *Emotional development and emotional intelligence: Implications for educators* (pp. 3–31). Basic Books.

Mitchell, R. K., Agle, B. R., & Wood, D. J. (1997). Toward a theory of stakeholder identification and salience: Defining the principle of who and what really counts. *Academy of Management Review*, *22*(4), 853–886. DOI: 10.2307/259247

Mittelstadt, B. D., Allo, P., Taddeo, M., Wachter, S., & Floridi, L. (2016). The ethics of algorithms: Mapping the debate. *Big Data & Society*, *3*(2), 1–21. DOI: 10.1177/2053951716679679

Moura-Leite, R., & Padgett, R. (2011). Historical background of corporate social responsibility. *Social Responsibility Journal*, *7*(4), 528–539. DOI: 10.1108/17471111111117511

Najimi, A., Doustmohamadi, P., & Omid, A. (2021). The relationship between emotional intelligence, social responsibility, and job performance in health service providers. *Journal of Education and Health Promotion*, *10*(1), 126. DOI: 10.4103/jehp.jehp_960_20 PMID: 34222501

Nonaka, I., & Takeuchi, H. (1996). The knowledge-creating company: How Japanese companies create the dynamics of innovation. *Long Range Planning*, *29*(4), 592. DOI: 10.1016/0024-6301(96)81509-3

Notari, M., Baumgartner, A., & Herzog, W. (2014). Social skills as predictors of communication, performance and quality of collaboration in project-based learning. *Journal of Computer Assisted Learning*, *30*(2), 132–147. DOI: 10.1111/jcal.12026

Ocasio, W., Laamanen, T., & Vaara, E. (2018). Communication and attention dynamics: An attention-based view of strategic change. *Strategic Management Journal*, *39*(1), 155–167. DOI: 10.1002/smj.2702

Odame, C., Pandey, M., & Pathak, P. (2020). Emotional intelligence and its importance in sustainable development of human resources: A conceptual model. In Dang, G. S., & Vyas-Doorgapersad, M. S. (Eds.), *Sustainable human resource management: Transforming organizations, societies and environment* (pp. 273–287). Springer. DOI: 10.1007/978-981-15-5656-2_17

Pant, I., & Yadav, R. K. (2016). Impact of emotional intelligence on the job performance of employee. *International Research Journal of Management. IT and Social Sciences*, *3*(1), 7–14.

Parsons, T. (1951). *The social system*. Free Press.

Partnership on AI. (2021). *The ethics of AI and emotional intelligence*. https://partnershiponai.org/wp-content/uploads/2021/08/PAI_The-ethics-of-AI-and-emotional-intelligence_073020.pdf

Podile, V., Reddy, K. P., Reddy, V. N. S., Babu, M. S., & Phani, A. K. (2024). Artificial intelligence and corporate social responsibility: Synergies, challenges, and future directions. *International Journal of Advanced Multidisciplinary Research Studies*, *4*(6), 95–99. DOI: 10.62225/2583049X.2024.4.6.3399

Porter, M. E., & Kramer, M. R. (2011). Creating shared value. *Harvard Business Review*, *89*(1/2), 62–77.

Ratka, A. (2018). Empathy and the development of affective skills. *American Journal of Pharmaceutical Education*, *82*(10), 7192. DOI: 10.5688/ajpe7192 PMID: 30643318

Rojas-Saffie, J. P., & García-Matte, N. (2024). Emotional self-regulation and personality in the light of Thomas Aquinas's philosophical anthropology. *Frontiers in Psychology*, *15*, 1419202. DOI: 10.3389/fpsyg.2024.1419202 PMID: 38882512

Ruisel, I. (1992). Social intelligence: Concepts and methodological problems. *Studia Psychologica*, *34*(4), 281.

Sachs, J. D. (2015). *The age of sustainable development*. Columbia University Press., DOI: 10.7312/sach17314

Salovey, P., & Mayer, J. D. (1990). Emotional intelligence. *Imagination, Cognition and Personality*, *9*(3), 185–211. DOI: 10.2190/DUGG-P24E-52WK-6CDG

Sandel, M. J. (2020, October 20). Ethical concerns mount as AI takes bigger decision-making role. *Harvard Gazette*. https://news.harvard.edu/gazette/story/2020/10/ethical-concerns-mount-as-ai-takes-bigger-decision-making-role/

Schaltegger, S., & Wagner, M. (2011). Sustainable entrepreneurship and sustainability innovation: Categories and interactions. *Business Strategy and the Environment*, *20*(4), 222–237. DOI: 10.1002/bse.682

Scott, W. R. (2014). Institutions and organizations: Ideas, interests, and identities. *Sage (Atlanta, Ga.)*.

Shimul, A. S., & Cheah, I. (2023). Consumers' preference for eco-friendly packaged products: Pride vs guilt appeal. *Marketing Intelligence & Planning*, *41*(2), 186–198. DOI: 10.1108/MIP-05-2022-0197

Silva, P., Moreira, A. C., & Mota, J. (2023). Employees' perception of corporate social responsibility and performance: The mediating roles of job satisfaction, organizational commitment and organizational trust. *Journal of Strategy and Management*, *16*(1), 92–111. DOI: 10.1108/JSMA-10-2021-0213

Stahl, B. C. (2021). Ethical issues of AI. In Stahl, B. C. (Ed.), *Artificial intelligence for a better future: An ecosystem perspective on the ethics of AI and emerging digital technologies* (pp. 35–53). Springer., DOI: 10.1007/978-3-030-69978-9_4

Strubell, E., Ganesh, A., & McCallum, A. (2019). Energy and policy considerations for deep learning in NLP. *Proceedings of the 57th Annual Meeting of the Association for Computational Linguistics*, 3645–3650. DOI: 10.18653/v1/P19-1355

Taddeo, M., & Floridi, L. (2018). How AI can be a force for good. *Science, 361*(6404), 751–752. DOI: 10.1126/science.aat5991 PMID: 30139858

Tamunomiebi, M. D., & Owhorji, S. (2018). Emotional self-awareness—a critical competency for managing excellence: A human factor. *American Journal of Humanities and Social Sciences Research, 2*(11), 129–136.

Teece, D. J., Pisano, G., & Shuen, A. (1997). Dynamic capabilities and strategic management. *Strategic Management Journal, 18*(7), 509–533. DOI: 10.1002/(SICI)1097-0266(199708)18:7<509::AID-SMJ882>3.0.CO;2-Z

Tretter, M. (2024). Equipping AI-decision-support-systems with emotional capabilities? Ethical perspectives. *Frontiers in Artificial Intelligence, 7*, 1398395. DOI: 10.3389/frai.2024.1398395 PMID: 38881951

Voldsgaard, A., & Rüdiger, M. (2022). Innovative enterprise, industrial ecosystems, and sustainable transition: The case of transforming DONG Energy to Ørsted. In *Handbook of climate change mitigation and adaptation* (pp. 3633–3684). Springer International Publishing. DOI: 10.1007/978-3-030-72579-2_160

Von Schomberg, R. (2013). A vision of responsible research and innovation. In Owen, R., Bessant, J., & Heintz, M. (Eds.), *Responsible innovation: Managing the responsible emergence of science and innovation in society* (pp. 51–74). Wiley., DOI: 10.1002/9781118551424.ch3

Wang, S., Liao, Y. K., Wu, W. Y., & Le, K. B. H. (2021). The role of corporate social responsibility perceptions in brand equity, brand credibility, brand reputation, and purchase intentions. *Sustainability (Basel), 13*(21), 11975. DOI: 10.3390/su132111975

Wong, P.-H. (2020). Democratizing algorithmic fairness. *Philosophy & Technology, 33*(2), 225–244. DOI: 10.1007/s13347-019-00355-w

World Business Council for Sustainable Development. (2020). *Corporate social responsibility: Making good business sense*. http://www.ceads.org.ar/downloads/Making%20good%20business%20sense.pdf

Wu, J. (2024). Social and ethical impact of emotional AI advancement: The rise of pseudo-intimacy relationships and challenges in human interactions. *Frontiers in Psychology*, *15*, 1410462. DOI: 10.3389/fpsyg.2024.1410462 PMID: 39564589

Yassin, Y., & Beckmann, M. (2024). CSR and employee outcomes: A systematic literature review. *Management Review Quarterly*, *75*(1), 595–641. DOI: 10.1007/s11301-023-00389-7

Zhang, C., & Yang, J. (2024). Artificial intelligence and corporate ESG performance. *International Review of Economics & Finance*, *96*, 103713. DOI: 10.1016/j.iref.2024.103713

Zhao, J., & Gómez Fariñas, B. (2023). Artificial intelligence and sustainable decisions. *European Business Organization Law Review*, *24*(1), 1–39. DOI: 10.1007/s40804-022-00262-2

Zhou, J. (2023). Higher expectations of artificial intelligence in terms of morality and humanity. *Journal of Education. Humanities and Social Sciences*, *20*, 279–284.

Zhu, Y. (2025). Authentic leadership: Fostering ethical cultures, employee engagement, and organizational resilience in complex environments. *Proceedings of the International Conference on Research in Humanities and Social Sciences,* *2*(1), 1–14. DOI: 10.33422/icrhs.v2i1.838

Chapter 7
Artificial Intelligence-Driven Corporate Social Responsibility Reporting:
Augmenting Transparency and Accountability

Swati Bhatia
http://orcid.org/0000-0003-3478-3640
Asian Business School, Noida, India

ABSTRACT

In a global environment where stakeholders believe ethical company practices, CSR reporting is vital for transparency. Traditional reporting methods often fail due to human data management, inaccuracies, and lack of real-time insights. AI has given businesses novel opportunities to rethink CSR strategy and reporting. This chapter examines how AI-driven systems might improve transparency and accountability through automated data gathering, better analytics, and insights that encourage corporate responsibility. It addresses the ethical implications, opportunities, and problems of AI-driven reporting systems and recommends best practices. The chapter discusses case studies of businesses using AI for CSR reporting to boost stakeholder confidence and uphold ethical leadership.

DOI: 10.4018/979-8-3693-4099-8.ch007

1 THE ROLE OF CSR REPORTING IN CORPORATE ACCOUNTABILIty

Theoretical Background and Definitions

Corporate Social Responsibility (CSR) has transitioned from a peripheral function to a fundamental pillar of strategic management. It is the pledge of businesses to contribute to sustainable development, which encompasses environmental protection, ethical labor practices, and community development (Carroll & Shabana, 2010). Freeman (1984)'s stakeholder theory functions as a fundamental framework for corporate social responsibility (CSR), emphasizing that organizations must be accountable to a diverse array of stakeholders, including employees, customers, suppliers, communities, and governments, in addition to shareholders.

On the flip side, corporate social responsibility (CSR) reporting refers to the process of systematically communicating a company's CSR actions and the results of such operations. At the same time as it serves as a foundation for stakeholder interaction, it guarantees openness. According to the research of academics such as Manetti and Becatti (2009), corporate social responsibility (CSR) reporting not only boosts the trust of stakeholders, but it also improves internal accountability and propels long-term company sustainability.

Accountability in this context refers to the fact that an organization is responsible for its activities, that it discloses those actions in an open and honest manner, and that it is evaluated and subjected to repercussions. According to Bovens (2007), the concept of corporate responsibility extends beyond the concept of financial disclosures to include ethical conduct, regulatory compliance, and governance standards. These practices are often defined through sustainability reports and other non-financial disclosures. A growing number of corporate governance frameworks, like the OECD Principles (2023) and the United Kingdom's Combined Code (FRC, 2018), have begun to integrate corporate social responsibility (CSR) disclosures as critical criteria for evaluating board accountability, stakeholder rights, and transparency procedures that are in place.

From Traditional to AI-Driven CSR Reporting

Traditional CSR reporting has historically relied on periodic, manual, and compliance-driven disclosures, often published annually in the form of sustainability reports. These reports, while valuable, are largely retrospective and static, limiting their ability to capture real-time organizational impact. In contrast, AI-driven CSR reporting represents a paradigm shift toward dynamic, data-driven, and predictive systems (Stone et al., 2023; Jarrahi, 2022). Artificial Intelligence enables organizations to collect, process, and analyze vast volumes of ESG-related data in real time, transforming CSR reporting from a descriptive exercise into a strategic decision-making tool. Unlike traditional approaches that depend on human interpretation and delayed reporting cycles, AI-powered systems facilitate continuous monitoring, automated reporting, and proactive risk identification. This transition not only enhances transparency but also aligns CSR reporting with the evolving expectations of stakeholders who demand timely, accurate, and actionable insights, reflecting broader organizational shifts toward human–AI collaboration and data-driven decision-making in governance and sustainability domains (Stone et al., 2023).

CSR Reporting as a Tool for Accountability

CSR reporting is an essential component in institutionalizing corporate accountability. It is possible for businesses to demonstrate their dedication to ethical practices and responsible leadership by documenting their performance in the areas of social, environmental, and governance. According to Eccles and Klimenko (2019), these disclosures make it possible for stakeholders to analyze the conduct of corporations and demand to make course corrections when they are required.

Furthermore, corporate social responsibility reporting helps connect the internal values of a company with the expectations of external regulators. Integrated reports mandated by global frameworks like the Global Reporting Initiative (GRI), Sustainability Accounting Standards Board (SASB), and the Task Force on Climate-related Financial Disclosures (TCFD) reflect this harmonization of internal strategy and external accountability (GRI, 2021; SASB, 2022).

The Role of ESG in Organizational Strategy

Environmental, Social, and Governance (ESG) aspects have emerged as the standard for contemporary CSR reporting. ESG reporting provides a detailed analysis of an organization's environmental effect, social equality efforts, and governance standards. These indicators assist investors in assessing long-term value and risk exposure (Eccles & Klimenko, 2019). For example, BlackRock and Vanguard now utilize ESG ratings to evaluate investment portfolios, while rules such as the EU's Corporate Sustainability Reporting Directive (CSRD, 2023) require ESG-based disclosures from big corporations.

The social aspect of ESG reporting has gained significance following COVID-19, emphasizing employee wellness, diversity, equality, and inclusion (DEI), along with equitable labor practices (Harvard Business Review, 2021).

Strategic Integration and Value Creation

The incorporation of ESG objectives into fundamental strategy converts CSR from a compliance-driven role into a competitive asset. Porter and Kramer's (2011) Shared benefit theory posit that firms may create economic benefit by tackling social issues that align with their operations. AI technology can facilitate this integration by analysing ESG patterns, forecasting stakeholder expectations, and producing automated dashboards for transparency (Deloitte, 2023). CSR reporting serves not just as a mechanism for stakeholder engagement, but as a facilitator of corporate responsibility, strategy coherence, and ethical governance. Its convergence with ESG standards enhances transparency and enables companies to manage the intricacies of contemporary business in a socially responsible environment.

Linking CSR Reporting to Corporate Accountability

CSR reporting is essential for maintaining corporate responsibility through the disclosure of ESG (Environmental, Social, and Governance) performance measures. CSR reports substantiate a company's dedication to responsible business practices by documenting initiatives and outcomes pertaining to sustainability, labor practices, community development, and ethical governance.

Transparent CSR reporting synchronizes internal business conduct with external stakeholder anticipations. It establishes standards for business performance, supplies data for decision-making, and encourages examination that fosters ongoing enhancement. When incorporated into governance standards, CSR reporting serves as a feedback mechanism that ensures corporate accountability for both immediate actions and long-term sustainability objectives.

Understanding ESG and Its Organizational Importance

ESG symbolizes Environmental, Social, and Governance. The three fundamental pillars employed by investors and stakeholders to assess a company's sustainability and ethical influence are as follows:

- **Environmental** includes energy use, waste management, pollution, conservation efforts, and climate change mitigation.
- **Social** encompasses labor practices, human rights, health and safety, and community engagement.
- **Governance** pertains to corporate structure, executive compensation, internal controls, auditing methods and practices, and shareholder rights.

ESG frameworks are essential for assessing a company's resilience, risk management proficiency, and ethical impact. Entities exhibiting robust ESG performance are progressively preferred by investors, regulators, and customers, since these firms are perceived as less hazardous, more sustainable, and better regulated (Eccles & Klimenko, 2019). Frameworks like the Global Reporting Initiative (GRI), Sustainability Accounting Standards Board (SASB), and Task Force on Climate-related Financial Disclosures (TCFD) assist corporations in organizing their CSR reports to accurately represent ESG criteria. The incorporation of these frameworks into business strategy facilitates compliance and fosters a culture of ethical leadership and sustainable value generation. CSR reporting is crucial for enhancing corporate accountability and governance. By associating CSR initiatives with ESG frameworks and concepts, firms guarantee transparency and conform with global sustainability standards. This alignment is further strengthened when supplemented by AI technologies, which improve data dependability, timeliness, and decision-making assistance.

Cross-Cultural Perspectives in CSR Reporting

CSR reporting practices vary significantly across cultural and regulatory contexts, influencing how organizations adopt and implement AI-driven reporting mechanisms. In Western economies such as the European Union and the United States, CSR reporting is often highly formalized, compliance-oriented, and guided by stringent regulatory frameworks like the Corporate Sustainability Reporting Directive (CSRD). In contrast, emerging economies such as India and other Asian countries emphasize a more stakeholder-centric and developmental approach, where CSR is closely linked to community engagement and socio-economic development. Cultural dimensions, including collectivism versus individualism and long-term orientation, also shape the prioritization of ESG factors. The integration of AI into CSR reporting must therefore be sensitive to these cross-cultural variations, ensuring that technological solutions are adaptable, inclusive, and aligned with local stakeholder expectations. This global perspective enhances the relevance and applicability of AI-driven CSR frameworks across diverse organizational environments.

While CSR reporting frameworks and ESG standards provide the structural foundation for corporate accountability, the increasing complexity and scale of sustainability data have created a need for more advanced analytical capabilities. This is where Artificial Intelligence emerges as a transformative enabler, redefining how organizations capture, interpret, and communicate their CSR performance. The following section explores how AI functions as a game-changer in CSR reporting by enhancing accuracy, efficiency, and strategic foresight.

2 ARTIFICIAL INTELLIGENCE AS A GAME-CHANGER IN CSR REPORTING

Artificial Intelligence (AI) denotes the emulation of human cognitive functions by technology, especially computer systems. The utilization of AI in CSR reporting is framed within the innovation diffusion theory and the resource-based view (RBV) of the organization (Barney, 1991). These theories highlight that the strategic utilization of technical resources, such as AI, may yield durable competitive benefits, particularly when matched with organizational ethics and corporate social responsibility objectives.

The use of AI into CSR initiatives and reporting frameworks beyond automation; it signifies a fundamental transformation in the generation, interpretation, and communication of data for accountability purposes. AI technologies facilitate the transition of companies from reactive to proactive CSR reporting through the provision of predictive analytics, risk modeling, and stakeholder sentiment analysis (Deloitte, 2023; McKinsey & Company, 2023).

Artificial Intelligence Capabilities in Corporate Social Responsibility Reporting

Artificial intelligence (AI) methods transform conventional reporting parameters in several significant manners:

- **Automated Data Collection and Integration**: AI consolidates data from many systems (e.g., ERP, HRM, CRM) and external sources (e.g., news feeds, IoT devices) to produce complete CSR insights. Schneider Electric using AI to monitor carbon emissions in real time throughout its production facilities (Schneider Electric, 2022).
- **Predictive Modeling**: Machine learning algorithms evaluate historical data to forecast environmental and social impact results, enabling firms to devise contingency plans and connect future CSR initiatives with emerging global challenges (World Economic Forum, 2023; Gartner, 2023).
- **Natural Language Processing (NLP)**: NLP examines text-based data from the media, regulatory updates, and public sentiment to assess reputational risks. IBM Watson has used NLP algorithms to extract CSR-related data from several internal reports and external articles (IBM, 2022).
- **Computer Vision**: This area of AI has been used in ESG applications such as monitoring deforestation using satellite images and identifying hazardous working conditions in workplaces via surveillance footage—efforts that enhance transparency.

- **Blockchain Integration**: In tandem with AI, blockchain improves data traceability and accountability. Walmart and Nestlé employ blockchain technology for supply chain transparency, while artificial intelligence oversees sustainability adherence (World Economic Forum, 2022).

AI-Driven Stakeholder Engagement

Beyond data processing and predictive analytics, Artificial Intelligence plays a crucial role in enhancing stakeholder engagement within CSR ecosystems. AI-powered tools such as chatbots, sentiment analysis engines, and digital feedback platforms enable organizations to interact with stakeholders in real time, capturing perceptions, concerns, and expectations related to sustainability initiatives. Natural Language Processing (NLP) techniques allow firms to analyze social media conversations, public disclosures, and stakeholder communications to assess trust levels and reputational risks. This continuous feedback loop transforms CSR reporting from a one-way communication process into an interactive and participatory model, enhancing transparency and stakeholder trust in line with emerging global ESG practices (World Economic Forum, 2023). By integrating stakeholder insights into decision-making, organizations can design more inclusive and responsive CSR strategies, thereby strengthening accountability and long-term stakeholder relationships.

Mechanisms and Platforms Augmenting CSR Reporting

Numerous industry-standard systems demonstrate AI's contribution to Corporate Social Responsibility (CSR):

- Microsoft Cloud for Sustainability provides predictive dashboards, ESG compliance maps, and customized APIs for data integration aligned with GRI and SASB standards.
- Tableau AI and Power BI integrated with Azure ML technologies facilitate the generation of automated sustainability visualizations and reports for management and stakeholders.
- Google Environmental Insights Explorer (EIE) integrates artificial intelligence with geographical data to assess carbon emissions at the municipal or neighbourhood scale.

Conformity With International Regulations and Legal Adherence

The European Union's Artificial Intelligence Act (2023), ISO/IEC 42001 AI Management Systems Standard, and OECD AI Principles offer systematic advice for the use of reliable AI in sustainability reporting (OECD, 2022). These regulations mandate that AI systems exhibit openness, explainability, and compliance with data privacy standards—principles that are closely aligned with ethical corporate social responsibility. Organizations using AI must also account for international legislative obligations such as GDPR, the Algorithmic Accountability Act (U.S. Congress, 2022), and India's Digital Personal Data Protection Bill (2023), all of which influence AI-driven CSR disclosures.

AI as a Strategic Facilitator of Corporate Social Responsibility

Eventually, AI serves as a disruptive catalyst for contemporary CSR strategy, enabling organizations to integrate sustainability with data-driven decision-making and competitive advantage (Deloitte, 2023). When implemented judiciously, AI enables organizations to foresee stakeholder requirements, uphold regulatory adherence, and cultivate a reputation for ethical leadership in a data-centric environment (Accenture, 2021).

Despite the transformative potential of AI in enhancing CSR reporting, its widespread adoption also raises critical ethical and governance concerns. Issues related to data privacy, algorithmic bias, and transparency necessitate a careful and responsible approach to AI implementation. The next section examines the ethical considerations that underpin AI-driven CSR reporting, highlighting the need for a balanced integration of technology and human values.

3 ETHICAL CONSIDERATIONS OF AI IN CSR REPORTING

The ethical implementation of Artificial Intelligence (AI) in Corporate Social Responsibility (CSR) reporting is regulated by a developing convergence of technological ethics, stakeholder theory, and digital rights frameworks (Virginia Dignum, 2023). Binns (2018) asserts that AI systems in business settings must adhere to ethical standards of justice, transparency, and responsibility. These principles align with Carroll's (1991) CSR Pyramid, which posits that ethical responsibility is a fundamental corporate requirement, equivalent to economic and legal responsibilities.

The European Union's Ethics Guidelines for Trustworthy AI (European Commission, 2019) delineate seven fundamental principles: human agency, technical robustness, privacy, openness, diversity, environmental sustainability, and responsibility. These rules are supported by global policy frameworks such as the OECD AI Principles (OECD, 2022) and UNESCO's guidance on ethical AI (UNESCO, 2023), along with laws such as the EU AI Act (2023).

Principal Ethical Concerns in AI-Driven CSR Reporting

1. Data Privacy and Consent

CSR reporting increasingly employs data about employee conduct, community demographics, and environmental trends—some of which are categorized as personal or sensitive information. The aggregation of data by AI poses significant problems regarding individual permission, particularly in regions regulated by data protection legislation like GDPR and India's Digital Personal Data Protection Bill (2023). Ethical CSR reporting must guarantee that data is anonymised, encrypted, and gathered with explicit stakeholder consent (Floridi & Cowls, 2019).

2. Algorithmic Bias and Fairness

AI algorithms educated on skewed data might unintentionally perpetuate prejudice in CSR storytelling. For example, predictive hiring or labor welfare models may harm specific groups due to past imbalances. IBM and Accenture have both deployed AI fairness auditing technologies to mitigate bias in sustainability reporting systems.

3. Clarity and Awareness

Black-box algorithms provide considerable ethical hazards, particularly when utilized in sustainability effect evaluations or resource distribution decisions. Doshi-Velez and Kim (2017) assert that enterprises must use explainable AI (XAI) methodologies to substantiate algorithmic judgments to internal stakeholders and external authorities. Ethical AI in CSR must provide traceability, ensuring that every automated insight is subject to scrutiny, justification, and correction as required.

4. Automation vs. Human Oversight

Excessive dependence on AI may result in a deterioration of human moral thinking. The precautionary principle posits that companies should establish "human-in-the-loop" mechanisms to verify AI outputs, particularly those affecting CSR disclosures, stakeholder rights, or ethical hazards. Prominent corporations such as

Microsoft and Unilever have instituted AI ethics committees to evaluate algorithmic processes associated with corporate social responsibility.

5. Environmental Ethics of AI Implementation

The implementation of high-performance AI models, such as large-scale natural language models, has environmental implications owing to substantial energy usage. Ethical CSR requires lifespan assessments of AI systems, a notion increasingly recognized within green AI policy.

Frameworks and Standards for Ethical CSR AI

- **IEEE P7000 Series**: Standards for ethical system design, algorithmic bias reduction, and data privacy incorporation.
- **ISO/IEC 38507:2022**: Offers recommendations on corporate governance for the ethical implementation of AI.
- **OECD AI Principles**: Address the importance of openness, robustness, and stakeholder engagement in AI systems (OECD, 2022).

By adhering to these principles and regulatory mandates, aligned with international frameworks such as OECD (2022) and UNESCO (2023), firms may reduce reputational risk, bolster stakeholder confidence, and guarantee that AI-driven CSR activities are both ethical and innovative.

Human-Centered Implications of AI in CSR Reporting

While ethical frameworks and regulatory guidelines provide a structural basis for responsible AI use, it is equally important to examine the human-centered implications of AI-driven CSR reporting. The increasing reliance on AI systems can influence employee perceptions, organizational culture, and stakeholder trust. Employees may experience concerns related to surveillance, job displacement, or reduced autonomy when AI tools are used to monitor performance or social impact metrics. Similarly, stakeholders may question the authenticity of CSR disclosures if they perceive them as overly automated or detached from human judgment. Therefore, organizations must adopt a human-in-the-loop approach, ensuring that AI augments rather than replaces human decision-making, as emphasized in responsible AI frameworks (Virginia Dignum, 2023). Building transparency, fostering digital trust, and promoting ethical leadership are essential to creating a balanced ecosystem where technological efficiency coexists with human values and organizational empathy.

4 CASE STUDIES IN AI-DRIVEN CSR REPORTING

Artificial Intelligence is currently revolutionizing the methods by which organizations execute, oversee, and disclose Corporate Social Responsibility (CSR) programs (McKinsey & Company, 2023). This collection of case studies demonstrates how prominent worldwide corporations have implemented AI-driven initiatives to improve sustainability, ethical governance, and transparency in social impact. These examples offer significant insights into the practical uses, problems, and scalable results of AI integration in corporate social responsibility.

Patagonia

Patagonia has cultivated a reputation for environmental advocacy, and artificial intelligence assists the brand in maintaining this image. The company employs AI-driven sensors and supply chain intelligence tools to monitor raw materials, guaranteeing ethical procurement from agricultural and manufacturing sources. These AI algorithms monitor energy use, labor conditions, and emissions in real time, allowing Patagonia to respond promptly to sustainability violations (Patagonia, 2022). Their CSR dashboard, driven by machine learning, automates the generation of sustainability disclosures aligned with the Global Reporting Initiative (GRI), establishing a standard for AI in ethical supply chain management.

Unilever

Unilever utilizes artificial intelligence throughout its worldwide operations to facilitate the attainment of its Sustainable Living Plan. The organization use artificial intelligence to evaluate ESG data gathered from more than 70,000 vendors. It forecasts sustainability risks and enhances buying decisions utilizing environmental and human rights criteria. AI algorithms analyze consumer comments from social media to evaluate brand impression of Unilever's CSR activities (Unilever, 2022). Their incorporation of AI conforms to the SASB and TCFD standards, enhancing investor transparency and stakeholder responsibility.

IBM (International Business Machines Corporation)

IBM has been a trailblazer in utilizing AI for corporate social responsibility governance. IBM used its Watson CSR Insights technology, utilizing Natural Language Processing (NLP) to analyze internal audit reports, compliance papers, and whistleblower submissions. These are examined for signs of ethical transgressions or labor disputes. IBM's predictive modeling assesses the social effect of business volunteer initiatives, research and development financing for community projects, and educational donations, in accordance with the UN Sustainable Development Goals (SDGs) (IBM, 2022).

Google

Google, through DeepMind, decreased cooling energy consumption in its data centres by 40% with AI algorithms that dynamically modify temperature controls according to load predictions. The corporation introduced the Environmental Insights Explorer (EIE), utilizing satellite data and machine learning to provide towns with precise carbon emissions predictions. Additionally, Google Cloud offers AI-powered ESG reporting tools to enterprises, broadening the application of AI in sustainability management across many sectors (Google Sustainability, 2023).

Tesla

Tesla employs artificial intelligence across its manufacturing chain. Tesla's AI systems oversee water use, trash emissions, and battery recycling efficiency, spanning from autonomous production to energy optimization. The organization incorporates these results into its yearly Impact Report, offering stakeholders clear, real-time information. Artificial intelligence is utilized to evaluate supply chain adherence to the Responsible Minerals Initiative (RMI) and Conflict-Free Sourcing Initiative (CFSI) requirements (Tesla, 2023).

Nestlé

Nestlé has introduced an AI-driven monitoring system for sustainable sourcing, specifically targeting cocoa and coffee supply chains. Satellite imagery and predictive algorithms evaluate deforestation, water scarcity, and soil deterioration, then relayed via blockchain-secured platforms. Nestlé's "T.R.A.C.E." platform offers customers and stakeholders immediate access to data about ingredient origins and environmental effects (Nestlé, 2022). This effort is consistent with the EU's Corporate Sustainability Due Diligence Directive.

Microsoft

Microsoft's AI for Earth project finances businesses and NGOs to create AI solutions in climate science, agriculture, and biodiversity. Microsoft use AI to predict energy requirements in data centres, minimize carbon emissions, and track Scope 1, 2, and 3 emissions. AI is integral to their objectives of achieving Carbon

Negativity and Water Positivity by 2030. Microsoft's CSR report employs AI to automatically create climate scenario analyses in accordance with TCFD criteria (Microsoft, 2023).

Danone

Danone utilizes artificial intelligence for monitoring social effect in developing regions. Their AI algorithms examine nutritional trends, accessibility of inexpensive food, and local community development via the Danone Communities project. AI further oversees waste reduction across product lines, assessing effects on food loss and packaging sustainability. These initiatives are recorded utilizing GRI-aligned standards and verified by independent ethical auditors (Danone, 2022).

These case studies illustrate how AI may improve all aspects of CSR, including data accuracy, traceability, decision-making, and global effect evaluation. They illustrate the scalability of AI-driven CSR solutions across many industries and regions, underscoring their strategic significance for corporate responsibility and ethical leadership. These trends reflect the growing adoption of AI-driven sustainability practices across industries, supported by global research and industry reports (World Economic Forum, 2023).

Managerial Insights from AI-Driven CSR Practices

The case studies discussed above offer valuable managerial insights into the practical implementation of AI in CSR reporting. A common theme across organizations is the strategic integration of AI with sustainability goals, enabling real-time monitoring, improved data accuracy, and enhanced transparency (Deloitte, 2023). These examples highlight that successful AI adoption in CSR is not solely dependent on technological capability but also on strong governance frameworks, ethical considerations, and stakeholder alignment. Managers can draw lessons on the importance of phased implementation, cross-functional collaboration, and continuous evaluation of AI systems. Furthermore, these cases underscore the need for organizations to balance innovation with responsibility, ensuring that AI-driven CSR initiatives deliver both business value and societal impact.

5 STRATEGIES FOR IMPLEMENTATION AND BEST PRACTICES

Strategic Frameworks for the Integration of Artificial Intelligence in Corporate Social Responsibility

Integrating Artificial Intelligence (AI) into Corporate Social Responsibility (CSR) is not only a technological endeavour; it requires strategic alignment, ethical consideration, and interdisciplinary cooperation. The socio-technical systems theory posits that successful technology adoption occurs only when it is congruent with organisational structures, cultural values, and stakeholder interactions. Connection guarantees that AI facilitates ethical decision-making, sustainability monitoring, and inclusive stakeholder engagement within the framework of CSR.

The Resource-Based View (RBV) hypothesis (Barney, 1991) is relevant in this context, characterising AI as a unique, precious, and non-replicable resource that, when effectively used, bolsters a company's sustainability-oriented competitive advantage.

Step-by-Step Implementation Strategic Plan

1. Needs Assessment and Readiness Audit

- Organizations should initiate a materiality evaluation to prioritise the CSR themes that are most pertinent to stakeholders (GRI, 2021).
- An AI-readiness audit assesses existing infrastructure, governance maturity, and data accessibility (PWC, 2022).

2. Selection of AI Platform and Alignment with Compliance

- Select AI solutions that provide compatibility with ESG frameworks, including the Global Reporting Initiative (GRI), Sustainability Accounting Standards Board (SASB), Task Force on Climate-related Financial Disclosures (TCFD), and Corporate Sustainability Reporting Directive (CSRD) (European Commission, 2023).
- Assess adherence to ethical AI standards, including ISO/IEC 42001 and IEEE P7000, as well as data protection regulations such as GDPR and the U.S. CCPA.

3. Workforce Training and Digital Ethics Education

- o Provide staff with training in AI literacy and digital ethics. Initiatives like as Microsoft's AI Business School and the UK Government's Digital Skills Framework can be tailored for CSR teams (UK DSF, 2022).
- o Formulate interdisciplinary CSR/AI teams of data scientists, legal specialists, and sustainability officers.

4. Stakeholder Engagement and Participatory Design

- o Engage investors, communities, suppliers, and NGOs in the formulation of AI-driven CSR KPIs.
- o Participatory data governance approaches guarantee that data gathering and algorithm design embody the different interests of stakeholders (OECD, 2022).

5. AI Governance and Risk Management

- o Establish specialised AI ethical boards or committees tasked with the monitoring of CSR algorithms.
- o Implement Explainable AI (XAI), conduct algorithmic effect evaluations, and provide continuous model monitoring for fairness and robustness.

6. Auditability and Third-Party Validation

- o Employ external auditors to evaluate AI systems for bias, data integrity, and impact precision.
- o Align CSR disclosures with integrated reporting systems to guarantee that AI findings are visible, actionable, and externally verifiable (IIRC, 2021).

Best Strategies from Industry Pioneers

- **Phased Deployment**: Initiate trial initiatives for AI in domains like as energy monitoring, ethical sourcing, or employee sentiment analysis prior to expansion.
- **Modular Infrastructure**: Employ cloud-based, API-driven AI solutions that can adjust to evolving CSR legislation or international standards.
- **Open Innovation**: Engage in collaboration with AI research consortia, academic institutions, and civil society to jointly build responsible AI tools for Corporate Social Responsibility (e.g., IBM Research, UNDP AI Labs).

Essential Tools and Platforms

- **AI for Good by ITU and UN**: Assists firms in aligning AI applications with the Sustainable Development Goals (SDGs).
- **ESG-AI dashboards (SASB, Refinitiv, Sustainalytics)**: Provide automated data analysis and visual reporting for Corporate Social Responsibility teams.
- **Audit Management Software**: Applications such as MetricStream or SAP GRC incorporate AI-driven audit trails for sustainability performance and risk reporting.

An effective AI-CSR deployment approach requires more than mere software. It necessitates an ethical perspective, strategic lucidity, inclusive governance, and a long-term vision for sustainable development. When executed correctly, it not only informs stakeholders but also empowers them.

6 CHALLENGES AND PROSPECTIVE TRAJECTORIES

Persistent Challenges in AI-Driven CSR Reporting

Notwithstanding the potential of Artificial Intelligence (AI) to improve Corporate Social Responsibility (CSR) reporting, organisations encounter significant technological, operational, ethical, and cultural obstacles. These restrictions not only impact AI adoption but also shape stakeholders' perceptions of the integrity and authenticity of CSR disclosures.

1. Technical Integration and Legacy Systems

- Many organisations function on disjointed legacy systems that do not integrate with AI-based platforms (Gartner, 2023). Integrating AI with diverse data sources, including spreadsheets, ERP, and supply chain systems, necessitates substantial infrastructure investment and customisation.
- Moreover, companies frequently lack standardised data ontologies crucial for machine-readable ESG measures (ISO, 2022).

2. Elevated Capital and Operational Expenditures

- The expenses associated with developing or acquiring AI-driven CSR technologies, together with the costs of employing data scientists and compliance experts, might be excessive for small- and medium-sized firms (SMEs) (PwC, 2024).

- o Training AI models also entails concealed expenses associated with data annotation, computing resources, and ethical verification (McKinsey & Company, 2023).

3. Regulatory Complexity and Compliance Risks

- o Companies must manoeuvre through a complex array of international and national AI rules. The EU AI Act (2023), U.S. Algorithmic Accountability Act (2022), India's Digital Data Protection Bill (2023), and China's AI Regulation Guidelines possess distinct standards, rendering worldwide compliance a formidable challenge.
- o These regulations also connect with established ESG frameworks like as the EU CSRD, SEC's ESG Disclosure Guidance (2022), and SASB requirements, necessitating dual-level reporting alignment.

4. Algorithmic Bias and Ethical Blind Spots

- o Even Even benevolent AI can mirror the historical biases ingrained in training data, possibly misrepresenting marginalised areas or disproportionately highlighting low-impact CSR projects (Eubanks, 2018).
- o Numerous organisations lack mechanisms to audit or elucidate algorithmic judgements, resulting in unclear CSR narratives that compromise transparency (Raji & Buolamwini, 2019).

5. Organizational Culture and Resistance to Change

- o Employee opposition, executive doubt, or insufficient AI knowledge might impede implementation. Organisational culture must transform to foster innovation based on responsibility and trust.
- o Leadership is essential in positioning AI not as a menace to employment but as an enhancement to human decision-making in corporate social responsibility situations (Brynjolfsson & McAfee, 2017).

6. Challenges Faced by SMEs in AI-Driven CSR Reporting

- o Small and Medium Enterprises (SMEs) face unique challenges in adopting AI-driven CSR reporting compared to large corporations. Limited financial resources, lack of technical expertise, and inadequate data infrastructure often hinder their ability to implement advanced AI solutions. Unlike multinational organizations that can invest in sophisticated ESG analytics platforms, SMEs may struggle with basic digital transformation, making AI integration a complex and resource-intensive process (PwC, 2024; McKinsey & Company, 2023). Additionally, SMEs often operate in less formalized regulatory environments, where CSR reporting practices are still evolving. To address these challenges, there is a growing need for scalable, cost-effective AI solutions and policy support mechanisms that enable SMEs to participate in sustainable and transparent business practices. Encouraging collaborative platforms, government incentives, and shared digital infrastructure can significantly enhance SME participation in AI-driven CSR ecosystems Prospective Trajectories for Artificial Intelligence in Corporate Social Responsibility

1. Predictive CSR and Sustainability Foresight

o Future Future AI systems will not only provide historical CSR outcomes but also anticipate upcoming risks, including climatic volatility, supply chain disruptions, and reputational crises, using real-time environmental, social, and geopolitical data (UNEP, 2023; McKinsey & Company, 2023).

2. Blockchain with AI for Tamper-Proof CSR Audits

o The integration of blockchain with AI will guarantee that CSR data is safe, verifiable, and decentralised. For example, the Trade Lens initiative by Maersk and IBM employs blockchain technology to record CSR-compliant supply chain information (World Bank, 2022).

3. Federated Learning and Privacy-Preserving AI

o To mitigate privacy issues, federated learning enables organisations to train AI models on decentralised data sources without consolidating sensitive stakeholder information (MIT Tech Review, 2022).

4. AI for SDG Alignment and Impact Valuation

o Advanced AI models are being customised to assess a corporation's contribution to the UN Sustainable Development Goals (SDGs), awarding weighted ratings to activities based on social return on investment (World Economic Forum, 2023).

5. External AI Audits and Accreditations

- o The future will likely have independent certification entities doing algorithm audits in accordance with ISO 42001 AI Management Systems, ensuring that CSR-related AI systems adhere to ethical, legal, and governance standards (ISO, 2023).
- o AI possesses the capacity to transform CSR; but, in the absence of effective risk mitigation techniques, this technology may undermine stakeholder trust. The future resides in ethical AI ecosystems characterised by openness, inclusion, and foresight that direct the digital transformation of sustainability.

7 CONCLUSION

Artificial Intelligence (AI) is transforming Corporate Social Responsibility (CSR) reporting by allowing organisations to progress beyond static, retroactive disclosures to dynamic, predictive, and ethically informed openness. This shift is not only technological; it is also geopolitical, ethical, and cultural. As stakeholders want enhanced responsibility, regulatory demands intensify, and societal expectations transform, AI surfaces as a formidable facilitator of sustainability, governance, and corporate ethics.

Enhancing Transparency and Stakeholder Confidence

AI improves transparency by automating data acquisition across intricate organisational frameworks and external contexts. Real-time dashboards, predictive analytics, and NLP-driven stakeholder sentiment evaluations enable firms to maintain continuous dialogues with stakeholders regarding impact and integrity. This degree of openness fosters confidence and enables stakeholders to hold firms responsible not just yearly but also continually (Floridi et al., 2018).

Furthermore, explainable AI (XAI) technologies guarantee that algorithmic judgements pertaining to CSR are comprehensible to both technical and non-technical audiences. This is particularly vital in sensitive domains like as labour rights oversight, environmental reporting, and ethical procurement. As AI elucidates the opaque characteristics of sustainability data, it simultaneously enhances the ethical representation of an organisation (Doshi-Velez & Kim, 2017).

Facilitating Strategic and Sustainable Value Creation

In addition to compliance, AI-driven CSR reporting corresponds with Porter and Kramer's (2011) shared value theory, which asserts that social impact and economic performance are inherently interconnected. When applied judiciously, AI fosters long-term value generation by improving operational efficiency (e.g., decreasing carbon emissions), alleviating reputational concerns (e.g., early warning systems), and facilitating innovation in ESG-compliant product development.

Furthermore, AI may assist organisations in synchronising their CSR initiatives with international frameworks like the UN Sustainable Development Goals (SDGs). AI solutions facilitate corporations in establishing more ambitious, evidence-based sustainability objectives by assessing CSR performance and forecasting future hazards or possibilities (World Economic Forum, 2023). These advancements are increasingly aligned with global reporting standards such as the Global Reporting Initiative (GRI, 2023), which emphasize transparency, comparability, and stakeholder inclusiveness in sustainability disclosures.

Reconciling Innovation with Ethical Standards and Governance

The incorporation of AI in CSR has ethical complexities. Concerns about data privacy, algorithmic bias, environmental impact, and explainability need the implementation of stringent AI governance frameworks. Prominent companies are using frameworks like ISO/IEC 42001, IEEE P7000, and the OECD AI Principles to formalize the appropriate utilization of AI within corporate social responsibility contexts.

AI governance must be inclusive, directed by ethical boards, stakeholder advisory groups, and interdisciplinary teams that embody a varied array of beliefs and life experiences. AI systems may genuinely embody the social contracts that CSR aims to maintain alone through participatory governance (OECD, 2022; EU AI Act, 2023; World Economic Forum, 2023).

Call to Action

AI does not replace ethical leadership; rather, it serves as a tool that, when developed and regulated judiciously, enhances human decision-making and strengthens corporate accountability. Organizations that integrate AI into their CSR reporting not only comply with legal standards but also distinguish themselves as proactive, transparent, and reliable leaders in a swiftly changing environment. As we go towards a future characterized by climate urgency, social fairness, and economic equity, Corporate Social Responsibility (CSR) must be astute, ethical, and inclusive—artificial intelligence may facilitate the realization of that vision.

While the above discussion highlights the transformative role of AI in CSR reporting across multiple dimensions, it is essential to consolidate these insights into a holistic perspective. The integration of Artificial Intelligence into CSR reporting represents a transformative shift toward more transparent, accountable, and strategic sustainability practices. However, the true potential of AI can only be realized when it is implemented within a framework that balances technological innovation with ethical responsibility and human values. Organizations must recognize that AI is not merely a reporting tool but a strategic enabler that shapes stakeholder relationships, organizational culture, and long-term value creation. Future research can further explore the role of AI in enhancing stakeholder inclusivity, addressing cross-cultural variations, and developing accessible solutions for SMEs. As businesses navigate an increasingly complex and data-driven environment, the convergence of AI, ethics, and sustainability will define the next generation of corporate responsibility and governance, as reinforced by evolving global ESG frameworks and reporting standards (World Economic Forum, 2023; GRI, 2023).

REFERENCES

Barney, J. (1991). Firm resources and sustained competitive advantage. *Journal of Management, 17*(1), 99–120. DOI: 10.1177/014920639101700108

Binns, R. (2018). Fairness in machine learning: Lessons from political philosophy. In *Proceedings of the 2020 Conference on Fairness, Accountability, and Transparency* (pp. 149–159). DOI: 10.1145/3287560.3287589

Bovens, M. (2007). Analysing and assessing accountability: A conceptual framework. *European Law Journal, 13*(4), 447–468. DOI: 10.1111/j.1468-0386.2007.00378.x

Brynjolfsson, E., & McAfee, A. (2017). The business of artificial intelligence. *Harvard Business Review*. https://hbr.org/2017/07/the-business-of-artificial-intelligence

Carroll, A. B., & Shabana, K. M. (2010). The business case for corporate social responsibility: A review of concepts, research and practice. *International Journal of Management Reviews, 12*(1), 85–105. DOI: 10.1111/j.1468-2370.2009.00275.x

Deloitte. (2023). AI for ESG: Driving sustainability through intelligent technologies. https://www.deloitte.com

Doshi-Velez, F., & Kim, B. (2017). Towards a rigorous science of interpretable machine learning. *arXiv preprint arXiv:1702.08608*. https://arxiv.org/abs/1702.08608

Eccles, R. G., & Klimenko, S. (2019). The investor revolution. *Harvard Business Review, 97*(3), 106–116. https://hbr.org/2019/05/the-investor-revolution

Eubanks, V. (2018). *Automating inequality: How high-tech tools profile, police, and punish the poor*. St. Martin's Press.

European Commission. (2019). *Ethics guidelines for trustworthy AI*. https://digital-strategy.ec.europa.eu/en/library/ethics-guidelines-trustworthy-ai

Floridi, L., & Cowls, J. (2019). A unified framework of five principles for AI in society. *Harvard Data Science Review, 1*(1). Advance online publication. DOI: 10.1162/99608f92.8cd550d1

Floridi, L., Cowls, J., Beltrametti, M., Chatila, R., Chazerand, P., Dignum, V., Luetge, C., Madelin, R., Pagallo, U., Rossi, F., Schafer, B., Valcke, P., & Vayena, E. (2018). AI4People—An ethical framework for a good AI society. *Minds and Machines, 28*(4), 689–707. DOI: 10.1007/s11023-018-9482-5 PMID: 30930541

Gartner. (2023). *Trends in responsible AI deployment*. https://www.gartner.com

Global Reporting Initiative. (2023). GRI standards update 2023. https://www.globalreporting.org

IBM. (2022). *IBM ESG and AI data platform*. https://www.ibm.com/sustainability

ISO. (2022). *ISO/IEC 42001: Artificial Intelligence Management System Standards*. Retrieved from https://www.iso.org

McKinsey & Company. (2023). The state of AI in 2023. https://www.mckinsey.com

Microsoft. (2023). *AI for Earth and Sustainability Reports*. https://www.microsoft.com/en-us/sustainability

Nestlé. (2022). *T.R.A.C.E. transparency platform.*

OECD. (2022). *OECD AI principles*. https://www.oecd.org

Patagonia. (2022). *Environmental & supply chain transparency report*. https://www.patagonia.com/our-footprint/

Porter, M. E., & Kramer, M. R. (2011). Creating shared value. *Harvard Business Review*, *89*(1/2), 62–77. https://hbr.org/2011/01/the-big-idea-creating-shared-value

PwC. (2024). *ESG and AI: From risk to opportunity*. https://www.pwc.com/gx/en/issues/data-and-analytics/publications/esg-reporting-and-ai.html

Raji, I. D., & Buolamwini, J. (2019). Actionable auditing: Investigating the impact of publicly naming biased performance results. *Proceedings of the 2019 AAAI/ACM Conference on AI, Ethics, and Society*, 429–435. DOI: 10.1145/3306618.3314244

SASB. (2022). *Sustainability Accounting Standards*. https://www.sasb.org

Schneider Electric. (2022). *Sustainability impact report*. https://www.se.com/ww/en/about-us/sustainability/

Tesla. (2023). *Impact report*. https://www.tesla.com/impact

UNESCO. (2023). Guidance for generative AI. https://www.unesco.org

Unilever. (2022). *Sustainability performance report*. https://www.unilever.com/sustainable-living/

Virginia Dignum, V. (2023). *Responsible artificial intelligence: How to develop and use AI in a responsible way*. Springer.

World Economic Forum. (2023). *AI governance frameworks for SDGs*. https://www.weforum.org/agenda/archive/artificial-intelligence/

Chapter 8
Organizational Strategic Implication Effect on Sustainable Business Practices Through Organizational Culture in the Horn of Africa

Wako Jio
http://orcid.org/0009-0003-6192-459X
Bule Hora University, Ethiopia

Shashi Kant
http://orcid.org/0000-0003-4722-5736
St. Joseph University in Tanzania, Tanzania

Zerihun Kinde Alemu
http://orcid.org/0000-0002-8546-2882
Ethiopian Civil Service University, Ethiopia

Hirut Assegid
http://orcid.org/0009-0003-6192-459X
Bule Hora University, Ethiopia

Mohit Verma
http://orcid.org/0009-0005-3036-3894
O.P. Jindal Global University, India

DOI: 10.4018/979-8-3693-4099-8.ch008

ABSTRACT

This section studies the strategic dimensions that Culture of Organizational plays for sustainable business practices through in the Horn of Africa which faces rapid economic development alongside special difficulties. The study analyzes data from 385 participants using KMO to check sample adequacy as well as CFA for measurement model validation as well as SEM based on AMOS software for variable relationship analysis. The study demonstrates that organizations through strong cultures lead the adoption of sustainable practices since they benefit from common values as well as shared organizational norms that drive environmental responsibility together through social equity standards. Organizations practicing adaptive cultures demonstrate better success rates in sustainability initiative implementation which strengthens their market position as well as organizational stability when encountering regional challenges. The study explores how these outcomes affect decision-making authorities as well as business executives who should establish sustainability as their fundamental strategy.

INTRODUCTION

The worldwide emphasis on responsible corporate practices has gained extraordinary focus because organizations need to face escalated demands for tackling environmental as well as social as well as economic issues (Odeyemi et al., 2024). The world's businesses have recognized the urgency to embed sustainability principles in their fundamental operational strategy because of climate change together through resource shortages as well as social disparities (Khaddage-Soboh et al., 2024). The sustainability transition leads to better community welfare as well as improved corporate image as well as sustainable financial success (Tadesse Bogale & Debela, 2024). Originating from the sustainable development discourse the business world adopted sustainability as an important concept toward the end of the 20th century. The framework combines economic growth through environmental stewardship together through social equity while maintaining their interdependent relationship (Wang & Zhang, 2024). The direction of Culture of Organizational emerges as a crucial factor for business success when organizations attempt to align through sound business principles (Lin et al., 2024). Study findings show that organizations through supportive cultures help businesses implement sustainable practices yet multiple organizations face challenges implementing sustainable practices throughout their operations (Tadesse Bogale & Debela, 2024). The growing comprehension about this relationship encounters multiple practical obstacles. Sustainability initiatives face challenges in integration because organizations encounter employee resistance to change combined through staff implementation difficulties regarding resources as well as lack of awareness (Khaddage-Soboh et al., 2024). The study community lacks sufficient evidence about cultural characteristics that support sustainable practices in regions through unique characteristics like the Horn of Africa despite their economic as well as social differences through developed areas (Channuwong et al., 2024).

The digital revolution is making sustainable business operations more viable in the Horn of Africa through increased efficiency, inclusion and transparency (Nwokolo et al., 2023; Plečko & Hojnik, 2024). A key area of impact is the growth in mobile banking and payments. East Africa now has more than 300 million registered mobile money accounts, with double-digit annual increases in the number of transactions in markets such as Ethiopia and its neighbours (Bigirimana et al., 2024; Kejela & Porath, 2022; Nwokolo et al., 2023). This expansion has led to increased financial inclusion through access to credit, savings and payments for rural and small businesses (Bonhoure, 2024; Mpofu, 2024; Shaikh et al., 2022). This helps to reduce transaction costs and cash-based transactions, which in turn supports economic sustainability and efficiency (Khaddage-Soboh et al., 2024; (Dudu et al., 2024; Tay et al., 2022)). Moreover, digital payments reduce transportation and paper-based transactions, which impacts carbon emissions and consumption (Dudu et al., 2024; Sethupathy, 2025). For example, mobile payments can lower transaction costs by up to 70% than other modes of payment, and increase transaction speed and efficiency. This is particularly relevant to regions where a lack of infrastructure makes transactions costly and cumbersome (Odeyemi et al., 2024).

Digital supply chains are also beginning to transform supply chains. With mobile enabled logistics and inventory management, real-time monitoring, reduction of losses, and planning of routes are all possible (Adama et al., 2024; Usuemerai et al., 2024). In the agricultural sector, a major part of the region's economies, digital technology has been shown to reduce post-harvest losses by 20-30% for increased profits and food security. Similarly, small farmers and traders with digital platforms can better match supply and demand, preventing overproduction and resource wastage (Channuwong et al., 2024). Furthermore, digital platforms are helping formalise the informal sector, which is prominent in the region (Choruma et al., 2024; Mohammad et al., 2025; Nwokolo et al., 2023). These platforms enable digital transactions and basic accounting systems, allowing informal businesses to move into formal markets and access to credit, enhancing transparency and sustainability (Hadizadeh et al., 2024; Malek, 2024; Mhlongo et al., 2024; Schilling et al., 2025). However, there are challenges, including digital literacy and access to internet (Lin et al., 2024).

To overcome these knowledge gaps, the study explores Culture of Organizational and sustainable business practices in the Horn of Africa. The study findings will be applicable for researchers and policymakers through the identification of key cultural factors that impact sustainability. The research question is: *"How does Culture of Organizational affect the uptake of sustainable business practices in the Horn of Africa, and what can organisations do to resolve the challenges?"* In addition to advancing scholarly discussion, answering this topic will provide useful advice for businesses looking to attain sustainability in a world that is changing quickly.

BACKGROUND OF STUDY

Organizations worldwide must urgently adopt sustainable business practices through their frameworks because this is especially important in the Horn of Africa region (Channuwong et al., 2024). Sustainability requires creative solutions in the Horn of Africa region because it encounters specific socio-economic obstacles consisting of economic scarcity together through political volatility as well as ecological damage. Organizational entities in the Horn of Africa need to adopt practices which combine environmental stewardship, social equity as well as economic resilience in their operations (Odeyemi et al., 2024). The path toward sustainability faces multiple obstacles that strongly obstruct execution efforts. A major agricultural cooperative in Ethiopia serves as a specific real-world test case to showcase the difficulties faced during sustainable farming implementation (Khaddage-Soboh et al., 2024). The sustainability initiative met opposition from farmers belonging to the local community because of their preference for traditional farming systems (Wang & Zhang, 2024). The failure to understand the extended rewards of sustainable methods along through minimal availability of training as well as resources stopped farmers from adopting new approaches. The situation demonstrates a regional phenomenon where traditional cultural customs oppose new environmental sustainability practices (Odeyemi et al., 2024).

The renewable energy sector in Kenya has implemented successful solar energy solutions through companies leading the way (Lin et al., 2024). Although some organizations have managed to implement solar systems into rural areas their success faced operational barriers from poor infrastructure as well as high investment costs as well as minimal community input (Tadesse Bogale & Debela, 2024). The combination of these factors caused both delayed implementation as well as decreased sustainability of initiatives because users lacked appropriate support systems for repairing as well as maintaining their received technologies (Khaddage-Soboh et al., 2024). The study studies demonstrate that organizations must analyze how their cultural dynamics affect the ongoing sustainability commitment of their members. The studies demonstrate that sustainable practices face failure because of resisting Culture of Organizational as well as practical obstacles such as employee resistance alongside inadequate training as well as insufficient stakeholder involvement. This investigation looks into ways that supportive Culture of Organizational decrease operational hurdles so organizations in the Horn of Africa can establish lasting sustainable business practices (Odeyemi et al., 2024). Study findings about these dynamics will serve organizations as well as policymakers who wish to establish sustainable changes in the Horn of Africa (Channuwong et al., 2024).

Customs are long-standing practices, beliefs and norms that influence how people think and behave in their work, in relation to authority and change. Customs are grounded in past experience, and are supported and encouraged through socialisation, norms and expectations. Given their entrenched nature, these practices have a preference for stability, predictability and familiarity, often relying on what has been tried and tested, rather than new ideas (Lin et al., 2024). Cultural resistance, here, is the inclination of individuals or groups to be wary, sceptical or even resistant to new practices that diverge from these practices and expectations. This resistance may not be negative or unwilling, but rather reflect a perceived unfit between the initiatives and the established norms and practices. For example, employees may perceive changes in practices, technology, and strategy as incompatible with familiar procedures, as uncertain, or as undermining their roles and identities. This can lead to more passive resistance patterns such as slow response, lack of participation or a preference for old ways of doing things, rather than outright resistance (Odeyemi et al., 2024).

Cultural resistance and traditional practices are not always barriers, they can also be stabilising forces, maintaining organisational unity and purpose. But when an organisation seeks to implement new strategies or sustainability practices, these norms may need to be aligned, and gradually shifted. Without this, well-intentioned initiatives may not take hold as employees apply the norms of the culture to their interpretation of initiatives.

STATEMENT OF THE PROBLEM

Sustainable business integration in the Horn of Africa meets considerable difficulties although the ideal situation involves effective sustainability operations that boost social equity through environmental stewardship as well as economic resilience (Odeyemi et al., 2024). The present situation demonstrates numerous hindering obstacles toward advancement. The literature contains contradictory evidence about multiple sustainability strategies as they relate to their actual effectiveness (Khaddage-Soboh et al., 2024). The study shows opposing outcomes regarding sustainable practices because cultural resistance among staff as well as deficient training as well as inadequate budgeting issues have led to varied outcomes among successful as well as unsuccessful sustainability implementations (Channuwong et al., 2024). Several theoretical shortcomings persist because few models explain the exact relationship among Culture of Organizational as well as sustainability (Tadesse Bogale & Debela, 2024). The existing models struggle to incorporate relevant features of Horn of Africa's socio-economic environment alongside its cultural traits that affect sustainable practice adoption. Insufficient knowledge exists about how specific local conditions shape organizational behavior regarding sustainability decision-making resulting in a shortage of appropriate methods for effective implementation (Odeyemi et al., 2024).

Most study studies about sustainability have focused on developed countries through distinct socio-economic systems as well as cultural conditions than those found in the Horn of Africa region (Lin et al., 2024). Applied study from the region remains limited which hampers the relevance of discovery insights as well as recommendation for the region. Organizations face practical implementation difficulties because their employees show resistance to change as well as lack awareness about sustainability while encountering logistical barriers (Wang & Zhang, 2024). The study initiative seeks to close these knowledge gaps by performing an extensive examination of Culture of Organizational effects on sustainable business practice adoption through in the Horn of Africa. The study analyzes regional-specific cultural elements to develop a theory which addresses specific business challenges organizations experience in this area. The study findings deliver practical recommendations which policymakers as well as business executives can use to develop sustainability fostering strategies. The study aims to establish an applied path for sustainability practitioners as well as researchers who aim to advance sustainable development in the Horn of Africa.

THEORETICAL FOUNDATION

Organizational Culture Theory: According to Culture of Organizational Theory organizational members enact their behavior as well as decision outputs through the collective values as well as beliefs as well as norms which exist through in their organization. Social scientists as well as anthropologists developed this theory during the 1980s to establish that Culture of Organizational directs how operations function while adopting new business practices. A sustainable organization through an environmental as well as social priority in its culture creates active employee participation as well as dedication to their sustainable programs. The theory enables us to understand the basic effects which cultural aspects create for sustainable practice introduction or prevention (Chourasia et al., 2024).

Diffusion of Innovations Theory: According to Everett Rogers' work from the 1960s the Diffusion of Innovations Theory demonstrates how new concepts as well as technical assessments move throughout organizational structures. According to this theory different variables determine how people accept new things through their evaluation of the advantages as well as their cultural alignment as well as their position in social frameworks. The factors affecting sustainability initiative diffusion need to be understood by organizations in the Horn of Africa as well as the Horn of Africa because of its significance to sustainable practices. This model supports organizations by providing insights to improve employee as well as stakeholder approval of sustainable practices implementation (Abdalla et al., 2024).

Stakeholder Theory: Stakeholder Theory defined by R. Edward Freeman during the 1980s declares organizations need to incorporate the interests of all stakeholders including employees, customers, suppliers, communities as well as environmental elements for their decision-making activities. Under this theory business success depends on stakeholder well-being because sustainable practices lead to better stakeholder relationships as well as continued business performance. The Horn of Africa demands organizations to focus on stakeholder-oriented strategies because this theory shows how businesses need to implement their goals alongside community expectations to establish sustainable progress (Awa et al., 2024).

Triple Bottom Line Theory: John Elkington introduced the Triple Bottom Line (TBL) Theory in the late 1990s which extends typical business profit focus toward social as well as environmental aspects. Organizations should embrace a framework which examines success through three distinct measurements consisting of economic performance as well as the effects they have on populace as well as natural ecosystems. Organizations can benefit from the TBL approach because it helps them examine their operations through economic viability as well as social equity as well as environmental stewardship. The theory applies directly to Horn of Africa organizations since it helps them achieve socially as well as environmentally sustainable development (Homer et al., 2025).

The study uses ***Organizational Culture Theory*** as its main theoretical framework. The selection stems from understanding that Culture of Organizational dominates the reception as well as adoption as well as sustainability of sustainability initiatives in companies. The investigation through cultural analysis reveals the essential beliefs as well as values that both help as well as hinder sustainable practice adoption in the specific Horn of Africa context (Chourasia et al., 2024).

DEFINITION AND ORIGIN OF CONCEPT

Organizational Culture: Through Culture of Organizational people inside an organization develop values along through beliefs as well as practices which determine their collective behavior. Study in anthropology originated this theory because it demonstrates how people develop organizational unity through their joint activities. An organization features multiple components from delegation routines to dialogue methods as well as unspoken protocols which control how workers cooperate through each other. Organizations through strong culture tend to achieve higher performance through innovation especially when implementing sustainable practices (Chourasia et al., 2024).

Sustainability: The definition of sustainability describes the present need fulfillment approach alongside the fulfillment of future generations. The environmental movement of the 1970s gave birth to the sustainability concept which gained significant prominence though the Brundtl and Commission's landmark report "Our Common Future" in 1987. The concept of sustainability dedicates its scope to the economic aspects as well as social aspects as well as environmental components often labeled as the triple bottom line. Business stakeholders should implement sustainable practices which support their enduring value preservation through equal attention to social as well as environmental operational effects (Rashid et al., 2024).

Stakeholders: Organizations include stakeholders as people or entities which maintain a personal interest in their actions as well as outcomes. This term encompasses a wide range of entities, including employees, customers, suppliers, investors, local communities, as well as regulatory bodies. Founder of the stakeholder concept in the 1960s developed it as a basis for recognizing multiple groups through different concerns in organizational decision-making processes. Organizations need to effectively involve stakeholders because this practice builds trust alongside sustainable business methods which respect social goals (Sanusi et al., 2024).

Triple Bottom Line: The Triple Bottom Line (TBL) refers to the three pillars of sustainability: economic, social, as well as environmental performance. The TBL approach developed by John Elkington in 1994 divides performance assessment into three pillars that encompass economic success together through social equity as well as environmental stewardship. Organizations should use this balanced method to determine their performance through economic, human as well as environmental measures in order to build responsible sustainable business operations. Organizations choose the TBL framework as their preferred methodology to unite their operations through worldwide sustainability targets (Liu et al., 2024).

EMPIRICAL LITERATURE REVIEW

Organizational Strategic Implication and Sustainable Business Practices

Empirical study focuses intensely on the relationship among organizational strategic implications as well as sustainable business practices because strategic alignment plays a fundamental role in sustainability development (Channuwong et al., 2024). Organizations achieving integration of sustainability through in their fundamental strategic goals tend to demonstrate higher performance rates as well as superior competitive position. When businesses apply their shared value approach to societal challenges they simultaneously boost their business success as well as deliver social advantages to their communities (Tadesse Bogale & Debela, 2024). The strategic linkage provides two major benefits that generate both increased profitability as well as beneficial social as well as environmental impacts. The implementation of sustainable business practices depends on multiple key factors which study has properly identified (Odeyemi et al., 2024). Study demonstrates that top-level organizational support determines the successful implementation of sustainability through in corporate strategies. Through their study the authors confirm that sustainability becomes stronger as leader emphasis increases because it shapes staff actions as well as creates sustainable organizational environments. The proper alignment of leadership through Culture of Organization acts as a key factor because it guarantees sustainability initiatives both get executed as well as continue across time periods (Lin et al., 2024).

Study investigations have thoroughly analyzed stakeholder engagement as a significant factor. Organizations gain better ability to address sustainability challenges when they engage their stakeholders in making decisions (Khaddage-Soboh et al., 2024). Companies which engage their stakeholders intensively demonstrate better sustainability outcomes through evidence-based data. Stakeholder relationships built by firms lead to better sustainable practices as well as innovation because these firms pay attention to stakeholder needs (Tadesse Bogale & Debela, 2024).

H1: Organizational Strategic Implication and Sustainable Business Practices having empirical association

Organizational Strategic Implication and Organizational Culture

In today's management literature, the relationship among Culture of Organizational as well as strategic consequences has become a crucial topic of study. Businesses are realizing more as well as more that their strategic goals need to be in line through the underlying cultural values as well as beliefs that influence employee conduct as well as decision-making (Odeyemi et al., 2024). Because culture acts as a guiding framework that affects how strategies are executed, study shows that businesses through a strong, coherent culture are better positioned to achieve their strategic goals. Artifacts, stated ideals, as well as underlying assumptions are the three layers of Culture of Organizational, according to one of the pioneering studies in this field (Tadesse Bogale & Debela, 2024). This approach demonstrates how deeply rooted cultural factors influence how strategic efforts are accepted as well as carried out (Wang & Zhang, 2024). For example, employees are more inclined to support strategic initiatives meant to promote creativity as well as change when the culture of the company values innovation as well as taking risks (Lin et al., 2024). According to a study that emphasizes how crucial it is to match Culture of Organizational through strategic goals in order to effectively drive change, on the other has well as, a culture that is resistant to change might make it difficult to successfully execute new strategies (Channuwong et al., 2024). The empirical evidence of the significant role of corporate culture on decision-making is also supported. A study confirms that companies with a customer-oriented culture through market-based strategies outperform other companies. This suggests that a more favourable market position is created in addition to greater efficiency when a cultural fit is achieved through strategic goals. Similarly, research shows the impact of culture on strategic choices, arguing that companies through adaptive cultures are best positioned to respond to opportunities as well as external changes (Khaddage-Soboh et al., 2024).

In addition, the notion of cultural intelligence has been in vogue in relation to how organisations manage the strategic implications in a cultural context. Research suggests companies through high cultural intelligence are better prepared to manage cultural differences, as well as take advantage of them when they execute strategies in the multicultural context (Wang & Zhang, 2024). This is particularly significant in global markets as companies need to work across cultural environments in order to align strategies. However, getting company culture aligned with strategic objectives is challenging (Tadesse Bogale & Debela, 2024). Research has found that misalignment can lead to low performance, low motivation, and also failed initiatives. For example, companies taking on ambitious growth strategies in cultures that prefer stability may encounter employee resistance, and this could lead to a loss of commitment to the strategic initiatives. This highlights the need for managers to assess as well as possibly change corporate culture to ensure alignment through strategic needs (Odeyemi et al., 2024).

H2: Empirical connection fond in OSI and OC.

Organizational Culture and Sustainable Business Practices

Empirical research has been more prominent in the relationship between corporate culture as well as sustainable business practices by highlighting the importance of cultural factors in shaping sustainable practices (Channuwong et al., 2024). Culture of Organizational refers to the shared values, norms, as well as behaviours that outline how employees communicate as well as engage in decision-making in an organisation. Research has shown that the implementation as well as application of sustainable practices rely on a supportive Culture of Organizational (Khaddage-Soboh et al., 2024). The Competing Values Framework (CVF) is an example of a paradigm used to understand this relationship. This theory classifies Culture of Organizational into four main quadrants: clan, adhocracy, market as well as hierarchy (Tadesse Bogale & Debela, 2024). According to empirical research, firms with a clan culture, which emphasises collaboration as well as a sense of community, are more likely to adopt sustainable practices. For instance, research indicates that companies with a collaborative culture promote employee engagement in sustainability-related initiatives, leading to innovative solutions to social and environmental challenges (Wang & Zhang, 2024).

Also, we can't underestimate the role of leadership in shaping corporate culture towards sustainability. In a study, the promotion of sustainable practices is positively related to transformational leadership practices that motivate as well as support employees (Khaddage-Soboh et al., 2024). When leaders that heavily value sustainability in their vision as well as values create a space for staff members to participate in sustainable initiatives, it enhances organisational commitment to sustainable goals. Further, research highlights the significance of cultural awareness as well as intelligence to the successful implementation of sustainable practices, particularly in diverse cultural organisations (Lin et al, 2024). A study found that for companies operating in multicultural contexts, it is important to develop cultural intelligence to successfully integrate sustainability into their corporate culture. This includes recognising and valuing different cultural perspectives towards sustainability, which can lead to more inclusive and effective sustainability strategies. Sustainable business practices are still challenging to align corporate culture, though (Channuwong et al., 2024). Research shows that cultural norms can be resistant to change, particularly in companies with a strong emphasis on short-term profits. A study shows that companies with a profit-oriented culture can struggle to introduce sustainable practices as employees may perceive that sustainability is less important than financial goals. This highlights the need for companies to proactively strive to shift their cultures to include equal weight on sustainability alongside profitability (Odeyemi et al., 2024).

H3: Empirical link between Organizational Culture and Sustainable Business Practices

OSI, Sustainable Business Practices mediated by OC

The empirical focus of research is the interdependency of Culture of Organizational, sustainable business practices and OSI (Channuwong et al., 2024). Research suggests that Culture of Organizational has a key mediation role in shaping how sustainable business-related strategic objectives are implemented and perceived within organisations (Tadesse Bogale & Debela, 2024). Given that organisational culture affects employees' perceptions as well as behaviours towards sustainability projects, strategy as well as culture need to be aligned to establish a conducive working environment for sustainable practices. Culture of Organizational affects the success of strategy implementation in addition to being a representation of the underlying values as well as beliefs of the firm (Khaddage-Soboh et al., 2024). In terms of sustainability, firms that have a socially as well as environmentally aware culture tend to incorporate sustainable practices into their strategy (Odeyemi et al., 2024). For example, one study found that employee involvement in sustainability activities was greater in firms that have a strong sustainability culture (Lin et al., 2024). It appears that cultural fit enhances the effectiveness of strategic sustainability approaches. Also, there is extensive research on the impact of strategic leadership on organisational culture and its impact on sustainable business practices (Channuwong et al., 2024). Research has shown that transformational leaders can have a significant impact on Culture of Organizational by cultivating beliefs that encourage sustainable practices when they prioritise sustainability in their strategic plans (Tadesse Bogale & Debela, 2024). The overall success of sustainability initiatives is enhanced by this leadership approach which not only fosters a collective commitment to the goal of sustainability but also inspires employees to adopt sustainability values (Wang & Zhang, 2024).

In addition, research has demonstrated the link among strategic implications as well as sustainable practices is moderated by corporate culture (Channuwong et al., 2024). For instance, one study found firms with a participatory and innovative culture were more successful in implementing sustainability strategies. This suggests that culture, by aligning employee attitudes as well as behaviours with corporate goals, acts as an enabler of sustainability, and helps companies effectively navigate the complexities of sustainability (Tadesse Bogale & Debela, 2024). However, it is very hard to comprehend the multiple ways in which culture moderates the relationship between strategy as well as sustainability. Research reveals that culture can undermine sustainability initiatives, particularly in firms through established practices that prioritise short-term profits over sustainability goals. This calls for CEOs to proactively engage in cultural change to ensure that strategic sustainability initiatives are successfully integrated into the corporate culture (Odeyemi et al., 2024).

H4: OSI, Sustainable Business Practices and OC Mediation having empirical association

CONCEPTUAL FRAMEWORK

Figure 1. Conceptual framework

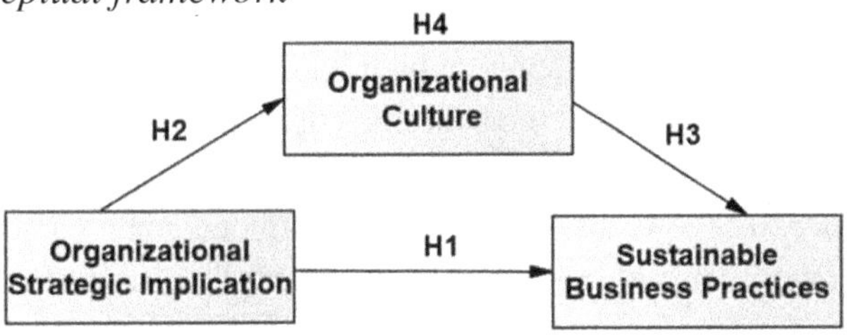

RESEARCH METHODOLOGY

The aim of this research was to apply a quantitative research approach to investigate the relationship between strategic implications for organizations, sustainable business practices, as well as Culture of Organizational (Ghanad, 2023). A convenience sampling approach was used to select 385 respondents to ensure representation of diverse businesses in the area of study. In the data gathering phase of the study, a structured questionnaire developed following a review of relevant literature was applied, with the inclusion of validated scales (Ghanad, 2023). To determine the underlying components associated with the construct of corporate culture, sustainable business practices and strategic outcomes of a business, EFA was used (Huang et al., 2023). The analysis was performed with a principal extraction (varimax) to avoid overlapping between components, and to highlight distinctive factors. The suggested inter-relationships between the components were then tested using AMOS software and SEM (Huang et al., 2023). SEM provided a robust approach to model the relationship between strategic implications, sustainable business practices and the mediating component of Culture of Organizational. The indices were used to assess the fit of the model to ensure it was a good representation of the data (Huang et al., 2023).

Scale Development

A comprehensive analysis of the body of study on Culture of Organizational, sustainable business practices, as well as strategic implications served as the foundation for the scale development process. First, pertinent constructs were found, as well as the validity as well as reliability of the current measuring scales was assessed. The items were modified from pre-existing scales, such as Triple Bottom Line framework for sustainability as well as Cameron as well as Quinn's Culture of Organizational scale (Literal & Guhao, 2021). Each construct was represented by several questions on the final scale, which had a Likert-type answer style. This method made it possible to record the subtleties of respondents' opinions about how corporate culture affects the execution of strategic goals as well as sustainable practices (Robie et al., 2022). As an outcome, the produced scale closely matched the theoretical frameworks presented in the literature while also guaranteeing validity as well as reliability. The thorough technique offered a strong basis for dissecting the complex connections among the components, making significant contributions to the fields of sustainability as well as organizational behavior (Robie et al., 2022).

DATA ANALYSIS

Table 1. Demographic

Variable	Category	Frequency (n)	Percentage (%)
Gender	Male	232	60.3
	Female	153	39.7
Age Group	Below 25 years	48	12.5
	25–34 years	146	37.9
	35–44 years	118	30.6
	45 years and above	73	19.0
Education Level	Diploma	72	18.7
	Bachelor's Degree	198	51.4
	Master's Degree	95	24.7
	PhD	20	5.2
Work Experience	Less than 5 years	104	27.0
	5–10 years	139	36.1
continued on following page	11–15 years	86	22.3

Table 1. Continued

Variable	Category	Frequency (n)	Percentage (%)
	Above 15 years	56	14.5
Sector	Public	167	43.4
	Private	218	56.6
Industry Type	Service	229	59.5
	Manufacturing	156	40.5
Position Level	Operational Staff	172	44.7
	Middle Management	139	36.1
	Top Management	74	19.2

The demographics in Table 1 help contextualise the findings of the study. The over-representation of private sector (56.6%) and service sector (59.5%) respondents in the sample indicates that the findings are likely to be more representative of market-oriented and customer-focused workplaces, in which sustainability initiatives are often linked to market competition and customer preferences. The even gender split and the relatively young (68.5% between 25 and 44 years old) sample suggest that the sample represents the views of an economically and professionally active population, making the study's insights about strategy and culture more relevant.

And the high educational background (over 75% have a bachelor degree or higher) suggests that respondents have the intellectual capability to grasp and assess sustainability practices, thus enhancing the reliability of the perceptual indicators. The representation of a balanced mix of experience and managerial roles also means that both operational and strategic considerations are taken into account, providing a comprehensive view of the dynamics at play. Theoretically, these characteristics support the use of Organizational Culture Theory and Stakeholder Theory, given that highly educated and experienced workforce are more likely to undertake sustainability-related practices if supported by a culture that endorses such initiatives. In practice, companies should understand that the human resource makeup (age, education, experience) of employees is important for the acceptance of sustainability strategies. Given the representativeness of the sample, the impacts of reliability and construct validity of the measures can now be explored.

Table 2. Construct reliability and validity

Construct	Items	Cronbach's Alpha	CR	AVE	Interpretation
OSI	6	0.93	0.92	0.65	Excellent reliability and convergent validity
OC	5	0.91	0.93	0.68	Strong internal consistency
SBP	6	0.89	0.91	0.64	Adequate convergent validity

The findings in Table 2 show that all the constructs are reliable and have strong convergent validity (Cronbach's alpha of 0.89 or higher and AVE of 0.50 or higher). This confirms that the measurement scales are not only consistent and conceptually coherent, but also that each construct is capturing its targeted construct. This research has methodological implications. First, they confirm that existing scales (e.g., culture and sustainability instruments) can be applied in the context of the Horn of Africa, overcoming a major weakness of previous studies that tend to use Western scales. Second, the high reliability indicates the constructs are reliable and consistent, enhancing the study's external validity in other emerging markets. Practically, the constructs can be used as measures to diagnose strategic fit, readiness to change and sustainability performance. This also enhances the validity of the structural relationships. The structural relationships between the constructs, based on the measurement model, yield valuable insights into the dynamics of strategy and culture on sustainability.

Figure 2. Structural equation model

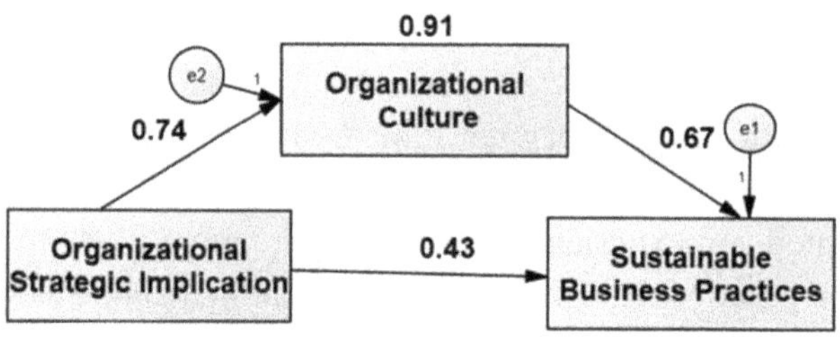

Table 3. Path estimates

Hypothesis	Path	Standardized β	t-value	p-value
H1	OSI → SBP	0.43	> 3.0	< 0.001
H2	OSI → OC	0.74	> 6.0	< 0.001
H3	OC → SBP	0.67	> 5.0	< 0.001

The results of the structural paths in Table 3 on base of figure 2 provide some important insights about sustainability implementation. The positive effect of OSI on OC (β = 0.74) confirms that strategy has an important influence on organisational culture. This is in line with the idea that strategy is a plan and culture is what makes the strategy happen. Moreover, the strong impact of OC on SBP (β = 0.67) demonstrates that OC is a crucial factor in the adoption of sustainability. This implies that sustainability is not just a matter of strategy and technology but of culture and behaviour. Although OSI also has a direct effect on SBP (β = 0.43), the effect is less significant, suggesting that strategy without cultural support is ineffective. The direct effects are important but to understand how strategy affects sustainability, it is necessary to explore the mediation effects.

Table 4. Mediation effect of OC (bootstrapping)

Effect Type	Path	β	Boot SE	t-value	p-value	95% CI (LL–UL)	Result
Direct Effect	OSI → SBP	0.43	0.052	8.27	< 0.001	0.328 – 0.532	Partial mediation
Indirect Effect	OSI → OC → SBP	0.496	0.061	8.13	< 0.001	0.377 – 0.615	Supported
Total Effect	OSI → SBP	0.926	—	—	—	—	Strong effect

The mediation effects in Table 4 and figure 2 are a key finding of this research. The result that the indirect effect (0.496) is larger than the direct effect (0.43) establishes that culture is a key mediation effect between strategy implication and sustainable business practices. This suggests that strategy has a more indirect impact on sustainability via a process of cultural change. This finding adds to the theoretical literature in that it shows culture is not simply a contextual factor but, rather, a conduit for strategy that either facilitates or hinders its outcomes. It supports the contention that sustainability programs are effective when embedded in the espoused and enacted values, norms and behaviours of organisational members. Practically, this finding means that managers should focus on culture-building initiatives, such as ensuring managers are supportive of sustainability programs, designing reward structures and encouraging sustainability and social values. A lack of this cultural fit could result in sustainability strategies and initiatives not delivering the expected results. The degree of mediation, however, varies across different organisational settings, and requires a comparative study.

Table 5. Comparative mediation strength across sectors

Sector Type	OSI → OC	OC → SBP	Indirect Effect	Mediation Strength	Key Insight
Public Sector	Moderate	Strong	Medium	Partial mediation	Bureaucratic rigidity limits strategic flexibility
Private Sector	Strong	Strong	High	Strong mediation	Culture aligns faster with strategic goals
Service Sector	Strong	Very Strong	Very High	Dominant mediation	Human-centric culture amplifies sustainability
Manufacturing Sector	Moderate	Moderate	Medium	Partial mediation	Operational constraints reduce cultural influence

The comparative study in Table 5 reveals that the mediation effect of the organisational culture differs among sectors. The private sector is found to have strong mediation, given the flexible nature and performance-oriented cultures that allow for a quick match between strategy and culture. However, public sector displays weak mediation, due to bureaucratic and procedural inflexibility that restrains cultural dynamics. Likewise, the strongest mediation effect is observed in the service sector, as it is heavily dependent on people, their actions and interactions with customers, which are all driven by culture. On the other hand, the manufacturing sector exhibits lower mediation, as sustainability strategies are more reliant on technological, infrastructural and regulatory factors rather than cultural factors. Thus, the power of culture as a mediation variable is sector-specific, influenced by the structure, nature of the industry and operations. This suggests that, for policy interventions, it's important to have sector-specific approaches to adopting sustainability practices, rather than a blanket approach. As we have identified variations across sectors, it is important to check if the model overall fits the data.

Table 6. Fit statistics

Fit Index	Value	Threshold	Interpretation
Chi-square/df	< 3.0	< 5.0	Acceptable fit
CFI	> 0.95	> 0.90	Excellent fit
RMSEA	< 0.06	< 0.08	Good fit
TLI	> 0.94	> 0.90	Strong fit

The model fit indices (CFI, TLI, RMSEA) shown in Table 6 indicate that the model fits the data very well (CFI, TLI > 0.90; RMSEA < 0.08). This suggests that the model is statistically and theoretically sound, and confirms the proposed relationships. The results have important research and managerial implications.

As a model, researchers can use it as a validated model to inform future research on the inter-relationships between strategy, culture and sustainability in emerging markets. For companies, the model can be a strategic readiness model to determine their sustainability readiness. Having a good model fit and empirical support, the discussion section can now discuss the implications from the findings for research and practice. Overall, the results indicate that culture is the instrument that enables strategy to be implemented sustainably and this is largely dependent on industry and other environmental factors, which has theoretical and practical implications for sustainable firms.

DISCUSSION

The findings demonstrate statistically significant relationships between the organisation's strategic implication, organisational culture and sustainability; but more importantly, they reveal insights regarding the operation of organisations in the Horn of Africa. While in the Western world institutional, regulatory and infrastructural systems create certainty in the environment and allow strategy to be implemented, in other nations (such as Ethiopia and Somalia) the situation is characterised by uncertainty, scarcity and poor institutional systems. The high influence of strategic implication on OC suggests that organisations in these countries require leaders who have to lead cultural norms and practices to respond to uncertainty. Rather than tradition, the desire for flexibility, adaptability and resilience calls for a dynamic culture.

This is particularly obvious in the case of adaptive culture. In emerging markets like Somalia, where there may not be formal mechanisms for rule-making and enforcement, and business may be conducted through informal networks and trust relationships, it is important to maintain legitimacy and viability through an adaptive culture. Similarly, in Ethiopia where businesses are plagued with policy uncertainty, foreign exchange shortages and poor infrastructure, the need for a rapid learning and adaptation requires the creation of an adaptive culture. In such settings, OC is not only developed, but nurtured and supported by organisational leaders to achieve their strategic intentions. This accounts for the strong association between strategy and culture, as leaders are the designers of culture, institutionalising strategic decision-making in organisational practices.

The study also reveals that culture is the key means by which sustainability is achieved. In many mature markets, sustainability programs are often motivated by regulatory and stakeholder pressures and formal governance structures. However, in the case of the Horn of Africa, where these external factors may be weak or absent, sustainability relies primarily on cultural factors. The high positive association between culture and sustainable business practices suggests that sustainability is more than a technical or procedural challenge, but a behavioural one. Companies that embed values of environmental and social responsibility and future-oriented thinking are more likely to succeed in implementing sustainable practices even without the presence of strong external pressures.

The mediation findings reveal even greater detail, with organisational culture being the primary avenue through which strategy plays out in terms of sustainability. The greater indirect effect over the direct effect implies that a strategy will not be effective unless it becomes embedded in the culture of the organisation. This is especially relevant in the Horn of Africa where institutional structures and processes may not be as robust as needed to guarantee operationalization. In these contexts, culture takes the place of formal institutional structures, by serving as a conduit to translate strategy into practice. When frontline workers adopt the sustainability narrative as part of their internal organisational narrative, they are more likely to continue to implement these practices even when external circumstances change, thus emphasising the need for cultural fit.

On the other hand, the differences in the strength of mediation across industries highlights the role of context. The private and service sectors' stronger cultural mediation is due to their greater human-centric focus and flexibility, allowing a greater influence of leadership on employees. On the other hand, the lower mediating effect in public and manufacturing sectors reflects the bureaucratic rigidities and infrastructural and technological demands of these sectors. These findings indicate that the role of culture as a mediator is not a universal, but more dependent on organisational and sectorial attributes and demands a nuanced approach to sustainability practices.

Overall, these insights move the focus from technical to leadership in the Horn of Africa. They indicate that leadership in this region must go beyond strategy to include the creation and maintenance of flexible organisational cultures that are in line with both internal and external environments. Therefore, leaders need to focus on cultural change as a key part of their strategy to ensure that sustainability is not viewed as a standalone project but as an intrinsic part of the organisation. In a context of uncertainty and weak institutional support, it is this fit between strategy, culture and action that ultimately will lead to success or failure in sustainability efforts.

CONCLUSION

The chapter provides a contextual and clear insight into the relationship between strategy, culture and sustainable business practices in the Horn of Africa. While previous research has shown that strategy and/or external institutional influence is the key driver of sustainability, in the Horn of Africa where resource constraints and uncertainty prevail, the key driver of sustainability is internal - culture. The results confirm that in addition to strategy being important in directing the organisation, it is the culture of the organisation that will influence the strategy. A significant finding of this analysis is that culture is the vehicle for strategy to influence sustainability. The significant mediating effect implies that if the culture of the organisation is not in line, strategies will not have a positive and long-term effect. This is especially significant in the Horn of Africa where institutional, infrastructural and regulatory issues result in weak formal systems. In this case, culture substitutes for external governance and controls employee behaviour, and sustainability programs. So, organisations with a culture that embraces sustainability are more capable of coping with uncertainty and maintaining performance.

The study also finds industry differences in the impact of culture. The higher mediation in the private and service sectors - sectors where adaptability, human relations and responsiveness to the market are high - suggest culture has a greater impact on sustainability. In contrast, the reduced impact in the public and manufacturing sectors is associated with the constraints from their structures and processes that limit the agility of culture. This suggests the need for different approaches in different sectors, and that a one-size-fits-all approach will not work. More broadly, the study contributes to theory by more clearly placing the role of organisational culture in the sustainability debate, in new or less-developed areas. It extends current models by demonstrating that culture is not only in the background of organisations and organisational activities, but that it can be a driver for change. Managers in the Horn of Africa need to move beyond traditional strategic management and focus on creating sustainable and flexible value-driven culture. This involves developing a shared understanding, providing opportunities for staff participation and leadership support for sustainability. Finally, the trick to success for sustainable business practices in the Horn of Africa is not having strategies but having strategies "fit" in the culture. It is this "fit" which enables organisations to implement strategies and fulfil their objectives in a dynamic and uncertain environment.

REFERENCES

Abdalla, A. A., Bhat, M. A., Tiwari, C. K., Khan, S. T., & Wedajo, A. D. (2024). Exploring ChatGPT adoption among business and management students through the lens of diffusion of Innovation Theory. *Computers and Education: Artificial Intelligence*, *7*, 100257. DOI: 10.1016/j.caeai.2024.100257

Awa, H. O., Etim, W., & Ogbonda, E. (2024). Stakeholders, stakeholder theory and corporate social responsibility (CSR). *International Journal of Corporate Social Responsibility*, *9*(1), 11. DOI: 10.1186/s40991-024-00094-y

Channuwong, S., Phudarat, B. S. S., Jirachottrakul, P., Pleansamai, J. L. K., Khamsom, S., & Kanhabutr, A. (2024). Strategic management for sustainable business development: Concepts, theories and practices. *Sciences of Conservation and Archaeology*, *36*(3), 11–22.

Chourasia, S., Dhama, A., & Bhardwaj, G. (2024). AI-Driven Organizational Culture Evolution: A Critical Review. *2024 International Conference on Communication, Computer Sciences and Engineering (IC3SE)*, 1839–1844. DOI: 10.1109/IC3SE62002.2024.10592949

Ghanad, A. (2023). An overview of quantitative research methods. *International Journal of Multidisciplinary Research and Analysis*, *6*(08), 3794–3803. DOI: 10.47191/ijmra/v6-i8-52

Homer, S. T., Lim, W. M., & Poon, W. C. (2025). A concentric locus of control and triple bottom line model for responsible management: Theory development inspired by students from the Global South. *International Journal of Management Education*, *23*(1), 101083. DOI: 10.1016/j.ijme.2024.101083

Huang, J.-F., Chen, C.-T. A., Chen, M.-H., Huang, S.-L., & Hsu, P.-Y. (2023). Structural Equation Modeling of the Marine Ecological System in Nanwan Bay Using SPSS Amos. *Sustainability (Basel)*, *15*(14), 11435. DOI: 10.3390/su151411435

Khaddage-Soboh, N., Yunis, M., Imran, M., & Zeb, F. (2024). Sustainable practices in Malaysian manufacturing: The influence of CSR, transformational leadership, and green organizational culture on environmental performance. *Economic Analysis and Policy*, *82*, 753–768. DOI: 10.1016/j.eap.2024.04.001

Lin, Z., Gu, H., Gillani, K. Z., & Fahlevi, M. (2024). Impact of Green Work–Life Balance and Green Human Resource Management Practices on Corporate Sustainability Performance and Employee Retention: Mediation of Green Innovation and Organisational Culture. *Sustainability (Basel)*, *16*(15), 6621. DOI: 10.3390/su16156621

Literal, V. J. I., & Guhao, E. S. (2021). *Structural equation model on triple bottom line performance of large manufacturing companies in Region XII*. Recent Developments in Asian Economics International Symposia in Economic Theory and Econometrics. DOI: 10.1108/S1571-038620210000028002

Liu, C., Dai, G., & Tu, H. (2024). Study of a triple bottom line perspective to reach a sustainable development model for critical minerals using financial development. *Resources Policy*, *90*, 104790. DOI: 10.1016/j.resourpol.2024.104790

Odeyemi, O., Usman, F. O., Mhlongo, N. Z., Elufioye, O. A., & Ike, C. U. (2024). Sustainable entrepreneurship: A review of green business practices and environmental impact. *World Journal of Advanced Research and Reviews*, *21*(2), 346–358. DOI: 10.30574/wjarr.2024.21.2.0461

Rashid, A., Rasheed, R., & Ngah, A. H. (2024). Achieving sustainability through multifaceted green functions in manufacturing. *Journal of Global Operations and Strategic Sourcing*, *17*(2), 402–428. DOI: 10.1108/JGOSS-06-2023-0054

Robie, C., Meade, A. W., Risavy, S. D., & Rasheed, S. (2022). Effects of response option order on Likert-type psychometric properties and reactions. *Educational and Psychological Measurement*, *82*(6), 1107–1129. DOI: 10.1177/00131644211069406 PMID: 36325125

Sanusi, I. T., Agbo, F. J., Dada, O. A., Yunusa, A. A., Aruleba, K. D., Obaido, G., Olawumi, O., & Oyelere, S. S.Centre for Multidisciplinary Research and Innovation (CEMRI). (2024). Stakeholders' insights on artificial intelligence education: Perspectives of teachers, students, and policymakers. *Computers and Education Open*, *7*, 100212. DOI: 10.1016/j.caeo.2024.100212

Tadesse Bogale, A., & Debela, K. L. (2024). Organizational culture: A systematic review. *Cogent Business & Management*, *11*(1), 2340129. Advance online publication. DOI: 10.1080/23311975.2024.2340129

Wang, S., & Zhang, H. (2024). Inter-organizational cooperation in digital green supply chains: A catalyst for eco-innovations and sustainable business practices. *Journal of Cleaner Production*, *472*, 143383. DOI: 10.1016/j.jclepro.2024.143383

ADDITIONAL READINGS

Adama, H. E., Popoola, O. A., Okeke, C. D., & Akinoso, A. E.Henry Ejiga AdamaOladapo Adeboye PopoolaChukwuekem David OkekeAbiodun Emmanuel Akinoso. (2024). ECONOMIC THEORY AND PRACTICAL IMPACTS OF DIGITAL TRANSFORMATION IN SUPPLY CHAIN OPTIMIZATION. *International Journal of Advanced Economics*, *6*(4), 95–107. DOI: 10.51594/ijae.v6i4.1072

Bigirimana, A., Ndikumagenge, J., & Tabbane, S. (2024). The Application of Mobile Money and Mobile Banking to Digital Transformation: State of Play in Burundi and within the Countries of the East African Community. *Open Journal of Business and Management*, *12*(3), 1619–1634. DOI: 10.4236/ojbm.2024.123087

Bonhoure, É. (2024). Indigenous knowledge and digital financial inclusion: A comparison between Europe and Sub-Saharan Africa. *Information Technology for Development*, *1*. Advance online publication. DOI: 10.1080/02681102.2024.2384716

Choruma, D. J., Dirwai, T. L., Mutenje, M., Mustafa, M. A., Chimonyo, V. G. P., Jacobs-Mata, I., & Mabhaudhi, T. (2024). Digitalisation in agriculture: A scoping review of technologies in practice, challenges, and opportunities for smallholder farmers in sub-saharan africa [Review of *Digitalisation in agriculture: A scoping review of technologies in practice, challenges, and opportunities for smallholder farmers in sub-saharan africa*]. *Journal of Agriculture and Food Research*, *18*, 101286. Elsevier BV. DOI: 10.1016/j.jafr.2024.101286

Dudu, O. F., Alao, O. B., & Alonge, E. O.Oritsematosan Faith DuduOlakunle Babatunde AlaoEnoch O. Alonge. (2024). Advancing financial inclusion through digital payment platforms in emerging markets. *Finance & Accounting Research Journal*, *6*(11), 2028–2060. DOI: 10.51594/farj.v6i11.1696

Hadizadeh, M., Feyzabadi, J. G., Fardi, Z., Mortazavi, S., Braga, V., & Salamzadeh, A. (2024). Digital Platforms as a Fertile Ground for the Economic Sustainability of Startups: Assaying Scenarios, Actions, Plans, and Players. *Sustainability (Basel)*, *16*(16), 7139. DOI: 10.3390/su16167139

Kejela, A. B., & Porath, D. (2022). Influence of attitude on mobile banking acceptance and factors determining attitude of end-users in Ethiopia. *Journal of Internet and Digital Economics*, *2*(1), 68–88. DOI: 10.1108/JIDE-08-2021-0007

Malek, N. A. (2024). Gig Economy: Is It a Trap or Stepping Stone for the Informal Sector? *Information Management and Business Review*, *16*(3S(I)a), 28–38. DOI: 10.22610/imbr.v16i3S(I)a.4201

Mhlongo, N. Z., Daraojimba, D. O., Olubusola, O., Ajayi-Nifise, A. O., & Falaiye, T. (2024). Reviewing the impact of digital platforms on entrepreneurship in Africa. *International Journal of Science and Research Archive, 11*(1), 1364–1375. DOI: 10.30574/ijsra.2024.11.1.0228

Mohammad, A. A. S., Mohammad, S. I., Daoud, K. I. A., Oraini, B. A., Qurneh, M., Vasudevan, A., & Wang, Y. (2025). *Digital Platforms and Agricultural Marketing: Bridging Gaps between Farmers and Consumers in Jordan*. Research on World Agricultural Economy., DOI: 10.36956/rwae.v6i3.1570

Mpofu, F. Y. (2024). Industry 4.0 in Finance, Digital Financial Services and Digital Financial Inclusion in Developing Countries: Opportunities, Challenges, and Possible Policy Responses. *International Journal of Economics and Financial Issues, 14*(2), 120–135. DOI: 10.32479/ijefi.15081

Nwokolo, S. C., Eyime, E., Obiwulu, A., & Ogbulezie, J. C. (2023). Africa's Path to Sustainability: Harnessing Technology, Policy, and Collaboration. *Trends in Renewable Energy, 10*(1), 98–131. DOI: 10.17737/tre.2024.10.1.00166

Plečko, S., & Hojnik, B. B. (2024). Sustainable Business Practices and the Role of Digital Technologies: A Cross-Regional Analysis. *Systems, 12*(3), 97. DOI: 10.3390/systems12030097

Schilling, L., Gleim, I.-M., Khalid, R. U., Wagner, R., & Seuring, S. (2025). Informal digital transactions: A path to value creation in base-of-the-pyramid supply chains. *International Journal of Operations & Production Management, 1*. Advance online publication. DOI: 10.1108/IJOPM-11-2024-1011

Sethupathy, U. K. A.Utham Kumar Anugula Sethupathy. (2025). Evolving Frameworks in Digital Payment Security: Technological Innovations, Economic Impact, and Consumer Trust Dynamics. *International Journal of Computational and Experimental Science and Engineering, 11*(3). Advance online publication. DOI: 10.22399/ijcesen.3893

Shaikh, A. A., Glavee-Geo, R., Karjaluoto, H., & Hinson, R. E. (2022). Mobile money as a driver of digital financial inclusion. *Technological Forecasting and Social Change, 186*, 122158. DOI: 10.1016/j.techfore.2022.122158

Tay, L.-Y., Tai, H.-T., & Tan, G.-S. (2022). Digital financial inclusion: A gateway to sustainable development. *Heliyon, 8*(6), e09766. Advance online publication. DOI: 10.1016/j.heliyon.2022.e09766 PMID: 35785228

Usuemerai, P. A., Ibikunle, O. E., Abass, L. A., Alemede, V., Nwankwo, E. I., & Mbata, A. O. (2024). Advanced supply chain optimization for emerging market healthcare systems. *International Journal of Management & Entrepreneurship Research*, *6*(10), 3321–3356. DOI: 10.51594/ijmer.v6i10.1637

KEY TERMS AND DEFINITIONS

Cultural Dimensions: The main components of cultural dimensions that impact organizational behavior as well as attitudes include individualism versus collectivism together through power distance as well as uncertainty avoidance as well as long-term orientation. The set of dimensions serves as tools to explain how cultural environments influence organizational operational practices.

Employee Engagement: Employee Engagement stands for the amount of enthusiasm along through dedication as well as investment workers demonstrate in their organizational duties. Higher employee engagement creates both increased worker productivity as well as better organizational goal fulfillment.

Mediation: In statistics mediation defines the situation when one variable changes through the impact of another variable that links them. The Culture of Organizational bridges the gap that connects strategic implications through sustainable practices.

Organizational Culture: Culture of Organizational represents the group-held beliefs along through shared values as well as standard procedures which determine member interactions both internally as well as toward external partners. Such constructs influence behaviors of employees as well as their decision-making processes as well as affect the organizational working environment.

Organizational Strategic Implication: Organizational Strategic Implication describes how an organization connects its core operational techniques as well as strategic objectives to generate desired operational outcomes through guiding decisions as well as allocating resources.

Stakeholder Collaboration: Organizations use stakeholder collaboration to activate discussions among employees as well as customers through suppliers as well as community members for achieving sustainability targets.

Sustainable Business Practices: The implementation of actions as well as strategies by organizations maintains environmental sustainability through social responsibility combined through financial viability to achieve enduring sustainability.

Chapter 9
Stock Market Reaction to Corporate Social Responsibility Measures Announcements

Chafik Massane
http://orcid.org/0009-0002-6684-4233
INSEEC-OMNES Education Research Center, France & IRGO-University of Bordeaux, France

Karim Remah
IRGO-University of Bordeaux, France

ABSTRACT

This study examines how financial markets react to CSR announcements by listed firms. Using event study methodology, we analyze abnormal returns and trading volumes around 237 CSR announcements by French companies between 2022 and 2024. Announcements fall into four categories: environmental, social, governance, and hybrid initiatives. Results show heterogeneous responses. Governance and hybrid announcements generate the strongest and most persistent abnormal returns and volumes, reflecting investor confidence. Environmental initiatives elicit moderate, delayed effects, while social ones trigger the weakest and most transient reactions. Findings highlight the market's differentiated valuation of CSR, favoring initiatives seen as strategically relevant or tied to governance. Evidence supports signaling and information asymmetry theories, indicating that transparent CSR communication enhances firm value by reducing investor uncertainty. The study also stresses the importance of aligning CSR with governance reforms and improving visibility of environmental and social efforts.

DOI: 10.4018/979-8-3693-4099-8.ch009

INTRODUCTION

With the growing awareness of environmental protection and the increasing importance of social dynamics within organizations, Corporate Social Responsibility (CSR) is becoming an area of significant interest for both business leaders and shareholders. In this context, balancing financial performance with CSR presents a unique challenge for managers, since they must handle not only their company's budgetary constraints but also the necessity of achieving profitability while honoring CSR commitments dictated by regulatory frameworks and the expectations of various stakeholders. As CSR continues to shape corporate agendas, its strategic alignment with financial goals remains a critical area of study.

Numerous studies have examined the effect of CSR initiatives on companies' economic and financial performance. These studies generally point to either the absence of a significant effect or a positive effect, particularly for firms that manage to integrate CSR into their long-term strategies and derive profitability from it (Waddock and Graves, 1997). However, the financial impact of CSR is highly dependent on several factors, such as the financial situation of the company, its industry sector, the specific context of the study, and the geographical region under consideration. This variability in findings highlights the complex relationship between CSR and financial outcomes, suggesting that CSR's impact is not uniform across all contexts.

Despite the broad range of literature on the economic effects of CSR, the domain focusing on the effects of CSR announcements specifically those regarding the potential or planned CSR measures on stock market performance remains relatively underexplored. Most studies related to CSR have focused on the effects of implementing CSR projects, rather than examining how announcements regarding these initiatives influence market reactions.

Our study focuses on stock market reactions to CSR announcements within the French stock market. The novelty of our study lies in its specific focus on the stock market performance of publicly listed companies in France in response to CSR related announcements. By analyzing stock price and trading volume movements following these announcements, our research seeks to provide a more nuanced understanding of how the market reacts to CSR information and to identify key variables that may influence stock returns following these announcements.

The results of our study hold important practical implications for investors, company managers, and regulators. Understanding how CSR announcements affect stock prices and trading volumes can help investors make more informed decisions about the long-term potential of companies with robust CSR strategies. For company managers, the findings highlight the value of communicating CSR initiatives effectively and aligning them with long-term business goals in order to enhance shareholder value. Furthermore, regulators may find the study's insights useful in designing policies that encourage transparency and the dissemination of relevant CSR information, thereby fostering more efficient and sustainable stock markets.

From section 1 to section 3 we analyze conceptual framework of CSR and its financial effects, then we explain our study methodology in section 4 before presenting results in section 5 and their discussion in section 6.

1. THE EVOLUTION OF CSR AND ITS CONCEPTUAL FRAMEWORK

The relationship between corporate social responsibility (CSR) and financial performance has been widely explored since the mid-20th century (Bowen, 1953). Despite extensive research, empirical findings remain inconclusive due to discrepancies in definitions and methodological approaches (Aldag and Bartol, 1978; Cochran and Wood, 1984; Ullmann, 1985; Waddock and Mahon, 1991; Griffin and Mahon, 1997; Orlitzky, 2015). Over time, CSR theories have oscillated between two dominant perspectives: profit maximization (Friedman, 2007) and ethical and social responsibility (Zenisek, 1979). The diversity of CSR conceptualizations (Bowen, 1953; Carroll, 1979; Epstein, 1987; Freeman, 1984; Wood, 1991) has contributed to ongoing methodological challenges in assessing its impact on corporate financial performance (CFP).

In response to this definitional ambiguity, Yassin and Beckmann (2024) examine the continuing debate surrounding CSR's conceptualization. Carroll (1991) defines CSR as encompassing economic, legal, ethical, and philanthropic responsibilities, creating a framework that seeks to balance profitability with social expectations. By contrast, the European Commission (CEC, 2001) adopts a more voluntary perspective, positioning CSR as the integration of social and environmental considerations into business operations and stakeholder engagements. These definitional inconsistencies illustrate CSR's dynamic nature, where classifications evolve based on research focus and stakeholder priorities (Yassin and Beckmann, 2024).

In the same side, Barnett (2007) critically examines the longstanding debate surrounding the ownership and obligations of corporations, interrogating whether firms exist solely to maximize shareholder wealth or also to uphold broader societal responsibilities. His analysis is situated in the context of increasingly high-profile instances of corporate misconduct, a reality that has intensified this debate without yielding a clear resolution. Rather than attempting to defuse this enduring tension, Barnett argues that society must continuously manage the dialectic between profit maximization and social responsibility. In doing so, he sheds light on the business case for corporate social responsibility (CSR) by introducing a contingent perspective that reconsiders the financial merits of CSR activities.

Barnett identifies a central methodological challenge faced by scholars: the difficulty in demonstrating a universal rate of return for CSR initiatives. For decades, researchers have been unable to establish clearly defined financial payoffs from CSR, a problem he likens to the traditional challenges of valuing investments in intangible assets such as research and development or advertising. In traditional accounting and financial practice, advances have gradually provided frameworks to justify investments that do not yield immediate financial returns. By analogy, Barnett argues that CSR, though ubiquitous as a corporate practice, requires a contingent model, one that acknowledges that while not all CSR initiatives are inherently profit maximizing, under certain conditions some CSR activities can indeed fulfill management's fiduciary responsibilities.

To support this contingent view, Barnett introduces the SIC construct and develops a conceptual framework aimed at specifying conditions under which CSR investments yield positive financial outcomes. He posits that the ambiguity in the financial merits of CSR does not necessarily stem from a fundamental flaw in the concept or practice of CSR, but rather from the failure to account for the contextual factors that condition its success. Thus, Barnett contends that CSR should be viewed as capable of generating financial returns in a contingent manner, depending on firm-specific, industry-specific, and temporal variables. In this light, CSR becomes comparable to other intangible investments whose eventual value is realized through careful, context-sensitive application.

Also, Barnett (2007) advances the literature by reframing the discussion of CSR from a debate to one that recognizes the conditional nature of its financial benefits. His work underscores that CSR cannot uniformly satisfy all firms at all times, but may contribute positively to financial performance when deployed under favorable conditions. This contingent perspective not only deepens our theoretical understanding of CSR but also aims to understand the specific circumstances under which CSR investments translate into tangible financial gains

1.1 The Interaction Between CSR, CFP, and Competitive Action

The relationship between corporate social responsibility (CSR), corporate governance (CG), and firm value has garnered significant attention from shareholders, practitioners, and government regulators. Despite its importance, empirical investigations into how these elements interrelate remain limited. Jo et al. (2011) address this gap by examining the determinants of CSR engagement and assessing whether CSR activities—when combined with robust corporate governance and effective monitoring mechanisms—enhance firm value.

Jo et al. (2011) extend existing scholarship in three notable ways. First, they offer a comprehensive analysis of CSR engagement determinants within the context of a full spectrum corporate governance system. Their findings indicate that several governance characteristics, consistent with both prior literature and economic intuition, positively influence a firm's likelihood to engage in CSR. This extension of the governance framework enriches our understanding of the antecedents that drive CSR initiatives.

Second, by rigorously controlling endogenous treatment effects and simultaneity bias, the study provides robust empirical evidence that CSR engagement is associated with an increase in firm value. The methodological care taken in addressing these econometric challenges is particularly valuable, given the long-standing difficulty in demonstrating a universal rate of return for CSR initiatives—a challenge that has historically obscured the financial merits of CSR, much like the valuation complexities of intangible investments such as RandD and advertising.

Third, the research highlights the significant role of external monitoring, specifically by security analysts, in enhancing firm value. The study finds that external oversight of a firm's CSR activities exerts a more pronounced impact on firm value than other internal mechanisms or alternative external monitoring systems. This insight emphasizes the importance of transparency and external validation in the corporate governance landscape, suggesting that market-based scrutiny can serve as a crucial complement to internal governance practices.

Jo et al. (2011) also provide practical implications for managers. They recommend that firms prioritize internal CSR initiatives—such as improving diversity, strengthening employee relations, and ensuring high product quality—as these have been empirically linked to enhanced firm value. Moreover, the study underscores the importance of incorporating rigorous governance practices alongside CSR efforts, as their synergistic effect appears to drive superior financial performance.

In the same vein, Kim et al. (2018) examine the complex relationship between corporate social responsibility (CSR) and corporate financial performance (CFP), incorporating competitive action (CA) as a crucial contingency. Their study distinguishes CSR into two forms: proactive CSR (PCSR), which represents socially responsible corporate behaviors, and non-proactive CSR (NCSR), which refers to practices that may have socially harmful effects. Through an analysis of U.S. software firms between 2000 and 2005, they investigate how CA interacts with these CSR dimensions to influence financial outcomes.

The results indicate that PCSR has a positive association with CFP, and this relationship is strengthened when firms actively engage in CA. This suggests that competitive initiatives complement socially responsible actions, enhancing their financial impact. Conversely, NCSR tends to negatively affect CFP when CA levels are high, but this detrimental effect is mitigated when firms engage in lower levels of CA. These findings highlight the complex dynamics between CSR and CA, demonstrating that NCSR, despite its negative social implications, may contribute to firm performance in specific contexts.

Kim et al. (2018) advance CSR literature in several key ways. First, their theoretical framework underscores the necessity of examining CSR's effects in conjunction with CA to fully understand its financial implications. Prior research has explored various contingencies affecting CSR-CFP relationships, including industry characteristics and stakeholder perceptions (Wang and Qian, 2011). This study builds upon those insights by identifying CA as an important boundary condition that shapes the financial impact of CSR.

Second, their empirical analysis contributes to ongoing discussions regarding the differentiation between PCSR and NCSR. Previous studies have emphasized that PCSR and NCSR are distinct concepts that should be analyzed separately to gain a more nuanced understanding of the CSR-CFP link (Kotchen and Moon, 2012). Kim et al.. (2018) provide empirical evidence supporting this claim, showing that PCSR enhances financial performance when complemented by CA, whereas NCSR may yield financial benefits when CA levels are low. This distinction underscores the need for firms to carefully evaluate their CSR strategies in light of their competitive positioning.

1.2 Implications for Corporate Strategy

The study also sheds new light on the implications of NCSR for firm performance. While NCSR is generally viewed as detrimental to social welfare, Kim et al.. (2018) argue that its financial impact is context-dependent. Specifically, firms engaging in NCSR may experience financial gains when CA is low, possibly due to strategic cost-cutting measures or efforts to obscure socially harmful actions through PCSR initiatives. However, the authors caution that sustained engagement in NCSR may lead to reputational damage and long-term financial consequences.

Beyond theoretical contributions, the study offers practical managerial implications. It suggests that firms should consider their level of CA when making CSR-related decisions. Although PCSR generally improves financial performance, its effects are maximized when firms actively engage in competitive initiatives. Conversely, when CA is insufficient, firms may opt for cost-saving strategies involving NCSR, though this approach carries significant reputational risks. The findings emphasize the strategic importance of aligning CSR efforts with competitive activities to optimize financial outcomes.

Wang et al. (2016) also present a meta-analytic study that examines the relationship between corporate social responsibility (CSR) and corporate financial performance (CFP), a subject that has been both central and contentious in the literature. The study aggregates 119 effect sizes from 42 independent studies to quantify the CSR–

CFP link. The overall effect size is found to be positive and statistically significant, thereby providing empirical support for the argument that CSR activity contributes to enhanced financial performance.

In addition to documenting the overall association between CSR and CFP, Wang et al. (2016) investigate the causal direction of this relationship. Their analysis indicates that subsequent financial performance is significantly associated with prior CSR engagement, while no evidence is found to support the reverse—namely, that superior financial performance leads to increased CSR activity. This unidirectional finding is consistent with instrumental stakeholder theory, which posits that CSR initiatives are strategically implemented to generate long-term shareholder value by addressing stakeholder interests.

The authors further address heterogeneity in prior research by examining the impact of measurement strategies. Variations in the operational definitions of CSR and CFP contribute to differences in reported effect sizes. This observation underscores the importance of methodological rigor and the potential benefits of standardizing measures in future empirical investigations.

Lastly, Wang et al. (2016) assess the moderating role of the environmental context on the CSR–CFP relationship. The meta-analysis reveals that the association is stronger for firms located in developed economies compared to those in developing economies. The authors attribute this difference to the more mature institutional frameworks, well-developed market mechanisms, and greater transparency of CSR activities in advanced economies, which enhance the visibility and effectiveness of CSR efforts.

2. CSR AND FINANCIAL PERFORMANCE: EMPIRICAL EVIDENCE AND METHODOLOGICAL CHALLENGES

Numerous studies have explored CSR's economic, social, and environmental implications, particularly in France. Chakroun and Ben Amar (2022) investigate the interplay between earnings management and financial performance, emphasizing CSR's moderating role. Their findings suggest that earnings management negatively impacts financial outcomes, but CSR commitments mitigate this effect by enhancing corporate sustainability and reducing volatility.

Expanding on this analysis, Miloud (2024) examines the determinants influencing firms' adoption of the Global Reporting Initiative (GRI) standards, focusing on governance structures and gender diversity. Drawing on cognitive theories, the study posits that gender diversity enhances decision-making by introducing a broad spectrum of cognitive resources influenced by socialization experiences. Utilizing a panel dataset of 91 firms from the SBF 120 index (2006–2017), Miloud (2024) finds that firms committed to GRI reporting prioritize transparency and stakeholder engagement. However, while governance structures play a pivotal role in shaping CSR disclosures, firm size emerges as a critical determinant, whereas leverage negatively affects GRI adoption, limiting governance's capacity to enhance transparency.

Further exploring governance's role in CSR policies, Toumi et al. (2022) investigate the influence of directors' regional backgrounds on CSR disclosure. Using panel data from firms listed on the SBF 120 (2008–2019), the study assesses the impact of Anglo-American, European, and French directors on CSR transparency. Findings indicate that Anglo-American directors are positively correlated with ESG and environmental disclosures, whereas European directors tend to underreport such aspects. Firms with exclusively French boards demonstrate a comprehensive approach to CSR disclosure, while other European directors exert a statistically significant negative influence. These results highlight the strategic importance of appointing directors with CSR expertise to enhance ESG performance.

In the context of regulatory frameworks, Chauvey et al. (2015) analyze the evolution of CSR reporting in France, focusing on transparency concerns and the effectiveness of legislative initiatives. Despite regulatory efforts between 2004 and 2010 to improve CSR reporting, findings indicate that disclosure quality has not significantly improved, suggesting that the Nouvelles Régulations Économiques (NRE) law has failed to fully achieve its objective of enhancing corporate transparency.

Although substantial research has been dedicated to examining CSR's implications for financial performance, methodological inconsistencies continue to hinder the development of a cohesive CSR assessment framework. Nizamuddin (2018) argues that CSR measurement tools are often selected based on data availability rather than theoretical rigor, leading to fragmented findings across empirical studies. Similarly, Barauskaite and Streimikiene (2021) emphasize that the absence of standardized CSR indicators complicates efforts to assess financial impact accurately. Addressing these challenges requires internationally recognized CSR assessment tools and guidelines to improve research reliability and enable more precise comparisons across studies.

Standardization would not only enhance methodological consistency but also provide businesses with a robust framework for integrating CSR into corporate strategy. Establishing uniform CSR evaluation metrics would facilitate a clearer understanding of CSR's financial implications while fostering long-term corporate sustainability and ethical accountability.

3. CSR AND FINANCIAL PERFORMANCE: A THEORETICAL AND EMPIRICAL PERSPECTIVE

CSR has increasingly been recognized as a critical component of modern business strategy, particularly within the context of globalization and sustainable development. Despite its growing prominence, CSR assessment methodologies remain fragmented due to the absence of a universally accepted conceptual framework (Barauskaite and Streimikiene, 2021). To evaluate CSR effectiveness, scholars have proposed various approaches, including reputation indices, content analysis, questionnaire surveys, and one-dimensional measures (Nizamuddin, 2018). However, methodological discrepancies continue to hinder the ability to establish definitive causal relationships between CSR and CFP.

Building on existing research, Nizamuddin (2018) critically examines CSR assessment methodologies by reviewing empirical studies that operationalize CSR within CFP analysis. Drawing upon Griffin and Mahon (1997), the study evaluates different research designs, highlighting their respective advantages and limitations. The findings emphasize that, while standardized financial reporting mechanisms facilitate consistent CFP evaluation, CSR measurement remains methodologically fragmented. This disparity complicates comparative analyses and limits the reliability of CSR-CFP linkages across empirical studies.

Barauskaite and Streimikiene (2021) extend this discussion by identifying four patterns in existing CSR-CFP research: positive, negative, neutral, and alternative relationships. While a significant number of studies report positive or neutral associations, negative and alternative relationships indicate that methodological refinement is required for conclusive results. These inconsistencies underscore the necessity for a more rigorous and empirically grounded CSR assessment framework.

Barauskaite and Streimikiene (2021) further emphasize CSR's strategic role in corporate decision-making, highlighting its capacity to enhance competitive advantage, reinforce brand reputation, and improve investor attractiveness. Although CSR initiatives often entail considerable financial investment, their long-term benefits—such as increased consumer trust and strengthened stakeholder relationships—contribute to overall business sustainability and market stability. Nonetheless, the absence of standardized CSR assessment tools continues to pose challenges in evaluating its precise impact on financial performance.

Literature underscores the complexity and evolving nature of CSR, as well as the methodological challenges associated with evaluating its financial implications. The absence of standardized CSR assessment frameworks complicates empirical analyses, leading to divergent findings regarding its financial impact. Establishing a uniform CSR evaluation framework would enhance research reliability and facilitate the strategic integration of CSR into corporate operations, reinforcing long-term sustainability and stakeholder engagement.

More recently, Coelho et al.. (2023) conducted a systematic review using the Web of Science database to explore the relationship between corporate social responsibility (CSR) and financial performance, with a special focus on the role of environmental, social, and governance (ESG) performance indicators. Their approach combined bibliometric and content analyses—employing the VOS viewer tool to generate co-citation clusters—to elucidate the intellectual structure of the field. Their descriptive analysis revealed that stakeholder theory emerged as a central pillar, with seminal contributions from authors like Waddock and Graves (1997), and Orlitzky (2015). Within this body of literature, the frequent co-occurrence of keywords like "financial performance" and "CSR" underscores a prevalent interest in understanding how sustainable practices influence economic outcomes.

The content analysis methodology provided compelling evidence that socially responsible practices—as measured by ESG indicators—tend to have a direct positive impact on a company's financial performance. A significant portion of the literature suggests that this positive relationship is curvilinear, reaching an optimal point when companies pay targeted attention to key stakeholders such as employees, customers, and the community. In addition, a separate cluster of research indicates that the CSR-financial performance link may be mediated by factors such as institutional strength in developed economies, a company's intangible resources, and investments in research and development or advertising. Moreover, the transparent disclosure of CSR practices, coupled with adherence to legal guidelines, is found to further enhance a firm's financial results.

The study by Coelho et al. (2023) makes several noteworthy contributions. It presents a range of theoretical and methodological approaches that not only enrich existing literature but also pave the way for future empirical inquiries. By integrating and organizing concepts into a coherent conceptual framework, the authors provide a valuable research agenda, highlighting urgent questions that could optimize subsequent investigations in the field. Practically, their review reinforces the view of CSR as an investment in sustainability that yields mutual benefits—enhancing trust and credibility among stakeholders while leading to superior financial performance—rather than as an additional cost.

However, Coelho et al. (2023) identifies importantes limitations. For example, the current absence of an objective, convergent, and robust measurement of CSR, which complicates the synthesis of previous findings. Additionally, the broad categorization of samples in past studies, which often overlooks company-specific or economy-specific differences, suggests the need for more nuanced future research. Coelho et al. (2023) recommend that subsequent studies examine the long-term consistency of CSR cycles, explore specific industry clusters, and assess cross-country and cross-cultural variations in the CSR–financial performance relationship. Further research should also consider whether external institutional pressures or internal organizational dynamics are more influential in promoting effective CSR practices.

Related to these matters, Krüger (2015) investigates the short-run shareholder value implications of both positive and negative corporate social responsibility (CSR) events. His study employs an event-study approach to discern how investors react to CSR-related news, thereby shedding light on the financial impact of corporate social (ir)responsibility. A central finding is that negative CSR events, particularly those concerning community issues and environmental matters, trigger markedly adverse reactions from investors. In quantifying these effects, Krüger estimates a median cost of approximately $76 million per event, suggesting that when a firm's actions harm its primary stakeholders, the resulting market response is both severe and financially significant.

The study further explores the asymmetry in market reactions to CSR events. While negative news produces a robustly negative market response, positive CSR events tend to elicit only slightly negative reactions from investors, and these positive effects are neither as strong nor as systematic. However, the research further refines this observation by accounting for underlying conditions such as agency problems. For firms where agency issues are less prevalent, or where positive CSR developments are interpreted as strategic managerial efforts to counteract previous missteps, the market reaction is comparatively more favorable. This nuance provides empirical support for the notion that CSR can enhance shareholder value under specific conditions, particularly in firms with a history of stakeholder-related controversies.

Krüger's (2015) incorporation of textual analysis, following the methodological spirit of Tetlock (2007), further enriches the study. By examining the economic and legal content within CSR-related disclosures, the analysis reveals that investors respond more strongly to news characterized by clear, substantive information. Additionally, the evidence suggests that the severity of the market reaction is contingent upon the intensity of the news, strongly positive or strongly negative events provoke a more pronounced response than those of a moderate nature.

Overall, the study contributes to the broader discourse on CSR and corporate governance by demonstrating that while negative CSR events clearly impose significant costs on shareholders, the benefits associated with positive CSR initiatives are conditional. Krüger (2015) argues that a sufficient condition for considering environmental and social responsibility in the shareholders' best interests is met, particularly in contexts where managerial efforts effectively mitigate prior social irresponsibility. This contingent perspective challenges the simplistic view that CSR universally enhances firm value, emphasizing instead that the financial merits of CSR are embedded within a complex framework of investor expectations, agency dynamics, and the informational content of CSR disclosures.

Overall, Krüger (2015) underscores the tangible financial penalties associated with corporate social irresponsibility and in the same time illustrates that under the right conditions, investments in CSR can yield dividend-like benefits for shareholders.

4. DATA AND METHODOLOGY

4.1 Event Study Methodology

To analyze the impact of CSR (Corporate Social Responsibility) announcements on publicly traded firms, we employ the event study methodology. This approach estimates the reaction of stock prices following the public disclosure of an event or announcement. Under the assumption of an efficient market, the stock price response at the announcement date provides a reliable estimator of the event's impact on the value of the firms concerned.

The event study methodology has its foundations in seminal works by Beaver (1968), Fama et al. (1969), and Brown and Warner (1980). Following an announcement or event, this method enables the calculation of abnormal returns generated and measures abnormal trading volumes. Brown and Warner (1980) define abnormal returns as the difference between the actual observed market return on the event day and the expected return that would have occurred in the absence of the event.

Formally, the abnormal return for stock i at time t is defined as follows:

$$ARit = Rit - E(Rit)$$

Where:

ARit: is the abnormal return of stock i at time t,

Rit: is the observed return of stock i at time t,

E(Rit): is the expected return of stock i at time t, in the absence of the event

In line with the recommendations of Brown and Warner (1985), the expected return is estimated using the market model:

$$E\,(Rit) = \alpha i + \beta i\ Rmt$$

Where:

Rmt: is the return of the market (approximated by a stock market index) at time t

αi and βi: are the market model parameters for stock i, estimated over a period prior to or following the event under consideration.

Abnormal trading volumes complement the analysis of abnormal returns by capturing the effect of the announcement on the visibility of eligible stocks. We measure trading volume by examining the amount of stock traded around the announcement window, which is the most commonly used approach in event studies (Ajinkya and Jain, 1989). By analyzing trading volumes in conjunction with price movements, we can gain a deeper understanding of how investors are processing CSR related information and the speed at which the market adjusts to new CSR announcements.

As with event studies based on returns, event studies focusing on volumes aim to determine the abnormal volume VAit for stock i at time t, following the release of an information-related announcement.

$$VAit = Vit - E(Vit)$$

Where:

VAit: is the abnormal trading volume of stock i at time t,

Vit: is the observed trading volume of stock i at time t

E(Vit): is the expected trading volume of stock i at time t, in the absence of the announcement.

In accordance with the recommendations of Mai and Tchemeni (1996), the expected volume is estimated as the average trading volume of the stock over the estimation window. We use the logarithm of the turnover rate as the measure of volume, defined as follows:

$$LOG.ROT = \frac{\text{Log}\ (1 + TRA)}{\text{Log}\ (1 + CAP)}$$

Where:

TRA: Trading volume in thousands of euros,

CAP: Market capitalization in thousands of euros.

4.2. CSR-Related Announcements

Publicly listed firms frequently issue announcements related to their corporate social responsibility (CSR) policies. Some of these announcements concern pre-existing or previously planned initiatives, which tend to have limited impact on firm valuation.

To conduct our analysis, we first identified the announcements most likely to be value-relevant. Drawing on the academic literature and reports from official institutions, we identified four main categories of CSR-related announcements that are considered the most significant in terms of their potential impact on firm value. These categories are summarized in Table 1.

Table 1. Categories and types of CSR announcements

CSR Announcement Category	Types of CSR Announcements	Examples
Environmental Announcements(Hart and Milstein, 2003; Porter and Kramer, 2011)	Carbon footprint reduction	Commitment to carbon neutrality by 2030; transition to 100% renewable energy.
	Sustainable resource management	Reduction in water usage; industrial waste recycling; circular economy initiatives.
	Green innovation	Development of environmentally friendly products; investment in clean technologies.
Social Announcements(Freeman, 1984; Carroll, 1991; ISO 26000)	Working conditions and employee well-being	Enhanced occupational health and safety standards; implementation of workplace quality-of-life programs.
	Diversity, equity, and inclusion	Introduction of gender or minority quotas; anti-discrimination initiatives; inclusion training.
	Local development and societal impact	Partnerships with local NGOs; support for social entrepreneurship.
Governance Announcements(Aguilera et al., 2007; OECD Guidelines, 2015; SASB Standards, 2018)	Transparency and ethical practices	Anti-corruption measures; publication of audited sustainability reports.
	Board diversity and independence	Appointment of women to the board of directors; increased representation of independent directors.
	Shareholder engagement	Implementation of advisory voting on CSR strategies; release of integrated reporting.
Strategic Hybrid Announcements(Pineda-Escobar, 2019; Eccles and Krzus, 2018; Stubbs, 2017; European Commission, 2022)	Integration of SDGs into corporate strategy	Alignment with the United Nations Sustainable Development Goals (SDGs).
	Integrated or non-financial reporting (CSRD, EU Green Taxonomy)	Publication of an integrated report in compliance with the Corporate Sustainability Reporting Directive (CSRD).
	Certification and labeling initiatives	Achievement of sustainability certifications such as B Corp, ISO 14001, or EcoVadis.

We identified 319 CSR-related announcements falling within the four categories outlined above, issued by French firms listed on Euronext Paris between 2022 and 2024. Some of these announcements occurred during periods that also featured other major corporate or geopolitical events—such as dividend declarations, the release of exceptional financial results, or the outbreak of the war in Ukraine. These overlapping events may distort abnormal return or volume measurements. Accordingly, such announcements were excluded from the final dataset. The resulting sample comprises 237 CSR announcements made by 185 listed French firms, distributed across the following categories:

Table 2. Number of announcements analyzed by category

CSR Announcement Category	Number of Announcements
Environmental Announcements	82
Social Announcements	57
Governance Announcements	48
Strategic Hybrid Announcements	50

The average abnormal returns and average abnormal trading volumes were computed for each of the four categories of CSR-related announcements over an event window spanning from five days before to five days after the announcement date.

These averages are calculated by taking the daily mean of abnormal returns and abnormal trading volumes for the stocks affected by each announcement.

5. EMPIRICAL RESULTS

5.1. Abnormal Returns Around CSR-Related Announcements

Table (3) reports the average abnormal returns (AARs) associated with CSR announcements, categorized into four distinct types: environmental, social, governance, and strategic hybrid initiatives.These abnormal returns are measured over a symmetric event window ranging from five days before the announcement (t−5 to t−1) to five days after the announcement (t+1 to t+5). Figure (1) illustrates the evolution of AARs throughout the event window.

Table 3. Average abnormal returns by CSR announcement category

Date	Environmental AARs	Social AARs	Governance AARs	Strategic Hybrid AARs
t−5	−0.000851	−0.000329	0.0001588	0.0001787
t−4	−0.000479	−0.000188	0.0003971	0.0004470
t−3	0.000392	−0.000169	0.0003003	0.0003380

continued on following page

Table 3. Continued

Date	Environmental AARs	Social AARs	Governance AARs	Strategic Hybrid AARs
t−2	0.000437	0.0001291	0.0007618	0.0008574
t−1	0.000471	0.0001426	0.0008258*	0.0009294*
t	0.007490*	0.0005125*	0.0107704**	0.0121225**
t+1	0.009540**	0.0015779*	0.0149634***	0.0168420***
t+2	0.008530**	0.0024068**	0.0147197***	0.0165676***
t+3	0.008480**	0.0034214**	0.0160180***	0.0180289***
t+4	0.007660**	0.0041337*	0.0168730***	0.0188657***
t+5	0.005120*	0.0025893*	0.0168759**	0.0189062**

AAR refers to the Average Abnormal Return. Asterisks *, **, and *** indicate significance at the 10%, 5%, and 1% levels, respectively, based on the Student's t-test.

Figure 1. Evolution of average abnormal return

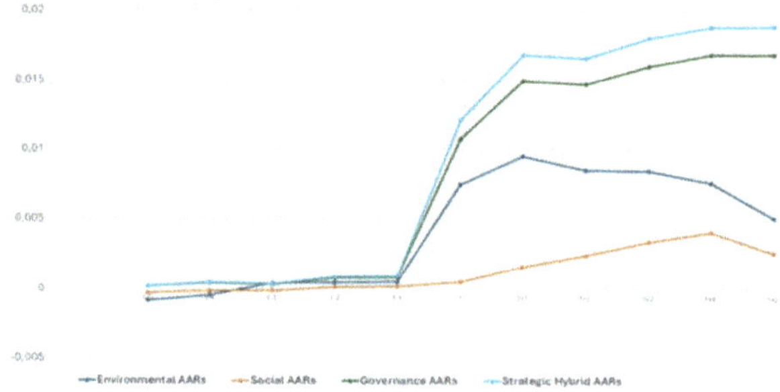

The analysis of average abnormal returns (AARs) observed over an eleven-day event window surrounding CSR-related announcements reveals differentiated dynamics depending on the nature of the initiatives disclosed. Four categories of CSR actions are considered: environmental, social, governance, and strategic hybrid initiatives. This classification enables a more nuanced understanding of how financial markets incorporate the various dimensions of corporate social responsibility into asset valuations.

Environmental announcements elicit a moderate but positive reaction from investors. AARs associated with this type of disclosure become statistically significant starting on the announcement day, with a return of +0.00749 significant at the 10% level. Returns peak at +0.00954 the following day (significant at the 5% level) and remain elevated for several days thereafter. The steady, albeit modest, increase in returns suggests that environmental initiatives are generally well received. However, their overall market impact appears limited—possibly due to partial anticipation by investors or the less immediately monetizable nature of environmental benefits.

In comparison, social announcements generate lower but occasionally significant abnormal returns. While no notable movements are observed in the pre-event period, AARs gradually rise after the announcement, reaching +0.00413 by the end of the window (significant at the 10% level). This pattern points to a cautious market response. Although social initiatives may enhance corporate reputation and talent attraction, their economic value is perceived as less tangible in the short term. As a result, investor valuation appears more diffuse and gradu*al.*

In contrast, governance-related announcements yield the strongest and most persistent abnormal returns. AARs rise sharply from +0.00082 (significant at 10%) on the day before the announcement to +0.01077 on the announcement day (5% level), peaking at +0.01687 four days later (significant at the 1% level). This sustained, high level of significance reflects increased investor confidence in actions related to transparency, control, and corporate decision-making processes. Governance initiatives are viewed as credible signals of long-term value creation, potentially improving organizational efficiency and mitigating agency risks resulting in immediate and persistent market revaluation.

Finally, strategic hybrid announcements, which combine multiple CSR dimensions and are integrated into the firm's broader strategy, elicit the strongest and most consistent market reactions. AARs show a steady and significant upward trend throughout the event window, rising from +0.00017 to +0.01890, with highly significant coefficients (*** at the 1% level). This reflects a robust and coherent positive perception among investors. The integrated nature of such announcements enhances their strategic clarity and credibility, likely being interpreted as transformational commitments that improve resilience, innovation capacity, and corporate reputation, all key drivers of sustainable competitive advantage.

Comparative analysis highlights a clear hierarchy in the way markets assess CSR dimensions. Governance and hybrid strategic initiatives receive particularly favorable treatment, both in terms of magnitude and duration of the market reaction. In contrast, environmental and social disclosures, while positive, trigger more moderate and short-lived responses. This suggests that the extent to which CSR actions are valued depends heavily on their strategic framing and perceived credibility.

These findings support the view that CSR, when embedded within the firm's strategic orientation, can serve as a powerful lever for shareholder value creation. Conversely, isolated or narrowly scoped CSR initiatives may require better contextualization or integration to be fully appreciated by the market.

Figure (1) illustrates the evolution of AARs for each category throughout the event window. It shows that governance and hybrid strategic announcements exhibit more pronounced and sustained post-event trajectories, whereas environmental and social announcements follow more subdued and ephemeral patterns. The divergence between these trajectories is visually apparent, reinforcing the idea that certain types of CSR initiatives generate stronger and more lasting investor reactions than others.

In sum, strategic hybrid and governance-related CSR announcements exert a greater impact on firm value than social or environmental disclosures. Interestingly, the market tends to quickly absorb the effects of environmental and social announcements—suggesting these actions may be perceived as standard or expected components of CSR, whereas governance and hybrid initiatives are seen as more strategic and potentially transformative.

5.2. Abnormal Trading Volumes Around CSR Announcement Events

The analysis of average abnormal volumes (AAV), computed using the logarithmic formula of the ratio between trading volume (TRA) and market capitalization (CAP), provides insights into market reactions in terms of liquidity and investor interest surrounding corporate social responsibility (CSR) announcements. The results are examined within an event window ranging from day -5 to day +5 relative to the announcement date (t). Table 4 presents the results of the event study focused on trading volumes.

Table 4. Average abnormal volumes by announcement

Dates	AAV for Environmental Announcements	AAV for Social Announcements	AAV for Governance Announcements	AAV for Strategic Hybrid Announcements
t-5	0,000564	0,000871	0,001076	0,001281
t-4	0,000974	0,001127	0,001794	0,002101
t-3	0,001691	0,001230	0,001896	0,001999
t-2	0,002152	0,001486	0,003433	0,003741
t-1	0,002460	0,002640	0,004048	0,004356
t	0,025308	0,003946	0,051809**	0,057907**
t+1	0,044166*	0,004066*	0,071333**	0,077892***
t+2	0,040227*	0,004018*	0,082409***	0,081377***
t+3	0,039510*	0,005630	0,088251***	0,098090***
t+4	0,035462	0,005851	0,083119**	0,091626**
t+5	0,024239	0,005196	0,083273**	0,092395**

AAV refers to the Average Abnormal Volume. Asterisks *, **, and *** indicate significance at the 10%, 5%, and 1% levels, respectively, based on the Student's t-test.

Abnormal average volumes (AAV) associated with environmental announcements show a steady increase from day t−5 (0.000564) up to the announcement date. On the event day (t), trading volume jumps to 0.025308, followed by a statistically significant rise on t+1 (0.044166, *), t+2 (0.040227, *), and t+3 (0.039510, *). This pattern indicates growing market attention to environmental disclosures, peaking slightly after the announcement. Although volumes slightly decline beyond t+3, they remain elevated through t+5 (0.024239), suggesting a lasting effect. The lack of significance prior to the event and the emergence of significant responses only afterward confirm that environmental announcements tend to attract ex post rather than ex ante market attention.

AAVs linked to social announcements display a more moderate trend. Volumes rise slightly from t−5 (0.000871) to t−1 (0.002640), without reaching statistical significance. The event day sees a modest increase (0.003946), followed by two statistically significant responses: t+1 (0.004066, *) and t+2 (0.004018, *). Compared to environmental events, the market reaction to social announcements is more subdued, both in magnitude and duration. This may reflect a lower investor priority for isolated social concerns, or a perception of their impact as more diffuse.

Governance-related announcements trigger the highest abnormal volumes in the sample. Starting from t−5, trading volumes gradually rise to reach 0.004048 at t−1. On the announcement day, the AAV surges to 0.051809, already statistically significant (**). Subsequent days confirm a strong reaction: t+1 (0.071333, **), t+2 (0.082409, ***), t+3 (0.088251, ***), t+4 (0.083119, **), and t+5 (0.083273, **). The persistence and significance of these volumes suggest heightened market sensitivity to governance issues, often viewed as key indicators of a firm's strategic and organizational robustness. The strength of the post-event response highlights the informational impact of such disclosures.

Strategic hybrid announcements—those combining multiple CSR dimensions—exhibit a dynamic similar to that of governance announcements, with slightly higher volume levels. AAV increases from 0.001281 at t−5 to 0.004356 at t−1. On the event day, volume reaches 0.057907 (**), followed by continued significant increases: t+1 (0.077892, ***), t+2 (0.081377, ***), t+3 (0.098090, ***), t+4 (0.091626, **), and t+5 (0.092395, **). The strong statistical significance and stability of volumes over several post-event days indicate a robust market reaction. These findings confirm that CSR announcements integrating multiple dimensions are perceived as particularly strategic and value-generating over the long term.

Among the four types of CSR disclosures, governance and strategic hybrid announcements elicit the strongest market responses in both intensity and duration. Environmental announcements trigger moderate but significant interest, primarily post-event, while social announcements generate a weaker and more transient reaction. These results reinforce the growing importance of governance and holistic CSR approaches in how financial markets assess corporate value.

Figure (2) shows the evolution of the trading volumes for each type of announcement after the announcement date.

Figure 2. Evolution of average abnormal volume

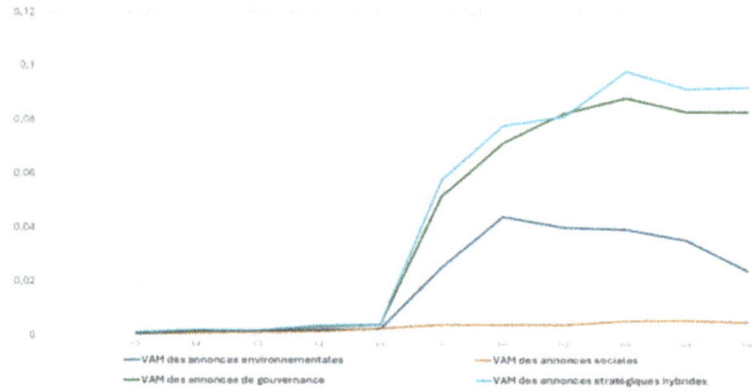

Visually, with the exception of the curve for social announcements, all event curves show a marked increase in abnormal trading volumes starting from the announcement date (t), indicating a systematic market reaction to CSR-related disclosures. This trend confirms that investors interpret such announcements as conveying financially relevant information, at least in the short term.

The two most prominent curves in figure (2) correspond to governance-related announcements and strategic hybrid measures. From day t onwards, volumes spike sharply and remain elevated through t+5, suggesting a persistent investor response. The peak occurs around t+3 for hybrid announcements, followed by a slight plateau—indicating a prolonged phase of information assimilation by the market. This sustained reaction may be explained by the cross-functional nature of these announcements, which often involve structural changes (e.g., executive turnover, mergers, or comprehensive CSR strategies) perceived as signals of strategic repositioning.

Governance and hybrid announcements dominate both in terms of volume intensity and the duration of post-announcement effects. Environmental announcements attract notable, albeit more short-lived, interest, whereas social announcements remain marginal. This suggests that the market differentially values CSR dimensions, attaching a premium to those perceived as strategically significant or directly affecting corporate governance.

6. RESULTS AND DISCUSSION

6.1 Market Reactions According to CSR Types of Announcements

The analysis of abnormal returns and abnormal volumes (AV) around corporate social responsibility (CSR) announcements provides compelling insights into how financial markets perceive different dimensions of CSR initiatives. By categorizing announcements into environmental, social, governance, and hybrid strategic initiatives, this study offers a nuanced understanding of market reactions, revealing significant heterogeneity in investor behavior and valuation patterns.

Our results indicate a clear hierarchy in market responsiveness. Governance and hybrid strategic announcements provoke the most substantial and persistent positive abnormal returns and volumes, while environmental and social announcements elicit more moderate and transient reactions. This finding aligns with prior research emphasizing governance as a critical signal for market confidence and firm value (Choi and Wang, 2009; Dhaliwal et al., 2011).

a. Governance announcements: Signals of strategic robustness and value creation:

Governance-related CSR announcements are distinguished by the strongest market impact, both in terms of intensity and persistence. Abnormal returns start to increase significantly even before the announcement, indicating some level of market anticipation. The surge on the announcement day and the sustained abnormal returns over the following days reflect investors' perception of governance initiatives as credible indicators of organizational strength, risk mitigation, and long-term strategic positioning (Eccles, Ioannou, and Serafeim, 2014).

This strong response corroborates the view that governance reforms—such as improvements in board structure, transparency, or executive accountability—are interpreted as credible commitments to reduce agency problems and enhance operational efficiency (Gompers, Ishii, and Metrick, 2003). Our findings also support prior evidence showing that governance measures lead to shareholder value creation by reinforcing trust and reducing informational asymmetries (Ferrell, Liang, and Renneboog, 2016).

b. Hybrid Strategic Announcements: The Value of Integrated CSR Approaches

Announcements combining multiple CSR dimensions elicit a reaction comparable to or even stronger than governance-only initiatives. This suggests that the market values an integrated approach to CSR as a strategic lever rather than isolated actions. The sustained significance of abnormal returns for hybrid announcements highlights investor recognition of the complexity and transformational potential embedded in multifaceted CSR strategies (Kiron and *al.,* 2013).

Hybrid announcements likely signal broader organizational commitment to sustainability and resilience, encompassing environmental stewardship, social responsibility, and governance reforms. This integrated narrative enhances the credibility and strategic clarity of CSR communication, thereby fostering investor confidence and driving value creation (Eccles and Klimenko, 2019).

c. Environmental Announcements: Moderate Yet Positive Market Reception

In contrast, environmental announcements trigger a more moderate, delayed market reaction, with significant abnormal returns emerging only on and after the announcement date. This pattern suggests that markets tend to integrate environmental news ex post rather than anticipate it. The relatively contained magnitude of abnormal returns might reflect partial anticipation of environmental initiatives or the perception that the financial benefits of such actions are less direct or more difficult to monetize in the short term (Clark and *al.*, 2015).

The persistence of abnormal returns for several days post-announcement implies a sustained, if modest, appreciation of environmental efforts. This aligns with studies indicating that environmental responsibility contributes to risk management and reputation, albeit with effects that may unfold over a longer horizon (Revelli and Viviani, 2015).

d. Social Announcements: Cautious and Transient Market Reaction

Social announcements exhibit the weakest and shortest-lived abnormal returns and volumes, signifying a cautious market stance. While social initiatives can enhance reputation and employee engagement, their economic impact appears more ambiguous or difficult to quantify promptly (Flammer, 2013). This might explain the gradual increase in abnormal returns only after the announcement and the lower overall magnitude.

Such results echo findings from studies highlighting the challenges investors face in valuing social CSR components due to their intangible nature and dispersed benefits (Margolis & Walsh, 2003). Moreover, social initiatives might be perceived as less directly linked to firm financial performance, resulting in slower and more moderate investor responses.

6.2 Comparative Insights and Theoretical Implications

Our findings offer important contributions to the literature on CSR valuation by demonstrating that the market's appraisal of CSR is not monolithic but varies by the nature of the initiatives. The stronger and more persistent reactions to governance and hybrid announcements validate the growing consensus that integrated and strategically aligned CSR efforts are more effective in signaling value creation to investors (Eccles and *al.*, 2014; Servaes and Tamayo, 2013).

This differential treatment also supports theories of signaling and information asymmetry. Governance and hybrid announcements provide clearer, more credible signals of future cash flows and risk mitigation, reducing uncertainty and encouraging investment. Environmental and social initiatives, while important, may be viewed as less immediate value drivers or as expected baseline commitments rather than sources of competitive advantage.

The observed temporal patterns in abnormal returns and volumes indicate how information about CSR initiatives is processed by markets. The absence of significant pre-announcement abnormal returns for environmental and social announcements suggests that these messages are largely unanticipated and processed reactively. Conversely, the early increase in volumes and returns for governance announcements suggests some degree of information leakage or anticipatory trading, reflecting higher market attention to governance changes.

The sustained abnormal volumes post-announcement, especially for governance and hybrid measures, highlight ongoing investor interest and reassessment of firm prospects based on CSR disclosures. These findings underscore the role of transparent and comprehensive CSR communication in shaping investor expectations and capital allocation.

6.3 Practical Implications for Managers and Policymakers

From a managerial perspective, the results emphasize the strategic importance of integrating governance reforms within CSR initiatives to maximize market impact. Firms aiming to enhance shareholder value through CSR should consider comprehensive, multidimensional approaches that combine environmental, social, and governance elements to signal commitment and create sustained investor confidence.

The moderate market response to environmental and social announcements suggests the need for better contextualization and communication of these initiatives' financial and strategic relevance. Enhanced disclosure standards and more precise quantification of the economic benefits of environmental and social efforts could improve market recognition and valuation.

Policymakers and regulators could also leverage these insights to promote reporting frameworks that encourage integrated CSR strategies and transparency in governance. Such measures may facilitate more efficient capital markets by reducing information asymmetries and enabling investors to better differentiate firms based on the quality and scope of their CSR commitments.

CONCLUSION

This study highlights the differentiated market valuation of CSR dimensions, with governance and integrated strategic initiatives commanding the most significant and persistent investor reactions. Environmental and social measures, while positively received, generate more muted responses, suggesting an evolving but still incomplete incorporation into market value. Findings underscore the strategic imperative for firms to adopt holistic CSR approaches that embed governance reforms and clearly communicate their transformative potenti*al.* Such strategies not only enhance reputation and stakeholder relations but also unlock shareholder value by signaling credible commitments to sustainable and resilient business practices. The study advances theoretical understanding of CSR as a multi-faceted construct and provides practical guidance for firms and policymakers striving to harness the full value of corporate responsibility in financial markets.

While this study provides valuable insights, it is not without limitations. The event study methodology captures short- to medium-term market reactions but may miss longer-term impacts of CSR initiatives. Future research could employ longitudinal designs or incorporate firm-level operational and financial performance data to assess sustained value creation. Additionally, the study focuses on a specific market and timeframe. Cross-country comparisons or analyses in different institutional contexts could reveal how regulatory environments and cultural factors influence market valuation of CSR.

Moreover, the classification of announcements into discrete categories, while useful for clarity, may oversimplify the complex, overlapping nature of CSR activities. Qualitative analyses or machine learning techniques applied to CSR disclosures could yield deeper understanding of how nuances in messaging affect investor perceptions.

REFERENCES

Aguilera, R. V., Williams, C. A., Conley, J. M., & Rupp, D. E. (2007). Corporate governance and social responsibility: A comparative analysis of the UK and the US. *Corporate Governance*, *15*(4), 386–399.

Ajinkya, B., & Jain, P. (1989). The behavior of daily stock market trading volume. *Journal of Accounting and Economics*, *11*(4), 331–359. DOI: 10.1016/0165-4101(89)90018-9

Aldag, R., & Bartol, K. (1978). Empirical Studies of Corporate Social Performance and Policy: A Survey of Problems and Results. In L. Research in Corporate Social Performance and Policy,10.

Barauskaite, G., & Streimikiene, D. (2021). Corporate social responsibility and financial performance of companies: The puzzle of concepts, definitions and assessment methods. *Corporate Social Responsibility and Environmental Management*, *28*(1), 278–287. DOI: 10.1002/csr.2048

Barnett, M. L. (2007). Stakeholder influence capacity and the variability of financial returns to corporate social responsibility. *Academy of Management Review*, *32*(3), 794–816. DOI: 10.5465/amr.2007.25275520

Beaver, W. H. (1968). The information content of annual earnings announcements. *Journal of Accounting Research*, *6*, 67–92. DOI: 10.2307/2490070

Bowen, H. R. (1953). Graduate education in economics. The American Economic Review, 43(4), IV 223.

Brown, S. J., & Warner, J. B. (1980). Measuring security price performance. *Journal of Financial Economics*, *8*(3), 205–258. DOI: 10.1016/0304-405X(80)90002-1

Brown, S. J., & Warner, J. B. (1985). Using daily stock returns: The case of event studies. *Journal of Financial Economics*, *14*(1), 3–31. DOI: 10.1016/0304-405X(85)90042-X

Carroll, A. B. (1979). A three-dimensional conceptual model of corporate performance. *Academy of Management Review*, *4*(4), 497–505. DOI: 10.2307/257850

Carroll, A. B. (1991). The pyramid of corporate social responsibility: Toward the moral management of organizational stakeholders. *Business Horizons*, *34*(4), 39–48. DOI: 10.1016/0007-6813(91)90005-G

Chakroun, S., & Ben Amar, A. (2022). Earnings management, financial performance and the moderating effect of corporate social responsibility: Evidence from France. *Management Research Review, 45*(3), 331–362. DOI: 10.1108/MRR-02-2021-0126

Chauvey, J.-N., Giordano-Spring, S., Cho, C. H., & Patten, D. M. (2015). The normativity and legitimacy of CSR disclosure: Evidence from France. *Journal of Business Ethics, 130*(4), 789–803. DOI: 10.1007/s10551-014-2114-y

Choi, J., & Wang, H. (2009). Stakeholder relations and the persistence of corporate financial performance. *Strategic Management Journal, 30*(8), 895–907. DOI: 10.1002/smj.759

Clark, G. L., Feiner, A., & Viehs, M. (2015). *From the stockholder to the stakeholder: How sustainability can drive financial outperformance*. University of Oxford, Smith School of Enterprise and the Environment.

Cochran, P. L., & Wood, R. A. (1984). Corporate social responsibility and financial performance. *Academy of Management Journal, 27*(1), 42–56. DOI: 10.2307/255956

Coelho, R., Jayantilal, S., & Ferreira, J. J. (2023). The impact of social responsibility on corporate financial performance: A systematic literature review. *Corporate Social Responsibility and Environmental Management, 30*(4), 1535–1560. DOI: 10.1002/csr.2446

Dhaliwal, D. S., Li, O. Z., Tsang, A., & Yang, Y. G. (2011). Voluntary nonfinancial disclosure and the cost of equity capital: The initiation of corporate social responsibility reporting. *The Accounting Review, 86*(1), 59–100. DOI: 10.2308/accr.00000005

Eccles, R. G., Ioannou, I., & Serafeim, G. (2014). The impact of corporate sustainability on organizational processes and performance. *Management Science, 60*(11), 2835–2857. DOI: 10.1287/mnsc.2014.1984

Eccles, R. G., & Klimenko, S. (2019). The investor revolution. *Harvard Business Review, 97*(3), 106–116.

Eccles, R. G., & Krzus, M. P. (2018). The Nordic model: An analysis of leading practices in ESG disclosure. *Nordic Journal of Business, 67*(4), 5–22.

Epstein, E. M. (1987). The corporate social policy process: Beyond business ethics, corporate social responsibility, and corporate social responsiveness. *California Management Review, 29*(3), 99–114. DOI: 10.2307/41165254

European Commission. (2022). *Corporate Sustainability Reporting Directive (CSRD)*. Official Journal of the European Union.

Fama, E. F., Fisher, L., Jensen, M. C., & Roll, R. (1969). The adjustment of stock prices to new information. *International Economic Review, 10*(1), 1–21. DOI: 10.2307/2525569

Ferrell, A., Liang, H., & Renneboog, L. (2016). Socially responsible firms. *Journal of Financial Economics, 122*(3), 585–606. DOI: 10.1016/j.jfineco.2015.12.003

Flammer, C. (2013). Corporate social responsibility and shareholder reaction: The environmental awareness of investors. *Academy of Management Journal, 56*(3), 758–781. DOI: 10.5465/amj.2011.0744

Freeman, R. E. (1984). Corporate Views of the Public Interest. Academy of Management Review (pre-1986), 9(000002), 366.

Freeman, R. E. (1984). *Strategic Management: A Stakeholder Approach.* Pitman.

Friedman, M. (2007). The social responsibility of business is to increase its profits. In Corporate ethics and corporate governance, 173–178. DOI: 10.1007/978-3-540-70818-6_14

Gompers, P., Ishii, J., & Metrick, A. (2003). Corporate governance and equity prices. *The Quarterly Journal of Economics, 118*(1), 107–156. DOI: 10.1162/00335530360535162

Griffin, J. J., & Mahon, J. F. (1997). The corporate social performance and corporate financial performance debate: Twenty-five years of incomparable research. *Business & Society, 36*(1), 5–31. DOI: 10.1177/000765039703600102

Hart, S. L., & Milstein, M. B. (2003). Creating sustainable value. *The Academy of Management Perspectives, 17*(2), 56–69. DOI: 10.5465/ame.2003.10025194

ISO 26000. (2010). *Guidance on social responsibility. International Organization for Standardization.*

Jo, H., & Harjoto, M. A. (2011). Corporate governance and firm value: The impact of corporate social responsibility. *Journal of Business Ethics, 103*, 351–383.

Kim, H., Woo, E., Uysal, M., & Kwon, N. (2018). The effects of corporate social responsibility (CSR) on employee well-being in the hospitality industry. *International Journal of Contemporary Hospitality Management, 30*(3), 1584–1600. DOI: 10.1108/IJCHM-03-2016-0166

Kiron, D., Kruschwitz, N., Reeves, M., & Goh, E. (2013). The innovation bottom line. *MIT Sloan Management Review, 54*(3), 69–73.

Kotchen, M., & Moon, J. J. (2012). Corporate social responsibility for irresponsibility. *The B.E. Journal of Economic Analysis & Policy*, *12*(1). Advance online publication. DOI: 10.1515/1935-1682.3308

Krüger, P. (2015). Corporate goodness and shareholder wealth. *Journal of Financial Economics*, *115*(2), 304–329. DOI: 10.1016/j.jfineco.2014.09.008

Mai, P., & Tchemeni, D. (1996). Volume et volatilité: Tests d'efficience du marché des actions. *Revue d'Economie Financiere*, *40*, 213–228.

Margolis, J. D., & Walsh, J. P. (2003). Misery loves companies: Rethinking social initiatives by business. *Administrative Science Quarterly*, *48*(2), 268–305. DOI: 10.2307/3556659

Miloud, T. (2024). Corporate governance and CSR disclosure: Evidence from French listed companies. *Global Finance Journal*, *59*, 100943. DOI: 10.1016/j.gfj.2024.100943

Nizamuddin, M. (2018). Corporate Social Responsibility and Corporate Financial Performance: An Exploratory Study of Measurement-Approach Selection Issues. IUP Journal of Corporate Governance, 17(2).

OECD. (2015). *G20/OECD Principles of Corporate Governance*. OECD Publishing.

Orlitzky, M. (2015). The politics of corporate social responsibility or: Why Milton Friedman has been right all along. *Annals in Social Responsibility*, *1*(1), 5–29. DOI: 10.1108/ASR-06-2015-0004

Pineda-Escobar, M. A. (2019). Moving the 2030 Agenda forward: SDG implementation in Colombia. *Corporate Governance (Bradford)*, *19*(1), 176–188. DOI: 10.1108/CG-11-2017-0268

Porter, M. E., & Kramer, M. R. (2011). Creating shared value. *Harvard Business Review*, *89*(1–2), 62–77.

Revelli, C., & Viviani, J. L. (2015). Financial performance of socially responsible investing (SRI): What have we learned? A meta-analysis. *Business Ethics (Oxford, England)*, *24*(2), 158–185. DOI: 10.1111/beer.12076

SASB. (2018). *Sustainability Accounting Standards Board Standards*. Value Reporting Foundation.

Servaes, H., & Tamayo, A. (2013). The impact of corporate social responsibility on firm value: The role of customer awareness. *Management Science*, *59*(5), 1045–1061. DOI: 10.1287/mnsc.1120.1630

Stubbs, W. (2017). Sustainable entrepreneurship and B Corps. *Business Strategy and the Environment*, *26*(3), 331–344. DOI: 10.1002/bse.1920

Toumi, N. B. F., Khemiri, R., & Makni, Y. F. (2022). Board directors' home regions and CSR disclosure: Evidence from France. *Journal of Applied Accounting Research*, *23*(2), 509–539. DOI: 10.1108/JAAR-02-2021-0032

Ullmann, A. A. (1985). Data in search of a theory: A critical examination of the relationships among social performance, social disclosure, and economic performance of US firms. *Academy of Management Review*, *10*(3), 540–557. DOI: 10.2307/258135

Waddock, S. A., & Graves, S. B. (1997). The corporate social performance–financial performance link. *Strategic Management Journal*, *18*(4), 303–319. DOI: 10.1002/(SICI)1097-0266(199704)18:4<303::AID-SMJ869>3.0.CO;2-G

Waddock, S. A., & Mahon, J. F. (1991). Corporate social performance revisited: Dimensions of efficacy, effectiveness, and efficiency. *Research in Corporate Social Performance and Policy*, *12*, 231–262.

Wang, H., & Qian, C. (2011). Corporate philanthropy and corporate financial performance: The roles of stakeholder response and political access. *Academy of Management Journal*, *54*(6), 1159–1181. DOI: 10.5465/amj.2009.0548

Wang, Q., Dou, J., & Jia, S. (2016). A meta-analytic review of corporate social responsibility and corporate financial performance: The moderating effect of contextual factors. *Business & Society*, *55*(8), 1083–1121. DOI: 10.1177/0007650315584317

Wood, D. J. (1991). Social issues in management: Theory and research in corporate social performance. *Journal of Management*, *17*(2), 383–406. DOI: 10.1177/014920639101700206

Yassin, Y., & Beckmann, M. (2024). CSR and employee outcomes: A systematic literature review. Management Review Quarterly, 1–47.

Zenisek, T. J. (1979). Corporate social responsibility: A conceptualization based on organizational literature. *Academy of Management Review*, *4*(3), 359–368. DOI: 10.2307/257192

Chapter 10

Data Ethics and Digital CSR in AI-Driven Learning Governance

Elif Sengun Oztas
http://orcid.org/0000-0001-5512-4869
Ufuk University, Turkey

ABSTRACT

The rapid integration of Artificial Intelligence (AI) into digital learning platforms has revolutionized educational approach through personalized learning paths and predictive analytics. However, this technological leap brings significant ethical challenges, particularly regarding data privacy, algorithmic bias, and user transparency. This chapter explores the intersection of AI, data ethics, and Corporate Social Responsibility (CSR) within the context of digital education. It argues that for platform providers, data ethics is no longer merely a legal compliance issue but a core element of Digital CSR. The chapter examines the risks of data exploitation in educational environments and proposes a Responsible AI framework that aligns corporate profit with social educational goals. By analyzing current industry standards and ethical guidelines, the study provides actionable recommendations for developers and policymakers to foster trust and equity in AI-driven education.

INTRODUCTION

The digital transformation of education has evolved beyond simply providing online content, transforming into an advanced ecosystem powered by Artificial Intelligence (AI). Today, digital learning platforms utilize AI technologies for personalized learning experiences, predictive student analytics, and automated assessment

DOI: 10.4018/979-8-3693-4099-8.ch010

tools (Luckin et al., 2016). As Holmes et al. (2019) emphasize, AI has the potential to provide every learner with an individual tutor, fundamentally altering the pedagogical landscape. While these innovations provide unprecedented opportunities for educational efficiency and inclusivity, they also bring forth a complex web of ethical dilemmas (Zawacki-Richter et al., 2019). The massive collection of data from students, the lack of transparency in "black box" algorithms, and the potential for systemic bias raise questions about the foundations of equity in education. In this context, Selwyn (2019) warns that the datafication of education may reinforce existing social inequalities rather than eliminate them, necessitating a critical re-examination of digital stewardship.

For a significant period, the accountability of EdTech providers was viewed through a reductionist lens, prioritizing legal adherence and system functionality over moral imperatives (Pangrazio and Selwyn, 2019). As Floridi and Taddeo (2016) suggest, such a 'checkbox' approach to digital responsibility emphasizes legislative compliance while often overlooking the nuanced ethical implications inherent in data-driven ecosystems.

However, as AI-driven educational tools evolve toward greater autonomy and algorithmic opacity, traditional reliance on regulatory compliance proves inadequate for safeguarding learner interests. To address this gap, this chapter proposes the Responsible Digital Learning Ecosystem (RDLE) framework, which conceptualizes ethical integrity not as an external liability, but as a core strategic asset. By embedding the UNESCO (2021) pillars of fairness and transparency into the organizational fabric, the RDLE framework transitions from a reactive, 'checkbox' compliance culture toward a proactive Digital Corporate Social Responsibility (D-CSR) paradigm (Herold et al., 2020). This shift redefines data ethics as a catalyst for value creation and stakeholder trust, rather than a mere restrictive barrier to innovation (Mittelstadt, 2019; Sjögren, 2021).

The primary objective of this chapter is to bridge the gap between AI development, ethical standards, and CSR strategies. By proposing the Responsible Digital Learning Ecosystem (RDLE) framework, the study examines how transparency, fairness, and accountability can be integrated into the business models of educational technology providers (Jobin et al., 2019). The following sections will analyze the critical ethical risks inherent in learning analytics and discuss how a robust CSR framework can transform these challenges into a competitive advantage based on trust and social impact. Besides, Siau and Wang (2018) argue, building trust is the fundamental prerequisite for the widespread adoption of AI; without it, even the most advanced educational technologies will face resistance from stakeholders. As highlighted by Vakkuri and Abrahamsson (2020), the successful operationalization of AI ethics requires moving beyond abstract principles and embedding them directly into the corporate and technical lifecycle.

BACKGROUND

The growing intersection of Artificial Intelligence (AI) and digital education represents both opportunity and challenge in today's learning environments. While AI provides extensive scalability and tailored learning pathways, it relies on data-heavy systems that generate complex ethical dilemmas. To situate the Responsible Digital Learning Ecosystem (RDLE) model within this context, it is important to analyze the current developments in AI ethics alongside the transforming role of Corporate Social Responsibility (CSR) in the digital landscape.

THE GLOBAL MANDATE FOR AI ETHICS

Today, AI ethics has become an integral part of corporate strategies, transforming into a strategic mandate within the framework of Digital Corporate Social Responsibility (D-CSR) to safeguard the societal presence of technological innovation (Siau & Wang, 2018; Vakkuri & Abrahamsson, 2020). Over the past decade, AI ethics has evolved from a narrow philosophical debate into a dynamic, interdisciplinary research field that systematically analyzes the socio-technical and moral consequences of algorithmic decision-making mechanisms (Mittelstadt et al., 2016). The increasing interference of AI systems in human experiences, social interactions, and corporate mechanisms has prompted both academics and industry actors to restructure these technologies around the principles of Fairness, Accountability, and Transparency (F.A.T.) (Ananny & Crawford, 2018; Shin & Park, 2019). This approach has reinforced the paradigm that ethical algorithmic governance is not merely a technical requirement, but also an ethical imperative in terms of democratic participation (Selwyn, 2019).

In this evolutionary process, the focus of ethical discussions has shifted from general principles to a solution-oriented 'application model' that attempts to manage the direct impact of algorithmic systems on social justice and fundamental rights; this indicates that theoretical ethics has been replaced by an applied ethics approach (Floridi et al., 2018; Jobin et al., 2019). As Barocas and Selbst (2016) emphasize, particularly in the context of educational technologies (EdTech), this highlights that algorithms should not only be efficiency-oriented, but also, as supported by UNESCO (2021), should have an ethically designed architecture that is "human-centered" (UNESCO, 2021) and minimizes bias.

FROM TRADITIONAL CSR TO DIGITAL CSR

As emphasized by Carroll (1999), corporate social responsibility (CSR) is a concept where organizations voluntarily focus on the social and environmental impacts of their activities, prioritizing work for society and the environment rather than profit-making. This is related to the ethical understanding or sense of responsibility between the firm and its stakeholders. Hopkins (2004) points out that in some organizations, corporate social responsibility is accepted as corporate philanthropy, while in others it is a corporate strategic framework that has begun to be adopted. Corporate social responsibility encompasses the social, environmental, and governmental goals of organizations for the future. The level of corporate social responsibility has different characteristics that can vary depending on the vision and mission of the organizations (Dudek et al. 2023). Popular digital tools are successfully used in finance, management, industry, and education (Muchiri et al. 2022; Pangalos 2023; Cinquepalmi et al. 2023; Richert and Dudek 2023; Sheel and Nath 2019). Digital technologies have the power to facilitate economic and social activities, thus enabling the creation of innovative ideas, activities, and business opportunities. Furthermore, promoting their efficient and effective use, ensuring their sustainability, and integrating them into corporate social responsibility structures has brought a new perspective to the vision of management.

In an environment where digitalization is increasing every day, organizations are supporting their operations with digital technologies as much as possible. Organizations that adapt to digitalization improve their business efficiency, communication methods, and competitive techniques, and enhance their corporate social responsibility (CSR) structures.

With the impact of digitalization, Corporate Social Responsibility (CSR), defined for many years as environmental sustainability and philanthropic activities, has transformed into a technology-integrated structure as Digital Corporate Social Responsibility (D-CSR). In this new paradigm, the most fundamental social responsibility is seen as the ethical handling of all data used (Herold et al., 2020). As Lobschat et al. (2020) emphasize, the concept of Digital Corporate Social Responsibility (D-CSR) suggests that organizations should integrate their moral obligations into all digital processes, from the data collection stage to the algorithmic output generation stage. This ensures that digital transformation processes do not compromise individual autonomy and do not jeopardize social equality (Lobschat et al., 2020; Floridi et al., 2018). In this context, D-CSR goes beyond mere legal compliance; It stands out as a strategic management paradigm that effectively and efficiently manages the impact of algorithmic systems on the social fabric and adopts the principle of ethics by design (Vakkuri & Abrahamsson, 2020; Siau & Wang, 2018).

For AI-powered learning platform providers, D-CSR includes commitment to data management. According to Knight and Ansell (2021), data management is critical to ensuring that data assets are used in socially effective, beneficial, and trust-motivating ways. Within the educational ecosystem, this approach requires technology providers to go beyond being mere data processors and position themselves as 'stewards' and trustworthy guardians of students' digital assets. As highlighted by Pansera et al. (2020), this management model necessitates that organizations systematically promote algorithmic accountability in both their internal processes and external stakeholder relationships. At this point, the long-term impact of data use on student autonomy and pedagogical development is prioritized over short-term commercial profitability goals (Selwyn, 2019; Pansera et al., 2020). This vision represents a proactive corporate stance that views student data as ethical assets that must be protected, rather than an approach that commodifies this data (Siau & Wang, 2018). Ultimately, integrating UNESCO's (2021) ethical principles into corporate social responsibility (D-CSR) strategies symbolizes a shift from merely adhering to the principle of 'non-maleficence' in technological interventions to a paradigm of 'actively doing good' (beneficence) for societal and individual well-being (Floridi et al., 2018; UNESCO, 2021).

IDENTIFICATION OF THE RESEARCH GAP

While there are high-level statements from sources such as UNESCO, much of the literature fails to address how these abstract principles can shape and currently impact the daily decisions and long-term corporate strategies of EdTech companies. As Mittelstadt (2019) and Morley et al. (2020) point out, much of the existing literature treats AI ethics as a technical constraint rather than a strategic corporate social responsibility opportunity. Consequently, there is a profound conceptual ambiguity regarding how these ethical principles on a global scale can be integrated into both the operational decision-making mechanisms shaping the daily workings and the long-term strategic visions of EdTech organizations.

Furthermore, traditional perspectives often reduce ethical compliance to a narrow framework, viewing it as a reactive, after thoughtful obligation, thus ignoring its potential as a proactive driver of Strategic CSR (Hagendorff, 2020). This reductionist approach results in a risky scenario, described in the literature as 'ethics washing,' where ethical standards are deprived of deep structural integration and remain merely symbolic elements (Floridi, 2019).

This chapter aims to address this conceptual gap by proposing the RDLE model, which integrates universal ethical principles into a structured corporate architecture and transforms them into a viable strategy. Moreover, the model goes beyond simply answering the question of 'what' ethical principles are; it transforms these principles into a robust institutional framework that synchronizes them with technological progress, institutional accountability, and pedagogical quality, presenting a structured 'how' paradigm for implementation.

THE CONCEPTUAL FRAMEWORK: THE RESPONSIBLE DIGITAL LEARNING ECOSYSTEM (RDLE)

As the integration of artificial intelligence in education increases, there is a need for a model where technological efficiency is implemented within an ethical framework. In this context, the Responsible Digital Learning Ecosystem (RDLE) is proposed, offering a multi-layered framework designed within the scope of data ethics and Digital Corporate Social Responsibility (D-CSR) for the integration of AI applications.

The RDLE model argues that ethical standards are not an afterthought independent of technological innovations, but rather a holistic management strategy maintained throughout the entire lifecycle, from the design phase to the implementation phase.

Figure 1. The Responsible Digital Learning Ecosystem (RDLE) model

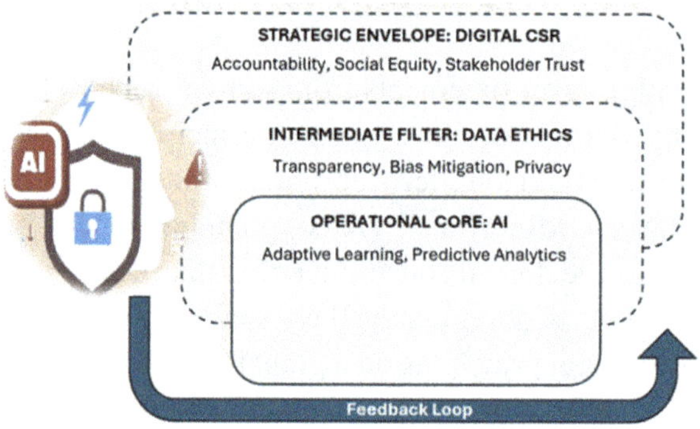

Figure 1 clearly summarizes the layered structure and operational mechanism of the Responsible Digital Learning Ecosystem (RDLE) model, conceived within the context of educational technologies (EdTech). This diagram is a hierarchical protective shield model showing how technical processes are surrounded by ethical and strategic values.

To operate the theoretical foundations of the proposed model, it is essential to categorize its functions into distinct yet interconnected dimensions. The Responsible Digital Learning Ecosystem (RDLE) does not operate as a monolithic structure;

rather, it functions as a modular framework where technical performance is continuously refined by ethical constraints and strategic social goals. While the Operational Core focuses on the immediate pedagogical needs through AI-driven analytics, the Intermediate Filter and the Strategic Envelope ensure that these activities remain within the boundaries of normative ethics and corporate accountability. To provide a comprehensive overview of this structural synergy, Figure 2 synthesizes the key components, ethical objectives, and the underlying academic literature supporting each layer of the RDLE framework.

Figure 2. Comparative analysis of the Responsible Digital Learning Ecosystem (RDLE) framework

Framework Layer	*Core Focus*	*Key Components*	*Ethical & Strategic Objective*	*Supporting Literature*
Layer 1: Operational Core (AI Engine)	Technical Infrastructure & Efficiency	Predictive Analytics, Adaptive Learning, Machine Learning Models	Enhancing Pedagogical Outcomes & Operational Excellence	Luckin et al. (2016); Holmes et al. (2019)
Layer 2: Intermediate Filter (Data Ethics)	Normative Regulation & Human-Centricity	Explainable AI (XAI), Algorithmic Fairness, Data Sovereignty	Mitigating Bias & Ensuring User Autonomy	UNESCO (2021); Floridi & Taddeo (2016); Jobin et al. (2019)
Layer 3: Strategic Envelope (Digital CSR)	Accountability & Corporate Vision	Stakeholder Trust, Social Equity, Impact Reporting	Aligning Profit with Social Good & Competitive Advantage	Siau & Wang (2018); Vakkuri & Abrahamsson (2020); Selwyn (2019)

As shown in Figure 2, accountability in educational technologies is integrated into a structured model with the RDLE framework, encompassing various approaches ranging from pedagogical artificial intelligence (Luckin et al., 2016) to data ethics (Floridi & Taddeo, 2016) and strategic corporate responsibility (Siau & Wang, 2018).

The layers in the RDLE model shown in Figure 1 are described in detail below.

Layer 1: The Operational Core (AI Engine)

The innermost layer of the RDLE model constitutes the technical backbone of the platform and houses artificial intelligence at its core. This operational core is managed by advanced machine learning algorithms that execute adaptive learning functions, which personalize learning processes, and predictive analytics, which provide data-driven predictions. The system's primary goal is to maximize pedagogical efficiency by analyzing student behavior, engagement processes, and learning outcomes (Luckin et al., 2016; Holmes et al., 2019). However, from a Digital CSR perspective, it is a strategic necessity that this technical structure is not only efficiency-focused but also fully compliant with 'Ethics by Design' principles, where ethical values are integrated into the system from the development stage. This approach aims to subject algorithms to rigorous scrutiny during their development phase and to prevent the systematic automation of historical biases ingrained in training datasets through artificial intelligence (Baker & Hawn, 2022; Barocas & Selbst, 2016).

Layer 2: The Intermediate Filter (Data Ethics)

Data ethics, the second layer of the RDLE model, acts as a regulatory bridge between technical operations and organizational strategy, integrating human-centered normative systems into efficiency and functionality-oriented algorithms. This layer focuses not only on the technical functionality of the system but also on its proper operation in accordance with the principles of justice, accountability, and transparency. This normative regulation, built upon technical operations, ensures that the pedagogical effects produced by artificial intelligence are aligned with human rights and global ethical standards (UNESCO, 2021). This approach ensures that technology centers on the human being as a subject, not an object (human-centeredness) (Floridi & Taddeo, 2016).

The layer is based on three fundamental components that transform abstract principles into concrete technical standards:

Explainable Artificial Intelligence (XAI): Rescuing artificial intelligence from being a 'black box' by making its answers and interpretations transparent and understandable for teachers and students (Jobin et al., 2019).

Algorithmic Justice: Preventing the system from discriminating against specific student groups by identifying biases in educational datasets (Barocas & Selbst, 2016).

Data Sovereignty: Protecting data autonomy by ensuring users have the right to control their own data.

In short, the main purpose of this layer is to prevent algorithms from automating and perpetuating historical inequalities (race, gender, socio-economic status, etc.) Bias reduction and safeguard users' data autonomy in the learning process. This ethical integration represents a critical transformation phase in terms of equipping AI-based systems not only with technical efficiency but also with a social and ethical approach.

Layer 3: The Strategic Envelope (Digital CSR)

The Strategic Envelope, the outermost layer of the RDLE model, provides a high-level strategic vision and accountability functions encompassing the entire ecosystem. In this layer, Accountability, Social Equity, and Stakeholder Trust are considered the most critical requirements for operational processes. At this level, technology is regarded not merely as a tool but as a corporate vision; this encompasses functions such as active social benefit creation and trust building, along with legal compliance (Siau & Wang, 2018). Similarly, within the framework of the RDLE model, Digital Corporate Social Responsibility (D-CSR) transforms from a voluntary philanthropic practice into a public benefit activity focused on education (Vakkuri & Abrahamsson, 2020). This approach is shaped by three fundamental characteristics:

Stakeholder Accountability: The scope of corporate responsibility extends beyond commercial stakeholders to a multi-dimensional societal level encompassing essential elements of the ecosystem, such as students, parents, and public educational institutions (Selwyn, 2019).

Social Equity and Inclusion: In line with the inclusivity principles emphasized by UNESCO (2023), D-CSR strategies prioritize closing the digital divide. In this context, developing AI models optimized for low-resource environments and providing algorithmic accessibility for individuals with disabilities are considered strategic outcomes of corporate success.

Strategic Stakeholder Trust: Stakeholder trust, a strategic layer of the RDLE model, is built on the principles of corporate transparency and radical integrity, ensuring the sustainability of the ecosystem. This environment of trust allows students and educators to be confident that their data will be meticulously protected and that algorithmic decisions will be made fairly (Siau & Wang, 2018). Within the framework of a digital CSR vision, stakeholder trust functions as a kind of "social enterprise license" for EdTech firms, transforming into strategic capital that secures the brand's long-term competitive advantage and social legitimacy (Siau & Wang, 2018; Vakkuri & Abrahamsson, 2020).

THE SYNERGISTIC INTERACTION OF THE RDLE

The fundamental strength of the RDLE model stems from the circular feedback loop that occurs between all layers. A strong Digital CSR (D-CSR) vision necessitates the application of a rigorous data ethics filter in operational processes; this ethical oversight mechanism, by its very nature, paves the way for the development of more transparent and fair AI algorithms. This circular interdependence triggers the creation of a trust environment, the most fundamental strategic capital within the ecosystem. A trust-based user experience strengthens the connection between students and educators and the platform; the rich data flow that naturally arises because of this high interaction creates a dynamic feedback loop that continuously improves the pedagogical effectiveness of AI algorithms. Consequently, ethical values go beyond being a passive requirement and become a dynamic force that enhances sustainable corporate growth, stakeholder trust, and the quality of pedagogical outcomes.

ADDRESSING CRITICAL ETHICAL CHALLENGES THROUGH THE RDLE MODEL

The proliferation of artificial intelligence in digital learning environments is more than just a technical advancement; it also represents a socio-technical intervention with critical risks. The Responsible Digital Learning Ecosystem (RDLE) framework offers a holistic and systematic methodology to address these complex problems in education.

1. Algorithmic Bias and Fairness

Instead of saying that algorithms in the educational technology ecosystem are value-independent constructs, it is more accurate to say that they reflect the assumptions of their designers and the datasets on which they are trained. If artificial intelligence systems are trained with data riddled with demographic inequalities (language, socioeconomic status, race, etc.), they can become mechanisms that deepen this bias in the processes of measuring student achievement and distributing educational opportunities (O'Neil, 2019; Noble, 2019). As emphasized by Eubanks (2018), this situation, instead of advocating equal opportunity, brings with it the danger of a 'digital caste system' that reproduces and structures existing injustices through technology.

The RDLE framework treats justice not as a static concept but as a dynamic management technique, and includes the following strategic approaches:

- *Continuous Bias Auditing:* Continuous Bias Auditing within the RDLE model represents a continuous process focused on monitoring and evaluating the impact of algorithms on marginalized students. Unlike traditional auditing mechanisms, this dynamic approach provides real-time monitoring, enabling the immediate detection and addressing of potential biases (Mittelstadt et al., 2016). Active monitoring throughout the entire AI lifecycle, from development to deployment, helps identify model deviations and unintended consequences (Rajesh et al., 2018). This proactive strategy promotes ethical accountability, safeguarding both social equity and pedagogical integrity. Ultimately, continuous bias auditing creates a more inclusive and equitable educational environment where technology serves all students equally. Barocas and Selbst (2016) emphasized that algorithms can unintentionally lead to discriminatory outcomes, often reflecting existing societal biases. To address this concern, the RDLE model offers continuous monitoring, enabling early detection of unfair effects before they become widespread. Such proactive oversight is vital in promoting fairness in automated decision-making processes. Selbst (2021) further underscores the importance of ongoing attentiveness and transparency to ensure that algorithms serve all individuals equitably, minimizing harm and fostering trust in technological systems. Holstein (2019) emphasizes the importance of integrating quantitative mathematical metrics with comprehensive socio-technical audits. They advocate for involving both students and teachers in this process to ensure a holistic assessment, fostering improved understanding and effective implementation of educational technologies within learning environments.

- *Inclusive Representativeness:* The RDLE model highlights the importance of diversifying training data to avoid the problem of algorithmic exclusion, where certain groups may be overlooked or misrepresented. By ensuring that datasets encompass a wide range of socio-cultural contexts, AI systems can be trained to recognize and serve all communities fairly. This approach promotes the development of ethical and inclusive artificial intelligence, fostering equality and respect. Ultimately, such practices help create AI technologies that acknowledge and honor the diversity of human experiences, leading to more just and equitable outcomes for everyone. Milan and Treré (2022) emphasize the importance of "Big Data from the South" warning that relying on datasets perpetuates data colonialism, which marginalizes voices from the Global South. They argue that such practices reinforce existing power imbalances and limit diverse perspectives in data collection. Similarly, Benjamin (2019) highlights that underrepresentation of marginalized groups in datasets leads to biased algorithms and unfair decision-making processes. Besides, these scholars underscore the urgent need for inclusive, equitable data practices that respect and amplify diverse voices worldwide. According to UNESCO (2021), cultural and linguistic diversity are fundamental human rights that must be protected and promoted worldwide. RDLE models operate these principles by providing frameworks that support inclusive policies, ensuring that diverse languages and cultures are preserved and valued within educational and societal contexts.
- *Pedagogical Equity by Design:* Rather than limiting algorithmic fairness to a strict technical approach such as mathematical equality, the RDLE model is built based on a teaching perspective that fits the way learning naturally happens. This approach considers how students use their brains and algorithms to achieve optimal outcomes rather than simply using past data. At this point Baker and Hawn (2022) point out, suggests that algorithms should

be designed not just to predict standard results like grades and success rates using past data, but also to help each student reach their own potential, learn at their own speed, and accommodate different ways of learning. The concept of "equity by design" implies that the construction of a system must account for individual needs when it is being constructed from the start. The system considers the differences as a crucial component in creating individualized learning experiences, rather than treating them as an impediment. Prinsloo and Slade (2017) say that in education systems that rely on data, ethics is not just about keeping data safe but also about taking responsibility to help students do better and be happier. This helps support RDLE's plan to improve algorithms with an emphasis on "student support." As Rose and Meyer (2002) point out, based on the "Universal Design Principles" (UDL) approach, they believe the system should be built in a way that is flexible enough to include even the weakest or most diverse students. RDLE uses this teaching idea in the goals that guide the AI's learning process.

2. Transparency and Explainability

In all educational activities, trust depends on the functioning of the system. When students and educators cannot analyze the logic behind critical AI-powered outcomes such as automated grading, risk analysis, or career recommendations, trust in the system is damaged, and the validity of the decisions is questioned. According to Burrell (2016), this situation is explained by the concept of "algorithmic opacity" in education and undermines the student's control over their own learning process. In his research titled "The Black Box Society," Pasquale (2015) emphasizes that algorithms that do not share decision-making processes cause social power imbalances. The RDLE model revises this opacity with the XAI feature, protecting the power balance in education in favor of students and teachers. According to Khoshnevisan and Rashtchi (2021), XAI in educational technologies is not only a technical necessity but also plays a supportive role for student motivation and self-regulation skills. This situation contributes to RDLE's feature of "using transparency as a pedagogical tool". In addition, Siemens (2012) states that for the learning analytics to be successful, stakeholders need to understand how the data is processed (interpretability). RDLE already provides an answer to this need in line with UNESCO (2021) standards.

To overcome this trust crisis, the RDLE framework places Explainable Artificial Intelligence (XAI) techniques at the heart of its enterprise architecture. The model's approach at this layer is as follows:

- *Human-Interpretability:* It is essential to provide not only technical but also "human-interpretable" justifications for the outputs of artificial intelligence.

This embodies UNESCO's (2021) principle of transparency, ensuring the ethical accountability of the platform.

- *Data Ethics Filter Integration:* Transparency is not a report added at the end of the product but is incorporated into the process from the very beginning of the design as a "Data Ethics Filter".
- *From Opacity to Pedagogy:* The RDLE model transforms opaque algorithms into pedagogical tools that encourage critical thinking. For example, when the system suggests a particular resource to a student, it allows the student to evaluate their own learning strategy by explaining "why" that resource was chosen.

3. Data Privacy and Constant Surveillance

In a modern educational landscape, EdTech platforms increasingly track biometric data such as eye movements and emotional responses. These innovations may be effective in enhancing learning experiences, but they could also turn classrooms into areas of surveillance. Surveillance capitalism threatens freedom of education because it prioritizes extensive data collection and continuous monitoring. This undermines privacy and autonomy and is incompatible with the fundamental principles of open and independent learning environments (Zuboff, 2019). The effects of this surveillance can hinder the development of 21st-century skills such as creativity and critical thinking, ultimately causing critical damage to the supportive environments necessary for educational development.

The RDLE model explores these risks based on the Digital CSR (Corporate Social Responsibility) approach in the following way:

- *Human Rights Instead of Commodity:* The RDLE model views data as a fundamental human right, emphasizing the importance of individual privacy and autonomy, and priotizing rights over commercial interests and unchecked data exploitation. Lupton and Williamson (2017) critically examine the reliance on data-driven approaches in education, highlighting potential drawbacks such as diminished teacher autonomy, loss of nuanced understanding and the risk of reducing students to mere metrics.
- *Data Minimization Protocol:* The framework focuses on data minimization principles, advocating for the collection of only data necessary for pedagogical development. All data collection processes whose necessity cannot be explained are considered unethical. Cavoukian (2010), a pioneer of the "Privacy by Design" concept, emphasizes that privacy is not a choice but a default setting. The RDLE framework operationalizes this principle as an institutional standard.

- *Sanctity of the Learning Space:* RDLE places critical importance on the privacy of learning processes, creating a safe space where students can practice learning activities multiple times without fear of making mistakes. Gilliard (2020) notes that intense observation and interaction on digital platforms create a "chilling effect" on students and educators and kill originality. RDLE's concept of "the sanctity of the learning space" aims to eliminate this effect.

SOLUTIONS AND RECOMMENDATIONS

Based on the RDLE framework, the following strategic recommendations are presented for education technology developers, education leaders, and policymakers to ensure that AI-powered educational technologies (EdTech) thrive on an ethical foundation and build societal trust.

1. Adopting Ethics by Design Approach

Ethical considerations should be treated as a fundamental technical requirement from the very beginning of the process, not as a "compliance check" performed in the final stage of the software development life cycle (SDLC). Implementation: Every organization should have "Ethics Leads" working within the development teams. These experts should integrate concepts such as fairness, accountability, and privacy into the system as "primary non-functional requirements" by conducting Algorithmic Impact Assessments (AIA) during the requirements analysis and architectural design phases (Vakkuri et al., 2020; Dignum, 2019).

2. Radical Transparency and User Empowerment

Instead of traditionally written, complex "Terms of Service" texts that are often not read by users, interactive and visually informative notices should be used. In terms of preserving human decision-making and preferences in educational processes, the explainability of AI decisions (XAI) is more than a technical necessity; it is a moral responsibility (Selwyn, 2019). Implementation: EdTech providers should include "Data Dashboards" that enable students and parents to quickly view AI-powered profiles, along with easy-to-use "opt-out" features for non-compulsory analytical monitoring.

3. Establishing Independent Ethical Audit Boards

In the context of Digital Corporate Social Responsibility (CSR), internal audits are not enough to ensure public confidence. The risk of "ethics washing" must be eliminated through external and independent verification processes (Mittelstadt, 2019). Implementation: Technology companies should plan annual "Ethics Audit" activities in collaboration with independent academic institutions or NGOs. To gain stakeholder trust, a "Transparency Report" should be published using the data obtained from these audits, thus providing the organization with a long-term strategic competitive advantage (Siau & Wang, 2018).

4. Closing the Digital Divide: A Strategic CSR Goal

The use of artificial intelligence technologies should not be limited to specific environments with high connection speeds. With an approach based on the principle of equality in education, the use of technological advancements should be considered a universal and broad umbrella (UNESCO, 2023).

Implementation: The creation of AI-Lite models that are specifically designed for low-resource settings and individuals with disabilities should be financed through Corporate Social Responsibility budgets. By implementing this approach, it is possible to provide education that benefits everyone, regardless of their socioeconomic background.

CONCLUSION

The widespread use of artificial intelligence technologies in digital learning processes has fundamentally changed current educational approaches, leading to a shift from static content delivery to dynamic, data-driven personalization. However, technological capabilities that do not adhere to ethical standards pose a risk that undermines the foundations of education in terms of equality, autonomy, and human dignity. The proposed RDLE framework is a strategic plan and emphasizes that ethical standards for educational technology providers are more important than data processing speeds.

By shifting from a technical compliance checklist to the fundamentals of Digital Corporate Social Responsibility (D-CSR), this study offers reassurance in the industry's approach to data ethics. The study suggests that a company's social responsibility in the 21st century is determined by its "digital manager". By integrating their AI with the human-centered principles promoted by UNESCO (2021), platform providers go beyond risk reduction and enhance corporate trust, which is the most crucial element in the digital economy.

In conclusion, the integration of AI and education necessitated a "social contract" that prioritizes the learner's rights rather than algorithmic effectiveness. This contract is based on the structural model of the RDLE, which makes sure that AI becomes a tool for universal empowerment rather than some instrument used to keep watch or exclude. Our success as digital learning platforms isn't going to come from their market share, but rather from our commitment to building an equitable, open-minded, and inclusive future for students everywhere.

FUTURE RESEARCH DIRECTIONS

While the RDLE (Responsible Digital Learning Ecosystems) model provides a strategic framework for responsible AI integration in educational settings, the field remains in a formative stage. Several substantive areas require deeper empirical investigation and theoretical development. The following directions outline priority avenues for future scholarly inquiry.

1. Generative AI and Academic Integrity

The rapid proliferation of Large Language Models (LLMs) and other generative AI tools has fundamentally altered the structure of academic production. Future research should systematically investigate how these technologies reshape the Corporate Social Responsibility (CSR) obligations of digital learning platforms, particularly with respect to content authenticity, originality verification, and the protection of intellectual property rights.

Academics should examine the extent to which platform providers have a responsibility to enable or mitigate AI-assisted academic fraud, and what institutional and technical safeguards are both feasible and ethically defensible. This area of research should also address the evolving normative boundaries between legitimate AI-assisted learning and the practice of academic fraud; current policy frameworks have not yet resolved these distinctions with sufficient precision. Future studies should investigate how the rise of Generative AI (e.g., LLMs) impacts platforms' corporate social responsibility obligations regarding content authenticity and intellectual property.

2. Long-Term Impact of Algorithmic Labeling

One particularly under-studied topic in AI-powered education systems is the lasting psychological impact of algorithmic categorization on students. As predictive analyses increasingly categorize students as "at risk," "struggling," or in need of intervention, there is an urgent need for longitudinal research to assess the consequences of such labeling on student motivation, academic self-concept, and long-term well-being.

Existing literature on stigma and labeling theory in educational psychology provides a preliminary theoretical foundation, but empirical studies tracking cohorts of students across multiple academic years are essential to establish causal claims. Research designs should account for mediating variables such as pedagogical context, instructor awareness, and the degree of transparency with which algorithmic outputs are communicated to students and their families.

3. Cross-Cultural Ethical Standards

The ethical norms and legal frameworks governing educational data are far from globally uniform. Future research should undertake rigorous comparative analysis of how CSR expectations, data sovereignty norms, and AI accountability standards vary across cultural and jurisdictional boundaries. While the European Union's Artificial Intelligence Law and the General Data Protection Regulation (GDPR) represent one end of the regulatory spectrum, their applicability, and even suitability, in the Global South, Southeast Asia, or the Middle East remains an open and important question.

Interdisciplinary collaboration between legal scholars, educational technologists, and cultural researchers will be necessary to develop frameworks that are both universally principled and locally sensitive. Such work should resist the uncritical export of Western regulatory models and instead foster co-developed standards that reflect the values, capacities, and structural conditions of diverse educational contexts.

4. Blockchain Technologies and Student Data Sovereignty

The RDLE framework's commitment to learner agency and data self-determination opens a promising avenue for technical innovation through decentralized architectures. Blockchain-based systems offer a theoretically compelling mechanism for granting students verifiable, immutable control over their educational records and behavioral data, eliminating the ambiguity and asymmetric power relations that characterize current platform-centric data governance.

Future research should evaluate the technical feasibility, scalability, and user accessibility of blockchain implementations within educational information systems. Equally important is the need to examine potential limitations: energy consumption, infrastructural demands, and the risk that technical complexity may itself become a barrier to equitable access. Pilot studies and proof-of-concept deployments in real institutional settings would meaningfully advance both the theoretical and practical dimensions of this research agenda.

Taken together, these directions reflect the multidisciplinary character of responsible AI in education encompassing fields such as computer science, educational psychology, legal theory, and ethics. Progress in each area will not only enrich the RDLE framework but contribute to the broader project of ensuring that digital learning environments serve the interests of all learners with rigor, fairness, and transparency.

REFERENCES

Ananny, M., & Crawford, K. (2018). Seeing without knowing: Limitations of the transparency ideal and its application to algorithmic accountability. *New Media & Society*, *20*(3), 973–989. DOI: 10.1177/1461444816676645

Baker, R. S., & Hawn, A. (2022). Algorithmic bias in education. *International Journal of Artificial Intelligence in Education*, *32*(4), 1052–1092. DOI: 10.1007/s40593-021-00285-9

Barocas, S., & Selbst, A. D. (2016). Big data's disparate impact. *California Law Review*, *104*, 671. DOI: 10.15779/Z38BG31

Benjamin, R. (2019). *Race After Technology: Abolitionist Tools for the New Jim Code*. Polity Press.

Burrell, J. (2016). How the machine 'thinks': Understanding opacity in machine learning algorithms. *Big Data & Society*, *3*(1), 2053951715622512. DOI: 10.1177/2053951715622512

Carroll, A. B. (1999). Corporate social responsibility: Evolution of a definitional construct. *Business & Society*, *38*(3), 268–295. DOI: 10.1177/000765039903800303

Cavoukian, A. (2010). Privacy by design: The definitive workshop. A foreword by Ann Cavoukian, Ph. D. *Identity in the Information Society*, *3*(2), 247–251. DOI: 10.1007/s12394-010-0062-y

Cinquepalmi, F., Paris, S., Pennacchia, E., & Tiburcio, V. A. (2023). Efficiency and sustainability: The role of digitization in re-inhabiting the existing building stock. *Energies*, *16*(9), 3613. DOI: 10.3390/en16093613

Dignum, V. (2019). *Responsible artificial intelligence: How to develop and use AI in a responsible way*. Springer Nature. DOI: 10.1007/978-3-030-30371-6

Dudek, M., Bashynska, I., Filyppova, S., Yermak, S., & Cichoń, D. (2023). Methodology for assessment of inclusive social responsibility of the energy industry enterprises. *Journal of Cleaner Production*, *394*, 136317. DOI: 10.1016/j.jclepro.2023.136317

Eubanks, V. (2018). *Automating inequality. How high-tech tools profile, police, and punish the poor*. St. Martin's Press.

Floridi, L. (2019). Translating principles into practices of digital ethics: Five risks of being unethical. *Philosophy & Technology*, *32*(2), 185–193. DOI: 10.1007/s13347-019-00354-x

Floridi, L., Cowls, J., Beltrametti, M., Chatila, R., Chazerand, P., Dignum, V., Luetge, C., Madelin, R., Pagallo, U., Rossi, F., Schafer, B., Valcke, P., & Vayena, E. (2018). AI4People—An ethical framework for a good AI society: Opportunities, risks, principles, and recommendations. *Minds and Machines*, *28*(4), 689–707. DOI: 10.1007/s11023-018-9482-5 PMID: 30930541

Floridi, L., & Taddeo, M. (2016). What is data ethics? *Philosophical Transactions. Series A, Mathematical, Physical, and Engineering Sciences*, *374*(2083), 20160360. DOI: 10.1098/rsta.2016.0360 PMID: 28336805

Gilliard, C. 2020. Caught in the Spotlight, Urban Omnibus, 9 January. Available at https://urbanomnibus.net/2020/01/caught-in-the-spotlight/

Hagendorff, T. (2020). The ethics of AI ethics: An evaluation of guidelines. *Minds and Machines*, *30*(1), 99–120. DOI: 10.1007/s11023-020-09517-8

Herold, D. M., Nowotny, S., Schuster, T., & Wortmann, J. (2020). The role of corporate social responsibility in the digital age. *Corporate Social Responsibility and Environmental Management*, *27*(5), 2341–2352. DOI: 10.1002/csr.1969

Holmes, W., Bialik, M., & Fadel, C. (2019). *Artificial intelligence in education: Promises and implications for teaching and learning*. Center for Curriculum Redesign.

Holstein, D. (2019). Quantitative Security Measures for Cyber Security Assurance.

Jobin, A., Ienca, M., & Vayena, E. (2019). The global landscape of AI ethics guidelines. *Nature Machine Intelligence*, *1*(9), 389–399. DOI: 10.1038/s42256-019-0088-2

Khoshnevisan, B., & Rashtchi, M. (2021). The First Field Experience: Perceptions of ESOL Pre-Service Teachers. *Advances in Language and Literary Studies*, *12*(5), 15–22. DOI: 10.7575/aiac.alls.v.12n.5.p.15

Knight, E., & Ansell, J. (2021). Data stewardship: A new imperative for business model innovation. *The Journal of Business Strategy*, *42*(3), 154–162.

Lobschat, L., Müller, B., Eggers, F., Brandimarte, L., Hui, S. K., Ozcan, G., & Verhoef, P. C. (2020). Corporate digital responsibility. *Journal of Business Research*, *122*, 875–888. DOI: 10.1016/j.jbusres.2019.10.006

Luckin, R., Holmes, W., Griffiths, M., & Forcier, L. B. (2016). *Intelligence unleashed: An argument for AI in education*. Pearson.

Lupton, D., & Williamson, B. (2017). The datafied child: The dataveillance of children and implications for their rights. *New Media & Society*, *19*(5), 780–794. DOI: 10.1177/1461444816686328

Milan, S., & Treré, E. (2022). Big Data from the South (s). *The Oxford handbook of digital media sociology, 76.*

Mittelstadt, B. (2019). Principles alone cannot guarantee ethical AI. *Nature Machine Intelligence, 1*(11), 501–507. DOI: 10.1038/s42256-019-0114-4

Mittelstadt, B. D., Allo, P., Taddeo, M., Wachter, S., & Floridi, L. (2016). The ethics of algorithms: Mapping the debate. *Big Data & Society, 3*(2), 2053951716679679. DOI: 10.1177/2053951716679679

Morley, J., Cowls, J., Taddeo, M., & Floridi, L. (2020). Ethical guidelines for COVID-19 tracing apps. *Nature, 582*(7810), 29–31. DOI: 10.1038/d41586-020-01578-0 PMID: 32467596

Muchiri, M. K., Erdei-Gally, S., & Fekete-Farkas, M. (2022). Effect of CSR on the financial performance of financial institutions in Kenya. *Economies, 10*(7), 174. DOI: 10.3390/economies10070174

Noble, A. (2019). *Exploring Solutions for Closing the Mathematics Achievement Gap between Elementary Students with and without Disabilities* (Doctoral dissertation, University of Massachusetts Lowell).

O'neil, L. R. (2019). *The Impact of Self-Assessment on the Learning Outcomes of African American Students in Geometry in a Rural School Setting* (Doctoral dissertation, Southern University and Agricultural and Mechanical College).

Pangalos, G. (2023). Financing for a sustainable dry bulk shipping industry: What are the potential routes for financial innovation in sustainability and alternative energy in the dry bulk shipping industry? *Journal of Risk and Financial Management, 16*(2), 101. DOI: 10.3390/jrfm16020101

Pangrazio, L., & Selwyn, N. (2019). 'Personal data practices' at school: The challenges of ethical and sustainable education data usage. *British Educational Research Journal, 45*(2), 414–436. DOI: 10.1002/berj.3502

Pansera, M., Owen, R., Meacham, D., & Kuh, V. (2020). Embedding responsible innovation within synthetic biology research and innovation: Insights from a UK multi-disciplinary research centre. *Journal of Responsible Innovation, 7*(3), 384–409. DOI: 10.1080/23299460.2020.1785678

Pasquale, F. (2015). The black box society: The secret algorithms that control money and information. In *The black box society*. Harvard University Press. DOI: 10.4159/harvard.9780674736061

Rajesh, S., Kandaswamy, M. U., & Rakesh, M. A. (2018). The impact of Artificial Intelligence in Talent Acquisition Lifecycle of organizations: A global perspective. *International Journal of Engineering Development and Research, 6*(2), 709–717.

Richert, M., & Dudek, M. (2023). Risk mapping: Ranking and analysis of selected, key risk in supply chains. *Journal of Risk and Financial Management, 16*(2), 71. DOI: 10.3390/jrfm16020071

Rose, D. H., & Meyer, A. (2002). *Teaching Every Student in the Digital Age: Universal Design for Learning*. Association for Supervision and Curriculum Development.

Selwyn, N. (2019). *Should robots replace teachers? AI and the future of education*. Polity Press.

Sheel, A., & Nath, V. (2019). Effect of blockchain technology adoption on supply chain adaptability, agility, alignment and performance. *Management Research Review, 42*(12), 1353–1374. DOI: 10.1108/MRR-12-2018-0490

Shin, D., & Park, Y. J. (2019). Role of fairness, accountability, and transparency in algorithmic affordability. *Computers in Human Behavior, 98*, 277–284. DOI: 10.1016/j.chb.2019.04.019

Siau, K., & Wang, W. (2018). Building trust in artificial intelligence, machine learning, and robotics. *Cutter Business Technology Journal, 31*(2), 47–53.

Siemens, G. (2012, April). Learning analytics: envisioning a research discipline and a domain of practice. In *Proceedings of the 2nd international conference on learning analytics and knowledge* (pp. 4-8). DOI: 10.1145/2330601.2330605

Sjögren, E. (2021). *The ethics of artificial intelligence in business: A guide to responsible management*. Routledge.

UNESCO. (2021). *Recommendation on the ethics of artificial intelligence*. https://unesdoc.unesco.org/ark:/48223/pf0000381115

UNESCO. (2023). *Guidance for generative AI in education and research*. https://unesdoc.unesco.org/ark:/48223/pf0000386693

Vakkuri, V., & Abrahamsson, P. (2020). The current state of AI ethics: Redesigning ethical AI for realization. *2020 IEEE International Conference on Engineering, Technology and Innovation (ICE/ITMC)*, 1-10. https://doi.org/DOI: 10.1109/ICE/ITMC49519.2020.9198576

Zawacki-Richter, O., Marín, V. I., Bond, M., & Gouverneur, F. (2019). Systematic review of research on artificial intelligence applications in higher education – where are the ethical domains? *International Journal of Educational Technology in Higher Education, 16*(39), 39. Advance online publication. DOI: 10.1186/s41239-019-0171-0

Zuboff, S. (2019). Surveillance capitalism and the challenge of collective action. []. Sage CA: Los Angeles, CA: Sage Publications.]. *New Labor Forum, 28*(1), 10–29. DOI: 10.1177/1095796018819461

KEY TERMS AND DEFINITIONS

Algorithmic Bias: Systematic and repeatable errors in a computer system that create unfair outcomes, such as privileging one arbitrary group of users over others.

Corporate Social Responsibility (CSR): A business model in which companies make a concerted effort to operate in ways that enhance rather than degrade society and the environment.

Data Ethics: A branch of ethics that evaluates moral problems related to data (including generation, recording, curation, processing, dissemination, sharing, and usage).

Data Stewardship: The formalization of accountability for the management and oversight of data assets, ensuring they are used ethically and securely.

Digital CSR (D-CSR): The extension of traditional CSR into the digital realm, focusing on responsible data handling, digital inclusion, and the ethical deployment of emerging technologies.

Explainable AI (XAI): A set of processes and methods that allow human users to comprehend and trust the results and output created by machine learning algorithms.

Responsible AI: A framework for developing, deploying, and relying on AI systems in a way that is ethical, transparent, and accountable to stakeholders.

Compilation of References

Abdalla, A. A., Bhat, M. A., Tiwari, C. K., Khan, S. T., & Wedajo, A. D. (2024). Exploring ChatGPT adoption among business and management students through the lens of diffusion of Innovation Theory. *Computers and Education: Artificial Intelligence*, *7*, 100257. DOI: 10.1016/j.caeai.2024.100257

Abdullah, K. H., Abd Aziz, F. S., Dani, R., Hammood, W. A., & Setiawan, E. (2023). Urban Pollution: A Bibliometric Review. *ASM Science Journal*, *18*, 1–16. DOI: 10.32802/asmscj.2023.1440

Abrams, F. W. (1951). Management's responsibilities in a complex world. *Harvard Business Review*, *29*(3), 29–34.

Acharya, A. (2020). The myth of the "civilization state": Rising powers and the cultural challenge to world order. *Ethics & International Affairs*, *34*(2), 139–156. DOI: 10.1017/S0892679420000192

Adekunle, B. I., Chukwuma-Eke, E. C., Balogun, E. D., & Ogunsola, K. O. (2023). Integrating AI-driven risk assessment frameworks in financial operations: A model for enhanced corporate governance. *International Journal of Scientific Research in Computer Science. Engineering and Information Technology*, *9*(6), 445–464.

Agarwal, P., & Sharma, S. (2023). Smart Urban Traffic Management System using Energy Efficient Optimized Path Discovery. *Proceedings of the 3rd International Conference on Artificial Intelligence and Smart Energy, ICAIS 2023*, 858 – 863. DOI: 10.1109/ICAIS56108.2023.10073840

Aggarwal, S., & Sharma, S. (2022). Voice Based Secured Smart Lock Design for Internet of Medical Things: An Artificial Intelligence Approach. *2022 International Conference on Wireless Communications, Signal Processing and Networking, WiSPNET 2022*, 1 – 9. DOI: 10.1109/WiSPNET54241.2022.9767113

Agrawal, A., Gans, J., & Goldfarb, A. (2019). Artificial intelligence: The ambiguous labor market impact of automating prediction. *The Journal of Economic Perspectives*, *33*(2), 31–50. DOI: 10.1257/jep.33.2.31

Aguilera, R. V., Williams, C. A., Conley, J. M., & Rupp, D. E. (2007). Corporate governance and social responsibility: A comparative analysis of the UK and the US. *Corporate Governance*, *15*(4), 386–399.

Ahani, A., Nilashi, M., Ibrahim, O., Sanzogni, L., & Weaven, S. (2019). Market segmentation and travel choice prediction in Spa hotels through TripAdvisor's online reviews. *International Journal of Hospitality Management*, *80*, 52–77. DOI: 10.1016/j.ijhm.2019.01.003

Ahmad, I., Sharma, S., Kumar, R., Dhyani, S., & Dumka, A. (2023). Data Analytics of Online Education during Pandemic Health Crisis: A Case Study. *2nd Edition of IEEE Delhi Section Owned Conference, DELCON 2023 - Proceedings*. DOI: 10.1109/DELCON57910.2023.10127423

Ahmed, R., Das Gupta, A., Krishnamurthy, R. M., Goyal, M., Kumar, K. S., & Gangodkar, D. (2022). The Role of Smart Grid Data Analytics in Enhancing the Paradigm of Energy Management for Sustainable Development. *2022 2nd International Conference on Advance Computing and Innovative Technologies in Engineering, ICACITE 2022*, 198 – 201. DOI: 10.1109/ICACITE53722.2022.9823542

Aiyappa, S., Kodikal, R., & Rahiman, H. U. (2024). Accelerating Gender Equality for Sustainable Development: A Case Study of Dakshina Kannada District, India. *Technical and Vocational Education and Training*, *38*, 335–349. DOI: 10.1007/978-981-99-6909-8_30

Ajay, D., Sharad, K., Singh, K. P., & Sharma, S. (2023). Impact of Prolonged Mental Torture on Housewives in Middle Class Families. *Journal for ReAttach Therapy and Developmental Diversities*, *6*(4), 1–7.

Ajinkya, B., & Jain, P. (1989). The behavior of daily stock market trading volume. *Journal of Accounting and Economics*, *11*(4), 331–359. DOI: 10.1016/0165-4101(89)90018-9

Akana, C. M. V. S., Kumar, A., Tiwari, M., Yunus, A. Z., Vijayakumar, E., & Singh, M. (2023). An Optimized DDoS Attack Detection Using Deep Convolutional Generative Adversarial Networks. *Proceedings of the 5th International Conference on Inventive Research in Computing Applications, ICIRCA 2023*, 668 – 673. DOI: 10.1109/ICIRCA57980.2023.10220745

Akberdina, V., Kumar, V., Kyriakopoulos, G. L., & Kuzmin, E. (2023). Editorial: What Does Industry's Digital Transition Hold in the Uncertainty Context? In K. V., K. G.L., A. V., & K. E. (Eds.), *Lecture Notes in Information Systems and Organisation: Vol. 61 LNISO* (pp. 1 – 4). Springer Science and Business Media Deutschland GmbH. DOI: 10.1007/978-3-031-30351-7_1

Akinsola, K. (2025). The Evolving Role of Corporate Governance in Shaping Business Practices and Legal Accountability in the 21st Century. *Available at SSRN* 5115523. DOI: 10.2139/ssrn.5115523

Alawamleh, H. K., Alkayed, I. Y., Albdour, A. W. M., & Shatnawi, H. A. (2025). The E-leadership transformation in corporate environment: A bibliometric study. *Human Systems Management*, *44*(2), 249–267.

Albert, E. T. (2019). AI in talent acquisition: A review of AI-applications used in recruitment and selection. *Strategic HR Review*, *18*(5), 215–221. DOI: 10.1108/SHR-04-2019-0024

Aldag, R., & Bartol, K. (1978). Empirical Studies of Corporate Social Performance and Policy: A Survey of Problems and Results. In L. Research in Corporate Social Performance and Policy,10.

Aljarah, A., Ibrahim, B., & López, M. (2024). *AI, we do not trust! The nexus between awareness of falsity in AI-generated CSR ads and online brand engagement*. Internet Research.

Al-kfairy, M., Mustafa, D., Kshetri, N., Insiew, M., & Alfandi, O. (2024). Ethical challenges and solutions of generative AI: An interdisciplinary perspective. *Informatics (MDPI)*, *11*(58), 58. DOI: 10.3390/informatics11030058

Alkhadra, W. A., Khawaldeh, S., & Aldehayyat, J. (2023). Relationship of ethical leadership, organizational culture, corporate social responsibility and organizational performance: A test of two mediation models. *International Journal of Ethics and Systems*, *39*(4), 737–760. DOI: 10.1108/IJOES-05-2022-0092

Al-Omari, A., & Al-Omari, H. (2006). E-government readiness assessment model. *Journal of Computational Science*, *2*(11), 841–845. DOI: 10.3844/jcssp.2006.841.845

Al-Ruithe, M., Benkhelifa, E., & Hameed, K. (2019). A systematic literature review of data governance and cloud data governance. *Personal and Ubiquitous Computing*, *23*(5-6), 839–859. DOI: 10.1007/s00779-017-1104-3

Ananny, M., & Crawford, K. (2018). Seeing without knowing: Limitations of the transparency ideal and its application to algorithmic accountability. *New Media & Society*, *20*(3), 973–989. DOI: 10.1177/1461444816676645

Ansari, M. F., & Afzal, A. (2022). Sensitivity and Performance Analysis of 10 MW Solar Power Plant Using MPPT Technique. *Lecture Notes in Electrical Engineering, 894 LNEE*, 512–518. DOI: 10.1007/978-981-19-1677-9_46

Antonopoulou, H. (2024). The value of emotional intelligence: Self-awareness, self-regulation, motivation, and empathy as key components. *Technium Education and Humanities*, *8*, 78–92. DOI: 10.47577/teh.v8i.9719

Arghode, V., Lathan, A., Alagaraja, M., Rajaram, K., & McLean, G. N. (2022). Empathic organizational culture and leadership: Conceptualizing the framework. *European Journal of Training and Development*, *46*(1/2), 239–256. DOI: 10.1108/EJTD-09-2020-0139

Argyris, C., & Schön, D. A. (1997). Organizational learning: A theory of action perspective. *Revista Española de Investigaciones Sociológicas*, (77/78), 345–348. DOI: 10.2307/40183951

Arora, A., Singh, R., Malik, K., & Kestwal, U. (2024). Association of sexual performance and intimacy with satisfaction in life in head and neck cancer patients: A review. *Oral Oncology Reports*, *11*, 100563. Advance online publication. DOI: 10.1016/j.oor.2024.100563

Arora, P. (2019). *The next billion users: Digital life beyond the West*. Harvard University Press. DOI: 10.4159/9780674238879

Arora, R., Singh, A. P., Sharma, R., & Chauhan, A. (2022). A remanufacturing inventory model to control the carbon emission using cap-and-trade regulation with the hexagonal fuzzy number. *Benchmarking*, *29*(7), 2202–2230. DOI: 10.1108/BIJ-05-2021-0254

Arora, S., Pargaien, S., Khan, F., Misra, A., Gambhir, A., & Verma, D. (2023). Smart Parking Allocation Using Raspberry Pi based IoT System. *Proceedings of the 5th International Conference on Inventive Research in Computing Applications, ICIRCA 2023*, 1457 – 1461. DOI: 10.1109/ICIRCA57980.2023.10220619

Arouri, M., & Pijourlet, G. (2017). CSR performance and the value of cash holdings: International evidence. *Journal of Business Ethics*, *140*(2), 263–284. DOI: 10.1007/s10551-015-2658-5

Ashkanasy, N. M., Humphrey, R. H., & Huy, Q. N. (2017). Integrating emotions and affect in theories of management. *Academy of Management Review*, *42*(2), 175–189. DOI: 10.5465/amr.2016.0474

Ashurov, S., Musse, O. S. H., & Abdelhak, T. (2024). Evaluating corporate social responsibility in achieving sustainable development and social welfare. *BRICS Journal of Economics*, *5*(2), 77–102. DOI: 10.3897/brics-econ.5.e121429

Awa, H. O., Etim, W., & Ogbonda, E. (2024). Stakeholders, stakeholder theory and corporate social responsibility (CSR). *International Journal of Corporate Social Responsibility*, *9*(1), 11. DOI: 10.1186/s40991-024-00094-y

Awal, G., & Khanna, R. (2019). Determinants of millennial online consumer behavior and prospective purchase decisions. *International Journal of Advanced Science and Technology*, *28*(18), 366–378.

Baba, C. (2024). Ethical Leadership and Accountability: Technology Innovation. [JURNAL KONSEP BISNIS DAN MANAJEMEN]. *JKBM*, *10*(2), 151–163.

Bahri, S. (2023). Long history of corporate social responsibility (CSR). In *Proceeding International Conference on Economics, Business Management, and Accounting (ICOEMA)*-2023 (Vol. 2, pp. 457–465).

Baker, R. S., & Hawn, A. (2022). Algorithmic bias in education. *International Journal of Artificial Intelligence in Education*, *32*(4), 1052–1092. DOI: 10.1007/s40593-021-00285-9

Banks, G. C., Fischer, T., Gooty, J., & Stock, G. (2020). Ethical leadership: Mapping the terrain for concept cleanup and a future research agenda. *The Leadership Quarterly*, *31*(6), 101471.

Bansal, S., Kumar, V., Kumari, A., & Kuzmin, E. (2023). Understanding the Role of Digital Technologies in Supply Chain Management of SMEs. In K. V., K. G.L., A. V., & K. E. (Eds.), *Lecture Notes in Information Systems and Organisation: Vol. 61 LNISO* (pp. 195 – 205). Springer Science and Business Media Deutschland GmbH. DOI: 10.1007/978-3-031-30351-7_16

Bansal, N., Bhatnagar, M., & Taneja, S. (2023). Balancing priorities through green optimism: A study elucidating initiatives, approaches, and strategies for sustainable supply chain management. In *Handbook of Research on Designing Sustainable Supply Chains to Achieve a Circular Economy*. IGI Global., DOI: 10.4018/978-1-6684-7664-2.ch004

Barauskaite, G., & Streimikiene, D. (2021). Corporate social responsibility and financial performance of companies: The puzzle of concepts, definitions and assessment methods. *Corporate Social Responsibility and Environmental Management*, *28*(1), 278–287. DOI: 10.1002/csr.2048

Barnea, A. (2020). How will AI change intelligence and decision-making? *Journal of Intelligence Studies in Business, 10*(1), 75–80. DOI: 10.37380/jisib.v10i1.564

Barnett, M. L. (2007). Stakeholder influence capacity and the variability of financial returns to corporate social responsibility. *Academy of Management Review, 32*(3), 794–816. DOI: 10.5465/amr.2007.25275520

Barney, J. (1991). Firm resources and sustained competitive advantage. *Journal of Management, 17*(1), 99–120. DOI: 10.1177/014920639101700108

Barocas, S., & Selbst, A. D. (2016). Big data's disparate impact. *California Law Review, 104*, 671. DOI: 10.15779/Z38BG31

Bar-On, R. (1997). *The Emotional Quotient Inventory (EQ-i): Technical manual*. Multi-Health Systems.

Bass, B. M. (1985). *Leadership and performance beyond expectations*. Free Press.

Bass, B. M. (1995). Theory of transformational leadership redux. *The Leadership Quarterly, 6*(4), 463–478. DOI: 10.1016/1048-9843(95)90021-7

Bayan, F. M. H. (2024). The Ethics of AI: Navigating the Moral dilemmas of Artificial Intelligence. Arab Journal for Scientific Publishing (AJSP). *ISSN, 2663*, 5798.

Beaver, W. H. (1968). The information content of annual earnings announcements. *Journal of Accounting Research, 6*, 67–92. DOI: 10.2307/2490070

Bechtsis, D., Tsolakis, N., Iakovou, E., & Vlachos, D. (2022). Data-driven secure, resilient and sustainable supply chains: Gaps, opportunities, and a new generalised data sharing and data monetisation framework. *International Journal of Production Research, 60*(14), 4397–4417. DOI: 10.1080/00207543.2021.1957506

Begum, S. J. P., Pratibha, S., Rawat, J. M., Venugopal, D., Sahu, P., Gowda, A., Qureshi, K. A., & Jaremko, M. (2022). Recent Advances in Green Synthesis, Characterization, and Applications of Bioactive Metallic Nanoparticles. *Pharmaceuticals (Basel, Switzerland), 15*(4), 455. Advance online publication. DOI: 10.3390/ph15040455 PMID: 35455452

Behera, A., & Singh Rawat, K. (2023). A brief review paper on mining subsidence and its geo-environmental impact. *Materials Today: Proceedings*. Advance online publication. DOI: 10.1016/j.matpr.2023.04.183

Bello, E. D. (2023). *Empowering Leaders: NAVIGATING CULTURE, COMMUNICATION, AND AI ETHICS IN NEGOTIATION*. BoD–Books on Demand.

Belwal, R., & Belwal, S. (2017). Employers' perception of women workers in Oman and the challenges they face. *Employee Relations*, *39*(7), 1048–1065. DOI: 10.1108/ER-09-2016-0183

Bender, E. M., Gebru, T., McMillan-Major, A., & Shmitchell, S. (2021). On the dangers of stochastic parrots: Can language models be too big? *Proceedings of the 2021 ACM Conference on Fairness, Accountability, and Transparency*, 610–623. DOI: 10.1145/3442188.3445922DOI: 10.1145/3442188.3445922

Benjamin, R. (2019). *Race After Technology: Abolitionist Tools for the New Jim Code*. Polity Press.

Bhamangol, B., Kaiwade, A., Pant, B., Rana, A., Kaiwade, A., & Shaikh, A. (2022). An Artificial Intelligence based Design and Implementation for classifying the Missing Data in IoT Applications. *Proceedings of 5th International Conference on Contemporary Computing and Informatics, IC3I 2022*, 1376 – 1382. DOI: 10.1109/IC3I56241.2022.10072634

Bhatnagar, M., Kumar, P., Taneja, S., Sood, K., & Grima, S. (2024). From digital overload to trading Zen: The role of digital detox in enhancing intraday trading performance. In *Business Drivers in Promoting Digital Detoxification*. IGI Global., DOI: 10.4018/979-8-3693-1107-3.ch010

Bhatnagar, M., Rajaram, R., Taneja, S., & Kumar, P. (2024). Balancing acts: The Yin and Yang of debit and credit on the stage of financial well-being. In *Emerging Perspectives on Financial Well-Being*. IGI Global., DOI: 10.4018/979-8-3693-1750-1.ch002

Bhatnagar, M., Taneja, S., & Kumar, P. (2023). The Effectiveness of Carbon Pricing Mechanism in Steering Financial Flows Toward Sustainable Projects. *International Journal of Environmental Impacts*, *6*(4), 183–196. DOI: 10.18280/ijei.060403

Bhatnagar, M., Taneja, S., Kumar, P., & Özen, E. (2024). Does financial education act as a catalyst for SME competitiveness? *International Journal of Education Economics and Development*, *15*(3), 377–393. DOI: 10.1504/IJEED.2024.139306

Bhatt, Y., & Ghuman, K. (2022). Managerial cognition and environmental behavioral intentions: A behavioral reasoning theory perspective. *Corporate Social Responsibility and Environmental Management*, *29*(5), 1315–1329. DOI: 10.1002/csr.2271

Binns, R. (2018). Fairness in machine learning: Lessons from political philosophy. In *Proceedings of the 2020 Conference on Fairness, Accountability, and Transparency* (pp. 149–159). DOI: 10.1145/3287560.3287589

Bisht, R. K., Bisht, I. P., & Joshi, B. C. (2022). Growth of Micro, Small and Medium Enterprises (MSMEs) in Uttarakhand (India). In D. N. & C. A. (Eds.), *AIP Conference Proceedings* (Vol. 2481). American Institute of Physics Inc. DOI: 10.1063/5.0103881

Bisht, B., Gururani, P., Aman, J., Vlaskin, M. S., Anna, I. K., Irina, A. A., Joshi, S., Kumar, S., & Kumar, V. (2023). A review on holistic approaches for fruits and vegetables biowastes valorization. *Materials Today: Proceedings*, *73*, 54–63. DOI: 10.1016/j.matpr.2022.09.168

Bist, A., Dobriyal, R., Gwalwanshi, M., & Avikal, S. (2022). Influence of Layer Height and Print Speed on the Mechanical Properties of 3D-Printed ABS. In D. N. & C. A. (Eds.), *AIP Conference Proceedings* (Vol. 2481). American Institute of Physics Inc. DOI: 10.1063/5.0107304

Black, J. S., & van Esch, P. (2021). AI-enabled recruiting: What is it and how should a manager use it? *Business Horizons*, *64*(2), 215–226. https://doi.org/10.1016/j.bushor.2019.12.001DOI: 10.1016/j.bushor.2019.12.001

Bordoloi, D., Singh, V., Sanober, S., Buhari, S. M., Ujjan, J. A., & Boddu, R. (2022). Deep Learning in Healthcare System for Quality of Service. *Journal of Healthcare Engineering*, *2022*, 1–11. Advance online publication. DOI: 10.1155/2022/8169203 PMID: 35281541

Bovens, M. (2007). Analysing and assessing accountability: A conceptual framework. *European Law Journal*, *13*(4), 447–468. DOI: 10.1111/j.1468-0386.2007.00378.x

Bowen, H. R. (1953). Graduate education in economics. The American Economic Review, 43(4), IV 223.

Bowen, Z. (1953). *Bowen. HR,(1953), Social Responsibilities of the Businessman.* Harper & Row.

Bowlby, J. (1982). Attachment and loss: Vol. 1. *Attachment* (2nd ed.). Basic Books.

Boyatzis, R. E., & Sala, F. (2004). Assessing emotional intelligence competencies. In Geher, G. (Ed.), *The measurement of emotional intelligence: Common ground and controversy* (pp. 147–180). Nova Science.

Brock, J. K. U., & von Wangenheim, F. (2019). Demystifying AI: What digital transformation leaders can teach you about realistic artificial intelligence. *California Management Review*, *61*(4), 110–134. DOI: 10.1177/1536504219865226

Brown, M. E., & Treviño, L. K. (2006). Ethical leadership: A review and future directions. *The Leadership Quarterly*, *17*(6), 595–616. DOI: 10.1016/j.leaqua.2006.10.004

Brown, S. J., & Warner, J. B. (1980). Measuring security price performance. *Journal of Financial Economics*, *8*(3), 205–258. DOI: 10.1016/0304-405X(80)90002-1

Brown, S. J., & Warner, J. B. (1985). Using daily stock returns: The case of event studies. *Journal of Financial Economics*, *14*(1), 3–31. DOI: 10.1016/0304-405X(85)90042-X

Brynjolfsson, E., & McAfee, A. (2017). The business of artificial intelligence. *Harvard Business Review*. https://hbr.org/2017/07/the-business-of-artificial-intelligence

Brynjolfsson, E., & Mcafee, A. N. D. R. E. W. (2017). The business of artificial intelligence. *Harvard Business Review*, *7*(1).

Bughin, J., Seong, J., Manyika, J., Chui, M., & Joshi, R. (2018). Notes from the AI frontier: Modeling the impact of AI on the world economy. McKinsey Global Institute Discussion Paper, 1-48.

Buhmann, A., & Fieseler, C. (2021). Towards a deliberative framework for responsible innovation in artificial intelligence. *Technology in Society*, *64*, 101475. DOI: 10.1016/j.techsoc.2020.101475

Bulińska-Stangrecka, H., & Bagieńska, A. (2021). The impact of employee training and development on tacit knowledge transfer and the mediating role of trust. *International Journal of Learning and Change*, *13*(4-5), 474–489. DOI: 10.1504/IJLC.2021.116668

Burrell, J. (2016). How the machine 'thinks': Understanding opacity in machine learning algorithms. *Big Data & Society*, *3*(1), 2053951715622512. DOI: 10.1177/2053951715622512

Bussin, M., & Christos, D. (2022). How to link TALENT MANAGEMENT and REMUNERATION. *HR Future*, (4), 42–44.

Caiado, R. G. G., Scavarda, L. F., Vidal, G., de Mattos Nascimento, D. L., & Garza-Reyes, J. A. (2023). A taxonomy of critical factors towards sustainable operations and supply chain management 4.0 in developing countries. *Operations Management Research*. DOI: 10.1007/s12063-023-00430-8

Camilleri, M. A. (2024). Artificial intelligence governance: Ethical considerations and implications for social responsibility. *Expert Systems: International Journal of Knowledge Engineering and Neural Networks*, *41*(7), e13406. DOI: 10.1111/exsy.13406

Cappelli, P., & Tavis, A. (2016). *Performance management revolution: The future of performance reviews*. Harvard Business Review Press.https://hbr.org/2016/10/the-performance-management-revolution

Carrasco, I. (2007). Corporate social responsibility, values, and cooperation. *International Advances in Economic Research, 13*(4), 454–460. DOI: 10.1007/s11294-007-9110-2

Carroll, A. B. (1979). A three-dimensional conceptual model of corporate performance. *Academy of Management Review, 4*(4), 497–505. DOI: 10.2307/257850

Carroll, A. B. (1991). The pyramid of corporate social responsibility: Toward the moral management of organizational stakeholders. *Business Horizons, 34*(4), 39–48. DOI: 10.1016/0007-6813(91)90005-G

Carroll, A. B. (1999). Corporate social responsibility: Evolution of a definitional construct. *Business & Society, 38*(3), 268–295. DOI: 10.1177/000765039903800303

Carroll, A. B., & Shabana, K. M. (2010). The business case for corporate social responsibility: A review of concepts, research and practice. *International Journal of Management Reviews, 12*(1), 85–105. DOI: 10.1111/j.1468-2370.2009.00275.x

Cascio, W., & Boudreau, J. (2010). *Investing in people: Financial impact of human resource initiatives*. Ft Press.

Cavaliere, L. P. L., Byloppilly, R., Khan, S. D., Othman, B. A., Muda, I., & Malhotra, R. K. (2024). Acceptance and effectiveness of Industry 4.0 internal and external organisational initiatives in Malaysian firms. *International Journal of Management and Enterprise Development, 23*(1), 1–25. DOI: 10.1504/IJMED.2024.138422

Cavoukian, A. (2010). Privacy by design: The definitive workshop. A foreword by Ann Cavoukian, Ph. D. *Identity in the Information Society, 3*(2), 247–251. DOI: 10.1007/s12394-010-0062-y

Chahar, A., & Christobel, Y. A. Ritika, Adakane, P. K., Sonal, D., & Tripathi, V. (2022). The Implementation of Big Data With Cloud and Edge Computing in Enhancing the Smart Grid Information Processes Through Sem Model. *2022 2nd International Conference on Advance Computing and Innovative Technologies in Engineering, ICACITE 2022*, 608 – 611. DOI: 10.1109/ICACITE53722.2022.9823896

Chakroun, S., & Ben Amar, A. (2022). Earnings management, financial performance and the moderating effect of corporate social responsibility: Evidence from France. *Management Research Review, 45*(3), 331–362. DOI: 10.1108/MRR-02-2021-0126

Chamorro-Premuzic, T., Akhtar, R., & D'Annunzio, P. (2019). The Future of Work: AI in Recruitment and Selection. Psychology Today.

Chandna, R., Saini, S., & Kumar, S. (2022). Selecting the Most Agile Manufacturing System with Respect to Agile Attribute-Technology: Fuzzy AHP Approach. In D. N. & C. A. (Eds.), *AIP Conference Proceedings* (Vol. 2481). American Institute of Physics Inc. DOI: 10.1063/5.0103804

Chandna, R. (2022). Selecting the most agile manufacturing system with respect to agile attribute-technology-fuzzy AHP approach. *International Journal of Operations Research, 43*(4), 512–532. DOI: 10.1504/IJOR.2022.122812

Chandran, G. C., Synthia Regis Prabha, D. M. M., Malathi, P., Kapila, D., Arunkumar, M. S., Verma, D., & Teressa, D. M. (2022). Built-In Calibration Standard and Decision Support System for Controlling Structured Data Storage Systems Using Soft Computing Techniques. *Computational Intelligence and Neuroscience, 2022*, 1–7. Advance online publication. DOI: 10.1155/2022/3476004 PMID: 36065369

Channuwong, S., Phudarat, B. S. S., Jirachottrakul, P., Pleansamai, J. L. K., Khamsom, S., & Kanhabutr, A. (2024). Strategic management for sustainable business development: Concepts, theories and practices. *Sciences of Conservation and Archaeology, 36*(3), 11–22.

Chatterjee, S., Rana, N. P., Dwivedi, Y. K., & Baabdullah, A. M. (2021). Understanding AI adoption in manufacturing and production firms using an integrated TAM-TOE model. *Technological Forecasting and Social Change, 170*, 120880. DOI: 10.1016/j.techfore.2021.120880

Chauvey, J.-N., Giordano-Spring, S., Cho, C. H., & Patten, D. M. (2015). The normativity and legitimacy of CSR disclosure: Evidence from France. *Journal of Business Ethics, 130*(4), 789–803. DOI: 10.1007/s10551-014-2114-y

Cheng, M. M., & Hackett, R. D. (2021). A critical review of algorithms in HRM: Definition, theory, and practice. *Human Resource Management Review, 31*(1), 100698. DOI: 10.1016/j.hrmr.2019.100698

Choi, J., & Wang, H. (2009). Stakeholder relations and the persistence of corporate financial performance. *Strategic Management Journal, 30*(8), 895–907. DOI: 10.1002/smj.759

Chourasia, S., Dhama, A., & Bhardwaj, G. (2024). AI-Driven Organizational Culture Evolution: A Critical Review. *2024 International Conference on Communication, Computer Sciences and Engineering (IC3SE)*, 1839–1844. DOI: 10.1109/IC3SE62002.2024.10592949

Cinquepalmi, F., Paris, S., Pennacchia, E., & Tiburcio, V. A. (2023). Efficiency and sustainability: The role of digitization in re-inhabiting the existing building stock. *Energies, 16*(9), 3613. DOI: 10.3390/en16093613

Clark, G. L., Feiner, A., & Viehs, M. (2015). *From the stockholder to the stakeholder: How sustainability can drive financial outperformance*. University of Oxford, Smith School of Enterprise and the Environment.

Cochran, P. L., & Wood, R. A. (1984). Corporate social responsibility and financial performance. *Academy of Management Journal, 27*(1), 42–56. DOI: 10.2307/255956

Coelho, R., Jayantilal, S., & Ferreira, J. J. (2023). The impact of social responsibility on corporate financial performance: A systematic literature review. *Corporate Social Responsibility and Environmental Management, 30*(4), 1535–1560. DOI: 10.1002/csr.2446

Cohen, W. M., & Levinthal, D. A. (1990). Absorptive capacity: A new perspective on learning and innovation. *Administrative Science Quarterly, 35*(1), 128–152. DOI: 10.2307/2393553

Coleman, J. S. (1988). Social capital in the creation of human capital. *American Journal of Sociology, 94*(Supplement), 95–120. DOI: 10.1086/228943

Collings, D. G., Mellahi, K., & Cascio, W. F. (2019). Global talent management and performance in multinational enterprises: A multilevel perspective. *Journal of Management, 45*(2), 540–566. DOI: 10.1177/0149206318757018

Conrow, E. H. (2011). Estimating technology readiness level coefficients. *Journal of Spacecraft and Rockets, 48*(1), 146–152. DOI: 10.2514/1.46753

Crawford, K. (2021). *Atlas of AI: Power, politics, and the planetary costs of artificial intelligence*. Yale University Press., DOI: 10.2307/j.ctv1ghv45t

Dahiya, K., & Taneja, S. (2023). To Analyse the Impact of Multi-Media Technology on the Rural Entrepreneurship Development. In *Contemporary Studies of Risks in Emerging Technology* (pp. 221–240). DOI: 10.1108/978-1-80455-562-020231015

Dangwal, A., Kaur, S., Taneja, S., & Ozen, E. (2022). A bibliometric analysis of green tourism based on the scopus platform. In *Developing Relationships, Personalization, and Data Herald in Marketing 5.0*. IGI Global., DOI: 10.4018/978-1-6684-4496-2.ch015

Darics, E. (2020). E-leadership or "how to be boss in instant messaging?" The role of nonverbal communication. *International Journal of Business Communication, 57*(1), 3–29. DOI: 10.1177/2329488416685068

Das, T., Thakur, R., Dhua, S., Teixeira-Costa, B. E., Beber Rodrigues, M., Pereira, M. M., Mishra, P., & Gupta, A. K. (2023). Processing of Cereals. In *Cereal Grains: Composition, Nutritional Attributes, and Potential Applications*. CRC Press., DOI: 10.1201/9781003252023-10

Dastin, J. (2018). Amazon scraps secret AI recruiting tool that showed bias against women. Reuters. https://www.reuters.com/article/us-amazon-com-jobs-automation-insight-idUSKCN1MK08G

Davenport, T. H., & Ronanki, R. (2018). Artificial intelligence for the real world. *HBR'S 10 MUST*, 67.

Davenport, T., & Harris, J. (2017). *Competing on analytics: Updated, with a new introduction: The new science of winning*. Harvard Business Press.

David, A., Yigitcanlar, T., Li, R. Y. M., Corchado, J. M., Cheong, P. H., Mossberger, K., & Mehmood, R. (2023). Understanding local government digital technology adoption strategies: A PRISMA review. *Sustainability (Basel)*, *15*(12), 9645. DOI: 10.3390/su15129645

Davuluri, S. K., Alvi, S. A. M., Aeri, M., Agarwal, A., Serajuddin, M., & Hasan, Z. (2023). A Security Model for Perceptive 5G-Powered BC IoT Associated Deep Learning. *6th International Conference on Inventive Computation Technologies, ICICT 2023 - Proceedings*, 118 – 125. DOI: 10.1109/ICICT57646.2023.10134487

De Hoogh, A. H., & Den Harog, D. N. (2009). Neuroticism and locus of control as moderators of the relationships of charismatic and autocratic leadership with burnout. *The Journal of Applied Psychology*, *94*(4), 1058–1067. DOI: 10.1037/a0016253 PMID: 19594244

De Vos, A., Jacobs, S., & Verbruggen, M. (2021). Career transitions and employability. *Journal of Vocational Behavior*, *126*, 1–13. DOI: 10.1016/j.jvb.2020.103475

Deloitte. (2023). AI for ESG: Driving sustainability through intelligent technologies. https://www.deloitte.com

Deluga, R. J. (2001). American presidential Machiavellianism: Implications for charismatic leadership and rated performance. *The Leadership Quarterly*, *12*(3), 339–363. DOI: 10.1016/S1048-9843(01)00082-0

Den Hartog, D. N. (2015). Ethical leadership. *Annual Review of Organizational Psychology and Organizational Behavior, 2*, 4.1–4.26.

Dhaliwal, D. S., Li, O. Z., Tsang, A., & Yang, Y. G. (2011). Voluntary nonfinancial disclosure and the cost of equity capital: The initiation of corporate social responsibility reporting. *The Accounting Review, 86*(1), 59–100. DOI: 10.2308/accr.00000005

Diddi, P. K., Sharma, P. K., Srivastava, A., Madduru, S. R. C., & Reddy, E. S. (2022). Sustainable Fast Setting Early Strength Self Compacting Concrete(FSESSCC) Using Metakaolin. *IOP Conference Series. Earth and Environmental Science, 1077*(1), 012009. Advance online publication. DOI: 10.1088/1755-1315/1077/1/012009

DiMaggio, P. J., & Powell, W. W. (1983). The iron cage revisited: Institutional isomorphism and collective rationality in organizational fields. *American Sociological Review, 48*(2), 147–160. DOI: 10.2307/2095101

Dimri, R., Mall, S., Sinha, S., Joshi, N. C., Bhatnagar, P., Sharma, R., Kumar, V., & Gururani, P. (2023). Role of microalgae as a sustainable alternative of biopolymers and its application in industries. *Plant Science Today, 10*, 8–18. DOI: 10.14719/pst.2460

Dixit, A. K., Kumar, T. V., Joshi, A., Bedi, H. S., Chakravarthi, M. K., & Singh, D. P. (2022). Trends in Robotics and Computer Integrated Manufacturing. *Proceedings of 5th International Conference on Contemporary Computing and Informatics, IC3I 2022*, 212 – 216. DOI: 10.1109/IC3I56241.2022.10072745

Donkers, T., Loepp, B., & Ziegler, J. (2017, August). Sequential user-based recurrent neural network recommendations. In *Proceedings of the eleventh ACM conference on recommender systems* (pp. 152-160). DOI: 10.1145/3109859.3109877

Doshi-Velez, F., & Kim, B. (2017). Towards a rigorous science of interpretable machine learning. *arXiv preprint arXiv:1702.08608*. https://arxiv.org/abs/1702.08608

Drucker, P. F. (1954). *The practice of management*. Collins. (Reprinted 2006)

Drucker, P. F. (1996). *Yönetim uygulaması* (Yarmalı, E. S., Trans.). İnkilap Kitabevi.

Dudek, M., Bashynska, I., Filyppova, S., Yermak, S., & Cichoń, D. (2023). Methodology for assessment of inclusive social responsibility of the energy industry enterprises. *Journal of Cleaner Production, 394*, 136317. DOI: 10.1016/j.jclepro.2023.136317

Duggan, T. J. (2023). Inflection Points and Forming a Leadership Identity: The Identity Work of Women Leaders in Organizations (Doctoral dissertation, Fielding Graduate University).

Dulebohn, J. H., & Johnson, R. D. (2013). Human resource metrics and decision support: A classification framework. *Human Resource Management Review, 23*(1), 71–83. DOI: 10.1016/j.hrmr.2012.06.005

Du, S., & Sen, S. (2023). AI through a CSR lens: Consumer issues and public policy. *Journal of Public Policy & Marketing*, *42*(4), 351–353. DOI: 10.1177/07439156231186573

Dutta, A., Singh, P., Dobhal, A., Mannan, D., Singh, J., & Goswami, P. (2023). Entrepreneurial Aptitude of Women of an Aspirational District of Uttarakhand. *Indian Journal of Extension Education*, *59*(2), 103–107. DOI: 10.48165/IJEE.2023.59222

Dyllick, T., & Hockerts, K. (2002). Beyond the business case for corporate sustainability. *Business Strategy and the Environment*, *11*(2), 130–141. DOI: 10.1002/bse.323

Eccles, R. G., Ioannou, I., & Serafeim, G. (2014). The impact of corporate sustainability on organizational processes and performance. *Management Science*, *60*(11), 2835–2857. DOI: 10.1287/mnsc.2014.1984

Eccles, R. G., & Klimenko, S. (2019). The investor revolution. *Harvard Business Review*, *97*(3), 106–116. https://hbr.org/2019/05/the-investor-revolution

Eccles, R. G., & Krzus, M. P. (2018). The Nordic model: An analysis of leading practices in ESG disclosure. *Nordic Journal of Business*, *67*(4), 5–22.

Ekren, B. Y., Stylos, N., Zwiegelaar, J., Turhanlar, E. E., & Kumar, V. (2023). Additive manufacturing integration in E-commerce supply chain network to improve resilience and competitiveness. *Simulation Modelling Practice and Theory*, *122*, 102676. Advance online publication. DOI: 10.1016/j.simpat.2022.102676

Elkington, J. (1997). *Cannibals with forks: The triple bottom line of 21st century business*. Capstone., DOI: 10.1002/tqem.3310080106

Epstein, E. M. (1987). The corporate social policy process: Beyond business ethics, corporate social responsibility, and corporate social responsiveness. *California Management Review*, *29*(3), 99–114. DOI: 10.2307/41165254

Escudero-Cipriani, C., García-del Junco, J., Chafloque-Céspedes, R., & Alvarez-Risco, A. (2024). Frugal innovation in the business environment: A literature review and future perspectives. *Frontiers in Artificial Intelligence*, *7*, 1385522. DOI: 10.3389/frai.2024.1385522 PMID: 39712468

Eswar, K. N. D. V. S., Doss, M. A. N., Vishnuram, P., Selim, A., Bajaj, M., Kotb, H., & Kamel, S. (2023). Comprehensive Study on Reduced DC Source Count: Multilevel Inverters and Its Design Topologies. *Energies*, *16*(1), 18. Advance online publication. DOI: 10.3390/en16010018

Eubanks, V. (2018). *Automating inequality. How high-tech tools profile, police, and punish the poor*. St. Martin's Press.

Eubanks, V. (2018). *Automating inequality: How high-tech tools profile, police, and punish the poor*. St. Martin's Press.

European Commission. (2019). *Ethics guidelines for trustworthy AI*. https://digital-strategy.ec.europa.eu/en/library/ethics-guidelines-trustworthy-ai

European Commission. (2021). Proposal for a regulation laying down harmonised rules on artificial intelligence (Artificial Intelligence Act). Brussels: European Commission. https://eur-lex.europa.eu/legal-content/EN/TXT/?uri=CELEX%3A52021PC0206

European Commission. (2022). *Corporate Sustainability Reporting Directive (CSRD)*. Official Journal of the European Union.

European Commission. (2023). *General Data Protection Regulation (GDPR): Official guidelines and regulations*. Retrieved from https://ec.europa.eu/info/law/law-topic/data-protection_en

Fama, E. F., Fisher, L., Jensen, M. C., & Roll, R. (1969). The adjustment of stock prices to new information. *International Economic Review*, *10*(1), 1–21. DOI: 10.2307/2525569

Farcane, N., & Bureana, E. (2015). History of corporate social responsibility concept. *Annales Universitatis Apulensis Series Oeconomica*, *17*(2), 31–48. DOI: 10.29302/oeconomica.2015.17.2.3

Fernandes, S., Sheeja, M. S., & Parivara, S. (2024). Potential of AI for a Sustainable, Inclusive, and Ethically Responsible Future. *Fostering Multidisciplinary Research for Sustainability*, 196.

Ferrell, A., Liang, H., & Renneboog, L. (2016). Socially responsible firms. *Journal of Financial Economics*, *122*(3), 585–606. DOI: 10.1016/j.jfineco.2015.12.003

Ferrell, O. C., & Ferrell, L. (2024). Building a Better World: The Role of AI Ethics and Social Responsibility. *Journal of Macromarketing*, *44*(4), 928–935. DOI: 10.1177/02761467241285793

Fioravante, R. (2024). Beyond the business case for responsible artificial intelligence: Strategic CSR in light of digital washing and the moral human argument. *Sustainability (Basel)*, *16*(3), 1232. DOI: 10.3390/su16031232

Fishbach, A., & Woolley, K. (2022). The structure of intrinsic motivation. *Annual Review of Organizational Psychology and Organizational Behavior*, *9*(1), 339–363. DOI: 10.1146/annurev-orgpsych-012420-091122

Fjelland, R. (2020). Why general artificial intelligence will not be realized. *Humanities & Social Sciences Communications*, *7*(1), 1–9. DOI: 10.1057/s41599-020-0494-4

Flammer, C. (2013). Corporate social responsibility and shareholder reaction: The environmental awareness of investors. *Academy of Management Journal*, *56*(3), 758–781. DOI: 10.5465/amj.2011.0744

Floridi, L. (2019). Establishing the rules for building trustworthy AI. *Nature Machine Intelligence*, *1*(6), 185–186. DOI: 10.1038/s42256-019-0055-y

Floridi, L. (2019). Translating principles into practices of digital ethics: Five risks of being unethical. *Philosophy & Technology*, *32*(2), 185–193. DOI: 10.1007/s13347-019-00354-x

Floridi, L., & Cowls, J. (2019). A unified framework of five principles for AI in society. *Harvard Data Science Review*, *1*(1), 1–15. DOI: 10.1162/99608f92.8cd550d1

Floridi, L., Cowls, J., Beltrametti, M., Chatila, R., Chazerand, P., Dignum, V., Luetge, C., Madelin, R., Pagallo, U., Rossi, F., Schafer, B., Valcke, P., & Vayena, E. (2018). AI4People—An ethical framework for a good AI society. *Minds and Machines*, *28*(4), 689–707. DOI: 10.1007/s11023-018-9482-5 PMID: 30930541

Floridi, L., & Taddeo, M. (2016). What is data ethics? *Philosophical Transactions. Series A, Mathematical, Physical, and Engineering Sciences*, *374*(2083), 20160360. DOI: 10.1098/rsta.2016.0360 PMID: 28336805

Fountaine, T., McCarthy, B., & Saleh, T. (2019). Building the AI-powered organization. *Harvard Business Review*, *97*(4), 62–73.

Frederick, W. C. (1960). The growing concern over business responsibility. *California Management Review*, *2*(4), 52–61. DOI: 10.2307/41165405

Freeman, R. E. (1984). Corporate Views of the Public Interest. Academy of Management Review (pre-1986), 9(000002), 366.

Freeman, R. E. (1984). *Strategic management: A stakeholder approach*. Cambridge University Press.

Freeman, R. E. (1984). *Strategic Management: A Stakeholder Approach*. Pitman.

Freeman, R. E., Harrison, J. S., Wicks, A. C., Parmar, B. L., & De Colle, S. (2010). *Stakeholder theory: The state of the art*. Cambridge University Press., DOI: 10.1017/CBO9780511815768

Friedman, M. (2007). The social responsibility of business is to increase its profits. In Corporate ethics and corporate governance, 173–178. DOI: 10.1007/978-3-540-70818-6_14

Gangwar, V. P., & Srivastva, S. P. (2020). Impact of micro finance in poverty eradication via SHGs: A study of selected districts in U.P. *International Journal of Advanced Science and Technology*, *29*(2), 3818–3829.

Gartner. (2023). *Trends in responsible AI deployment*. https://www.gartner.com

Gaurav, G., Singh, A. B., Khandelwal, C., Gupta, S., Kumar, S., Meena, M. L., & Dangayach, G. S. (2023). Global Development on LCA Research: A Bibliometric Analysis From 2010 to 2021. *International Journal of Social Ecology and Sustainable Development*, *14*(1), 1–19. Advance online publication. DOI: 10.4018/IJSESD.327791

Ghanad, A. (2023). An overview of quantitative research methods. *International Journal of Multidisciplinary Research and Analysis*, *6*(08), 3794–3803. DOI: 10.47191/ijmra/v6-i8-52

Ghotbi, N. (2023). The ethics of emotional artificial intelligence: A mixed method analysis. *Asian Bioethics Review*, *15*(4), 417–430. DOI: 10.1007/s41649-022-00237-y PMID: 37808444

Giaccardi, E., & Bendor, R. (2024). Rethink design: a vocabulary for designing with AI.

Gilliard, C. 2020. Caught in the Spotlight, Urban Omnibus, 9 January. Available at https://urbanomnibus.net/2020/01/caught-in-the-spotlight/

Global Reporting Initiative. (2023). GRI standards update 2023. https://www.globalreporting.org

Gloor, P., Fronzetti Colladon, A., & Grippa, F. (2022). Measuring ethical behavior with AI and natural language processing to assess business success. *Scientific Reports*, *12*(1), 10228. DOI: 10.1038/s41598-022-14101-4 PMID: 35715458

Godbole, V., Kukrety, S., Gautam, P., Bisht, M., & Pal, M. K. (2023). Bioleaching for Heavy Metal Extraction from E-waste: A Sustainable Approach. In *Microbial Technology for Sustainable E-waste Management*. Springer International Publishing., DOI: 10.1007/978-3-031-25678-3_4

Goleman, D. (1995). *Emotional intelligence: Why it can matter more than IQ*. Bantam Books.

Goleman, D., Boyatzis, R. E., & McKee, A. (2013). *Primal leadership: Unleashing the power of emotional intelligence*. Harvard Business Press.

Gompers, P., Ishii, J., & Metrick, A. (2003). Corporate governance and equity prices. *The Quarterly Journal of Economics, 118*(1), 107–156. DOI: 10.1162/00335530360535162

Gonfa, Y. H., Tessema, F. B., Tadesse, M. G., Bachheti, A., & Bachheti, R. K. (2023). Medicinally Important Plant Roots and Their Role in Nanoparticles Synthesis and Applications. In *Secondary Metabolites from Medicinal Plants: Nanoparticles Synthesis and their Applications*. CRC Press., DOI: 10.1201/9781003213727-11

Gopal, S., Gupta, P., & Minocha, A. (2023). Advancements in Fin-Tech and Security Challenges of Banking Industry. *4th International Conference on Intelligent Engineering and Management, ICIEM 2023*. DOI: 10.1109/ICIEM59379.2023.10165876

Goswami, S., & Sharma, S. (2022). Industry 4.0 Enabled Molecular Imaging Using Artificial Intelligence Technique. *2022 1st International Conference on Computational Science and Technology, ICCST 2022 - Proceedings*, 455–460. DOI: 10.1109/ICCST55948.2022.10040406

Griffin, J. J., & Mahon, J. F. (1997). The corporate social performance and corporate financial performance debate: Twenty-five years of incomparable research. *Business & Society, 36*(1), 5–31. DOI: 10.1177/000765039703600102

Grover, D., Sharma, S., Kaur, P., Mittal, A., & Sharma, P. K. (2024). Societal Elements that Impact the Performance of Women Entrepreneurs in Tier-II Cities: A Study of Rohilkhand Region of Uttar Pradesh. *2024 IEEE Zooming Innovation in Consumer Technologies Conference. ZINC, 2024*, 114–117. DOI: 10.1109/ZINC61849.2024.10579316

Grover, P., Kar, A. K., & Dwivedi, Y. K. (2022). Understanding artificial intelligence adoption in operations management: Insights from the review of academic literature and social media discussions. *Annals of Operations Research, 308*(1), 177–213. DOI: 10.1007/s10479-020-03683-9

Gupta, C., Jindal, P., & Malhotra, R. K. (2022). A Study of Increasing Adoption Trends of Digital Technologies - An Evidence from Indian Banking. In D. N. & C. A. (Eds.), *AIP Conference Proceedings* (Vol. 2481). American Institute of Physics Inc. DOI: 10.1063/5.0104572

Gupta, R., Jain, A., & Singh, K. (2025). AI-Driven Sustainable Business in CSR Reporting Regime: A Systematic Literature Review. *Corporate Social Responsibility Approaches to Ethical AI in Business*, 277-292.

Gupta, A., & Kumar, H. (2022). Multi-dimensional perspectives on electric vehicles design: A mind map approach. *Cleaner Engineering and Technology*, *8*, 100483. Advance online publication. DOI: 10.1016/j.clet.2022.100483

Gupta, H., Taluja, R., Shaw, S., Chari, S. L., Deepak, A., & Rana, A. (2023). Internet of Things Based Reduction of Electricity Theft in Urban Areas. *Proceedings of International Conference on Contemporary Computing and Informatics, IC3I 2023*, 2642 – 2645. DOI: 10.1109/IC3I59117.2023.10397868

Gupta, M., Arora, K., & Taneja, S. (2023). Bibliometric analysis on employee engagement and human resource management. In *Enhancing Customer Engagement Through Location-Based Marketing*. IGI Global., DOI: 10.4018/978-1-6684-8177-6.ch013

Gupta, M., Verma, P. K., Verma, R., & Upadhyay, D. K. (2023). Applications of Computational Intelligence Techniques in Communications. In *Applications of Computational Intelligence Techniques in Communications*. CRC Press., DOI: 10.1201/9781003452645

Gururani, P., Bhatnagar, P., Bisht, B., Jaiswal, K. K., Kumar, V., Kumar, S., Vlaskin, M. S., Grigorenko, A. V., & Rindin, K. G. (2022). Recent advances and viability in sustainable thermochemical conversion of sludge to bio-fuel production. *Fuel*, *316*, 123351. Advance online publication. DOI: 10.1016/j.fuel.2022.123351

Hagendorff, T. (2020). The ethics of AI ethics: An evaluation of guidelines. *Minds and Machines*, *30*(1), 99–120. DOI: 10.1007/s11023-020-09517-8

Hajoary, P. K., Balachandra, P., & Garza-Reyes, J. A. (2023). Industry 4.0 maturity and readiness assessment: An empirical validation using Confirmatory Composite Analysis. *Production Planning and Control*. Advance online publication. DOI: 10.1080/09537287.2023.2210545

Hanna, M., Pantanowitz, L., Jackson, B., Palmer, O., Visweswaran, S., Pantanowitz, J., & Rashidi, H. (2024). Ethical and Bias considerations in artificial intelligence (AI)/machine learning. *Modern Pathology*, , 100686. PMID: 39694331

Haque, E. (2024). *AI Horizons: Shaping a Better Future Through Responsible Innovation and Human Collaboration*. Walter de Gruyter GmbH & Co KG. DOI: 10.1515/9781501518430

Hart, S. L. (1995). A natural-resource-based view of the firm. *Academy of Management Review*, *20*(4), 986–1014. DOI: 10.2307/258963

Hart, S. L., & Milstein, M. B. (2003). Creating sustainable value. *The Academy of Management Perspectives*, *17*(2), 56–69. DOI: 10.5465/ame.2003.10025194

Herath, S. K., & Herath, L. M. (2024). Embedding Ethical Practices: Overcoming the Challenges of Corporate Social Responsibility Implementation. *Social and Ethical Implications of AI in Finance for Sustainability*, 1-40.

Herold, D. M., Nowotny, S., Schuster, T., & Wortmann, J. (2020). The role of corporate social responsibility in the digital age. *Corporate Social Responsibility and Environmental Management*, *27*(5), 2341–2352. DOI: 10.1002/csr.1969

Hmoud, B., & Laszlo, V. (2019). Will artificial intelligence take over human resources recruitment and selection? *Network Intelligence Studies*, *7*(13), 21–30.

Holm, E. A. (2019). In defense of the black box. *Science*, *364*(6435), 26–27. DOI: 10.1126/science.aax0162 PMID: 30948538

Holmes, W., Bialik, M., & Fadel, C. (2019). *Artificial intelligence in education: Promises and implications for teaching and learning*. Center for Curriculum Redesign.

Holstein, D. (2019). Quantitative Security Measures for Cyber Security Assurance.

Homans, G. C. (1961). *Social behavior: Its elementary forms*. Harcourt, Brace & World.

Homer, S. T., Lim, W. M., & Poon, W. C. (2025). A concentric locus of control and triple bottom line model for responsible management: Theory development inspired by students from the Global South. *International Journal of Management Education*, *23*(1), 101083. DOI: 10.1016/j.ijme.2024.101083

House, R. J. (1977). A 1976 theory of charismatic leadership. In Hunt, J. G., & Larson, L. L. (Eds.), *Leadership: the cutting edge* (pp. 189–207). Southern Illinois Univ. Press.

Hsieh, Y. C., Weng, J., Pham, N. T., & Yi, L. H. (2022). What drives employees to participate in corporate social responsibility? A personal characteristics-CSR capacity-organizational reinforcing model of employees' motivation for voluntary CSR activities. *International Journal of Human Resource Management*, *33*(18), 3703–3735. DOI: 10.1080/09585192.2021.1967422

Huang, J.-F., Chen, C.-T. A., Chen, M.-H., Huang, S.-L., & Hsu, P.-Y. (2023). Structural Equation Modeling of the Marine Ecological System in Nanwan Bay Using SPSS Amos. *Sustainability (Basel)*, *15*(14), 11435. DOI: 10.3390/su151411435

Iansiti, M., & Lakhani, K. R. (2020). Competing in the age of AI: Strategy and leadership when algorithms and networks run the world. Harvard Business Review Press, 60-75.

IBM. (2022). *IBM ESG and AI data platform*. https://www.ibm.com/sustainability

IEA. (2025). *World energy outlook 2025*. International Energy Agency.

Ihuah, A. S. (2024). African endogenous knowledge and sustainable development: Evolving an African agrarian philosophy. In *African agrarian philosophy* (pp. 287–310). Springer International Publishing.

Ikart, E. (2023). Emotional intelligence: Why it matters in change leadership and innovation in the 21st century styles of work. *International Journal of Business Innovation*, *2*, e34732.

Imran, M. K., Ilyas, M., Aslam, U., & Ubaid-Ur-Rahman, U.-U.-R. (2016). Organizational learning through transformational leadership. *The Learning Organization*, *23*(4), 232–248. DOI: 10.1108/TLO-09-2015-0053

Indu, R., Dimri, S. C., & Kumar, B. (2023). Identification of Location for Police Headquarters to Deal with Crime Against Women in India Using Clustering Based on K-Means Algorithm. *International Journal of Computing and Digital Systems*, *14*(1), 965–974. DOI: 10.12785/ijcds/140175

ISO 26000. (2010). *Guidance on social responsibility. International Organization for Standardization.*

ISO. (2022). *ISO/IEC 42001: Artificial Intelligence Management System Standards*. Retrieved from https://www.iso.org

Janssen, M., Brous, P., Estevez, E., Barbosa, L. S., & Janowski, T. (2020). Data governance: Organizing data for trustworthy Artificial Intelligence. *Government Information Quarterly*, *37*(3), 101493. DOI: 10.1016/j.giq.2020.101493

Jayadeva, S. M., Prasad Krishnam, N., Raja Mannar, B., Prakash Dabral, A., Buddhi, D., & Garg, N. (2023). An Investigation of IOT-Based Consumer Analytics to Assist Consumer Engagement Strategies in Evolving Markets. *2023 3rd International Conference on Advance Computing and Innovative Technologies in Engineering, ICACITE 2023*, 487 – 491. DOI: 10.1109/ICACITE57410.2023.10183310

Jeeva, M., Leelavathi, R., Philip, B., Kalaivani, S., & Raj, R. R. (2024). A Study on Technological Revolutions in Dynamic Educational Sector Post-covid-19. In *Artificial Intelligence (AI) and Customer Social Responsibility (CSR)* (pp. 591–601). Springer Nature Switzerland. DOI: 10.1007/978-3-031-50939-1_45

Jena, S., & Gairola, A. (2022). Numerical Method to Generate and Evaluate Environmental Wind Over Hills: Comparison of Pedestrian Winds Over Hills and Plains. *CFD Letters*, *14*(10), 56–67. DOI: 10.37934/cfdl.14.10.5667

Jindal, T., Sheoliha, N., Kishore, K., Uike, D., Khurana, S., & Verma, D. (2022). A Conceptual Analysis on the Impact of Internet of Things (IOT) Towards on Digital Marketing Transformation. *2022 2nd International Conference on Advance Computing and Innovative Technologies in Engineering, ICACITE 2022*, 1943 – 1947. DOI: 10.1109/ICACITE53722.2022.9823714

Jobin, A., Ienca, M., & Vayena, E. (2019). *Artificial intelligence: The global landscape of ethics guidelines. Preprint version. Health Ethics & Policy Lab*. ETH Zurich.

Jobin, A., Ienca, M., & Vayena, E. (2019). The global landscape of AI ethics guidelines. *Nature Machine Intelligence*, *1*(9), 389–399. DOI: 10.1038/s42256-019-0088-2

Jo, H., & Harjoto, M. A. (2011). Corporate governance and firm value: The impact of corporate social responsibility. *Journal of Business Ethics, 103*, 351–383.

Johri, S., Singh Sidhu, K., Jafersadhiq, A., Mannar, B. R., Gehlot, A., & Goyal, H. R. (2023). An investigation of the effects of the global epidemic on Crypto Currency returns and volatility. *2023 3rd International Conference on Advance Computing and Innovative Technologies in Engineering, ICACITE 2023*, 345 – 348. DOI: 10.1109/ICACITE57410.2023.10182988

Jones, T. M., & Wicks, A. C. (1999). Convergent stakeholder theory. *Academy of Management Review*, *24*(2), 206–221. DOI: 10.2307/259075

Joshi, S., Sharma, M., & Barve, A. (2023). Implementation challenges of blockchain technology in closed-loop supply chain: A Waste Electrical and Electronic Equipment (WEEE) management perspective in developing countries. *Supply Chain Forum, 24*(1), 59 – 80. DOI: 10.1080/16258312.2022.2135972

Joshi, K., Patil, S., Gupta, S., & Khanna, R. (2022). Role of Pranayma in emotional maturity for improving health. *Journal of Medical Pharmaceutical and Allied Sciences*, *11*(2), 4569–4573. DOI: 10.55522/jmpas.V11I2.2033

Joshi, K., Sharma, R., Singh, N., & Sharma, B. (2023). Digital World of Cloud Computing and Wireless Networking: Challenges and Risks. In *Applications of Artificial Intelligence in Wireless Communication Systems*. IGI Global., DOI: 10.4018/978-1-6684-7348-1.ch003

Joshi, S., & Sharma, M. (2022). Sustainable Performance through Digital Supply Chains in Industry 4.0 Era: Amidst the Pandemic Experience. *Sustainability (Basel)*, *14*(24), 16726. Advance online publication. DOI: 10.3390/su142416726

Joshi, S., & Sharma, M. (2023). Strategic challenges of deploying LARG approach for sustainable manufacturing: Research implications from Indian SMEs. *International Journal of Internet Manufacturing and Services*, *9*(2–3), 373–397. DOI: 10.1504/IJIMS.2023.132791

Josphineleela, R., Jyothi, M., Natrayan, L., Kaviarasu, A., & Sharma, M. (2023). Development of IoT based Health Monitoring System for Disables using Microcontroller. *Proceedings - 7th International Conference on Computing Methodologies and Communication, ICCMC 2023*, 1380 – 1384. DOI: 10.1109/ICCMC56507.2023.10084026

Josphineleela, R., Siva Reddy, K. V., Reddy, M. V. S. S., & Rawat, R. S. (2023). Design and Development of a Smart Sprinkler Device for IoT-Integrated Plants Irrigation. *Proceedings of the 2023 2nd International Conference on Electronics and Renewable Systems, ICEARS 2023*, 498 – 501. DOI: 10.1109/ICEARS56392.2023.10084960

Judge, T. A., & Piccolo, R. F. (2004). Transformational and transactional leadership: A meta-analytic test of their relative validity. *The Journal of Applied Psychology*, *89*(5), 755–768. DOI: 10.1037/0021-9010.89.5.755 PMID: 15506858

Juneja, P. J., Sunori, S., Sharma, A., Sharma, A., & Joshi, V. (2020). Modeling, Control and Instrumentation of Lime Kiln Process: A Review. In S. S. & D. P. (Eds.), *Proceedings - 2020 International Conference on Advances in Computing, Communication and Materials, ICACCM 2020* (pp. 399 – 403). Institute of Electrical and Electronics Engineers Inc. DOI: 10.1109/ICACCM50413.2020.9212948

Juneja, P. K., Kumar Sunori, S., Manu, M., Joshi, P., Sharma, S., Garia, P., & Mittal, A. (2022). Potential Applications of Fuzzy Logic Controller in the Pulp and Paper Industry - A Review. *5th International Conference on Inventive Computation Technologies, ICICT 2022 - Proceedings*, 399 – 401. DOI: 10.1109/ICICT54344.2022.9850626

Kaleem, S., Ahmad, B., & Tabassam, A. (2025). An Exploratory Study of the Relationship Between Corporate Social Responsibility and Financial Performance: The Role of Artificial Intelligence in Enhancing CSR and Financial Outcomes. *Social Science Review Archives*, *3*(1), 1571–1581. DOI: 10.70670/sra.v3i1.458

Kaliappan, S., Natrayan, L., & Garg, N. (2023). Checking and Supervisory System for Calculation of Industrial Constraints using Embedded System. *Proceedings of the 4th International Conference on Smart Electronics and Communication, ICOSEC 2023*, 87 – 90. DOI: 10.1109/ICOSEC58147.2023.10275952

Kalshoven, K. A. R. I. A. N. N. E., & Den Hartog, D. (2013). Ethical and unethical leader behaviors and their impact on individual well-being and deviance. *Handbook of unethical work behavior: Implications for individual well-being*, 140-154.

Kamra, J., Mani, A. P., & Tripathi, V. M. (2023). Decarbonization Trajectory in Cement Industry. In S. P., N. S., R. J.J.P.C., R. J.J.P.C., R. J.J.P.C., L.-I. G.-A. D., P. T., C. L., & P. L. (Eds.), *2023 8th International Conference on Smart and Sustainable Technologies, SpliTech 2023*. Institute of Electrical and Electronics Engineers Inc. DOI: 10.23919/SpliTech58164.2023.10193682

Kandasamy, U. C. (2024). Ethical Leadership in the Age of AI Challenges, Opportunities and Framework for Ethical Leadership. *arXiv preprint arXiv:2410.18095.*

Kane, G. C., Nguyen Phillips, A., Copulsky, J., & Andrus, G. (2019). How digital leadership is(n't) different. *MIT Sloan Management Review*, *60*(3), 34–39.

Kannan, P. R., Periasamy, K., Pravin, P., & Vinod Kumaar, J. R. (2022). An experimental investigation of wire breakage and performance optimisation of WEDM process on machining of recycled aluminium alloy metal matrix composite. *Materials Science Poland*, *40*(3), 12–26. DOI: 10.2478/msp-2022-0030

Kanojia, P., Malhotra, R. K., & Uniyal, A. K. (2022a). Impact of Organizational Commitment Components on the Teachers of Higher Education in Uttarakhand: An Emperical Analysis. *Proceedings - 2022 International Conference on Recent Trends in Microelectronics, Automation, Computing and Communications Systems, ICMACC 2022*, 360–364. DOI: 10.1109/ICMACC54824.2022.10093606

Kanojia, P., Malhotra, R. K., & Uniyal, A. K. (2022b). Organizational Commitment and the Academic Staff in HEI's in North West India. *Proceedings - 2022 International Conference on Recent Trends in Microelectronics, Automation, Computing and Communications Systems, ICMACC 2022*, 365–370. DOI: 10.1109/ICMACC54824.2022.10093347

Kaplan, A., & Haenlein, M. (2020). Rulers of the world, unite! The challenges and opportunities of artificial intelligence. *Business Horizons*, *63*(1), 37–50. DOI: 10.1016/j.bushor.2019.09.003

Karatzoglou, A., Amatriain, X., Baltrunas, L., & Oliver, N. (2010, September). Multiverse recommendation: n-dimensional tensor factorization for context-aware collaborative filtering. In *Proceedings of the fourth ACM conference on Recommender systems* (pp. 79-86). DOI: 10.1145/1864708.1864727

Kathir, I., Haribabu, K., Kumar, A., Kaliappan, S., Patil, P. P., Dhanalakshmi, C. S., Madhu, P., & Birhanu, H. A. (2022). Utilization of Tea Industrial Waste for Low-Grade Energy Recovery: Optimization of Liquid Oil Production and Its Characterization. *Advances in Materials Science and Engineering*, *2022*, 1–9. Advance online publication. DOI: 10.1155/2022/7852046

Kaur, J., Khanna, R., Kumar, R., & Sunil, G. (2024). Role of Blockchain Technologies in Goods and Services Tax. *Proceedings - 2024 3rd International Conference on Sentiment Analysis and Deep Learning, ICSADL 2024*, 607–612. DOI: 10.1109/ICSADL61749.2024.00104

Kaur, A., Kumar, P., Taneja, S., & Ozen, E. (2023). Fintech emergence – an opportunity or threat to banking. *International Journal of Electronic Finance, 13*(1), 1–19. DOI: 10.1504/IJEF.2024.135163

Kaur, H., Thacker, C., Singh, V. K., Sivashankar, D., Patil, P. P., & Gill, K. S. (2023). An implementation of virtual instruments for industries for the standardization. *2023 International Conference on Artificial Intelligence and Smart Communication, AISC 2023*, 1110 – 1113. DOI: 10.1109/AISC56616.2023.10085547

Kaur, N., & Hirudayaraj, M. (2021). The role of leader emotional intelligence in organizational learning: A literature review using 4I framework. *New Horizons in Adult Education and Human Resource Development, 33*(1), 51–68. DOI: 10.1002/nha3.20305

Kaushal, D., Kumar, S., Raj, R., & Negi, A. (2022). Understanding the effect of entrepreneurial orientation, innovation capability and differentiation strategy on firm performance: A study on small and medium enterprises. *International Journal of Business and Globalisation, 30*(1), 57–80. DOI: 10.1504/IJBG.2022.122280

Kayyali, M. (2025a). Leadership's Role in Fostering a Resilient Organizational Culture. In *Enhancing Resilience in Business Continuity Management* (pp. 267–294). IGI Global Scientific Publishing. DOI: 10.4018/979-8-3693-8809-9.ch009

Kayyali, M. (2025b). The Role of Leadership in Promoting Workplace Happiness. In *Insights on Wellbeing and Happiness in the Workplace* (pp. 233–254). IGI Global Scientific Publishing. DOI: 10.4018/979-8-3693-2939-9.ch012

Kergel, D., Heidkamp-Kergel, B., Nørreklit, H., & Paulsen, M. (Eds.). (2022). *Agile Learning and Management in a Digital Age: Dialogic Leadership*. Taylor & Francis. DOI: 10.4324/9781003188728

Khaddage-Soboh, N., Yunis, M., Imran, M., & Zeb, F. (2024). Sustainable practices in Malaysian manufacturing: The influence of CSR, transformational leadership, and green organizational culture on environmental performance. *Economic Analysis and Policy, 82*, 753–768. DOI: 10.1016/j.eap.2024.04.001

Khan, A. N., Mehmood, K., & Ali, A. (2024). Maximizing CSR impact: Leveraging artificial intelligence and process optimization for sustainability performance management. *Corporate Social Responsibility and Environmental Management, 31*(5), 4849–4861. DOI: 10.1002/csr.2832

Khandelwal, C., Kumar, S., Tripathi, V., & Madhavan, V. (2023). Joint impact of corporate governance and risk disclosures on firm value: Evidence from emerging markets. *Research in International Business and Finance, 66*, 102022. Advance online publication. DOI: 10.1016/j.ribaf.2023.102022

Khan, M. A. S., Du, J., Anwar, F., Khan, H. S. U. D., Shahzad, F., & Qalati, S. A. (2021). Corporate social responsibility and the reciprocity between employee perception, perceived external prestige, and employees' emotional labor. *Psychology Research and Behavior Management, 14*, 61–75. DOI: 10.2147/PRBM.S277850 PMID: 33500672

Khan, M. R. (2024). Application of artificial intelligence for talent management: Challenges and opportunities. *Intelligent Human Systems Integration (IHSI 2024). Integrating People and Intelligent Systems, 119*, 324–329. DOI: 10.54941/ahfe1004496

Khanna, L. S., Yadav, P. S., Maurya, S., & Vimal, V. (2023). Integral Role of Data Science in Startup Evolution. *Proceedings - 2023 15th IEEE International Conference on Computational Intelligence and Communication Networks, CICN 2023*, 720 – 726. DOI: 10.1109/CICN59264.2023.10402129

Khanna, R., Jindal, P., & Noja, G. G. (2023). Blockchain technologies, a catalyst for insurance sector. In *The Application of Emerging Technology and Blockchain in the Insurance Industry*. DOI: 10.1201/9781032630946-19

Khoshnevisan, B., & Rashtchi, M. (2021). The First Field Experience: Perceptions of ESOL Pre-Service Teachers. *Advances in Language and Literary Studies, 12*(5), 15–22. DOI: 10.7575/aiac.alls.v.12n.5.p.15

Khoury, G., Rostami, J., & Turnbull, P. L. (1999). *Corporate social responsibility: Turning words into action*. Conference Board of Canada.

Kilcullen, M., & Ohles Kooistra, J. (1999). At least do no harm: Sources on the changing role of business ethics and corporate social responsibility. *RSR. Reference Services Review, 27*(2), 158–178. DOI: 10.1108/00907329910275150

Kim, H., Woo, E., Uysal, M., & Kwon, N. (2018). The effects of corporate social responsibility (CSR) on employee well-being in the hospitality industry. *International Journal of Contemporary Hospitality Management, 30*(3), 1584–1600. DOI: 10.1108/IJCHM-03-2016-0166

Kirkpatrick, J. D., & Kirkpatrick, W. K. (2023). *Kirkpatrick's four levels of training evaluation* (2nd ed.). ATD Press.

Kiron, D., Kruschwitz, N., Reeves, M., & Goh, E. (2013). The innovation bottom line. *MIT Sloan Management Review, 54*(3), 69–73.

Kitchin, R. (2014). The data revolution: Big data, open data, data infrastructures and their consequences. *Sage (Atlanta, Ga.)*. Advance online publication. DOI: 10.4135/9781473909472

Knight, E., & Ansell, J. (2021). Data stewardship: A new imperative for business model innovation. *The Journal of Business Strategy, 42*(3), 154–162.

Köchling, A., & Wehner, M. C. (2020). Discriminated by an algorithm: A systematic review of discrimination and fairness by algorithmic decision-making in the context of HR recruitment and HR development. *Business Research, 13*(3), 795–848. DOI: 10.1007/s40685-020-00134-w

Köchling, A., Wehner, M. C., & Ruhle, S. A. (2025). This (AI) n't fair? Employee reactions to artificial intelligence (AI) in career development systems. *Review of Managerial Science, 19*(4), 1195–1228. DOI: 10.1007/s11846-024-00789-3

Kohli, P., Sharma, S., & Matta, P. (2022). Secured Privacy Preserving Techniques Analysis of 6G Driven Vehicular Communication Network in Industry 5.0 Internet-of-Everything (IoE) Applications. *2022 International Conference on Smart Generation Computing, Communication and Networking, SMART GENCON 2022*. DOI: 10.1109/SMARTGENCON56628.2022.10084289

Komkowski, T., Antony, J., Garza-Reyes, J. A., Tortorella, G. L., & Pongboonchai-Empl, T. (2023a). A systematic review of the integration of Industry 4.0 with quality-related operational excellence methodologies. *The Quality Management Journal, 30*(1), 3–15. DOI: 10.1080/10686967.2022.2144783

Komkowski, T., Antony, J., Garza-Reyes, J. A., Tortorella, G. L., & Pongboonchai-Empl, T. (2023b). Integrating Lean Management with Industry 4.0: An explorative Dynamic Capabilities theory perspective. *Production Planning and Control*. Advance online publication. DOI: 10.1080/09537287.2023.2294297

Kotchen, M., & Moon, J. J. (2012). Corporate social responsibility for irresponsibility. *The B.E. Journal of Economic Analysis & Policy, 12*(1). Advance online publication. DOI: 10.1515/1935-1682.3308

Kour, M., Taneja, S., Özen, E., Sood, K., & Grima, S. (2025). *Financial Landscape Transformation Technological Disruptions.*

Kowsalya, K., & Rani, R. P. J. Ritu, Bhiyana, M., Saini, M., & Patil, P. P. (2023). Blockchain-Internet of things-Machine Learning: Development of Traceable System for Multi Purposes. *2023 3rd International Conference on Advance Computing and Innovative Technologies in Engineering, ICACITE 2023*, 1112 – 1115. DOI: 10.1109/ICACITE57410.2023.10183065

Krishna, S. H., Upadhyay, A., Tewari, M., Gehlot, A., Girimurugan, B., & Pundir, S. (2022). Empirical investigation of the key machine learning elements promoting e-business using an SEM framework. *Proceedings of 5th International Conference on Contemporary Computing and Informatics, IC3I 2022*, 1960 – 1964. DOI: 10.1109/IC3I56241.2022.10072712

Krüger, P. (2015). Corporate goodness and shareholder wealth. *Journal of Financial Economics, 115*(2), 304–329. DOI: 10.1016/j.jfineco.2014.09.008

Kukreti, A., Shriyal, A., Sharma, S., & Bhadula, S. (2023). Internet-of-Things Enabled Smart and Portable Terrace Garden Protection Shed. *2023 4th IEEE Global Conference for Advancement in Technology, GCAT 2023*. DOI: 10.1109/GCAT59970.2023.10353281

Kumari, J., Singh, P., Mishra, A. K., Singh Meena, B. P., Singh, A., & Ojha, M. (2024). Challenges Hindering Women's Involvement in the Hospitality Industry as Entrepreneurs in the Era of Digital Economy. In *Revolutionizing the AI-Digital Landscape: A Guide to Sustainable Emerging Technologies for Marketing Professionals*. Taylor and Francis., DOI: 10.4324/9781032688305-9

Lade, J., Mohammed, K. A., Singh, D., Prasad Verma, R., Math, P., Saraswat, M., & Raj Gupta, L. (2023). A critical review of fabrication routes and their effects on mechanical properties of AMMCs. *Materials Today: Proceedings*. Advance online publication. DOI: 10.1016/j.matpr.2023.03.041

Lapatoura, C. (2025). The Role of Leadership in Shaping. *Leadership Studies in the Turbulent Business Ecosystem*, 73.

Latonero, M. (2018). Governing artificial intelligence: Upholding human rights & dignity. *Data & Society, 38*.

Lawler, E. E., & Boudreau, J. W. (2009). *Achieving excellence in human resources management: An assessment of human resource functions*. Stanford University Press.

Lee, C. K. H., Suh, A., Roy, D., & Baucus, M. (2019). Emerging technology and business model innovation: The case of artificial intelligence. *Journal of Open Innovation*, *5*(3), 1–13. DOI: 10.3390/joitmc5030044

Lievens, F., & Chan, D. (2017). Practical intelligence, emotional intelligence, and social intelligence. In Farr, J. L., & Tippins, N. T. (Eds.), *Handbook of employee selection* (2nd ed., pp. 342–364). Routledge. DOI: 10.4324/9781315690193-15

Lin, W. L., Yip, N., Ho, J. A., & Sambasivan, M. (2020). The adoption of technological innovations in a B2B context and its impact on firm performance: An ethical leadership perspective. *Industrial Marketing Management*, *90*, 320–329. DOI: 10.1016/j.indmarman.2019.12.009

Lin, Z., Gu, H., Gillani, K. Z., & Fahlevi, M. (2024). Impact of Green Work–Life Balance and Green Human Resource Management Practices on Corporate Sustainability Performance and Employee Retention: Mediation of Green Innovation and Organisational Culture. *Sustainability (Basel)*, *16*(15), 6621. DOI: 10.3390/su16156621

Literal, V. J. I., & Guhao, E. S. (2021). *Structural equation model on triple bottom line performance of large manufacturing companies in Region XII*. Recent Developments in Asian Economics International Symposia in Economic Theory and Econometrics. DOI: 10.1108/S1571-038620210000028002

Liu, C., Dai, G., & Tu, H. (2024). Study of a triple bottom line perspective to reach a sustainable development model for critical minerals using financial development. *Resources Policy*, *90*, 104790. DOI: 10.1016/j.resourpol.2024.104790

Liu, S. C., Luu, T. T., Pham, N. T., & Tang, A. D. (2024). Internal CSR and work-family facilitation: A dual mechanism of organizational citizenship behaviors and moderating role of emotional intelligence. *Journal of Hospitality and Tourism Management*, *58*, 394–408. DOI: 10.1016/j.jhtm.2024.02.008

Lobschat, L., Müller, B., Eggers, F., Brandimarte, L., Hui, S. K., Ozcan, G., & Verhoef, P. C. (2020). Corporate digital responsibility. *Journal of Business Research*, *122*, 875–888. DOI: 10.1016/j.jbusres.2019.10.006

Lokanadham, D., Sharma, R. C., Palli, S., & Bhardawaj, S. (2022). Wear Rate Modelling and Analysis of Limestone Slurry Particulate Composites Using the Fuzzy Method. *International Journal on Recent and Innovation Trends in Computing and Communication*, *10*(1), 133–143. DOI: 10.17762/ijritcc.v10i1s.5818

Lombana Diaz, C. (2025). AI Ethics. In *Human-Centered AI: An Illustrated Scientific Quest* (pp. 439–474). Springer Nature Switzerland. DOI: 10.1007/978-3-031-61375-3_5

Luckin, R., Holmes, W., Griffiths, M., & Forcier, L. B. (2016). *Intelligence unleashed: An argument for AI in education*. Pearson.

Luhmann, N. (2018). *Organization and decision*. Cambridge University Press. DOI: 10.1017/9781108560672

Lupton, D., & Williamson, B. (2017). The datafied child: The dataveillance of children and implications for their rights. *New Media & Society*, *19*(5), 780–794. DOI: 10.1177/1461444816686328

Luthra, S., Sharma, M., Kumar, A., Joshi, S., Collins, E., & Mangla, S. (2022). Overcoming barriers to cross-sector collaboration in circular supply chain management: A multi-method approach. *Transportation Research Part E, Logistics and Transportation Review*, *157*, 102582. Advance online publication. DOI: 10.1016/j.tre.2021.102582

Luusua, A., & Ylipulli, J. (2020, July). Artificial intelligence and risk in design. In *Proceedings of the 2020 ACM designing interactive systems conference* (pp. 1235-1244). DOI: 10.1145/3357236.3395491

Mai, N. K., An Nguyen, K. T., Do, T. T., & Phan, L. N. (2023). Corporate social responsibility strategy practices, employee commitment, reputation as sources of competitive advantage. *SAGE Open*, *13*(4), 1–17. DOI: 10.1177/21582440231216248

Mai, P., & Tchemeni, D. (1996). Volume et volatilité: Tests d'efficience du marché des actions. *Revue d'Economie Financiere*, *40*, 213–228.

Malhotra, R. K., Gupta, C., & Jindal, P. (2022). Blockchain and Smart Contracts for Insurance Industry. In *Blockchain Technology in Corporate Governance*. Transforming Business and Industries., DOI: 10.1002/9781119865247.ch11

Manjunatha, B. N., Chandan, M., Kottu, S., Rappai, S., Hema, P. K., Singh Rawat, K., & Sarkar, S. (2023). A Successful Spam Detection Technique for Industrial IoT Devices based on Machine Learning Techniques. *Proceedings of the 2nd International Conference on Applied Artificial Intelligence and Computing, ICAAIC 2023*, 363 – 369. DOI: 10.1109/ICAAIC56838.2023.10141275

Manyika, J., Chui, M., Miremadi, M., Bughin, J., George, K., Willmott, P., & Dewhurst, M. (2017). *Harnessing automation for a future that works*. McKinsey Global Institute.

Marchegiani, L. (2023). AI, corporate governance and sustainability. In Monteduro, M., Marchegiani, L., & Saraceno, F. (Eds.), *Digital economy, sustainability and international economic law* (pp. 65–88). Bentham Science Publishers. DOI: 10.2174/9789815124064123030006

Margolis, J. D., & Walsh, J. P. (2003). Misery loves companies: Rethinking social initiatives by business. *Administrative Science Quarterly*, *48*(2), 268–305. DOI: 10.2307/3556659

Mary Joshitta, S., & Sunil, M. P. Badriasulaimanalfurhood, Bodhankar, A., Ch.Sreedevi, & Khanna, R. (2023). The Integration of Machine Learning Technique with the Existing System to Predict the Flight Prices. *2023 3rd International Conference on Advance Computing and Innovative Technologies in Engineering, ICACITE 2023*, 398–402. DOI: 10.1109/ICACITE57410.2023.10182539

Masal, V., Pavithra, P., Tiwari, S. K., Singh, R., Panduro-Ramirez, J., & Gangodkar, D. (2022). Deep Learning Applications for Blockchain in Industrial IoT. *Proceedings of 5th International Conference on Contemporary Computing and Informatics, IC3I 2022*, 276 – 281. DOI: 10.1109/IC3I56241.2022.10073357

Mathipurani, V. B., & Narayanaswamy, K. (2024). Ethical Entrepreneurship in the Age of AI: Balancing Innovation and Social Responsibility. *Library of Progress-Library Science, Information Technology & Computer, 44*(3).

Mathur, S.(2024) Digital Sovereignty: Balancing Security, Identity And Global Hegemony. *Navigation the digital frontiers: new paradigms of technology and society*, 19.

Matten, D., & Crane, A. (2005). Corporate citizenship: Toward an extended theoretical conceptualization. *Academy of Management Review*, *30*(1), 166–179. DOI: 10.5465/amr.2005.15281448

Maurya, S. K., Ghosal, A., & Manna, A. (2022). Experimental investigations during fabrication and electrical discharge machining of hybrid Al/(SiC+ZrO2+NiTi) MMC. *International Journal of Machining and Machinability of Materials*, *24*(3–4), 215–230. DOI: 10.1504/IJMMM.2022.125195

Mayer, J. D., & Salovey, P. (1997). What is emotional intelligence? In Salovey, P., & Sluyter, D. (Eds.), *Emotional development and emotional intelligence: Implications for educators* (pp. 3–31). Basic Books.

McKinsey & Company. (2023). The state of AI in 2023. https://www.mckinsey.com

Medhi, M. K., Ambust, S., Kumar, R., & Das, A. J. (2023). Characterization and Purification of Biosurfactants. In *Advancements in Biosurfactants Research*. Springer International Publishing., DOI: 10.1007/978-3-031-21682-4_4

Mehershilpa, G., Prasad, D., Sai Kiran, C., Shaikh, A., Jayashree, K., & Socrates, S. (2023). EDM machining of Ti6Al4V alloy using colloidal biosilica. *Materials Today: Proceedings*. Advance online publication. DOI: 10.1016/j.matpr.2023.02.443

Microsoft. (2023). *AI for Earth and Sustainability Reports*. https://www.microsoft.com/en-us/sustainability

Milan, S., & Treré, E. (2022). Big Data from the South (s). *The Oxford handbook of digital media sociology, 76*.

Miloud, T. (2024). Corporate governance and CSR disclosure: Evidence from French listed companies. *Global Finance Journal, 59*, 100943. DOI: 10.1016/j.gfj.2024.100943

Mishra, A. K., & Wazid, M. (2023). Design of a cloud-based security mechanism for Industry 4.0 communication. *ICSCCC 2023 - 3rd International Conference on Secure Cyber Computing and Communications*, 337 – 343. DOI: 10.1109/ICSCCC58608.2023.10176702

Mishra, D., Kandpal, V., Agarwal, N., & Srivastava, B. (2024). Financial Inclusion and Its Ripple Effects on Socio-Economic Development: A Comprehensive Review. *Journal of Risk and Financial Management, 17*(3), 105. Advance online publication. DOI: 10.3390/jrfm17030105

Mitchell, R. K., Agle, B. R., & Wood, D. J. (1997). Toward a theory of stakeholder identification and salience: Defining the principle of who and what really counts. *Academy of Management Review, 22*(4), 853–886. DOI: 10.2307/259247

Mitra, D., Mondal, R., Khoshru, B., Senapati, A., Radha, T. K., Mahakur, B., Uniyal, N., Myo, E. M., Boutaj, H., Sierra, B. E. G. U. E. R. R. A., Panneerselvam, P., Ganeshamurthy, A. N., Elković, S. A. N. Đ. J., Vasić, T., Rani, A., Dutta, S., & Mohapatra, P. K. D. A. S.MITRA. (2022). Actinobacteria-enhanced plant growth, nutrient acquisition, and crop protection: Advances in soil, plant, and microbial multifactorial interactions. *Pedosphere, 32*(1), 149–170. DOI: 10.1016/S1002-0160(21)60042-5

Mittelstadt, B. (2019). Principles alone cannot guarantee ethical AI. *Nature Machine Intelligence, 1*(11), 501–507. DOI: 10.1038/s42256-019-0114-4

Mittelstadt, B. D., Allo, P., Taddeo, M., Wachter, S., & Floridi, L. (2016). The ethics of algorithms: Mapping the debate. *Big Data & Society, 3*(2), 1–21. DOI: 10.1177/2053951716679679

Mohav, Y. (2023). Ethical leadership in AI-driven organizations: Balancing innovation and responsibility. *International Journal of Advanced Engineering Technologies and Innovations, 1*(4), 204–210.

Mohd, N., Kumar, I., & Khurshid, A. A. (2023). Changing Roles of Intelligent Robotics and Machinery Control Systems as Cyber-Physical Systems (CPS) in the Industry 4.0 Framework. *2023 International Conference on Communication, Security and Artificial Intelligence, ICCSAI 2023*, 647 – 651. DOI: 10.1109/ICCSAI59793.2023.10421085

Morley, J., Cowls, J., Taddeo, M., & Floridi, L. (2020). Ethical guidelines for COVID-19 tracing apps. *Nature, 582*(7810), 29–31. DOI: 10.1038/d41586-020-01578-0 PMID: 32467596

Moura-Leite, R., & Padgett, R. (2011). Historical background of corporate social responsibility. *Social Responsibility Journal, 7*(4), 528–539. DOI: 10.1108/17471111111117511

Muchiri, M. K., Erdei-Gally, S., & Fekete-Farkas, M. (2022). Effect of CSR on the financial performance of financial institutions in Kenya. *Economies, 10*(7), 174. DOI: 10.3390/economies10070174

Nadeem, S. P., Garza-Reyes, J. A., & Anosike, A. I. (2023). A C-Lean framework for deploying Circular Economy in manufacturing SMEs. *Production Planning and Control.* Advance online publication. DOI: 10.1080/09537287.2023.2294307

Najimi, A., Doustmohamadi, P., & Omid, A. (2021). The relationship between emotional intelligence, social responsibility, and job performance in health service providers. *Journal of Education and Health Promotion, 10*(1), 126. DOI: 10.4103/jehp.jehp_960_20 PMID: 34222501

Nardin, T., & Mapel, D. R. (2021). International Society: Diverse. *Ethical Perspectives.*

Negi, D., Sah, A., Rawat, S., Choudhury, T., & Khanna, A. (2021). Block Chain Platforms and Smart Contracts. *EAI/Springer Innovations in Communication and Computing*, 65 – 76. DOI: 10.1007/978-3-030-65691-1_5

Neha, M., S., Alfurhood, B. S., Bakhare, R., Poongavanam, S., & Khanna, R. (2023). The Role and Impact of Artificial Intelligence on Retail Business and its Developments. *2023 International Conference on Artificial Intelligence and Smart Communication, AISC 2023*, 1098–1101. DOI: 10.1109/AISC56616.2023.10085624

Nestlé. (2022). *T.R.A.C.E. transparency platform.*

Nethravathi, K., Tiwari, A., Uike, D., Jaiswal, R., & Pant, K. (2022). Applications of Artificial Intelligence and Blockchain Technology in Improved Supply Chain Financial Risk Management. *Proceedings of 5th International Conference on Contemporary Computing and Informatics, IC3I 2022*, 242 – 246. DOI: 10.1109/IC3I56241.2022.10072787

Nicholson, J., & Kurucz, E. (2019). Relational leadership for sustainability: Building an ethical framework from the moral theory of 'ethics of care'. *Journal of Business Ethics, 156*(1), 25–43. DOI: 10.1007/s10551-017-3593-4

Nizamuddin, M. (2018). Corporate Social Responsibility and Corporate Financial Performance: An Exploratory Study of Measurement-Approach Selection Issues. IUP Journal of Corporate Governance, 17(2).

Noble, A. (2019). *Exploring Solutions for Closing the Mathematics Achievement Gap between Elementary Students with and without Disabilities* (Doctoral dissertation, University of Massachusetts Lowell).

Noe, R. A., & Kodwani, A. D. (2018). *Employee training and development, 7e*. McGraw-Hill Education.

Nonaka, I., & Takeuchi, H. (1996). The knowledge-creating company: How Japanese companies create the dynamics of innovation. *Long Range Planning, 29*(4), 592. DOI: 10.1016/0024-6301(96)81509-3

Northouse, P. G. (2025). *Leadership: Theory and practice*. Sage publications.

Notari, M., Baumgartner, A., & Herzog, W. (2014). Social skills as predictors of communication, performance and quality of collaboration in project-based learning. *Journal of Computer Assisted Learning, 30*(2), 132–147. DOI: 10.1111/jcal.12026

O'neil, L. R. (2019). *The Impact of Self-Assessment on the Learning Outcomes of African American Students in Geometry in a Rural School Setting* (Doctoral dissertation, Southern University and Agricultural and Mechanical College).

Ocasio, W., Laamanen, T., & Vaara, E. (2018). Communication and attention dynamics: An attention-based view of strategic change. *Strategic Management Journal, 39*(1), 155–167. DOI: 10.1002/smj.2702

Odame, C., Pandey, M., & Pathak, P. (2020). Emotional intelligence and its importance in sustainable development of human resources: A conceptual model. In Dang, G. S., & Vyas-Doorgapersad, M. S. (Eds.), *Sustainable human resource management: Transforming organizations, societies and environment* (pp. 273–287). Springer. DOI: 10.1007/978-981-15-5656-2_17

Odeyemi, O., Usman, F. O., Mhlongo, N. Z., Elufioye, O. A., & Ike, C. U. (2024). Sustainable entrepreneurship: A review of green business practices and environmental impact. *World Journal of Advanced Research and Reviews, 21*(2), 346–358. DOI: 10.30574/wjarr.2024.21.2.0461

OECD. (2015). *G20/OECD Principles of Corporate Governance*. OECD Publishing.

OECD. (2022). *OECD AI principles*. https://www.oecd.org

Orlitzky, M. (2015). The politics of corporate social responsibility or: Why Milton Friedman has been right all along. *Annals in Social Responsibility*, *1*(1), 5–29. DOI: 10.1108/ASR-06-2015-0004

Otto, B. (2011). A morphology of the organisation of data governance.

Ozkan, B. (2024). The Transformative Impact of AI on CSR, ESG, and Sustainability: Critical Review and Case Studies. In *Responsible Firms: CSR, ESG, and Global Sustainability* (Vol. 23, pp. 203-218). Emerald Publishing Limited.

Padhi, B. K., Singh, S., Gaidhane, A. M., Abu Serhan, H., Khatib, M. N., Zahiruddin, Q. S., Rustagi, S., Sharma, R. K., Sharma, D., Arora, M., & Satapathy, P. (2024). Inequalities in cardiovascular disease among elderly Indians: A gender perspective analysis using LASI wave-I (2017-18). *Current Problems in Cardiology*, *49*(7), 102605. Advance online publication. DOI: 10.1016/j.cpcardiol.2024.102605 PMID: 38692448

Pai, H. A., Almuzaini, K. K., Ali, L., Javeed, A., Pant, B., Pareek, P. K., & Akwafo, R. (2022). Delay-Driven Opportunistic Routing with Multichannel Cooperative Neighbor Discovery for Industry 4.0 Wireless Networks Based on Power and Load Awareness. *Wireless Communications and Mobile Computing*, *2022*(1), 5256133. Advance online publication. DOI: 10.1155/2022/5256133

Pai, V., & Chandra, S. (2022). Exploring factors influencing organizational adoption of artificial intelligence (AI) in corporate social responsibility (CSR) initiatives. *Pacific Asia Journal of the Association for Information Systems*, *14*(5), 4. DOI: 10.17705/1pais.14504

Pallavi, B., Othman, B., Trivedi, G., Manan, N., Pawar, R. S., & Singh, D. P. (2022). The Application of the Internet of Things (IoT) to establish a technologically advanced Industry 4.0 for long-term growth and development. *2022 2nd International Conference on Advance Computing and Innovative Technologies in Engineering, ICACITE 2022*, 1927 – 1932. DOI: 10.1109/ICACITE53722.2022.9823481

Pande, S. D., Bhatt, A., Chamoli, S., Saini, D. K. J. B., Kute, U. T., & Ahammad, S. H. (2023). Design of Atmel PLC and its Application as Automation of Coal Handling Plant. *2023 International Conference on Sustainable Emerging Innovations in Engineering and Technology, ICSEIET 2023*, 178 – 183. DOI: 10.1109/ICSEIET58677.2023.10303627

Pandey, N. K., Kashyap, S., Sharma, A., & Diwakar, M. (2023). Contribution of Cloud-Based Services in Post-Pandemic Technology Sustainability and Challenges: A Future Direction. In *Evolving Networking Technologies: Developments and Future Directions*. wiley. DOI: 10.1002/9781119836667.ch4

Pandey, K., Joshi, H., Paliwal, S., Pawar, S., & Kumar, N. (2020). Technology transfer: An overview of process transfer from development to commercialization. *International Journal of Current Research and Review*, *12*(19), 188–192. DOI: 10.31782/IJCRR.2020.121913

Pandey, K., Paliwal, S., Joshi, H., Bisht, N., & Kumar, N. (2022). A review on change control: A critical process of the pharmaceutical industry. *Journal of Medical Pharmaceutical and Allied Sciences*, *11*(2), 4588–4592. DOI: 10.55522/jmpas.V11I2.2077

Pangalos, G. (2023). Financing for a sustainable dry bulk shipping industry: What are the potential routes for financial innovation in sustainability and alternative energy in the dry bulk shipping industry? *Journal of Risk and Financial Management*, *16*(2), 101. DOI: 10.3390/jrfm16020101

Pangrazio, L., & Selwyn, N. (2019). 'Personal data practices' at school: The challenges of ethical and sustainable education data usage. *British Educational Research Journal*, *45*(2), 414–436. DOI: 10.1002/berj.3502

Pansera, M., Owen, R., Meacham, D., & Kuh, V. (2020). Embedding responsible innovation within synthetic biology research and innovation: Insights from a UK multi-disciplinary research centre. *Journal of Responsible Innovation*, *7*(3), 384–409. DOI: 10.1080/23299460.2020.1785678

Pant, I., & Yadav, R. K. (2016). Impact of emotional intelligence on the job performance of employee. *International Research Journal of Management. IT and Social Sciences*, *3*(1), 7–14.

Parsons, T. (1951). *The social system*. Free Press.

Partnership on AI. (2021). *The ethics of AI and emotional intelligence*. https://partnershiponai.org/wp-content/uploads/2021/08/PAI_The-ethics-of-AI-and-emotional-intelligence_073020.pdf

Pasquale, F. (2015). The black box society: The secret algorithms that control money and information. In *The black box society*. Harvard University Press. DOI: 10.4159/harvard.9780674736061

Patagonia. (2022). *Environmental & supply chain transparency report*. https://www.patagonia.com/our-footprint/

Pathania, A., & Srivastava, A. (2025). Navigating the Role of Artificial Intelligence (AI) in Transforming Corporate Social Responsibility (CSR) Strategies. In *Corporate Social Responsibility Approaches to Ethical AI in Business* (pp. 89-102). IGI Global Scientific Publishing.

Pineda-Escobar, M. A. (2019). Moving the 2030 Agenda forward: SDG implementation in Colombia. *Corporate Governance (Bradford), 19*(1), 176–188. DOI: 10.1108/CG-11-2017-0268

Podile, V., Reddy, K. P., Reddy, V. N. S., Babu, M. S., & Phani, A. K. (2024). Artificial intelligence and corporate social responsibility: Synergies, challenges, and future directions. *International Journal of Advanced Multidisciplinary Research Studies, 4*(6), 95–99. DOI: 10.62225/2583049X.2024.4.6.3399

Porter, M. E., & Kramer, M. R. (2011). Creating shared value. *Harvard Business Review, 89*(1/2), 62–77.

Posner, B. Z., & Kouzes, J. M. (1988). Relating leadership and credibility. *Psychological Reports, 63*(2), 527–530. DOI: 10.2466/pr0.1988.63.2.527

PwC. (2024). *ESG and AI: From risk to opportunity*. https://www.pwc.com/gx/en/issues/data-and-analytics/publications/esg-reporting-and-ai.html

Raghavan, M., Barocas, S., Kleinberg, J., & Levy, K. (2020). Mitigating bias in algorithmic hiring: Evaluating claims and practices. Proceedings of the 2020 Conference on Fairness, Accountability, and Transparency (FAT* '20), 469-481. https://doi.org/DOI: 10.1145/3351095.3372828

Raisch, S., & Krakowski, S. (2021). Artificial intelligence and management: The automation–augmentation paradox. *Academy of Management Review, 46*(1), 192–210. DOI: 10.5465/amr.2018.0072

Raja, S., Agrawal, A. P. P., Patil, P., Thimothy, P., Capangpangan, R. Y., Singhal, P., & Wotango, M. T. (2022). Optimization of 3D Printing Process Parameters of Polylactic Acid Filament Based on the Mechanical Test. *International Journal of Chemical Engineering, 2022*(1), 5830869. Advance online publication. DOI: 10.1155/2022/5830869

Rajbalaji, S., Raman, R., Pant, B., Rathour, N., Rajagopa, B. R., & Prasad, C. R. (2023). Design of deep learning models for the identifications of harmful attack activities in IIOT. *2023 International Conference on Artificial Intelligence and Smart Communication, AISC 2023*, 609 – 613. DOI: 10.1109/AISC56616.2023.10085088

Rajesh, S., Kandaswamy, M. U., & Rakesh, M. A. (2018). The impact of Artificial Intelligence in Talent Acquisition Lifecycle of organizations: A global perspective. *International Journal of Engineering Development and Research, 6*(2), 709–717.

Rajeswari, M., Kumar, N., Raman, P., Patjoshi, P. K., Singh, V., & Pundir, S. (2022). Optimal Analysis for Enterprise Financial Management Based on Artificial Intelligence and Parallel Computing Method. *Proceedings of 5th International Conference on Contemporary Computing and Informatics, IC3I 2022*, 2081 – 2086. DOI: 10.1109/IC3I56241.2022.10072851

Raji, I. D., & Buolamwini, J. (2019). Actionable auditing: Investigating the impact of publicly naming biased performance results. *Proceedings of the 2019 AAAI/ACM Conference on AI, Ethics, and Society*, 429–435. DOI: 10.1145/3306618.3314244

Raji, I. D., Smart, A., White, R. N., Mitchell, M., Gebru, T., Hutchinson, B., & Smith-Loud, J. (2022). *Closing the AI accountability gap: Defining an end-to-end framework for internal algorithmic auditing. Proceedings of the 2022 ACM Conference on Fairness, Accountability, and Transparency*, 33-44.

Raju, K., Balakrishnan, M., Prasad, D. V. S. S. S. V., Nagalakshmi, V., Patil, P. P., Kaliappan, S., Arulmurugan, B., Radhakrishnan, K., Velusamy, B., Paramasivam, P., & El-Denglawey, A. (2022). Optimization of WEDM Process Parameters in Al2024-Li-Si3N4MMC. *Journal of Nanomaterials, 2022*(1), 2903385. Advance online publication. DOI: 10.1155/2022/2903385

Rakhra, M., Bhargava, A., Bhargava, D., Singh, R., Bhanot, A., & Rahmani, A. W. (2022). Implementing Machine Learning for Supply-Demand Shifts and Price Impacts in Farmer Market for Tool and Equipment Sharing. *Journal of Food Quality, 2022*, 1–19. Advance online publication. DOI: 10.1155/2022/4496449

Ramachandran, K. K., Lamba, F. L. R., Rawat, R., Gehlot, A., Raju, A. M., & Ponnusamy, R. (2023). An Investigation of Block Chains for Attaining Sustainable Society. *2023 3rd International Conference on Advance Computing and Innovative Technologies in Engineering, ICACITE 2023*, 1069 – 1076. DOI: 10.1109/ICACITE57410.2023.10182462

Raman, R., Kumar, R., Ghai, S., Gehlot, A., Raju, A. M., & Barve, A. (2023). A New Method of Optical Spectrum Analysis for Advanced Wireless Communications. *2023 3rd International Conference on Advance Computing and Innovative Technologies in Engineering, ICACITE 2023*, 1719 – 1723. DOI: 10.1109/ICACITE57410.2023.10182414

Ram, M., Negi, G., Goyal, N., & Kumar, A. (2022). Analysis of a Stochastic Model with Rework System. *Journal of Reliability and Statistical Studies, 15*(2), 553–582. DOI: 10.13052/jrss0974-8024.1527

Ram, M., & Xing, L. (2023). Reliability Modeling in Industry 4.0. In *Reliability Modeling in Industry 4.0*. Elsevier., DOI: 10.1016/C2021-0-01679-5

Rana, M. S., Cavaliere, L. P. L., Mishra, A. B., Padhye, P., Singh, R. R., & Khanna, R. (2022). Internet of Things (IOT) Based Assessment for Effective Monitoring Data Against Malicious Attacks on Financial Collectors. *2022 2nd International Conference on Advance Computing and Innovative Technologies in Engineering, ICACITE 2022*, 177–181. DOI: 10.1109/ICACITE53722.2022.9823612

Rashid, A., Rasheed, R., & Ngah, A. H. (2024). Achieving sustainability through multifaceted green functions in manufacturing. *Journal of Global Operations and Strategic Sourcing, 17*(2), 402–428. DOI: 10.1108/JGOSS-06-2023-0054

Ratka, A. (2018). Empathy and the development of affective skills. *American Journal of Pharmaceutical Education, 82*(10), 7192. DOI: 10.5688/ajpe7192 PMID: 30643318

Rawat, R., Sharma, S., & Goyal, H. R. (2023). Intelligent Digital Financial Inclusion System Architectures for Industry 5.0 Enabled Digital Society. *Winter Summit on Smart Computing and Networks. WiSSCoN, 2023*, 1–5. Advance online publication. DOI: 10.1109/WiSSCoN56857.2023.10133858

Rawat, S. S., Pant, S., Kumar, A., Ram, M., Sharma, H. K., & Kumar, A. (2022). A State-of-the-Art Survey on Analytical Hierarchy Process Applications in Sustainable Development. *International Journal of Mathematical. Engineering and Management Sciences, 7*(6), 883–917. DOI: 10.33889/IJMEMS.2022.7.6.056

Reddy, P. N., Umaeswari, P., Natrayan, L., & Choudhary, A. (2023). Development of Programmed Autonomous Electric Heavy Vehicle: An Application of IoT. *Proceedings of the 2023 2nd International Conference on Electronics and Renewable Systems, ICEARS 2023*, 506 – 510. DOI: 10.1109/ICEARS56392.2023.10085492

Reepu, R., Taneja, S., Ozen, E., & Singh, A. (2023). A globetrotter to the future of marketing: Metaverse. In *Cultural Marketing and Metaverse for Consumer Engagement*. IGI Global., DOI: 10.4018/978-1-6684-8312-1.ch001

Resick, C. J., Hanges, P. J., Dickson, M. W., & Mitchelson, J. K. (2006). A cross-cultural examination of the endorsement of ethical leadership. *Journal of Business Ethics, 63*(4), 345–359. DOI: 10.1007/s10551-005-3242-1

Revelli, C., & Viviani, J. L. (2015). Financial performance of socially responsible investing (SRI): What have we learned? A meta-analysis. *Business Ethics (Oxford, England), 24*(2), 158–185. DOI: 10.1111/beer.12076

Richert, M., & Dudek, M. (2023). Risk mapping: Ranking and analysis of selected, key risk in supply chains. *Journal of Risk and Financial Management, 16*(2), 71. DOI: 10.3390/jrfm16020071

Riggio, R. E., Zhu, W., Reina, C., & Maroosis, J. A. (2010). Virtue-based measurement of ethical leadership: The leadership virtues questionnaire. *Consulting Psychology Journal, 62*(4), 235–250. DOI: 10.1037/a0022286

Robie, C., Meade, A. W., Risavy, S. D., & Rasheed, S. (2022). Effects of response option order on Likert-type psychometric properties and reactions. *Educational and Psychological Measurement, 82*(6), 1107–1129. DOI: 10.1177/00131644211069406 PMID: 36325125

Robinson, G. M., Magnusen, M., & Kim, J. W. (2019). The socially effective leader: Exploring the relationship between athletic director political skill and coach commitment and job satisfaction. *International Journal of Sports Science & Coaching, 14*(2), 197–204. DOI: 10.1177/1747954119834118

Rojas-Saffie, J. P., & García-Matte, N. (2024). Emotional self-regulation and personality in the light of Thomas Aquinas's philosophical anthropology. *Frontiers in Psychology, 15*, 1419202. DOI: 10.3389/fpsyg.2024.1419202 PMID: 38882512

Rose, D. H., & Meyer, A. (2002). *Teaching Every Student in the Digital Age: Universal Design for Learning*. Association for Supervision and Curriculum Development.

Ruisel, I. (1992). Social intelligence: Concepts and methodological problems. *Studia Psychologica, 34*(4), 281.

Sacavém, A., Cruz, R. N., Sousa, M. J., & Rosário, A. M. (2019). An integrative literature review on leadership models for innovative organizations. *International Journal of Innovation and Economic Development, 5*(6), 43–53.

Sachs, J. D. (2015). *The age of sustainable development*. Columbia University Press., DOI: 10.7312/sach17314

Sahu, S. R., & Rawat, K. S. (2023). Analysis of Land subsidencein coastal and urban areas by using various techniques– Literature Review. *The Indonesian Journal of Geography, 55*(3), 488–495. DOI: 10.22146/ijg.83675

Salama, R., Al-Turjman, F., Bordoloi, D., & Yadav, S. P. (2023). Wireless Sensor Networks and Green Networking for 6G communication- An Overview. *2023 International Conference on Computational Intelligence, Communication Technology and Networking, CICTN 2023*, 830 – 834. DOI: 10.1109/CICTN57981.2023.10141262

Salovey, P., & Mayer, J. D. (1990). Emotional intelligence. *Imagination, Cognition and Personality*, *9*(3), 185–211. DOI: 10.2190/DUGG-P24E-52WK-6CDG

Salvador-Carulla, L., Woods, C., de Miquel, C., & Lukersmith, S. (2024). Adaptation of the technology readiness levels for impact assessment in implementation sciences: The TRL-IS checklist. *Heliyon*, *10*(9), e29930. DOI: 10.1016/j.heliyon.2024.e29930 PMID: 38726201

Sandel, M. J. (2020, October 20). Ethical concerns mount as AI takes bigger decision-making role. *Harvard Gazette*. https://news.harvard.edu/gazette/story/2020/10/ethical-concerns-mount-as-ai-takes-bigger-decision-making-role/

Sanusi, I. T., Agbo, F. J., Dada, O. A., Yunusa, A. A., Aruleba, K. D., Obaido, G., Olawumi, O., & Oyelere, S. S.Centre for Multidisciplinary Research and Innovation (CEMRI). (2024). Stakeholders' insights on artificial intelligence education: Perspectives of teachers, students, and policymakers. *Computers and Education Open*, *7*, 100212. DOI: 10.1016/j.caeo.2024.100212

SASB. (2018). *Sustainability Accounting Standards Board Standards*. Value Reporting Foundation.

SASB. (2022). *Sustainability Accounting Standards*. https://www.sasb.org

Sathyaseelan, K., Vyas, T., Madala, R., Chamundeeswari, V., Rai Goyal, H., & Jayaraman, R. (2023). Blockchain Enabled Intelligent Surveillance System Model with AI and IoT. *Proceedings of 8th IEEE International Conference on Science, Technology, Engineering and Mathematics, ICONSTEM 2023*. DOI: 10.1109/ICONSTEM56934.2023.10142303

Saxena, R. (2024). Artificial intelligence and sustainable social development. In Jorasia, A., & Kumar, R. (Eds.), *Navigation the digital frontiers: New paradigms of technology and society* (pp. 1–8). Career Point University.

Schaltegger, S., & Wagner, M. (2011). Sustainable entrepreneurship and sustainability innovation: Categories and interactions. *Business Strategy and the Environment*, *20*(4), 222–237. DOI: 10.1002/bse.682

Schneider Electric. (2022). *Sustainability impact report*. https://www.se.com/ww/en/about-us/sustainability/

Schneider, S., & Leyer, M. (2019). Me or information technology? Adoption of artificial intelligence in the delegation of personal strategic decisions. *MDE. Managerial and Decision Economics*, *40*(3), 223–231. DOI: 10.1002/mde.2982

Scott, W. R. (2014). Institutions and organizations: Ideas, interests, and identities. *Sage (Atlanta, Ga.)*.

Selvaraj, J. T. (2024). Aligning AI systems with corporate sustainability and CSR strategies: Providing Actionable Insights and Guidelines for Enhanced Integration.

Selwyn, N. (2019). *Should robots replace teachers? AI and the future of education*. Polity Press.

Sen Thapa, B., Pandit, S., Patwardhan, S. B., Tripathi, S., Mathuriya, A. S., Gupta, P. K., Lal, R. B., & Tusher, T. R. (2022). Application of Microbial Fuel Cell (MFC) for Pharmaceutical Wastewater Treatment: An Overview and Future Perspectives. *Sustainability (Basel)*, *14*(14), 8379. Advance online publication. DOI: 10.3390/su14148379

Servaes, H., & Tamayo, A. (2013). The impact of corporate social responsibility on firm value: The role of customer awareness. *Management Science*, *59*(5), 1045–1061. DOI: 10.1287/mnsc.1120.1630

Shabbiruddin, Kanwar, N., Jadoun, V. K., Jayalakshmi, N. S. J., Afthanorhan, A., Fatema, N., Malik, H., & Hossaini, M. A. (2023). Industry - Challenge to Pro-Environmental Manufacturing of Goods Replacing Single-Use Plastic by Indian Industry: A Study Toward Failing Ban on Single-Use Plastic Access. *IEEE Access : Practical Innovations, Open Solutions*, *11*, 77336–77346. DOI: 10.1109/ACCESS.2023.3296097

Shah, J. K., Sharma, R., Misra, A., Sharma, M., Joshi, S., Kaushal, D., & Bafila, S. (2023). Industry 4.0 Enabled Smart Manufacturing: Unleashing the Power of Artificial Intelligence and Blockchain. *2023 1st DMIHER International Conference on Artificial Intelligence in Education and Industry 4.0, IDICAIEI 2023*. DOI: 10.1109/IDICAIEI58380.2023.10406671

Shamim, S., Cang, S., & Yu, H. (2017). Supervisory orientation, employee goal orientation, and knowledge management among front line hotel employees. *International Journal of Hospitality Management*, *62*, 21–32. DOI: 10.1016/j.ijhm.2016.11.013

Sharma, M., Hagar, A. A., Krishna Murthy, G. R., Beyane, K., Gawali, B. W., & Pant, B. (2022). A Study on Recognising the Application of Multiple Big Data Technologies and its Related Issues, Difficulties and Opportunities. *2022 2nd International Conference on Advance Computing and Innovative Technologies in Engineering, ICACITE 2022*, 341 – 344. DOI: 10.1109/ICACITE53722.2022.9823623

Sharma, S., Gupta, A., & Tyagi, R. (2023). Sustainable Natural Resources Utilization Decision System for Better Society Using Vedic Scripture, Cloud Computing, and IoT. In B. R.C., S. K.M., & D. M. (Eds.), *Proceedings of IEEE 2023 5th International Conference on Advances in Electronics, Computers and Communications, ICAECC 2023*. Institute of Electrical and Electronics Engineers Inc. DOI: 10.1109/ICAECC59324.2023.10560335

Sharma, A., & Sharma, T. (2017). HR analytics and performance appraisal system: A conceptual framework for employee performance improvement. *Management Research Review*, *40*(6), 684–697. DOI: 10.1108/MRR-04-2016-0084

Sharma, E., Rana, S., Sharma, I., Sati, P., & Dhyani, P. (2023). Organic polymers for CO2 capture and conversion. In *CO2-Philic Polymers, Nanocomposites and Solvents: Capture, Conversion and Industrial Products*. Elsevier., DOI: 10.1016/B978-0-323-85777-2.00002-0

Sharma, H., Verma, D., Rana, A., Chari, S. L., Kumar, R., & Kumar, N. (2023). Enhancing Network Security in IoT Using Machine Learning- Based Anomaly Detection. *Proceedings of International Conference on Contemporary Computing and Informatics, IC3I 2023*, 2650 – 2654. DOI: 10.1109/IC3I59117.2023.10397636

Sharma, K., Pandit, S., Sen Thapa, B., & Pant, M. (2022). Biodegradation of Congo Red Using Co-Culture Anode Inoculum in a Microbial Fuel Cell. *Catalysts*, *12*(10), 1219. Advance online publication. DOI: 10.3390/catal12101219

Sharma, P., Malhotra, R. K., Ojha, M. K., & Gupta, S. (2022). Impact of meditation on mental & physical health and thereby on academic performance of students: A study of higher educational institutions of Uttarakhand. *Journal of Medical Pharmaceutical and Allied Sciences*, *11*(2), 4641–4644. DOI: 10.55522/jmpas.V11I2.2309

Sharma, P., Taneja, S., Kumar, P., Özen, E., & Singh, A. (2024). Application of the UTAUT model toward individual acceptance: Emerging trends in artificial intelligence-based banking services. *International Journal of Electronic Finance*, *13*(3), 352–366. DOI: 10.1504/IJEF.2024.139584

Sharma, R. C., Palli, S., & Sharma, S. K. (2023). Ride analysis of railway vehicle considering rigidity and flexibility of the carbody. *Zhongguo Gongcheng Xuekan, 46*(4), 355–366. DOI: 10.1080/02533839.2023.2194918

Sharma, S., & Bhadula, S. (2023). Secure Federated Learning for Intelligent Industry 4.0 IoT Enabled Self Skin Care Application System. *Proceedings of the 2nd International Conference on Applied Artificial Intelligence and Computing, ICAAIC 2023*, 1164 – 1170. DOI: 10.1109/ICAAIC56838.2023.10141028

Shashikala, R., Singh, B. P., Azam, M., & Magesh, C. R. Rajat, & Singh, D. P. (2022). IoT Engineering Nanomaterial's Approach To Sustainable Advance Crop Production Management. *2022 2nd International Conference on Advance Computing and Innovative Technologies in Engineering, ICACITE 2022*, 2284 – 2288. DOI: 10.1109/ICACITE53722.2022.9823573

Sheel, A., & Nath, V. (2019). Effect of blockchain technology adoption on supply chain adaptability, agility, alignment and performance. *Management Research Review, 42*(12), 1353–1374. DOI: 10.1108/MRR-12-2018-0490

Shen, H., DeVos, A., Eslami, M., & Holstein, K. (2021). Everyday algorithm auditing: Understanding the power of everyday users in surfacing harmful algorithmic behaviors. Proceedings of the ACM on Human-Computer Interaction, 5(CSCW2), 1-29.

Shimul, A. S., & Cheah, I. (2023). Consumers' preference for eco-friendly packaged products: Pride vs guilt appeal. *Marketing Intelligence & Planning, 41*(2), 186–198. DOI: 10.1108/MIP-05-2022-0197

Shin, D., Chotiyaputta, V., & Zaid, B. (2022). The effects of cultural dimensions on algorithmic news: How do cultural value orientations affect how people perceive algorithms? *Computers in Human Behavior, 126*, 107007. DOI: 10.1016/j.chb.2021.107007

Shin, D., & Park, Y. J. (2019). Role of fairness, accountability, and transparency in algorithmic affordability. *Computers in Human Behavior, 98*, 277–284. DOI: 10.1016/j.chb.2019.04.019

Shoker, A. (2022). Digital sovereignty strategies for every nation. *Applied Cybersecurity & Internet Governance, 1*(1), 1–17. DOI: 10.5604/01.3001.0016.0943

Shrestha, Y. R., Ben-Menahem, S. M., & von Krogh, G. (2019). Organizational decision-making structures in the age of artificial intelligence. *California Management Review, 61*(4), 66–83. DOI: 10.1177/0008125619862257

Shrivastava, A., Usha, R., Kukreti, R., Sharma, G., Srivastava, A. P., & Khan, A. K. (2023). Women Safety Precaution. *2023 1st International Conference on Circuits, Power, and Intelligent Systems, CCPIS 2023*. DOI: 10.1109/CCPIS59145.2023.10291594

Siau, K., & Wang, W. (2018). Building trust in artificial intelligence, machine learning, and robotics. *Cutter Business Technology Journal, 31*(2), 47–53.

Sidgwick, H. (2022). *The methods of ethics*. DigiCat.

Siemens, G. (2012, April). Learning analytics: envisioning a research discipline and a domain of practice. In *Proceedings of the 2nd international conference on learning analytics and knowledge* (pp. 4-8). DOI: 10.1145/2330601.2330605

Silva, P., Moreira, A. C., & Mota, J. (2023). Employees' perception of corporate social responsibility and performance: The mediating roles of job satisfaction, organizational commitment and organizational trust. *Journal of Strategy and Management, 16*(1), 92–111. DOI: 10.1108/JSMA-10-2021-0213

Simmons, S. V., & Yawson, R. M. (2022). Developing leaders for disruptive change: An inclusive leadership approach. *Advances in Developing Human Resources, 24*(4), 242–262. DOI: 10.1177/15234223221114359

Singamaneni, K. K., Dhiman, G., Juneja, S., Muhammad, G., AlQahtani, S. A., & Zaki, J. (2022). A Novel QKD Approach to Enhance IIOT Privacy and Computational Knacks. *Sensors (Basel), 22*(18), 6741. Advance online publication. DOI: 10.3390/s22186741 PMID: 36146089

Singh, K. D., Singh, P., Chhabra, R., Kaur, G., Bansal, A., & Tripathi, V. (2023). Cyber-Physical Systems for Smart City Applications: A Comparative Study. In K. R., K. R., G. M., G. M., S. R., & S. R. (Eds.), *2023 International Conference on Advancement in Computation and Computer Technologies, InCACCT 2023* (pp. 871 – 876). Institute of Electrical and Electronics Engineers Inc. DOI: 10.1109/InCACCT57535.2023.10141719

Singh, K. D., Singh, P., Tripathi, V., & Khullar, V. (2022). A Novel and Secure Framework to Detect Unauthorized Access to an Optical Fog-Cloud Computing Network. In R. H.S., B. R., G. P.K., & S. V.K. (Eds.), *PDGC 2022 - 2022 7th International Conference on Parallel, Distributed and Grid Computing* (pp. 618 – 622). Institute of Electrical and Electronics Engineers Inc. DOI: 10.1109/PDGC56933.2022.10053223

Singh, P., & Singh, K. D. (2023). Fog-Centric Intelligent Surveillance System: A Novel Approach for Effective and Efficient Surveillance. In K. R., K. R., G. M., G. M., S. R., & S. R. (Eds.), *2023 International Conference on Advancement in Computation and Computer Technologies, InCACCT 2023* (pp. 762 – 766). Institute of Electrical and Electronics Engineers Inc. DOI: 10.1109/InCACCT57535.2023.10141802

Singh, A. K., Singh, R., & Singh, S. (2024). A review on factors affecting and performance of nutritional security of women and children in India. In *Impact of Women in Food and Agricultural Development*. IGI Global., DOI: 10.4018/979-8-3693-3037-1.ch019

Sjögren, E. (2021). *The ethics of artificial intelligence in business: A guide to responsible management*. Routledge.

Soubhari, T., Jayaprakasan, P. P., Shobha, C. V., Mannarath, A. K., & Nanda, S. S. (2025). "AI-Driven Green Growth and Carbon–Neutral Solutions"—The CSR Spectrum Redefined. In *Integrating Environmental Sustainability and Corporate Social Responsibility: A Move Beyond Profit: Corporate Social Responsibility for Environmental Sustainability* (pp. 245-271). Cham: Springer Nature Switzerland. zhou Hua, X., Hasan, N. A. M., De Costa, F., & Qiao, W. (2024). Opportunities or Challenges? The Interplay between Artificial Intelligence and Corporate Social Responsibility Communication. *Business Systems Research: International journal of the Society for Advancing Innovation and Research in Economy, 15*(1), 131-157.

Sousa, M. J., & Rocha, Á. (2019). Skills for disruptive digital business. *Journal of Business Research, 94*, 257–263. DOI: 10.1016/j.jbusres.2017.12.051

Squires, V. (2018). Northouse, PG (2016). Leadership: Theory and practice. Thousand Oaks, CA: Sage. Pages: 494. *Canadian Journal of Educational Administration and Policy*, •••, 185.

Srivastava, A., Jawaid, S., Singh, R., Gehlot, A., Akram, S. V., Priyadarshi, N., & Khan, B. (2022). Imperative Role of Technology Intervention and Implementation for Automation in the Construction Industry. *Advances in Civil Engineering, 2022*(1), 6716987. Advance online publication. DOI: 10.1155/2022/6716987

Srivastava, B., Kandpal, V., & Jain, A. K. (2024). Financial well-being of women self-help group members: A qualitative study. *Environment, Development and Sustainability, 27*(12), 29471–29492. Advance online publication. DOI: 10.1007/s10668-024-04879-w

Stahl, B. C. (2021). Ethical issues of AI. In Stahl, B. C. (Ed.), *Artificial intelligence for a better future: An ecosystem perspective on the ethics of AI and emerging digital technologies* (pp. 35–53). Springer., DOI: 10.1007/978-3-030-69978-9_4

Stahl, G. K., Brewster, C. J., Collings, D. G., & Hajro, A. (2020). Enhancing the role of human resource management in corporate sustainability and social responsibility: A multi-stakeholder, multidimensional approach to HRM. *Human Resource Management Review*, *30*(3), 1–16. DOI: 10.1016/j.hrmr.2019.100708

Stogdill, R. M. (1948). Personal factors associated with leadership: A survey of the literature. *The Journal of Psychology*, *25*(1), 35–71. DOI: 10.1080/00223980.1948.9917362 PMID: 18901913

Strubell, E., Ganesh, A., & McCallum, A. (2019). Energy and policy considerations for deep learning in NLP. *Proceedings of the 57th Annual Meeting of the Association for Computational Linguistics*, 3645–3650. DOI: 10.18653/v1/P19-1355

Stubbs, W. (2017). Sustainable entrepreneurship and B Corps. *Business Strategy and the Environment*, *26*(3), 331–344. DOI: 10.1002/bse.1920

Subramani, R., Kaliappan, S., Kumar, P. V. A., Sekar, S., De Poures, M. V., Patil, P. P., & Raj, E. S. E. (2022). A Recent Trend on Additive Manufacturing Sustainability with Supply Chain Management Concept, Multicriteria Decision Making Techniques. *Advances in Materials Science and Engineering*, *2022*, 1–12. Advance online publication. DOI: 10.1155/2022/9151839

Subramani, R., Kaliappan, S., Sekar, S., Patil, P. P., Usha, R., Manasa, N., & Esakkiraj, E. S. (2022). Polymer Filament Process Parameter Optimization with Mechanical Test and Morphology Analysis. *Advances in Materials Science and Engineering*, *2022*, 1–8. Advance online publication. DOI: 10.1155/2022/8259804

Sunori, S. K., Kant, S., Agarwal, P., & Juneja, P. (2023). Development of Rainfall Prediction Models using Linear and Non-linear Regression Techniques. *2023 4th IEEE Global Conference for Advancement in Technology, GCAT 2023*. DOI: 10.1109/GCAT59970.2023.10353508

Taddeo, M., & Floridi, L. (2018). How AI can be a force for good. *Science*, *361*(6404), 751–752. DOI: 10.1126/science.aat5991 PMID: 30139858

Tadesse Bogale, A., & Debela, K. L. (2024). Organizational culture: A systematic review. *Cogent Business & Management*, *11*(1), 2340129. Advance online publication. DOI: 10.1080/23311975.2024.2340129

Tagscherer, F., & Carbon, C.-C. (2023). Leadership for successful digitalization: A literature review on companies' internal and external aspects of digitalization. *Sustainable Technology and Entrepreneurship*, *2*(2), 100039. DOI: 10.1016/j.stae.2023.100039

Tambe, P., Cappelli, P., & Yakubovich, V. (2019). Artificial intelligence in human resources management: Challenges and a path forward. *California Management Review, 61*(4), 15–42. DOI: 10.1177/0008125619867910

Tamunomiebi, M. D., & Owhorji, S. (2018). Emotional self-awareness—a critical competency for managing excellence: A human factor. *American Journal of Humanities and Social Sciences Research, 2*(11), 129–136.

Taneja, S., Gupta, S., Singh, A., Bhatnagar, M., & Gaur, A. (2023). Green management - A new paradigm in the world of business. *Green Management - A New Paradigm in the World of Business*, 1–230. DOI: 10.52305/DLIH6622

TANEJA. S., KUMAR, P., REEPU, KUKRETI, M., & OZEN, E. ¨. (2024). *Data Alchemy in the Insurance Industry*. Emerald Publishing Limited. https://doi.org/https://doi.org/10.1108/978-1-83608-582-920241033

Taneja, S., Bhatnagar, M., Kumar, P., & Grima, S. (2023). A Panel Analysis of the Effectiveness of the Asset Management in Indian Agricultural Companies. *International Journal of Sustainable Development and Planning, 18*(3), 653–660. DOI: 10.18280/ijsdp.180301

Taneja, S., Bhatnagar, M., Kumar, P., & Rupeika-apoga, R. (2023). India ' s Total Natural Resource Rents (NRR) and GDP : An Augmented Autoregressive Distributed Lag (ARDL) Bound Test. *Journal of Risk and Financial Management, 16*(2), 91. https://doi.org/doi.org/10.3390/jrfm16020091. DOI: 10.3390/jrfm16020091

Taneja, S., & Özen, E. (2023). To analyse the relationship between bank's green financing and environmental performance. *International Journal of Electronic Finance, 12*(2), 163–175. DOI: 10.1504/IJEF.2023.129919

Teece, D. J., Pisano, G., & Shuen, A. (1997). Dynamic capabilities and strategic management. *Strategic Management Journal, 18*(7), 509–533. DOI: 10.1002/(SICI)1097-0266(199708)18:7<509::AID-SMJ882>3.0.CO;2-Z

Tesla. (2023). *Impact report*. https://www.tesla.com/impact

Toumi, N. B. F., Khemiri, R., & Makni, Y. F. (2022). Board directors' home regions and CSR disclosure: Evidence from France. *Journal of Applied Accounting Research, 23*(2), 509–539. DOI: 10.1108/JAAR-02-2021-0032

Trache, D., Tarchoun, A. F., Abdelaziz, A., Bessa, W., Hussin, M. H., Brosse, N., & Thakur, V. K. (2022). Cellulose nanofibrils-graphene hybrids: Recent advances in fabrication, properties, and applications. *Nanoscale, 14*(35), 12515–12546. DOI: 10.1039/D2NR01967A PMID: 35983896

Tretter, M. (2024). Equipping AI-decision-support-systems with emotional capabilities? Ethical perspectives. *Frontiers in Artificial Intelligence*, *7*, 1398395. DOI: 10.3389/frai.2024.1398395 PMID: 38881951

Tripathi, V. M., & Mohan, A. (2016). Microfinance and empowering rural women in the Terai, Uttarakhand, India. *International Journal of Agricultural and Statistics Sciences*, *12*(2), 523–530.

Uike, D., Agarwalla, S., Bansal, V., Chakravarthi, M. K., Singh, R., & Singh, P. (2022). Investigating the Role of Block Chain to Secure Identity in IoT for Industrial Automation. In D. R.K., S. A.Kr., K. G., & B. S. (Eds.), *Proceedings of the 2022 11th International Conference on System Modeling and Advancement in Research Trends, SMART 2022* (pp. 837 – 841). Institute of Electrical and Electronics Engineers Inc. DOI: 10.1109/SMART55829.2022.10047385

Ullmann, A. A. (1985). Data in search of a theory: A critical examination of the relationships among social performance, social disclosure, and economic performance of US firms. *Academy of Management Review*, *10*(3), 540–557. DOI: 10.2307/258135

Umamaheswaran, S. K., Singh, G., Dixit, A. K., Mc, S. C., Chakravarthi, M. K., & Singh, D. P. (2023). IOT-Based Analysis for Effective Continuous Monitoring Prevent Fraudulent Intrusions in Finance and Banking. *2023 International Conference on Artificial Intelligence and Smart Communication, AISC 2023*, 548 – 552. DOI: 10.1109/AISC56616.2023.10084920

UNESCO. (2021). *Recommendation on the ethics of artificial intelligence*. https://unesdoc.unesco.org/ark:/48223/pf0000381115

UNESCO. (2023). *Guidance for generative AI in education and research*. https://unesdoc.unesco.org/ark:/48223/pf0000386693

UNESCO. (2023). Guidance for generative AI. https://www.unesco.org

Unhelkar, B., Joshi, S., Sharma, M., Prakash, S., Mani, A. K., & Prasad, M. (2022). Enhancing supply chain performance using RFID technology and decision support systems in the industry 4.0–A systematic literature review. *International Journal of Information Management Data Insights*, 2(2), 100084. Advance online publication. DOI: 10.1016/j.jjimei.2022.100084

Unilever. (2022). *Sustainability performance report*. https://www.unilever.com/sustainable-living/

Uniyal, A. K., Kanojia, P., Khanna, R., & Dixit, A. K. (2022). Quantitative Analysis of the Impact of Demography and Job Profile on the Organizational Commitment of the Faculty Members in the HEI'S of Uttarakhand. *Communications in Computer and Information Science, 1742 CCIS*, 24–35. DOI: 10.1007/978-3-031-23647-1_3

Uniyal, S., Sarma, P. R. S., Kumar Mangla, S., Tseng, M.-L., & Patil, P. (2022). ICT as "Knowledge Management" for Assessing Sustainable Consumption and Production in Supply Chains. In *Research Anthology on Measuring and Achieving Sustainable Development Goals* (Vol. 3). IGI Global. DOI: 10.4018/978-1-6684-3885-5.ch048

Uniyal, A., Prajapati, Y. K., Ranakoti, L., Bhandari, P., Singh, T., Gangil, B., Sharma, S., Upadhyay, V. V., & Eldin, S. M. (2022). Recent Advancements in Evacuated Tube Solar Water Heaters: A Critical Review of the Integration of Phase Change Materials and Nanofluids with ETCs. *Energies*, *15*(23), 8999. Advance online publication. DOI: 10.3390/en15238999

Upreti, H., & Malhotra, R. K. (2024). Bridging The Urban-Rural Education Gap In India Through CSR (Corporate Social Responsibility) Initiatives: A Conceptual Study With Special Reference To Sustainable Development Goal 4 (Quality Education). In P. P.K. (Ed.), *E3S Web of Conferences* (Vol. 556). EDP Sciences. DOI: 10.1051/e3sconf/202455601032

Vakkuri, V., & Abrahamsson, P. (2020). The current state of AI ethics: Redesigning ethical AI for realization. *2020 IEEE International Conference on Engineering, Technology and Innovation (ICE/ITMC)*, 1-10. https://doi.org/DOI: 10.1109/ICE/ITMC49519.2020.9198576

Vaswani, G. (2024). Dawn of The Digital Era. *NAVIGATION THE DIGITAL FRONTIERS: NEW PARADIGMS OF TECHNOLOGY AND SOCIETY*, 9.

Venkatesh, J., Shukla, P. K., Ahanger, T. A., Maheshwari, M., Pant, B., Hemamalini, R. R., & Halifa, A. (2023). A Complex Brain Learning Skeleton Comprising Enriched Pattern Neural Network System for Next Era Internet of Things. *Journal of Healthcare Engineering*, *2023*(1), 2506144. Advance online publication. DOI: 10.1155/2023/2506144

Verma, M., Ahmad, W., Park, J.-H., Kumar, V., Vlaskin, M. S., Vaya, D., & Kim, H. (2022). One-step functionalization of chitosan using EDTA: Kinetics and isotherms modeling for multiple heavy metals adsorption and their mechanism. *Journal of Water Process Engineering*, *49*, 102989. Advance online publication. DOI: 10.1016/j.jwpe.2022.102989

Verma, P., Chaudhari, V., Dumka, A., & Singh, R. P. (2022). A Meta-Analytical Review of Deep Learning Prediction Models for Big Data. In *Encyclopedia of Data Science and Machine Learning*. IGI Global., DOI: 10.4018/978-1-7998-9220-5.ch023

Verma, P., Kumar, V., Daim, T., Sharma, N. K., & Mittal, A. (2022). Identifying and prioritizing impediments of industry 4.0 to sustainable digital manufacturing: A mixed method approach. *Journal of Cleaner Production*, *356*, 131639. Advance online publication. DOI: 10.1016/j.jclepro.2022.131639

Virginia Dignum, V. (2023). *Responsible artificial intelligence: How to develop and use AI in a responsible way*. Springer.

Voigt, P., & Von dem Bussche, A. (2017). *The EU General Data Protection Regulation (GDPR): A practical guide*. Springer International Publishing., DOI: 10.1007/978-3-319-57959-7

Voldsgaard, A., & Rüdiger, M. (2022). Innovative enterprise, industrial ecosystems, and sustainable transition: The case of transforming DONG Energy to Ørsted. In *Handbook of climate change mitigation and adaptation* (pp. 3633–3684). Springer International Publishing. DOI: 10.1007/978-3-030-72579-2_160

Von Schomberg, R. (2013). A vision of responsible research and innovation. In Owen, R., Bessant, J., & Heintz, M. (Eds.), *Responsible innovation: Managing the responsible emergence of science and innovation in society* (pp. 51–74). Wiley., DOI: 10.1002/9781118551424.ch3

Waddock, S. A., & Graves, S. B. (1997). The corporate social performance–financial performance link. *Strategic Management Journal*, *18*(4), 303–319. DOI: 10.1002/(SICI)1097-0266(199704)18:4<303::AID-SMJ869>3.0.CO;2-G

Waddock, S. A., & Mahon, J. F. (1991). Corporate social performance revisited: Dimensions of efficacy, effectiveness, and efficiency. *Research in Corporate Social Performance and Policy*, *12*, 231–262.

Wamba, S. F., Gunasekaran, A., Akter, S., Ren, S. J. F., Dubey, R., & Childe, S. J. (2017). Big data analytics and firm performance: Effects of dynamic capabilities. *Journal of Business Research*, *70*, 356–365. DOI: 10.1016/j.jbusres.2016.08.009

Wang, H., & Qian, C. (2011). Corporate philanthropy and corporate financial performance: The roles of stakeholder response and political access. *Academy of Management Journal*, *54*(6), 1159–1181. DOI: 10.5465/amj.2009.0548

Wang, Q., Dou, J., & Jia, S. (2016). A meta-analytic review of corporate social responsibility and corporate financial performance: The moderating effect of contextual factors. *Business & Society*, *55*(8), 1083–1121. DOI: 10.1177/0007650315584317

Wang, S., Liao, Y. K., Wu, W. Y., & Le, K. B. H. (2021). The role of corporate social responsibility perceptions in brand equity, brand credibility, brand reputation, and purchase intentions. *Sustainability (Basel), 13*(21), 11975. DOI: 10.3390/su132111975

Wang, S., & Zhang, H. (2024). Inter-organizational cooperation in digital green supply chains: A catalyst for eco-innovations and sustainable business practices. *Journal of Cleaner Production, 472*, 143383. DOI: 10.1016/j.jclepro.2024.143383

Wang, Y., & Hajli, N. (2017). Exploring the path to big data analytics success in healthcare. *Journal of Business Research, 70*, 287–299. DOI: 10.1016/j.jbusres.2016.08.002

Westerman, G., Bonnet, D., & McAfee, A. (2014). *Leading digital: Turning technology into business transformation*. Harvard Business Press.

Williams, J. J., & Seaman, A. E. (2016). The influence of ethical leadership on managerial performance: Mediating effects of mindfulness and corporate social responsibility. *Journal of Applied Business Research, 32*(3), 815–828. DOI: 10.19030/jabr.v32i3.9659

Wilson, H. J., & Daugherty, P. R. (2018). Collaborative intelligence: Humans and AI are joining forces. *Harvard Business Review, 96*(4), 114–123.

Winston, M. D. (2001). The importance of leadership diversity: The relationship between diversity and organizational success in the academic environment. *College & Research Libraries, 62*(6), 517–526. DOI: 10.5860/crl.62.6.517

Wong, P.-H. (2020). Democratizing algorithmic fairness. *Philosophy & Technology, 33*(2), 225–244. DOI: 10.1007/s13347-019-00355-w

Wood, D. J. (1991). Social issues in management: Theory and research in corporate social performance. *Journal of Management, 17*(2), 383–406. DOI: 10.1177/014920639101700206

World Business Council for Sustainable Development. (2020). *Corporate social responsibility: Making good business sense*. http://www.ceads.org.ar/downloads/Making%20good%20business%20sense.pdf

World Economic Forum. (2023). *AI governance frameworks for SDGs*. https://www.weforum.org/agenda/archive/artificial-intelligence/

Wu, J. (2024). Social and ethical impact of emotional AI advancement: The rise of pseudo-intimacy relationships and challenges in human interactions. *Frontiers in Psychology, 15*, 1410462. DOI: 10.3389/fpsyg.2024.1410462 PMID: 39564589

Wu, Y. (2014). Protecting personal data in E-government: A cross-country study. *Government Information Quarterly*, *31*(1), 150–159. DOI: 10.1016/j.giq.2013.07.003

Yassin, Y., & Beckmann, M. (2024). CSR and employee outcomes: A systematic literature review. Management Review Quarterly, 1–47.

Yassin, Y., & Beckmann, M. (2024). CSR and employee outcomes: A systematic literature review. *Management Review Quarterly*, *75*(1), 595–641. DOI: 10.1007/s11301-023-00389-7

Yeruva, A. R., Vijaya Durga, C. S. L., Gokulavasan, B., Pant, K., Chaturvedi, P., & Srivastava, A. P. (2022). A Smart Healthcare Monitoring System Based on Fog Computing Architecture. *Proceedings of International Conference on Technological Advancements in Computational Sciences, ICTACS 2022*, 904 – 909. DOI: 10.1109/ICTACS56270.2022.9987881

Zahari, A. I., Said, J., Muhamad, N., & Ramly, S. M. (2024). Ethical culture and leadership for sustainability and governance in public sector organisations within the ESG framework. *Journal of Open Innovation*, *10*(1), 100219. DOI: 10.1016/j.joitmc.2024.100219

Zawacki-Richter, O., Marín, V. I., Bond, M., & Gouverneur, F. (2019). Systematic review of research on artificial intelligence applications in higher education – where are the ethical domains? *International Journal of Educational Technology in Higher Education*, *16*(39), 39. Advance online publication. DOI: 10.1186/s41239-019-0171-0

Zenisek, T. J. (1979). Corporate social responsibility: A conceptualization based on organizational literature. *Academy of Management Review*, *4*(3), 359–368. DOI: 10.2307/257192

Zhai, C., Wibowo, S., & Li, L. D. (2024). Evaluating the AI dialogue System's intercultural, humorous, and empathetic dimensions in English language learning: A case study. *Computers and Education: Artificial Intelligence*, *7*, 100262. DOI: 10.1016/j.caeai.2024.100262

Zhang, C., & Yang, J. (2024). Artificial intelligence and corporate ESG performance. *International Review of Economics & Finance*, *96*, 103713. DOI: 10.1016/j.iref.2024.103713

Zhang, Y., Cao, C., Gu, J., & Garg, H. (2023). The Impact of Top Management Team Characteristics on the Risk Taking of Chinese Private Construction Enterprises. *Systems*, *11*(2), 67. Advance online publication. DOI: 10.3390/systems11020067

Zhao, J., & Gómez Fariñas, B. (2023). Artificial intelligence and sustainable decisions. *European Business Organization Law Review*, *24*(1), 1–39. DOI: 10.1007/s40804-022-00262-2

Zhou, J. (2023). Higher expectations of artificial intelligence in terms of morality and humanity. *Journal of Education. Humanities and Social Sciences*, *20*, 279–284.

Zhu, Y. (2025). Authentic leadership: Fostering ethical cultures, employee engagement, and organizational resilience in complex environments. *Proceedings of the International Conference on Research in Humanities and Social Sciences,* *2*(1), 1–14. DOI: 10.33422/icrhs.v2i1.838

Zuboff, S. (2019). Surveillance capitalism and the challenge of collective action. []. Sage CA: Los Angeles, CA: Sage Publications.]. *New Labor Forum*, *28*(1), 10–29. DOI: 10.1177/1095796018819461

About the Contributors

Çağlar Doğru is a Professor of Management and Strategy at Ufuk University, Ankara, Türkiye. He received his bachelor's degree in Business Administration from Hacettepe University, his master's degree in Human Resources Management, and his Ph.D. in Business Administration from Gazi University. Professor Doğru's research focuses on strategic management, organizational behavior, leadership, corporate governance, human resource management, artificial intelligence in management, corporate social responsibility, sustainability, and digital transformation. He has taught a wide range of undergraduate, graduate, and doctoral courses in these fields and has supervised numerous master's and doctoral theses. His academic work has been published extensively in leading national and international peer-reviewed journals, conference proceedings, and edited volumes published by internationally recognized publishers. He is the author and editor of several academic books and book chapters covering leadership, management, organizational studies, artificial intelligence, and sustainability. Professor Doğru serves as editor, associate editor, and editorial board member for several prestigious international journals and edited book projects. His research and editorial activities emphasize the integration of ethical leadership, strategic management, corporate social responsibility, and emerging technologies to promote sustainable organizational development.

***

Uğur Berdibek is an Assistant Professor at Bingöl University, Turkey, affiliated with the Faculty of Economics and Administrative Sciences.

Swati Bhatia is presently working as Professor and Head Research & Development Cell with Asian Business School under the aegis of Asian Education Group, Noida. With assignments in areas of Administration, Human Resource Management, Liaison Coordination, Team Management, Training & Development,

Swati has a noteworthy cross-functional experience of over 22 years in Strategic & Tactical Planning, Problem Resolution, Connexion, Performance Management and Onboarding. An out-of-the-box thinker with a flair education while identifying & adopting emerging trends and addressing industry requirements to achieve objectives bearing adherence to norms, her insightful experience in technical activities including scoping, planning, outlook finalization, resource administration & quality management. She has to her credit notable Books, Book Chapters, Research papers in several National and International Publications.

Koray Gündüz is an Assistant Professor at Bingöl University, Turkey, affiliated with the Faculty of Economics and Administrative Sciences.

Saadet Nur Karadenizli Sinap is a Research Assistant in the Department of Business Administration at Hacettepe University and a Ph.D. candidate in Business Administration. Her research focuses on organizational behavior, leadership, motivation, creativity, knowledge sharing, and management. She investigates how cognitive, emotional, and social mechanisms influence employee behaviors and organizational processes, with particular emphasis on the effects of leadership styles, interpersonal relationships, motivational factors, performance pressures, and organizational culture on employee attitudes and organizational behaviors. Her work examines concepts such as spiritual leadership, knowledge sharing, psychological capital, cultural values, workplace loneliness, communication quality, and perceived organizational support, and how these factors relate to employees' adaptation, creativity, innovativeness, and performance. In addition, she explores the impact of digital transformation, artificial intelligence, and emerging organizational structures on employee attitudes and leadership processes. By integrating quantitative and qualitative analysis methods with psychometric validation studies, her research aims to develop a comprehensive understanding of the psychological and contextual foundations of effective, innovative, and human-centered management systems in contemporary organizations.

Mustafa Kayyali is an ardent advocate for excellence in higher education, driven by a relentless pursuit of quality, recognition, and innovation. Their journey in academia started with a Master's in Quality Management and Evaluation in Higher Education from Universitat Oberta de Catalunya, followed by a Ph.D. in Quality Management from Azteca University. These academic pursuits have laid a strong foundation for their expertise in Accreditation, Quality Assurance, and Higher Education Rankings. As an entrepreneur, researcher, translator, and publisher, they are deeply involved in various facets of the academic world. Their diverse interests encompass Management, Translation, Interpretation, and Academic consulting, contributing to a well-rounded understanding of the industry. Throughout their career, they have made significant contributions to academic literature, with more than 40 published papers and 30 book chapters to my name. Additionally, they take pride in having translated 6 books, bridging language gaps, and promoting knowledge exchange on a global scale. They are committed to fostering positive change in higher education and contributing to its continuous improvement.

Grazia Murtarelli is an associate professor at IULM, an expert in strategic and digital communication, online reputation and measurement of digital activities.

Stefania Romenti is Full Professor in Strategic communication and PR at IULM university (Milan, Italy) and Chair of the Master of Science in Strategic Communication (taught in English Language). She is Pro-Rector for Educational Affairs and Track Chair of Sustainable Marketing of Società Italiana Marketing (SIM). She is Director of the Executive Master in Corporate Public Relations (IULM University) and Coordinator of the PhD program in Communication, Markets and Society at IULM University. She is Past President of EUPRERA (European Public Relations Education and Research Association). She is Director of the Research Center in Strategic Communication (CECOMS) at IULM University. Her research combines a communicative perspective with a concern for contemporary managerial issues and challenges. She published two monographs, 11 edited volumes and dozens articles in top international peer-reviewed management journals (i.e. Journal of Business Ethics, MIT Sloan Review, Journal of Business Research, TQM Journal) and communication journals (i.e. International Journal of Strategic Communication, Journal of Communication Management, Corporate Communication: an International Journal, Public Relations Review).

Vahid Sinap is an Associate Professor in the Department of Management Information Systems at Ufuk University, Ankara, Türkiye. He holds a Ph.D. in Educational Technology from Ankara University. His scholarly work focuses on the integration of machine learning, deep learning, and predictive analytics into organizational decision-making and digital transformation processes. Dr. Sinap's research interests encompass artificial intelligence applications, data-driven management, and intelligent decision support systems. He has published numerous articles and book chapters addressing algorithmic optimization, data mining, and AI-supported forecasting models. He also serves as a book editor and editorial board member in various international journals and academic publishing initiatives, contributing to the advancement of interdisciplinary research on technology and management. His recent publications and edited volumes explore the evolving role of AI in management information systems, innovation, and knowledge management, aiming to bridge the gap between technological advancement and organizational strategy.

Index

A

C

D

E

F

G

H

I

L

O

www.ingramcontent.com/pod-product-compliance
Lightning Source LLC
LaVergne TN
LVHW080903300926
849162LV00003B/537